D1476595

HONDA

FOURTRAX 200SX and ATC200X • 1986-1988
SERVICE • REPAIR • MAINTENANCE

By
ED SCOTT

ALAN AHLSTRAND
Editor

CLYMER PUBLICATIONS

*World's largest publisher of books devoted exclusively
to automobiles and motorcycles*

**A division of INTERTEC PUBLISHING CORPORATION
P.O. Box 12901, Overland Park, Kansas 66212**

FIRST EDITION
First Printing December, 1988

Printed in U.S.A.

ISBN: 0-89287-436-8

MOTORCYCLE INDUSTRY COUNCIL

COVER: Photographed by Mark Clifford. Fourtrax 200SX courtesy of Honda Santa Monica, Santa Monica, California.

3 1235 00563 6019   wsP

CONTENTS

QUICK REFERENCE DATA

TIRE INFLATION PRESSURE (COLD) *

Model	Tire size	Standard kPa	psi	Tire pressure Minimum kPa	psi	Maximum kPa	psi
3-wheeled models							
Front	23.5×11.0-8	25	3.6	22	3.2	28	4.1
Rear	22×10-9	17	2.5	14	2.0	20	2.9
4-wheeled models							
Front	20×7.0-8	21	3.0	18	2.6	24	3.5
Rear	22×11-8	17	2.5	14	2.0	20	2.9

* Tire inflation pressure for factory equipped tires. Aftermarket tires may require different inflation pressure.

MAINTENANCE TORQUE SPECIFICATIONS

Item	N·m	ft.-lb.
Oil drain plug	35-40	25-29
Front fork top cap bolt (3-wheeled)	15-30	11-22
Disc brake—parking brake adjuster locknut	15-20	11-15
Clutch mechanism adjust locknut (4-wheeled)	19-25	14-18
Fuel strainer cup	3-5	2-4
Rear axle housing pinch bolts		
3-wheeled models	18-24	13-17
4-wheeled models	80-110	58-72
Valve adjuster lockbolt	10-14	7.2-10
Spark plug	12-19	9-14

ENGINE OIL CAPACITY

Model	Draining Liter	U.S. qt.	After engine disassembly Liter	U.S. qt.
3-wheeled	1.5	1.6	1.8	1.9
4-wheeled	1.6	1.7	1.9	2.0

FORK OIL CAPACITY (3-WHEELED MODELS)

Year	Capacity cc	oz.	Dimension from top mm	in.
1986	216-221	7.3-7.5	178	7.0
1987	226-231	7.6-7.8	160	6.25

DRIVE CHAIN REPLACEMENT NUMBERS

Model	Drive chain number	Number of links
3-wheeled		
1986	DID 520 V-S	86
	RK 520 HMO	86
1987	DID 520 V-6	86
	RK 520 SMOZ10	86
4-wheeled	DID 520 V-S	80
	RK 520 HMOX-LE	80

TUNE-UP SPECIFICATIONS

Valve clearance (intake and exhaust)	0.08 mm (0.003 in.)
Spark plug	NGK DR8ES-L, ND X24ESR-U
Spark plug gap	0.6-0.7 mm (0.024-0.028 in.)
Compression pressure (at sea level)	1,200-1,400 kPa (170-198 psi)
Idle speed	1,300-1,500 rpm

REPLACEMENT BULBS

Item and model	Voltage/wattage
Headlight	
3-wheeled models	12V 60/55W
4-wheeled models	12V 45/45W
Taillight	
3-wheeled models	
1986	12V 5W
1987	12V 8W
4-wheeled models	12V 5W
NEUTRAL indicator	12V 3W
REVERSE indicator	12V 3W

HONDA

FOURTRAX 200SX and ATC200X • 1986-1988
SERVICE • REPAIR • MAINTENANCE

CHAPTER ONE

GENERAL INFORMATION

This detailed, comprehensive manual covers the Honda Fourtrax 200SX and ATC200X from 1986-on. The expert text gives complete information on maintenance, tune-up, repair and overhaul. Hundreds of photos and drawings guide you through every step. The book includes all you need to know to keep your Honda running right.

A shop manual is a reference. You want to be able to find information fast. As in all Clymer books, this one is designed with you in mind. All chapters are thumb tabbed. Important items are extensively indexed at the rear of the book. All procedures, tables, photos, etc., in this manual are for the reader who may be working on the vehicle for the first time or using this manual for the first time. All the most frequently used specifications and capacities are summarized in the *Quick Reference Data* pages at the front of the book.

Keep the book handy in your tool box or tow vehicle. It will help you better understand how your bike runs, lower repair costs and generally improve your satisfaction with the bike.

Tables 1-3 are at the end of this chapter.

MANUAL ORGANIZATION

All dimensions and capacities are expressed in English units familiar to U.S. mechanics as well as in metric units.

This chapter provides general information and discusses equipment and tools useful both for preventive maintenance and troubleshooting.

Chapter Two provides methods and suggestions for quick and accurate diagnosis and repair of problems. Troubleshooting procedures discuss typical symptoms and logical methods to pinpoint the trouble.

Chapter Three explains all periodic lubrication and routine maintenance necessary to keep your Honda running well. Chapter Three also includes recommended tune-up procedures, eliminating the need to constantly consult chapters on the various assemblies.

Subsequent chapters describe specific assemblies and systems such as the engine, clutch, transmission, fuel and exhaust systems, suspension and brakes. Each chapter provides disassembly, repair and assembly procedures in simple step-by-step form.

If a repair is impractical for a home mechanic, it is so indicated. It is usually faster and less expensive to take such repairs to a dealer or competent repair shop.

Specifications concerning a particular system are included at the end of the appropriate chapter.

Some of the procedures in this manual specify special tools. In most cases, the tool is illustrated either in actual use or alone. Well equipped mechanics may find they can substitute similar tools already on hand or can fabricate their own.

NOTES, CAUTIONS AND WARNINGS

The terms NOTE, CAUTION and WARNING have specific meanings in this manual. A NOTE provides additional information to make a step or procedure easier or clearer. Disregarding a NOTE could cause inconvenience, but would not cause equipment damage or personal injury.

A CAUTION emphasizes areas where equipment damage could occur. Disregarding a CAUTION could cause mechanical damage; however, personal injury is unlikely.

A WARNING emphasizes areas where personal injury or even death could result from negligence. Mechanical damage may also occur. WARNINGS *are to be taken seriously.* In some cases, serious injury or death has resulted from disregarding similar warnings.

Throughout this manual keep in mind 2 conventions. "Front" refers to the front of the vehicle. The front of any component, such as the engine, is the end which faces toward the front of the vehicle. The "left-" and "right-hand" sides refer to the position of the parts as viewed by a rider sitting on the seat facing forward. For example, the throttle control is on the right-hand side. These rules are simple, but even experienced mechanics occasionally become disoriented.

SERVICE HINTS

Most of the service procedures covered are straightforward and can be performed by anyone reasonably handy with tools. However, you should consider your own capabilities carefully before attempting any operation involving major disassembly of the engine.

Some operations, for example, require the use of a press. It would be wiser to have these performed by a shop equipped for such work, rather than trying to do the job yourself with makeshift equipment. Other procedures require precise measurements. Unless you have the skills and equipment required, it would be better to have a qualified repair shop make the measurements for you.

There are many items available that can be used on your hands before and after working on your vehicle. A little preparation before getting "all greased up" will help when cleaning up later.

Before starting out, work Vaseline, soap or a product such as Invisible Glove (**Figure 1**) onto

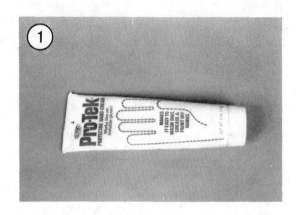

your forearms, into your hands and under your fingernails and cuticles. This will make cleanup a lot easier. For cleanup, use a waterless hand soap such as Sta-Lube and then finish up with powdered Boraxo and a fingernail brush. Repairs go much faster and easier if the vehicle is clean before you begin work. There are special cleaners, such as Gunk or Bel-Ray Degreaser, for washing the engine and related parts. Just spray or brush on the cleaning solution, let it stand, then rinse it away with a garden hose. Clean all oily or greasy parts with cleaning solvent as you remove them.

> *WARNING*
> *Never use gasoline as a cleaning agent. It presents an extreme fire hazard. Be sure to work in a well-ventilated area when using cleaning solvent. Keep a fire extinguisher, rated for gasoline fires, handy in any case.*

Special tools are required for some repair procedures. These may be purchased from a dealer or motorcycle shop, rented from a tool rental dealer or fabricated by a mechanic or machinist (often at a considerable savings). Much of the labor charged for by mechanics is to remove and disassemble other parts to reach the defective unit. It is usually possible to perform the preliminary operations yourself and then take the defective unit in to the dealer for repair.

Once you have decided to tackle the job yourself, read the entire applicable section in this manual, making sure you have identified the proper one. Study the illustrations and text until you have a good idea of what is involved in completing the job satisfactorily. If special tools or replacement parts are required, make arrangements to get them before you start. It is frustrating and time-consuming to get part way into a job and then be unable to complete it.

Simple wiring checks can be easily made at home, but knowledge of electronics is almost a necessity for performing tests with complicated electronic testing gear.

During disassembly of parts keep a few general cautions in mind. Force is rarely needed to get things apart. If parts are a tight fit, such as a bearing in a case, there is usually a tool designed to separate them. Never use a screwdriver to pry parts with machined surfaces such as crankcase halves. You will mar the surfaces and end up with leaks.

Make diagrams or take a Polaroid picture wherever similar-appearing parts are found. For instance, crankcase bolts are often not the same length. You may think you can remember where everything came from, but mistakes are costly. There is also the possibility you may be sidetracked and not return to work for days or even weeks, in which interval carefully laid out parts may have become disturbed.

Tag all similar internal parts for location and mark all mating parts for position. Record number and thickness of any shims as they are removed. Small parts such as bolts can be identified by placing them in plastic sandwich bags. Seal and label the bags with masking tape.

Wiring should be tagged with masking tape and marked as each wire is removed. Again, do not rely on memory alone.

Protect finished surfaces from physical damage or corrosion. Keep gasoline and hydraulic brake fluid off plastic parts and painted surfaces.

Frozen or very tight bolts and screws can often be loosened by soaking with penetrating oil, such as WD-40 or Liquid Wrench, then sharply striking the bolt head a few times with a hammer and punch (or screwdriver for screws). Avoid heat unless absolutely necessary, since it may melt, warp or remove the temper from many parts.

No parts, except those assembled with a press fit, require unusual force during assembly. If a part is hard to remove or install, find out why before proceeding.

Cover all openings after removing parts to keep dirt, small tools, etc., from falling in.

When assembling 2 parts, start all fasteners, then tighten evenly.

Electrical wire connectors and brake components should be kept clean and free of grease and oil.

When assembling parts, be sure all shims and washers are installed exactly as they came out. Whenever a rotating part butts against a stationary part, look for a shim or washer. Use new gaskets if there is any doubt about the condition of the old ones. A thin coat of oil on gaskets may help them seal effectively.

Cold heavy grease can be used to hold small parts in place if they tend to fall out during assembly. However, keep grease and oil away from electrical and brake components.

High spots may be sanded off a piston with sandpaper, but fine emery cloth and oil will do a much more professional job.

Carbon can be removed from the head, the piston crown and the exhaust ports with a dull screwdriver. Do *not* scratch machined surfaces. Wipe off the surface with a clean cloth when finished.

Carburetors are best cleaned by disassembling them and soaking the parts in a commercial carburetor cleaner. Never soak gaskets and rubber parts in these cleaners. Never use wire to clean out jets and air passages; they are easily damaged. Use compressed air to blow out the carburetor *after* the float has been removed.

A baby bottle makes a good measuring device for adding oil to the front forks. Get one that is graduated in fluid ounces and cubic centimeters. After it has been used for this purpose, do not let a small child drink out of it as there will always be an oil residue in it.

Take your time and do the job right. Do not forget that a newly rebuilt engine must be broken in the same as a new one. Keep the rpm within the limits given in your owner's manual when you get back on the road.

TORQUE SPECIFICATIONS

Torque specifications throughout this manual are given in Newton meters (N•m) and foot-pounds (ft.-lb.). Newton meters have been adopted in place of meter kilograms (mkg) in accordance with the International Modernized Metric System. Tool manufacturers offer torque wrenches calibrated in both values.

Existing torque wrenches calibrated in meter kilograms can be used by performing a simple conversion. All you have to do is move the decimal point one place to the right; for example, 4.7 mkg-47 N•m. This conversion is accurate enough for mechanical work, even though the exact mathematical conversion is 3.5 mkg = 34.3 N•m.

Refer to **Table 1** for standard torque specifications for fasteners which are not covered in tables at the end of each chapter.

SAFETY FIRST

Professional mechanics can work for years and never sustain a serious injury. If you observe a few rules of common sense and safety, you can enjoy

many hours servicing your own machine. If you
ignore these rules you can hurt yourself or damage
the vehicle.

1. Never use gasoline as a cleaning solvent.

2. Never smoke or use a torch in the vicinity of
flammable liquids such as cleaning solvent in open
containers.

3. If welding or brazing is required on the
machine, remove the fuel tank to a safe distance, at
least 50 feet away.

4. Use the proper size wrenches to avoid damage
to nuts and injury to yourself.

5. When loosening a tight or stuck nut, think
about what would happen if the wrench should
slip. Be careful; protect yourself accordingly.

6. Keep your work area clean and uncluttered.

7. Wear safety goggles during all operations
involving drilling, grinding or the use of a cold
chisel.

8. Never use worn tools.

9. Keep a fire extinguisher handy and be sure it is
rated for gasoline and electrical fires.

SPECIAL TIPS

Because of the extreme demands placed on the
vehicle, several points should be kept in mind
when performing service and repair. The following
items are general suggestions that may improve the
overall life of the machine and help avoid costly
failures.

1. Use a locking compound such as Loctite Lock
N' Seal No. 242 (blue Loctite) on all bolts and nuts,
even if they are secured with lockwashers. This
type of Loctite does not harden completely and
allows easy removal of the bolt or nut. A screw or
bolt lost from an engine cover or bearing retainer
could easily cause serious and expensive damage
before its loss is noticed. When applying Loctite,
use a small amount. If too much is used, it can
work its way down the threads and stick parts
together not meant to be stuck. Keep a tube of
Loctite in your tool box; when used properly it is
cheap insurance.

2. Use a hammer-driven impact tool to remove
and install all bolts and screws, particularly engine
cover screws. These tools help prevent damage to
bolt and screw heads and ensure a tight
installation.

> *NOTE*
> *When a torque is specified, use a torque*
> *wrench to tighten fasteners.*

3. When replacing missing or broken fasteners
(bolts, nuts and screws), especially on the engine or
frame components, always use Honda replacement

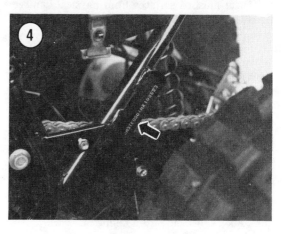

parts. They are specially hardened for each
application. The wrong fastener could easily cause
serious and expensive damage, not to mention
rider injury.

4. When installing gaskets in the engine, always
use Honda replacement gaskets *without* sealer,
unless designated. These gaskets are designed to
swell when they come in contact with oil. Gasket
sealer will prevent the gaskets from swelling as
intended, which can result in oil leaks. These
Honda gaskets are cut from material of the precise

thickness needed. Installation of a too-thick or too-thin gasket in a critical area could cause engine damage.

EXPENDABLE SUPPLIES

Certain expendable supplies are required during maintenance and repair work. These include grease, oil, gasket cement, wiping rags and cleaning solvent. Ask your dealer for the special locking compounds, silicone lubricants and other products (**Figure 2**) which make vehicle maintenance simpler and easier. Cleaning solvent or kerosene is available at some service stations or hardware stores.

PARTS REPLACEMENT

Honda makes frequent changes during a model year—some minor, some relatively major. When you order parts from the dealer or other parts distributor, always order by engine and frame number. Write the numbers down and carry them with you. Compare new parts to old before purchasing them. If they are not alike, have the parts manager explain the difference to you.

SERIAL NUMBERS

You must know the model serial number (frame and/or engine) and vehicle identification number (VIN) for registration purposes and when ordering replacement parts.

The frame serial number is located as follows:
 a. 3-wheeled models: stamped on the right-hand side of the steering head (**Figure 3**).
 b. 4-wheeled models: stamped on the left-hand frame down tube under the seat (**Figure 4**).

The engine serial number is located on the lower left-hand side of the crankcase behind the gear shift lever (**Figure 5**). The carburetor serial number is located on the right-hand side of the carburetor body above the float bowl (**Figure 6**).

BASIC HAND TOOLS

A number of tools are required to maintain an ATV in top riding condition. You may already have some of these tools for home or car repairs. There are also tools made especially for motorcycle and ATV repairs; these you will have to purchase. In any case, a wide variety of quality tools will make ATV repairs easier and more effective.

Top quality tools are essential; they are also more economical in the long run. If you are now starting to build your tool collection, stay away from the "advertised specials" featured at some parts houses, discount stores and chain drug stores. These are usually a poor grade tool that can be sold cheaply and that is exactly what they are—*cheap*. They are usually made of inferior material and are thick, heavy and clumsy. Their rough finish makes them difficult to clean and they usually don't last very long. Quality tools are made of alloy steel and are heat treated for greater strength. They are lighter and better balanced than cheap ones. Their surface is smooth, making them a pleasure to work with and easy to clean. The initial cost of good quality tools may be more, but it is cheaper in the long run. Don't try to buy everything in all sizes in the beginning; do it a little at a time until you have the necessary tools.

Keep your tools clean and in a tool box. Keep them organized with the sockets and related drives together and the open end and box wrenches together, etc. After using a tool, wipe off dirt and grease with a clean cloth and place the tool in its correct place. Doing this will save a lot of time you would have spent trying to find a socket buried in a bunch of clutch parts.

The following tools are required to perform virtually any repair job on an ATV. Each tool is described and the recommended size given for starting a tool collection. **Table 2** includes the tools that should be on hand for simple home repairs and/or major overhaul as shown in **Figure 7**. Additional tools and some duplicates may be added as you become more familiar with the ATV. Almost all motorcycles and ATV's (with the exception of the U.S. built Harley and some English bikes) use metric size bolts and nuts. If you are starting your collection now, buy metric sizes.

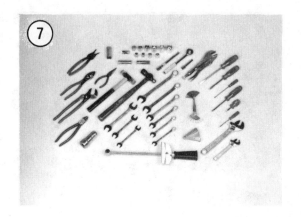

Screwdrivers

The screwdriver is a very basic tool, but if used improperly it will do more damage than good. The slot on a screw has a definite dimension and shape. A screwdriver must be selected to conform with that shape. Use a small screwdriver for small screws and a large one for large screws or the screw head will be damaged.

Two basic types of screwdriver are required to repair the bike—a common (flat blade) screwdriver and the Phillips screwdriver.

Screwdrivers are available in sets which often include an assortment of common and Phillips blades. If you buy them individually, buy at least the following:

    a. Common screwdriver—5/16×6 in. blade.
    b. Common screwdriver—3/8×12 in. blade.
    c. Phillips screwdriver—size 2 tip, 6 in. blade.

Use screwdrivers only for driving screws. Never use a screwdriver for prying or chiseling. Do not try to remove a Phillips or Allen head screw with a common screwdriver; you can damage the head so that the proper tool will be unable to remove it. Keep screwdrivers in the proper condition and they will last longer and perform better. Always keep the tip of a common screwdriver in good condition. **Figure 8** shows how to grind the tip to the proper shape if it becomes damaged. Note the symmetrical sides of the tip.

Pliers

Pliers come in a wide range of types and sizes. Pliers are useful for cutting, bending and crimping. They should never be used to cut hardened objects or to turn bolts or nuts. **Figure 9** shows several pliers useful in ATV repairs.

Each type of pliers has a specialized function. Gas pliers are general purpose pliers and are used mainly for holding things and for bending. Vise Grips are used as pliers or to hold objects very tight like a vise. Needlenose pliers are used to hold or bend small objects. Channel lock pliers can be adjusted to hold various sizes of objects; the jaws remain parallel to grip around objects such as pipe or tubing. There are many more types of pliers.

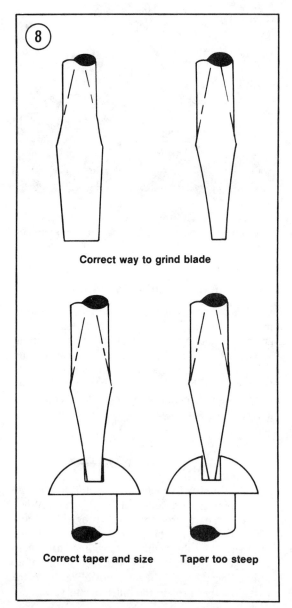

Correct way to grind blade

Correct taper and size   Taper too steep

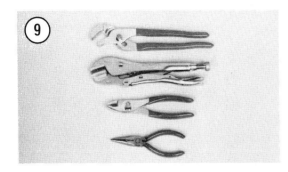

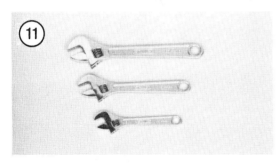

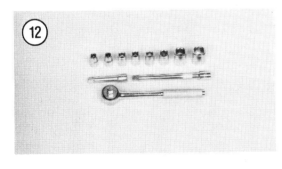

The ones described here are most suitable for ATV repairs.

Box and Open-end Wrenches

Box and open-end wrenches are available in sets or separately in a variety of sizes (**Figure 10**). The size number stamped near the end refers to the distance between 2 parallel flats on the hex head bolt or nut.

Box wrenches are usually superior to open-end wrenches. Open-end wrenches grip the nut on only 2 flats. Unless it fits well, it may slip and round off the points on the nut. The box wrench grips all 6 flats. Both 6-point and 12-point openings on box wrenches are available. The 6-point gives superior holding power; the 12-point allows a shorter swing.

Combination wrenches which are open on one side and boxed on the other are also available. Both ends are the same size.

Adjustable (Crescent) Wrenches

An adjustable wrench (also called a crescent wrench) can be adjusted to fit nearly any nut or bolt head. See **Figure 11**. However, it can loosen and slip, causing damage to the nut and injury to your knuckles. Use an adjustable wrench only when other wrenches are not available.

Crescent wrenches come in sizes ranging from 4-18 in. overall. A 6 or 8 in. wrench is recommended as an all-purpose wrench.

Socket Wrenches

This type is undoubtedly the fastest, safest and most convenient to use. See **Figure 12**. Sockets which attach to a ratchet handle are available with 6-point or 12-point openings and 1/4, 3/8, 1/2 and 3/4 inch drives. The drive size indicates the size of the square hole which mates with the ratchet handle.

Torque Wrench

A torque wrench is used with a socket to measure how tightly a nut or bolt is installed. They come in a wide price range and with either 3/8 or 1/2 in. square drive. The drive size indicates the size of the square drive which mates with the socket. Purchase one that measures 0-140 N•m (0-100 ft.-lb.).

Impact Driver

This tool might have been designed with the ATV in mind. See **Figure 13**. It makes removal of engine and clutch parts easy and eliminates damage to bolts and screw slots. This tool is available at most large hardware, motorcycle or auto parts stores.

Circlip Pliers

Circlip pliers (sometimes referred to as snap-ring pliers) are necessary to remove the circlips used on the transmission shaft assemblies. See **Figure 14**.

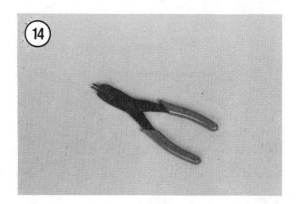

Hammers

The correct hammer is necessary for ATV repairs. Use only a hammer with a face (or head) of rubber or plastic or the soft-faced type that is filled with buckshot. These are sometimes necessary in engine teardowns. *Never* use a metal-faced hammer on the ATV as severe damage will result in most cases. You can always produce the same amount of force with a soft-faced hammer.

Ignition Gauge

This tool has both flat and wire measuring gauges and is used to measure spark plug gap (**Figure 15**). This device is available at most auto or motorcycle supply stores.

Other Special Tools

A few other special tools may be required for major service. These are described in the appropriate chapters and are available from Honda dealers or other manufacturers as indicated.

TUNE-UP AND TROUBLESHOOTING TOOLS

Multimeter or Volt-ohm Meter

This instrument (**Figure 16**) is invaluable for electrical system troubleshooting and service. A few of its functions may be duplicated by homemade test equipment, but for the serious mechanic it is a must. Its uses are described in the applicable sections of the book.

Strobe Timing Light

This instrument is necessary for checking the ignition timing. By flashing a light at the precise instant the spark plug fires, the position of the timing mark can be seen. Marks on the starter clutch assembly line up with the stationary mark on the crankcase cover while the engine is running.

Suitable lights range from inexpensive neon bulb types to powerful xenon strobe lights. See **Figure 17**. Neon timing lights are difficult to see and must be used in dimly lit areas. Xenon strobe timing lights can be used outside in bright sunlight. Both types work on the bike; use according to the manufacturer's instructions.

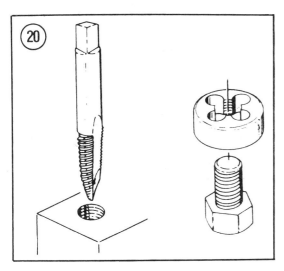

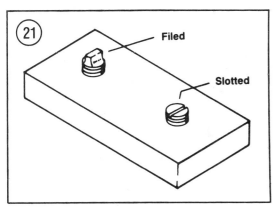

Filed

Slotted

Portable Tachometer

A portable tachometer is necessary for tuning. See **Figure 18**. Ignition timing checks and carburetor adjustments must be performed at the specified idle speed. The best instrument for this purpose is one with a low range of 0-1,000 or 0-2,000 rpm and a high range of 0-4,000 rpm. Extended range (0-6,000 or 0-8,000 rpm) instruments lack accuracy at lower speeds. The instrument should be capable of detecting changes of 25 rpm on the low range.

Compression Gauge

A compression gauge measures the engine compression. The one shown in **Figure 19** is the type used for the Honda ATV's covered in this manual. They are available from motorcycle or auto supply stores and mail order outlets.

MECHANIC'S TIPS

Removing Frozen Nuts and Screws

When a fastener rusts and cannot be removed, several methods may be used to loosen it. First, apply penetrating oil such as Liquid Wrench or WD-40 (available at any hardware or auto supply store). Apply it liberally and let it penetrate for 10-15 minutes. Rap the fastener several times with a small hammer; do not hit it hard enough to cause damage. Reapply the penetrating oil if necessary.

For frozen screws, apply penetrating oil as described, then insert a screwdriver in the slot and rap the top of the screwdriver with a hammer. This loosens the rust so the screw can be removed in the normal way. If the screw head is too chewed up to use a screwdriver, grip the head with Vise Grips and twist the screw out.

Remedying Stripped Threads

Occasionally, threads are stripped through carelessness or impact damage. Often the threads can be cleaned up with a tap (for internal threads on nuts) or die (for external threads on bolts). See **Figure 20**.

Removing Broken Screws or Bolts

When the head breaks off a screw or bolt, several methods are available for removing the remaining portion.

If a large portion of the remainder projects out, try gripping it with Vise Grips. If the projecting portion is too small, file it to fit a wrench or cut a slot in it to fit a screwdriver. See **Figure 21**.

If the head breaks off flush, use a screw extractor. To do this, centerpunch the remaining portion of the screw or bolt. Drill a small hole in the screw and tap the extractor into the hole. Back the screw out with a wrench on the extractor. See **Figure 22**.

"OFF THE ROAD" RULES

Areas set aside by government or local agencies for off-road riding are continuing to disappear. The loss of many of these areas is usually due to the few who really don't care and therefore ruin the sport of off-road fun for those who do. Many areas are closed off to protect wildlife habitat, vegetation and geological structures. Do not enter into these areas as it can result in an expensive citation and adds to the anti-off-road vehicle sentiment that can result in further land closures. By following these basic rules you and others will always have an area open for this type of recreational use.

1. When riding, always observe the basic practice of good sportsmanship and recognize that other people will judge all off-road vehicle owners by your actions.

2. Don't litter the trails or camping areas. Leave the area cleaner than it was before you came.

3. Don't pollute lakes, streams or the ocean.

4. Be careful not to damage living trees, shrubs or other natural terrain.

5. Respect other people's rights and property.

6. Help anyone in distress.

7. Make yourself and your vehicle available for assistance in any search and rescue parties.

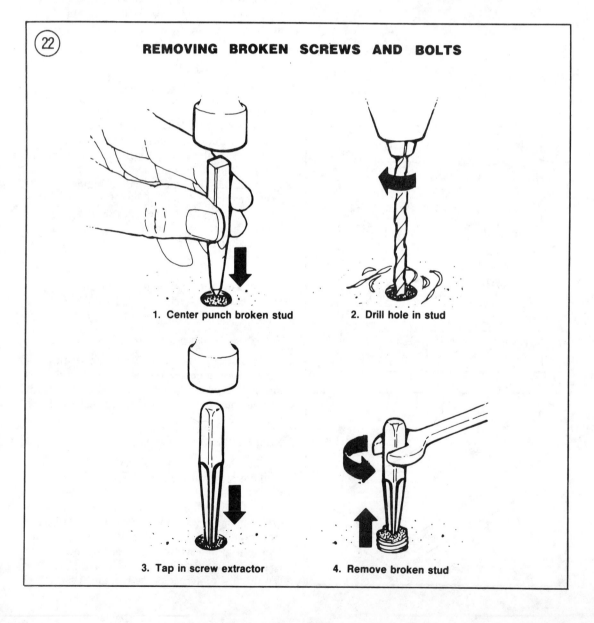

22

REMOVING BROKEN SCREWS AND BOLTS

1. Center punch broken stud

2. Drill hole in stud

3. Tap in screw extractor

4. Remove broken stud

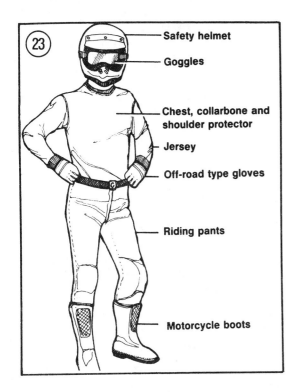

- Safety helmet
- Goggles
- Chest, collarbone and shoulder protector
- Jersey
- Off-road type gloves
- Riding pants
- Motorcycle boots

WINTER PROTECTIVE CLOTHING

Inner layers   **Outer layers**

- Face mask
- Wool shirt
- Glove liners
- Thermal underwear
- Heavy pants
- Wool socks

- Safety helmet
- Goggles
- Insulated suit
- Leather gloves
- Motorcycle or snowmobile boots

8. Don't harass other people using the same area as you are. Respect the rights of others enjoying the recreation area.

9. Be sure to obey all federal, state, provincial and other local rules regulating the operation of the ATV.

10. Inform public officials when using public lands.

11. Don't harass wildlife and stay out of areas posted for the protection and feeding of wildlife.

12. Keep your exhaust noise to a minimum.

13. When riding in the snow, stay away from carefully groomed snowmobile trails. Snowmobilers get pretty upset and rightfully so when ATV's spoil the trails that they have worked hard to make.

SAFETY

General Tips

1. Read your owner's manual and know your machine.

2. Check the throttle and brake controls before starting the engine.

3. Know how to make an emergency stop.

4. Know all state, federal and local laws concerning the ATV. Respect private property.

NOTE
*The Honda ATV is designed and manufactured for off-road use **only**. It does not conform to Federal Motor Vehicle Safety Standards and it is illegal to operate it on public streets, roads or highways.*

5. Never add fuel while anyone is smoking in the area or when the engine is running.

6. Never wear loose scarves, belts or boot laces that could catch on moving parts or tree limbs.

7. Always wear protective clothing to protect your *entire* body. **Figure 23** shows a well equipped off-road rider who is ready for almost any riding condition. Today's riding apparel is very stylish and you will be ready for action as will as being well protected.

8. Riding in the winter months requires a good set of clothes to keep your body dry and warm, otherwise your entire trip may be miserable. If you dress properly, moisture will evaporate from your body. If you become too hot and if your clothes trap the moisture, you will become cold. **Figure 24** shows some recommended inner and outer layers of cold weather clothing. Even mild temperatures can be very uncomfortable and dangerous when combined with a strong wind or high-speed travel.

See **Table 3** for wind chill factors. Always dress according to what the wind chill factor is, not the ambient temperature.

9. Never allow anyone to operate the ATV without proper instruction. This is for their bodily protection and to keep your machine from damage or destruction.

CAUTION
*Do **not** "pop wheelies" and run any distance with the ATV. The oil capacity is relatively small and the oil will drain out of the oil pump area, causing a loss of oil pressure and costly engine damage.*

10. Use the "buddy system" for long trips, just in case you have a problem or run out of gas.
11. Never carry a passenger. The ATV is designed to carry only one person.
12. Never attempt to repair your machine with the engine running except when necessary for certain tune-up procedures.
13. Check all of the machine components and hardware frequently, especially the wheels and the steering.
14. Push the ATV onto a truck or trailer bed—never ride it on. Secure it firmly to the truck or trailer and if towing a trailer be sure that the trailer lights operate properly.

Operating Tips

1. Never operate the machine in crowded areas or steer toward persons.

2. Avoid dangerous terrain.
3. Cross highways (where permitted) at a 90 degree angle after looking in both directions. Post traffic guards if crossing in groups.
4. Do not ride the vehicle on or near railroad tracks. The ATV engine and exhaust noise can drown out the sound of an approaching train.
5. Keep the headlight free of dirt and never ride at night without the headlight on.
6. Do not ride the ATV without the seat/fender assembly in place.
7. Always steer with both hands.
8. Be aware of the terrain and avoid operating the ATV at excessive speed.
9. Do not panic if the throttle sticks. Turn the engine stop switch to the OFF position.
10. Do not speed through wooded areas. Hidden obstructions, hanging tree limbs, unseen ditches and even wild animals and hikers can cause injury and damage to the ATV.
11. Do not tailgate. Rear end collisions can cause injury and machine damage.
12. Do not mix alcoholic beverages or drugs with riding—ride straight.
13. Keep both feet on the footpegs. Do not permit your feet to hang out to stabilize the machine when making turns or in near spill situations; broken limbs could result.
14. Check your fuel supply regularly. Do not travel farther than your fuel supply will permit you to return.
15. Check to make sure that the parking brake is *completely* released while riding. If it is left on, the rear brake shoes or pads will be damaged.

Table 1 STANDARD TORQUE SPECIFICATIONS

Item	N·m	ft.-lb.
5 mm bolt and nut	4.5-6	3-4
6 mm bolt and nut	8-12	6-9
8 mm bolt and nut	18-25	13-18
10 mm bolt and nut	30-40	22-29
12 mm bolt and nut	50-60	36-43
5 mm screw	3.5-5	2-4
6 mm screw and 6 mm bolt with 8 mm head	7-11	5-8
6 mm flange bolt and nut	10-14	7-10
8 mm flange bolt and nut	24-30	17-22
10 mm flange bolt and nut	35-45	25-33

1

Table 2 WORKSHOP TOOLS

Tool	Size or Specifications
Screwdriver	
Common	5/16×8 in. blade
Common	3/8×12 in. blade
Phillips	Size 2 tip, 6 in. overall
Pliers	
Gas pliers	6 in. overall
Vise Grips	10 in. overall
Needlenose	6 in. overall
Channel lock	12 in. overall
Snap ring	–
Wrenches	
Box-end set	5-17 mm (24 and 28 mm)
Open-end set	5-17 mm (24 and 28 mm)
Crescent	6 in. and 12 in. overall
Socket set	1/2 in. drive ratchet with 5-17 mm sockets
Other special tools	
Strap wrench	–
Impact driver	1/2 in. drive with assorted bits
Torque wrench	1/2 in. drive 0-100 ft.-lb.
Ignition gauge	–

Table 3 WIND CHILL FACTOR

Estimated Wind Speed in MPH	Actual Thermometer Reading (° F)											
	50	40	30	20	10	0	—10	—20	—30	—40	—50	—60
	Equivalent Temperature (° F)											
Calm	50	40	30	20	10	0	—10	—20	—30	—40	—50	—60
5	48	37	27	16	6	—5	—15	—26	—36	—47	—57	—68
10	40	28	16	4	—9	—21	—33	—46	—58	—70	—83	—95
15	36	22	9	—5	—18	—36	—45	—58	—72	—85	—99	—112
20	32	18	4	—10	—25	—39	—53	—67	—82	—96	—110	—124
25	30	16	0	—15	—29	—44	—59	—74	—88	—104	—118	—133
30	28	13	—2	—18	—33	—48	—63	—79	—94	—109	—125	—140
35	27	11	—4	—20	—35	—49	—67	—82	—98	—113	—129	—145
40	26	10	—6	—21	—37	—53	—69	—85	—100	—116	—132	—148

*

Little Danger (for properly clothed person)	Increasing Danger	Great Danger
	• Danger from freezing of exposed flesh •	

*Wind speeds greater than 40 mph have little additional effect.

CHAPTER TWO

TROUBLESHOOTING

Diagnosing mechanical problems is relatively simple if you use orderly procedures and keep a few basic principles in mind. The troubleshooting procedures in this chapter analyze typical symptoms and show logical methods of isolating causes. These are not the only methods. There may be several ways to solve a problem, but only a systematic, methodical approach can guarantee success. Never assume anything. Do not overlook the obvious. If you are riding along and the engine suddenly quits, check the easiest, most accessible problems first. Is there gasoline in the tank? Is the fuel shutoff valve in the ON position? Has the spark plug wire fallen off? If nothing obvious turns up in a quick check, look a little further. Learning to recognize and describe symptoms will make repairs easier for you or a mechanic at the shop. Describe problems accurately and fully. Saying that "it won't run" isn't the same as saying "it quit at high speed and won't start" or that "it sat in my garage for 3 months and then wouldn't start."

Gather as many symptoms together as possible to aid in diagnosis. Note whether the engine lost power gradually or all at once. Remember that the more complicated a machine is, the easier it is to troubleshoot because symptoms point to specific problems.

After the symptoms are defined, areas which could cause the problems are tested and analyzed.

Guessing at the cause of a problem may provide the solution, but it can easily lead to frustration, wasted time and a series of expensive, unnecessary parts replacements.

You do not need fancy equipment or complicated test gear to determine whether repairs can be attempted at home. A few simple checks could save a large repair bill and time lost while the bike sits in a dealer's service department. On the other hand, be realistic and don't attempt repairs beyond your abilities. Service departments tend to charge a lot for putting together a disassembled engine that may have been abused. Some dealers won't even take on such a job—so use common sense and don't get in over your head.

OPERATING REQUIREMENTS

An engine needs 3 basics to run properly: correct fuel/air mixture, compression and a spark at the correct time. If one or more are missing, the engine just won't run. The electrical system is the weakest link of the 3 basics. More problems result from electrical breakdowns than from any other source. Keep that in mind before you begin tampering with carburetor adjustments and the like.

If the vehicle has been sitting for any length of time and refuses to start, check and clean the spark plug and then look to the gasoline delivery system.

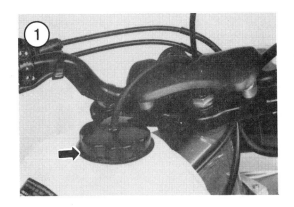

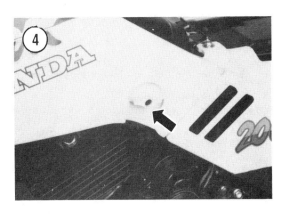

This includes the fuel tank, fuel shutoff valve and integral fuel filter and the fuel line to the carburetor. Gasoline deposits may have formed and gummed up the carburetor's jets and air passages. Gasoline tends to lose its potency after standing for long periods. Condensation may contaminate the fuel with water. Drain the old fuel and try starting with a fresh tankful.

EMERGENCY TROUBLESHOOTING

When the vehicle is difficult to start or won't start at all, it does not help to keep trying. Check for obvious problems even before getting out your tools. Go down the following list step by step. Do each one. You may be embarrassed to find your kill switch is stuck in the OFF position, but that is better than wearing down the battery. If it still will not start, refer to the appropriate troubleshooting procedure which follows in this chapter.

1. Is there fuel in the tank? Open the filler cap. Refer to **Figure 1** for 3-wheeled models or **Figure 2** for 4-wheeled models. Rock the vehicle and listen for fuel sloshing around.

> *WARNING*
> *Do not use an open flame to check in the tank. A serious explosion is certain to result.*

2. Is the fuel shutoff valve in the ON position? Refer to **Figure 3** for 3-wheeled models or **Figure 4** for 4-wheeled models.
3. Make sure the kill switch (**Figure 5**) is not stuck in the OFF position.

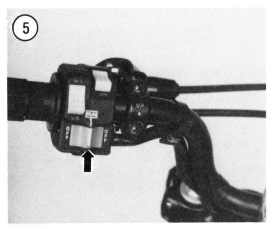

4. Is the spark plug wire (**Figure 6**) on tight? Push it on and slightly rotate it to clean the electrical connection between the plug and the connector.

5A. On models so equipped, is the choke knob (**Figure 7**) in the right position? The knob should be pulled *up* for a cold engine and pushed *down* for a warm engine.

5B. On all other models, is the choke lever (**Figure 8**) in the right position? The lever should be *raised* for a cold engine or *lowered* for a warm engine.

ENGINE STARTING

An engine that refuses to start or is difficult to start is very frustrating. More often than not, the problem is very minor and can be found with a simple and logical troubleshooting approach.

The following items show a beginning point from which to isolate engine starting problems.

Engine Fails to Start

Perform the following spark test to determine if the ignition system is operating properly.

1. Remove the spark plug from the cylinder.

2. Connect the spark plug wire and connector to the spark plug and touch the spark plug's base to a good ground such as the engine cylinder head (**Figure 9**). Position the spark plug so you can see the electrodes.

> *WARNING*
> *If it is necessary to hold the high voltage lead in the next step, do so with an insulated pair of pliers. The high voltage generated by the ignition pulse generator and CDI unit could produce serious or fatal shocks.*

3. Crank the engine over with the recoil starter, kickstarter or with the starter. A fat blue spark should be evident across the plug's electrodes.

4. If the spark is good, check for one or more of the following possible malfunctions:

   a. Obstructed fuel line.
   b. Low compression.
   c. Leaking head gasket.
   d. Choke not operating properly.
   e. Throttle not operating properly.

5. If spark is not good, check for one or more of the following:

   a. Weak ignition coil.
   b. Weak CDI pulse generator.
   c. Broken or shorted high tension lead to the spark plug.
   d. Loose electrical connections.
   e. Loose or broken ignition coil ground wire.

Engine Is Difficult to Start

Check for one or more of the following possible malfunctions:

   a. Fouled spark plug.
   b. Improperly adjusted choke.
   c. Contaminated fuel system.
   d. Improperly adjusted carburetor.
   e. Weak ignition coil.
   f. Weak CDI pulse generator.
   g. Incorrect type ignition coil.
   h. Poor compression.

Engine Will Not Crank

Check for one or more of the following possible malfunctions:

   a. Discharged battery (models so equipped).
   b. Defective starter motor, starter solenoid or start switch (models so equipped).
   c. Defective or broken recoil starter mechanism (models so equipped).
   d. Defective or broken kickstarter mechanism (models so equipped).
   e. Seized piston.
   f. Seized crankshaft bearings.
   g. Broken connecting rod.
   h. Locked-up transmission or clutch assembly.

ENGINE PERFORMANCE

In the following checklist, it is assumed that the engine runs, but is not operating at peak performance. This will serve as a starting point from which to isolate a performance malfunction.

The possible causes for each malfunction are listed in a logical sequence and in order of probability.

Engine Will Not Start or Is Hard to Start

a. Fuel tank empty.
b. Obstructed fuel line or fuel shutoff valve.
c. Sticking float valve in carburetor.
d. Carburetor incorrectly adjusted.
e. Improper choke operation.
f. Fouled or improperly gapped spark plug.
g. Weak CDI pulse generator.
h. Ignition timing incorrect (faulty component in system).
i. Broken or shorted ignition coil.
j. Weak or faulty spark unit or pulse generator.
k. Improper valve timing.
l. Improper valve clearance.
m. Excessive decompression lever free play (models so equipped).
n. Clogged air filter element.
o. Contaminated fuel.

Engine Will Not Idle or Idles Erratically

a. Carburetor incorrectly adjusted.
b. Fouled or improperly gapped spark plug.
c. Leaking head gasket or vacuum leak.
d. Weak CDI pulse generator.
e. Ignition timing incorrect (faulty component in system).
f. Improper valve timing.
g. Improper valve clearance.
h. Insufficient decompression lever free play (models so equipped).
i. Obstructed fuel line or fuel shutoff valve.

Engine Misses at High Speed

a. Fouled or improperly gapped spark plug.
b. Improper ignition timing (faulty component in system).
c. Improper carburetor main jet selection.
d. Clogged jets in the carburetor.
e. Weak ignition coil.
f. Weak CDI pulse generator.
g. Improper valve timing.
h. Obstructed fuel line or fuel shutoff valve.

Engine Continues to Run with Ignition Off

a. Excessive carbon build-up in engine.
b. Vacuum leak in intake system.
c. Contaminated or incorrect fuel octane rating.

Engine Overheating

a. Obstructed cooling fins on the cylinder and cylinder head.
b. Improper ignition timing (faulty component in system).
c. Improper spark plug heat range.

Engine Misses at Idle

a. Fouled or improperly gapped spark plug.
b. Spark plug cap faulty.
c. Ignition cable insulation deteriorated (shorting out).
d. Dirty or clogged air filter element.
e. Carburetor incorrectly adjusted (too lean or too rich).
f. Choke valve stuck.
g. Clogged jet(s) in the carburetor.
h. Carburetor float height incorrect.

**Engine Backfires—
Explosions in Mufflers**

  a. Fouled or improperly gapped spark plug.

  b. Spark plug cap faulty.

  c. Ignition cable insulation deteriorated (shorting out).

  d. Ignition timing incorrect.

  e. Improper valve timing.

  f. Contaminated fuel.

  g. Burned or damaged intake and/or exhaust valves.

  h. Weak or broken intake and/or exhaust valve springs.

**Pre-ignition (Fuel Mixture
Ignites Before Spark Plug Fires)**

  a. Hot spot in combustion chamber (piece of carbon).

  b. Valve(s) stuck in guide.

  c. Overheating engine.

Smoky Exhaust and Engine Runs Roughly

  a. Fuel mixture too rich.

  b. Choke not operating correctly.

  c. Water or other contaminants in fuel.

  d. Clogged fuel line.

  e. Clogged air filter element.

**Engine Loses Power at
Normal Riding Speed**

  a. Carburetor incorrectly adjusted.

  b. Engine overheating.

  c. Improper ignition timing (faulty component in system).

  d. Weak CDI pulse generator.

  e. Incorrectly gapped spark plug.

  f. Weak ignition coil.

  g. Weak CDI pulse generator.

  h. Obstructed muffler.

  i. Dragging brake(s).

Engine Lacks Acceleration

  a. Mixture too lean.

  b. Clogged fuel line.

  c. Improper ignition timing (faulty component in system).

  d. Improper valve clearance.

  e. Dragging brake(s).

ENGINE NOISES

1. *Knocking or pinging during acceleration—* Caused by using a lower octane fuel than recommended. May also be caused by poor fuel. Pinging can also be caused by a spark plug of the wrong heat range. Refer to *Spark Plug Selection* in Chapter Three.

2. *Slapping or rattling noises at low speed or during acceleration—*May be caused by piston slap (excessive piston to cylinder wall clearance).

3. *Knocking or rapping while decelerating—* Usually caused by excessive rod bearing clearance. bearing clearance.

4. *Persistent knocking and vibration—*Usually caused by excessive main bearing clearance.

5. *Rapid on-off squeal—*Compression leak around cylinder head gasket or spark plug.

EXCESSIVE VIBRATION

Usually this is caused by loose engine mounting hardware. If not, it can be difficult to find without disassembling the engine.

FRONT SUSPENSION AND STEERING

Poor handling may be caused by improper tire pressure, a damaged or bent frame or front steering components, a worn front fork assembly, worn wheel bearings or dragging brakes.

BRAKE PROBLEMS

A sticking drum brake may be caused by worn or weak return springs, dry pivot and cam bushings or improper adjustment.

Sticking disc brakes may be caused by a stuck piston(s) in the caliper assembly or warped disc(s).

Grabbing brakes may be caused by greasy linings or pads which must be replaced. Brake grab may also be due to an out-of-round drum or warped disc. Glazed linings or pads will cause loss of stopping power.

CHAPTER THREE

LUBRICATION, MAINTENANCE AND TUNE-UP

If this is your first experience with an ATV or motorcycle, you should become acquainted with products that are available in auto or motorcycle parts and supply stores. Look into the tune-up tools and parts and check out the different fluids such as motor oil, locking compounds and greases. Also check engine degreasers, like Gunk or Bel-Ray Degreaser, for cleaning your engine before working on it.

The more you get involved with your ATV the more you will want to work on it. Start out by doing simple tune-up, lubrication and maintenance. Tackle more involved jobs as you gain experience.

The Honda ATV is a relatively simple machine but to gain the utmost in safety, performance and useful life from it, it is necessary to make periodic inspections and adjustments. Minor problems are often found during such inspections that are simple and inexpensive to correct at the time, but which could lead to major problems if not corrected.

This chapter explains lubrication, maintenance and tune-up procedures required for the Honda ATV's covered in this book. **Table 1** is a suggested factory maintenance schedule. **Tables 1-8** are at the end of this chapter.

PRE-CHECKS

The following checks should be performed before the first ride of the day.

1. Inspect all fuel lines and fittings for wetness.
2. Make sure the fuel tank is full of fresh gasoline.
3. Make sure the engine oil level is correct. Add oil if necessary.
4. Make sure the air filter element is clean.
5. Check the operation of the clutch and adjust if necessary.
6. Check the throttle and the brake levers. Make sure they operate properly with no binding.
7. On models so equipped, check the brake fluid level in the front master cylinder reservoir. Add fluid if necessary.
8. Inspect the front and rear suspension; make sure it has a good solid feel with no looseness.
9. Check tire pressure or circumference measurement. Refer to **Table 2**.
10. Check the exhaust system for damage.
11. Check the tightness of all fasteners, especially engine mounting hardware.
12. Make sure the headlight and taillight work.

SERVICE INTERVALS

The services and intervals shown in **Table 1** are recommended by the factory. Strict adherence to these recommendations will ensure long service from your Honda ATV. However, if the vehicle is run in an area of high humidity, the lubrication services must be done more frequently to prevent possible rust damage. This is particularly true if you have run the ATV through water (especially salt water).

For convenience when maintaining your vehicle, most of the services shown in **Table 1** are described in this chapter. However, some procedures which require more than minor disassembly or adjustment are covered elsewhere in the appropriate chapter.

TIRES AND WHEELS

Tire Pressure

Tire pressure should be checked and adjusted to maintain the smoothness of the tire, good traction and handling and to get the maximum life out of the tire. A simple, accurate gauge (**Figure 1**) can be purchased for a few dollars and should be carried in your tool box in the tow vehicle. The appropriate tire pressures are shown in **Table 2**.

> *WARNING*
> *Always inflate both rear tires to the same pressure. If the ATV is run with unequal air pressures, the vehicle will always run toward one side and handle poorly.*

> *CAUTION*
> *Do not overinflate the stock tires as they will be permanently distorted and damaged. If overinflated, they will bulge out like an inner tube that is not within the constraints of a tire. If this happens the tire will **not** return to its original contour.*

Tire Inspection

The tires take a lot of punishment due to the variety of terrain they are subject to. Inspect them periodically for excessive wear, cuts, abrasions, etc. If you find a nail or other object in the tire, mark its location with a light crayon before removing it. This will help locate the hole for repair. Refer to Chapter Nine for tire changing and repair information.

Rim Inspection

Frequently inspect the condition of the wheel rims, especially the outer side (**Figure 2**). If the wheel has hit a tree or large rock, rim damage may be sufficient to cause an air leak or misalignment. Improper wheel alignment can cause severe vibration and result in an unsafe riding condition.

Make sure that the cotter pins (**Figure 3**) are securely in place on all wheels (models so equipped). If they are lost and the castellated nut works loose—it's good-bye wheel.

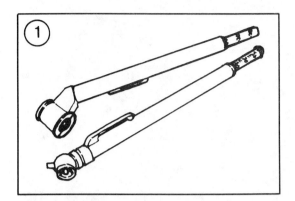

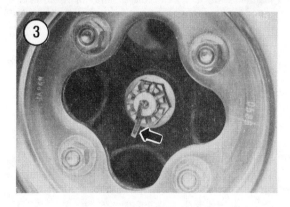

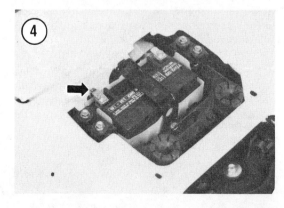

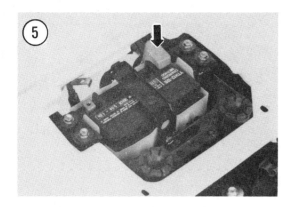

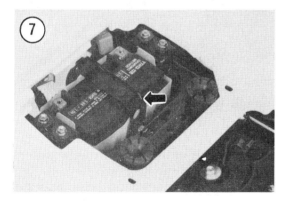

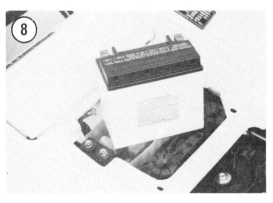

3

BATTERY (MODELS SO EQUIPPED)

The original equipment battery is a sealed type. There is no routine upkeep on the sealed battery other than to keep the terminals free of corrosion and keep the terminal screws securing the leads to the battery tight.

The electrolyte level cannot be corrected on a sealed battery as the battery top is not removable.

Battery
Removal/Installation

1. Remove the seat as described in Chapter Fifteen.
2. First disconnect the battery negative (−) lead (**Figure 4**) then the positive (+) lead (**Figure 5**) from the battery.
3. Remove the bolt (**Figure 6**) securing the battery holder and remove the holder (**Figure 7**).
4. Pull the battery up and out of its tray (**Figure 8**). Wipe off any of the highly corrosive residue that may have dripped from the battery during removal.

> *CAUTION*
> *Be careful not to spill battery electrolyte on painted surfaces. The liquid is highly corrosive and will damage the finish. If it is spilled, wash it off immediately with soapy water and thoroughly rinse with clean water.*

5. Install by reversing these removal steps.

Charging

> *CAUTION*
> ***Never*** *connect a battery charger to the battery with the leads still connected.* ***Always*** *disconnect the leads from the battery. During the charging procedure the charger may damage the diodes within the voltage regulator/rectifier.*

1. Connect the positive (+) charger lead to the positive (+) battery terminal (or lead) and the negative (−) charger lead to the negative (−) battery terminal (or lead).

> *CAUTION*
> *Do not exceed the recommended charging amperage rate or charging time listed in **Table 3** or the battery will be damaged.*

2. Set the charger at 12 volts. If the output of the charger is variable, it is best to select a low setting. Refer to **Table 3** for charging amperage and length of charging time. Switch the charger on.

3. After the battery has been charged for the time listed in **Table 3**, turn the charger off and disconnect the charger leads.

4. Connect a voltmeter across the battery negative and positive terminals and measure the battery voltage. A fully charged battery should read 13.1 volts. If the voltage is 12.4 or less the battery is undercharged.

5. If the battery voltage remains stable for 1 hour, the battery is considered charged.

6. Clean the battery terminals and surrounding case and reinstall the battery as described in this chapter. Coat the battery terminals with Vaseline or silicone spray to retard corrosion and decomposition of the terminals.

New Battery Installation

Always replace the battery with another sealed-type battery. The charging system is designed for this type of battery.

When replacing the old battery with a new one, be sure to charge it completely before installing it in the ATV. Failure to do so will permanently damage the new battery.

PERIODIC LUBRICATION

Drive Chain Cleaning and Lubrication

Drive chain cleaning and lubrication are covered in Chapter Eleven or Chapter Twelve.

Engine Oil Level Check

Engine oil level is checked with the dipstick/oil fill cap, located on the right-hand crankcase cover. Refer to **Figure 9** for 3-wheeled models or **Figure 10** for 4-wheeled models.

1. Start the engine and let it warm up approximately 2-3 minutes.

2. Shut off the engine and let the oil settle.

3. Unscrew the dipstick/oil fill cap and wipe it clean. Reinsert it onto the threads in the hole; do not screw it in. Remove it and check the oil level. The ATV must be level for a correct reading.

4. The level should be between the 2 lines and not above the upper one (**Figure 11**). If necessary, add the recommended type oil to correct the level. Install the dipstick/oil fill cap and tighten it securely.

Engine Oil Change

Regular oil changes will contribute more to engine longevity than any other maintenance performed. The factory recommended oil change interval and the cleaning of the oil filter screen and

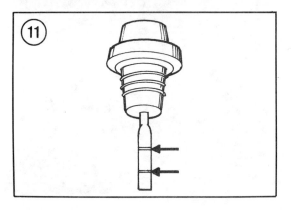

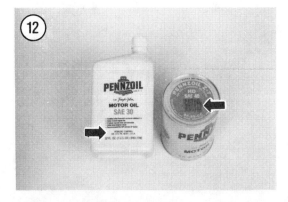

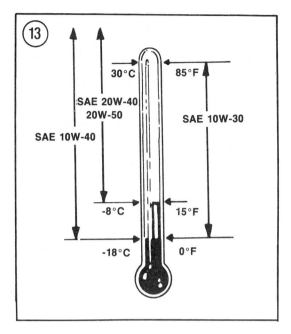

3

rotor is listed in **Table 1**. This assumes that the vehicle is operated in moderate climates. If it is operated under dusty conditions, the oil will get dirty more quickly and should be changed more frequently than recommended.

Use only a high quality detergent motor oil with an API rating of SE or SF. The quality rating is stamped or printed on top of the can or label on plastic bottles (**Figure 12**). Try to use the same brand of oil at each oil change. Refer to **Figure 13** for correct oil weight to use under anticipated ambient temperatures (not engine oil temperature).

> *CAUTION*
> *Do not add any friction reducing additives to the oil as they will cause clutch slippage. Also, do not use an engine oil with graphite added. The use of graphite oil will void any applicable Honda warranty. It is not established at this time if graphite will build up on the clutch friction plates and cause clutch problems. Until further testing is done by the oil and motorcycle industries, do not use this type of oil.*

To change the engine oil you will need the following:
   a. Drain pan.
   b. Funnel.
   c. Can opener or pour spout.
   d. 17 mm wrench (supplied in the owner's tool kit).
   e. 2 quarts of oil.
There are several ways to discard the old oil safely. Some service stations and oil retailers will accept your used oil for recycling; some may even give you money for it. Never drain the oil onto the ground.
1. Place the ATV on level ground.
2. Set the parking brake, start the engine and let it reach operating temperature.
3. Shut it off and place a drain pan under the engine.
4. Remove the 17 mm drain plug. Refer to **Figure 14** for 3-wheeled models or **Figure 15** for 4-wheeled models. Remove the dipstick/oil fill cap; this will speed up the flow of oil.

> *CAUTION*
> *Do not let the engine start and run without oil in the crankcase. Make sure the engine kill switch is in the OFF position.*

5. Let the oil drain for at least 15-20 minutes. During this time, pull on the recoil starter or kick

the kickstarter a couple of times to help drain any remaining oil.

6. Inspect the O-ring seal on the drain plug. Replace it if its condition is in doubt.

7. Tighten the drain plug to the torque specification listed in **Table 4**.

8. At the indicated interval (see **Table 1**), perform *Oil Filter Screen and Rotor Cleaning* as described in this chapter.

9. Insert a funnel into the oil fill hole and fill the engine with the correct weight and quantity oil as listed in **Figure 13** and **Table 5**.

10. Install and tighten the dipstick/oil fill cap securely.

11. If the engine has been rebuilt or disassembled, turn the engine kill switch to the OFF position and use the recoil starter or kickstarter a couple of times to help distribute the oil throughout the engine.

12. Start the engine and let the engine run at moderate speed and check for leaks.

13. Turn the engine off and check for correct oil level; adjust as necessary.

Oil Filter Screen and Rotor Cleaning

3-wheeled models

1. Remove the right-hand crankcase cover as described in Chapter Four.

2. Carefully withdraw the oil filter screen (**Figure 16**) from the crankcase.

3. Thoroughly clean the oil filter screen with a soft toothbrush and solvent.

4. Inspect the oil filter screen (**Figure 17**) for damage or broken areas. Replace the screen if damaged.

5. Clean the oil filter screen receptacle in the crankcase with solvent. Scrape out any oil sludge with a broad-tipped, dull screwdriver.

6. Install the oil filter screen with the *thick* end facing toward the outside.

7. Remove the screws securing the oil filter rotor cover (**Figure 18**) and remove the cover and gasket.

8. Clean the inside of the rotor in solvent and scrape out any oil sludge with a broad-tipped, dull screwdriver.

9. Disassemble the rotor cover as follows:

   a. Remove the spring clip (**Figure 19**) securing the oil pipe and spring.

   b. Remove the oil pipe and spring (**Figure 20**) from the cover.

   c. Clean out the oil pipe with solvent and dry thoroughly.

   d. Install the oil pipe and spring.

   e. Install the spring clip.

10. Install a new gasket (**Figure 21**) on the cover.

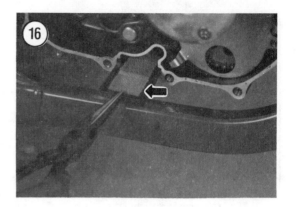

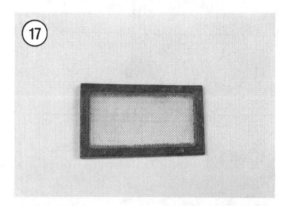

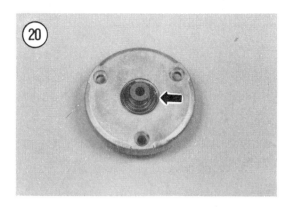

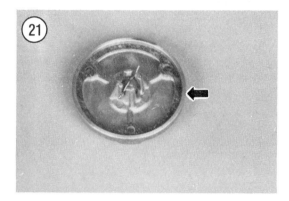

11. Install the oil filter rotor cover and tighten the screws securely.

12. Install the right-hand crankcase cover as described in Chapter Four.

13. Refill the crankcase with the recommended type and quantity of engine oil as described in this chapter.

3

4-wheeled models

1. Remove the right-hand crankcase cover as described in Chapter Four.

> *NOTE*
> *Figure 22 is shown with the engine partially disassembled for clarity. It is not necessary to disassemble the engine to perform this procedure.*

2. Carefully withdraw the oil filter screen (**Figure 22**) from the crankcase.

3. Thoroughly clean the oil filter screen with a soft toothbrush and solvent.

4. Inspect the oil filter screen (**Figure 17**) for damage or broken areas. Replace the screen if damaged.

5. Clean the oil filter screen receptacle in the crankcase with solvent. If necessary scrape out any oil sludge with a broad-tipped, dull screwdriver.

6. Install the oil filter screen with the *thick* end facing toward the outside.

7. Remove the bolts (**Figure 23**) securing the oil filter rotor cover and remove the cover and gasket from the centrifugal clutch assembly.

> *CAUTION*
> *Do not allow any dirt or foreign matter to enter the oil passageway in the end of the crankshaft.*

> *CAUTION*
> *Do not use compressed air to clean the oil filter rotor assembly.*

8. Clean the inside of the rotor and cover with a lint-free cloth.

9. Install a new gasket on the cover.

10. Install the oil filter rotor cover and tighten the screws securely.

11. Install the right-hand crankcase cover as described in Chapter Four.

12. Refill the crankcase with the recommended type and quantity of engine oil as described in this chapter.

**Front Fork Oil Change
(3-wheeled Models)**

Change the fork oil at the interval indicated in **Table 1** or when it becomes contaminated.

1. Place the ATV on level ground and set the parking brake.

2. Place wood blocks under the frame to support the ATV with the front wheel off the ground.

> *WARNING*
> *Release the air pressure gradually in the following step. If released too fast, fork oil will spurt out with the air. Protect your eyes and clothing accordingly.*

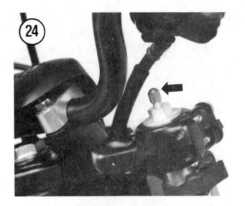

3. Remove the air valve cap (**Figure 24**) and bleed off *all* air pressure by depressing the valve stem (**Figure 25**). Reinstall the air valve cap.

> *WARNING*
> *Always bleed off all air pressure; failure to do so may cause personal injury when disassembling the fork assembly.*

4. Slowly unscrew the fork cap bolt (**Figure 26**), as it is under spring pressure from the fork springs.

5. Place a drain pan under the drain screw (**Figure 27**) and remove the drain screw. Allow the oil to drain for at least 5 minutes. *Never* reuse the oil.

> *CAUTION*
> *Do not allow the fork oil come in contact with any of the brake components.*

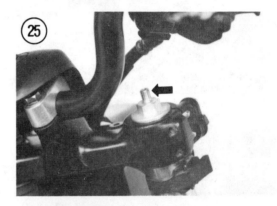

6. Inspect the gasket on the drain screw and replace if necessary. Install the drain screw and tighten securely.

7. Repeat for the other fork.

8. Remove the upper fork spring "A," spring seat and the lower fork spring "B" from the fork tube.

9. Repeat Steps 3-8 for the other fork assembly.

10. Remove the wood blocks from under the frame and set the front wheel on the ground. Gradually lower the front of the ATV until the front forks are completely compressed (bottomed out at the end of their travel).

11. Refill each fork leg with the specified quantity of Dexron automatic transmission fluid or 10W fork oil. Refer to **Table 6** for specified quantity and oil level and to **Figure 28**.

> *NOTE*
> *To measure the correct amount of fluid, use a plastic baby bottle. These have measurements in cubic centimeters (cc) and fluid ounces (oz.) on the side.*

12. Raise the front of the ATV and place wood blocks under the frame so the front wheel is off the ground.

13. Inspect the O-ring seal on the fork cap bolt and replace if necessary.

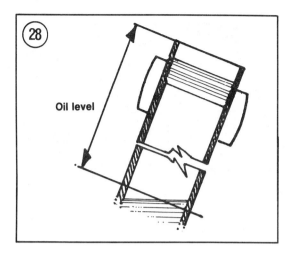

Oil level

14. Install the lower fork spring "B" with the tapered end going in first.
15. Install the spring seat and the upper fork spring "A."
16. Install the fork cap bolt while pushing down on the fork springs. Start the fork cap bolt slowly—don't crossthread it. Tighten to the torque specification listed in **Table 4**.
17. Remove the wood blocks from under the frame. Road test the ATV and check for leaks.

Throttle Housing Lubrication

1. Remove the screws (**Figure 29**) securing the throttle housing cover and remove the cover and gasket.
2. Straighten the tab (**Figure 30**) on the lockwasher.
3. Remove the nut (**Figure 31**) securing the throttle arm.
4. Remove the lockwasher, the throttle arm (**Figure 32**) and spring from the throttle lever shaft.
5. Disconnect the throttle cable from the throttle arm (**Figure 33**).

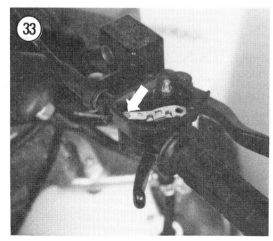

6. Withdraw the throttle lever and shaft (**Figure 34**) from the housing.

7. Lubricate the throttle cable as described in this chapter.

8. Apply a light coat of multipurpose grease to all pivoting areas of the throttle housing and to the throttle arm shaft.

9. Attach the throttle cable to the throttle arm (**Figure 33**).

10. Install the throttle arm return spring onto the throttle housing post (**Figure 35**).

11. Align the flats of the throttle arm with the flats on the throttle shaft. Hold the throttle shaft in place and install the throttle arm.

12. Hook the spring onto the throttle arm as shown in **Figure 36**.

13. Install the lockwasher (**Figure 37**) onto the throttle shaft.

14. Install the nut (**Figure 31**) securing the throttle arm. Tighten the nut securely.

15. Operate the throttle lever several times to make sure it is operating correctly. Correct any problems that may exist at this time.

16. Bend the locking tab up against one of the flats on the nut (**Figure 30**).

17. Install a new gasket (**Figure 38**) onto the housing or cover.

18. Align the holes in the cover with the locating dowels in the housing and install the cover. Tighten the cover screws (**Figure 29**) securely.

Control Cables

The control cables should be lubricated at the interval indicated in **Table 1**. They should also be inspected at this time for fraying and the cable sheath should be checked for chafing. The cables are relatively inexpensive and should be replaced when found to be faulty.

The control cables can be lubricated either with oil or with any of the popular cable lubricants and a cable lubricator. The first method requires more time and complete lubrication of the entire cable is less certain.

Oil method

1. Disconnect the cable from the throttle, choke, rear brake, and parking brake lever.

2. Make a cone of stiff paper and tape it to the end of the cable sheath (**Figure 39**).

NOTE
To avoid a mess, place a shop cloth at the end of the cable to catch the oil as it runs out.

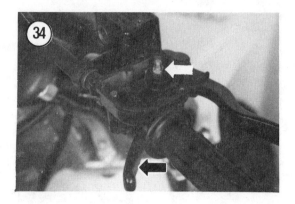

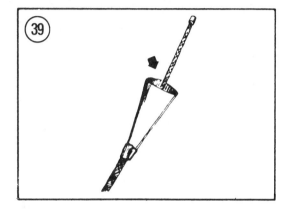

3. Hold the cable upright and pour a small amount of light oil (SAE 10W/30) into the cone. Work the cable in and out of the sheath for several minutes to help the oil work its way down to the end of the cable.

4. Remove the cone, reconnect the cable and adjust the cable(s) as described in this chapter.

Lubricator method

1. Disconnect the cables from the throttle, choke, rear brake lever and parking brake lever.

2. Attach a lubricator following the manufacturer's instructions.

NOTE
To avoid a mess, place a shop cloth at the end of the cable to catch the oil as it runs out.

3. Insert the nozzle of the lubricant can in the lubricator, press the button on the can and hold it down until the lubricant begins to flow out of the other end of the cable.

4. Remove the lubricator, reconnect the cable(s) and adjust the cable(s) as described in this chapter.

Miscellaneous Lubrication Points

Lubricate the front brake lever, rear brake lever and rear brake pedal pivot points.

PERIODIC MAINTENANCE

Drive Chain Adjustment

The drive chain should be checked at every fuel stop or at the beginning of each riding day. Clean, lubricate and adjust the drive chain at the intervals indicated in **Table 1**. Refer to procedures in this chapter and Chapter Eleven or Chapter Twelve. A properly lubricated and adjusted drive chain will provide maximum service life and reliability.

The correct amount of drive chain free play, when pushed up midway on the upper chain run, is 25-35 mm (1-1 3/8 in.). See **Figure 40**.

1. Place the vehicle on level ground and set the parking brake.

2. Shift the transmission into NEUTRAL.

3A. On 3-wheeled models, adjust the tension by performing the following:

   a. Loosen the swing arm pinch bolts (A, **Figure 41**) securing the axle holder.

   b. Insert a drift or round bar into one of the holes (B, **Figure 41**) in the axle holder.

   c. To increase drive chain tension, pull the drift toward the rear of the vehicle, rotating the top of the axle holder to the rear. To decrease drive chain tension, push the drift toward the front of the vehicle, rotating the top of the axle holder toward the front.

d. Rotate the axle holder until the correct amount of drive chain slack is obtained.

e. Tighten the pinch bolts to the torque specification listed in **Table 4**.

3B. On 4-wheeled models, adjust the tension by performing the following:

a. Loosen the axle housing pinch bolts (**Figure 42**) on each side, securing the axle holder.

b. Turn the adjuster nuts (**Figure 43**) in either direction until the correct amount of drive chain tension is achieved.

c. Tighten the pinch bolts to the torque specification listed in **Table 4**.

4. Release the parking brake and push the ATV forward to move the chain to another position and recheck the adjustment. Chains rarely wear or stretch evenly. As a result, the free play will not remain constant over the entire chain.

5. If the chain cannot be adjusted within these limits, it is excessively worn and stretched and should be replaced as described in Chapter Eleven or Chapter Twelve. Drive chain replacement numbers are listed in **Table 7**. Always replace both sprockets when replacing the drive chain; never install a new chain over worn sprockets.

> *WARNING*
> *Excess free play can result in chain breakage which could cause a serious accident.*

6. After the drive chain has been adjusted, the rear brake pedal free play must be adjusted as described in this chapter.

> *NOTE*
> *If the side plates of the drive chain are very dirty and covered with sand and grit, the chain should be removed and cleaned as described in Chapter Eleven or Chapter Twelve.*

7. Thoroughly lubricate the drive chain with SAE 80W-90 gear oil or a good grade of chain lubricant (specifically formulated for O-ring chains), following the manufacturer's instructions.

**Drive Chain Slider and Roller
(3-Wheeled Models)**

Inspect the drive chain slider (**Figure 44**) and roller for wear. When the depth of the groove in the slider reaches 2.0 mm (0.08 in.) or greater, remove the material to lower the height of the center ridge between the grooves to less than 2.0 mm (0.08 in.) as shown in **Figure 45**.

If the drive chain has worn a groove 6.0 mm (0.24 in.) through the slider (**Figure 46**) it should be

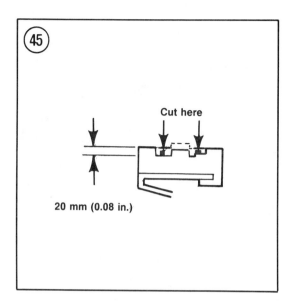

Cut here

20 mm (0.08 in.)

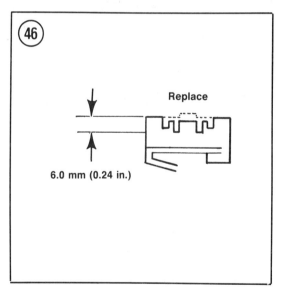

Replace

6.0 mm (0.24 in.)

replaced. To remove the slider, the swing arm must be removed as described in Chapter Eleven or Chapter Twelve.

Front Drum Brake Lining Inspection

The front drum brakes are not equipped with wear indicators.

1. Move the ATV in either direction until the rubber inspection caps are horizontal. This will align the wheel and brake drum inspection holes with the brake linings.

> *NOTE*
> *The 2 rubber inspection caps are spaced at different distances from the center of the wheel. The outer hole is the inspection hole as it aligns with the brake shoes. The inner hole is for adjusting as it aligns with the adjustment wheels of the front brake wheel cylinder.*

2. Remove the outer rubber inspection cap (**Figure 47**) from the front wheel brake drum.

3. Using a vernier caliper, measure the lining thickness. If either brake lining is worn to within 2.0 mm (0.08 in.) of the metal backing plate, both brake shoes must be replaced as described in Chapter Thirteen. Replace both brake shoes in each front wheel at the same time even though only one requires replacement.

> *CAUTION*
> *If the inspection caps are not completely seated in the brake drum, they will allow water to enter the brake drum leading to brake failure and damage.*

4. Install the rubber inspection cap. Make sure it is pressed completely into the brake drum for a good water-tight seal.

Rear Drum Brake Lining Inspection

At the interval indicated in **Table 1**, inspect the rear brake lining wear indicator. Apply the rear brake fully, if the index line on the brake arm camshaft aligns with the index mark on the brake backing plate, replace the rear brake shoes as described in Chapter Thirteen.

Disc Brakes

The hydraulic brake fluid in each disc brake master cylinder should be checked at the interval indicated in **Table 1**. The brake pads should also be checked for wear at the same time. Brake service is covered in Chapter Fourteen.

Disc Brake Fluid Level

The hydraulic brake fluid in the reservoir should be up to the upper line. Refer to **Figure 48** for the front brake and **Figure 49** for the rear brake. If necessary, correct the level by adding fresh brake fluid.

1. Clean any dirt from the area around the cover before removing the cover.

2. Remove the screws securing the cover and remove the cover, diaphragm plate and the diaphragm. Refer to **Figure 50** for the front master cylinder and **Figure 51** for the rear master cylinder.

> *WARNING*
> *Use brake fluid marked DOT 3 or DOT 4 (specified for disc brakes). Others may vaporize and cause brake failure. Do not intermix different brands or types of brake fluid as they may not be compatible. Do not intermix silicone based (DOT 5) brake fluid as it can cause brake component damage leading to brake system failure.*

> *CAUTION*
> *Be careful when adding brake fluid. Do not spill it on painted or plated surfaces as it will destroy the finish. Wash off the area immediately with soapy water and thoroughly rinse it off with clean water.*

3. Reinstall the diaphragm, diaphragm plate and cover. Tighten the cover screws securely.

Disc Brake Lines

Check the brake lines between the master cylinder(s) and the brake caliper assembly(ies). If there is any leakage, tighten the connections and bleed the brakes as described under *Bleeding the System* in Chapter Fourteen. If tightening the connection does not stop the leak or if the brake line is obviously damaged, cracked or chafed, replace the brake line(s) and bleed the system as described in Chapter Fourteen.

Disc Brake Pad Wear

Inspect the brake pads for excessive or uneven wear or scoring of the disc. Replace the brake pads if the wear groove on the brake pad reaches the brake disc. If brake pad replacement is necessary, refer to Chapter Fourteen.

> *NOTE*
> *Always replace both pads at the same time to maintain even pressure on the brake disc.*

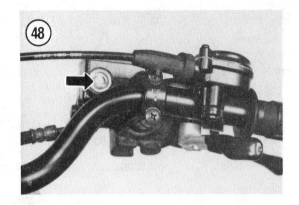

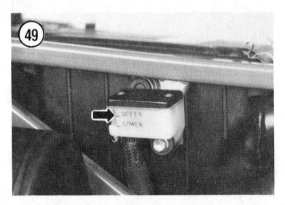

3

Disc Brake Fluid Change

Every time the reservoir cap is removed, a small amount of dirt and moisture enters the brake fluid system. The same thing happens if a leak occurs or any part of the hydraulic brake system is loosened or disconnected. Dirt can clog the system and cause unnecessary wear. Water in the brake fluid vaporizes at high temperature, impairing the hydraulic action and reducing the brake's stopping ability.

To maintain peak braking efficiency, change the brake fluid every year. To change brake fluid, follow the *Bleeding the System* procedure in Chapter Fourteen. Continue adding new brake fluid to the master cylinder(s) and bleed the fluid out at the caliper(s) until the brake fluid leaving the caliper(s) is clean and free of contaminants.

> *WARNING*
> *Use brake fluid marked DOT 3 or DOT 4 (specified for disc brakes). Others may vaporize and cause brake failure. Do not intermix different brands or types of brake fluid as they may not be compatible. Do not intermix silicone based (DOT 5) brake fluid as it can cause brake component damage leading to brake system failure.*

Front Drum Brake Lever Adjustment

The front brake lever should be inspected at the interval indicated in **Table 1** and adjusted if necessary to maintain the proper amount of free play.

The brake lever should travel about 25-30 mm (1-1 1/4 in.) before the brake shoes make contact with the brake drum, but must not be adjusted so closely that the brake shoes contact the brake drum with the lever relaxed.

1. Place the ATV on level ground and set the parking brake. Block the rear wheels so the vehicle will not roll in either direction.
2. Place wood block(s) under the frame to support the vehicle with both front wheels off the ground.
3. Rotate the wheel until the rubber inspection caps are vertical. This will align one of the wheel inspection holes with the brake adjuster.

> *NOTE*
> *The 2 rubber inspection caps are spaced at different distances from the center of the wheel. The one inner hole is for adjusting as it aligns with the adjustment wheels of the front brake wheel cylinder. The outer hole is the inspection hole as it aligns with the brake shoes.*

4. Remove the *inner* rubber inspection cap (**Figure 52**) from the front wheel brake drum.
5. Insert a flat-bladed screwdriver through the hole in the wheel and onto the notches of the adjuster (**Figure 53**). Move the screwdriver handle *down* and rotate the adjusters *up*.
6. Continue to rotate the adjuster up while rotating the wheel. Rotate the adjuster until the wheel is locked in place and cannot rotate.
7. Now move the screwdriver handle in the opposite way and rotate the adjusters down, three notches. At this time the wheel should rotate freely without any brake shoe drag.
8. Perform Steps 3-7 for the other wheel.

> *CAUTION*
> *When rotating the wheels and applying the brakes, if there is a metal-to-metal sound, the brake lining may be worn down to the metal backing plate. Refer to Chapter Thirteen and inspect the brake linings. Replace as necessary.*

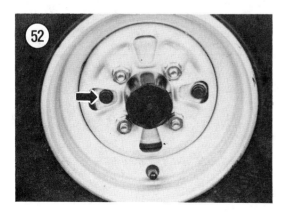

52

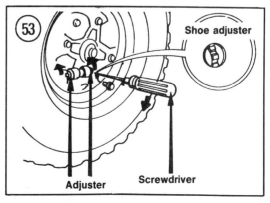

53 Shoe adjuster

Adjuster   Screwdriver

9. Rotate both front wheels and apply the brakes several times. Both wheels should stop at the same time.

10. Rotate each wheel and make sure the brakes are not dragging; readjust if necessary.

> *CAUTION*
> *If the inspection cap is not completely seated in the brake drum it will allow water to enter the brake drum leading to brake failure and damage.*

11. Install the rubber inspection cap. Make sure it is pressed completely into the brake drum for a good water-tight seal.

Rear Drum Brake Adjustment

> *NOTE*
> *Adjust the rear brake pedal free play before adjusting the rear brake lever.*

Rear drum brake lever free play

The rear brake lever adjustment should be inspected at the interval indicated in **Table 1** and adjusted if necessary to maintain the proper amount of free play. Free play is the distance the lever travels from the at-rest position to the applied position when the lever is lightly pulled by hand toward the hand grip.

The brake lever should travel about 15-20 mm (5/8-3/4 in.) before the brake shoes come in contact with the brake drum, but must not be adjusted so closely that the brake shoes contact the brake drum with the lever relaxed.

Minor adjustments should be made at the upper adjuster (brake lever) and major adjustments made at the lower adjuster (rear brake arm).

If adjustment is necessary, perform the following:

1. Slide the rubber boot (A, **Figure 54**) off the hand lever adjuster.

2. Loosen the locknut (B, **Figure 54**) and turn the adjuster (C, **Figure 54**) all the way in toward the hand grip. Hold onto the adjuster and tighten the locknut.

3. At the rear brake pivot arm, turn the *upper* adjustment nut (A, **Figure 55**) in or out to achieve the correct amount of free play.

> *NOTE*
> *Make sure the cutout relief in the adjustment nut is properly seated on the brake arm pivot pin.*

4. Minor adjustment can be made at the hand lever adjuster. Tighten the locknut securely.

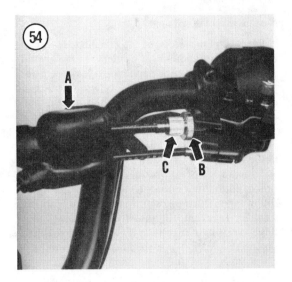

Rear drum brake pedal adjustment

The rear brake pedal adjustment should be inspected at the interval indicated in **Table 1** and adjusted, if necessary, to maintain the proper amount of free play. Free play is the distance the pedal travels from the at-rest position to the applied position when the pedal is lightly depressed by hand.

The brake pedal should travel about 15-20 mm (5/8-3/4 in.) before the brake shoes come in contact with the brake drum, but must not be adjusted so closely that the brake shoes contact the brake drum with the pedal released. If adjustment is necessary, turn the *lower* adjustment nut (B, **Figure 55**) in or out to achieve the correct amount of free play.

> *NOTE*
> *Make sure the cutout relief in the adjustment nut is properly seated on the brake arm pivot pin.*

Parking Brake Adjustment
(Disc Brake Models)

The parking brake lever adjustment should be inspected at the interval indicated in **Table 1** and adjusted if necessary to maintain the proper amount of free play. Free play is the distance the

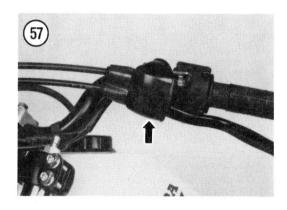

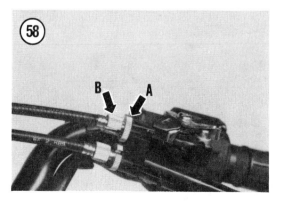

lever travels from the at-rest position to the applied position when the lever is lightly pulled by hand toward the hand grip.

The parking brake lever should travel the following amount before the brake pads come in contact with the brake disc.

   a. 1986 models: 31-39 mm (1 3/16-1 1/2 in.).
   b. 1987 models: 25-30 mm (1-1 1/8).
1. Disconnect the clutch cable from the clutch actuating arm on the engine.
2. Press the parking brake button and pull in the clutch/parking lever.
3. Measure the free play at the tip of the lever. If adjustment is necessary, perform the following.

1986 models

1. At the brake caliper assembly, loosen the locknut (A, **Figure 56**).

> *NOTE*
> *Loosen the locknut far enough so the locknut will not touch the caliper mounting bracket during Step 2. If the locknut touches the mounting bracket it will give a false resistance reading and the adjustment will be incorrect.*

2. Screw in the adjuster bolt (B, **Figure 56**) until resistance is felt, then stop. Tighten the locknut to the torque specification listed in **Table 4**.
3. Recheck the brake lever free play and readjust if necessary.

1987 models

1. Temporarily adjust the clutch lever free play to more than 30 mm (1 1/8 in.) as described in this chapter.
2. Slide the rubber boot (**Figure 57**) off the hand lever adjuster.
3. Loosen the locknut (A, **Figure 58**) and turn the adjuster (B, **Figure 58**) all the way in toward the hand grip. Hold onto the adjuster and tighten the locknut securely.
4. At the brake caliper assembly, loosen the locknut (A, **Figure 56**).

> *NOTE*
> *Loosen the locknut sufficiently so the locknut will not touch the caliper mounting bracket during Step 5. If the locknut touches the mounting bracket it will give a false resistance reading and the adjustment will be incorrect.*

5. Screw in the adjuster bolt (B, **Figure 56**) until resistance is felt, then stop. Back the adjuster bolt out 1/8 of a turn. Tighten the locknut to the torque specification listed in **Table 4**.

6. Press down on the parking brake button and apply the clutch/parking brake lever until a firm resistance is felt.

7. Measure the distance the lever has traveled. The specified distance is 25-30 mm (1-1 1/8 in.).

8. Loosen the locknut (A, **Figure 56**) and turn the adjuster (B, **Figure 56**) until the correct amount of travel is obtained. Tighten the locknut.

9. Readjust the clutch lever as described in this chapter.

Rear Disc Brake Pedal Height Adjustment

The rear brake pedal height should be adjusted so the brake pedal is 20 mm (3/4 in.) above the top surface of the foot peg (**Figure 59**).

1. Place the ATV on level ground and set the parking brake.

2. To change height position, loosen the locknut (A, **Figure 60**) and turn the master cylinder pushrod (B, **Figure 60**) in either direction until the desired height is obtained.

3. Tighten the locknut securely.

Clutch Adjustment (3-wheeled Models)

The clutch free play adjustment should be inspected at the interval indicated in **Table 1** and adjusted if necessary to maintain the proper amount of free play. Free play is the distance the lever travels from the at-rest position to the applied position when the lever is lightly pulled by hand toward the hand grip.

The proper amount of free play is 10-20 mm (3/8-3/4 in.) at the tip of the clutch lever before the clutch starts to engage.

If the proper amount of free play cannot be achieved by using this adjustment procedure, either the clutch cable has stretched to the point that it needs to be replaced or the clutch friction discs are worn and need replacing. Refer to Chapter Five for these service procedures.

1. At the clutch hand lever, slide the rubber boot (**Figure 57**) off the hand lever adjuster.

2. Loosen the locknut (A, **Figure 61**) and turn the adjuster (B, **Figure 61**) all the way in toward the hand grip. Hold onto the adjuster and tighten the locknut.

3. On the right-hand side of the engine at the clutch mechanism, loosen the locknut (A, **Figure 62**) and turn the adjusting nut (B, **Figure 62**) in either direction, until the proper amount of free play is obtained at the hand lever. Hold onto the adjusting nut and tighten the locknut.

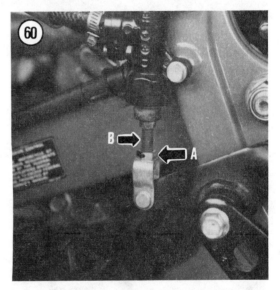

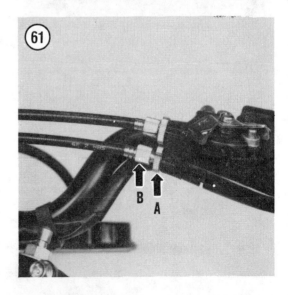

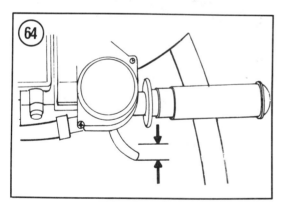

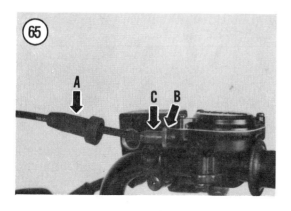

4. Minor adjustment can be made at the hand lever adjuster. Tighten the locknut securely.

**Clutch Mechanism Adjustment
(4-wheeled Models)**

The clutch mechanism free play should be checked at the interval indicated in **Table 1**.

This adjustment pertains only to the manual clutch as the centrifugal clutch requires no adjustment. Since there is no clutch cable the mechanism is the only component requiring adjustment. This adjustment takes up slack due to clutch component wear.

This procedure is to be performed with the engine off.

1. Place the ATV on level ground and set the parking brake.
2. Loosen the locknut (A, **Figure 63**) and turn the adjusting screw (B, **Figure 63**) *counterclockwise* until resistance is felt, then *stop*.
3. From this point, turn the adjusting screw *clockwise* 1/4 of a turn. Hold onto the adjusting screw and tighten the locknut to the torque specification listed in **Table 4**.

> *NOTE*
> *Make sure the adjusting screw does not move when tightening the locknut.*

4. After adjustment is completed, check that the locknut is tight.
5. On models so equipped, install the rubber cover.
6. Test ride the ATV and make sure the clutch is operating correctly; readjust if necessary.

Throttle Lever Adjustment

The throttle cable free play should be checked at the interval indicated in **Table 1**. The throttle cable should have 3-8 mm (1/8-5/16 in.) of free play measured at the tip of the throttle lever (**Figure 64**).

1. At the throttle lever, slide back the rubber boot (A, **Figure 65**).
2. Loosen the locknut (B, **Figure 65**) and turn the adjuster (C, **Figure 65**) in either direction until the correct amount of free play is achieved.
3. Hold onto the adjuster and tighten the locknut securely.
4. If the proper amount of free play cannot be achieved by using this adjustment procedure, the cable has stretched to the point that it needs to be replaced. Refer to Chapter Seven for this service procedure.
5. Slide the rubber boot back onto the adjuster.

6. Check the throttle cable from grip to carburetor. Make sure it is not kinked or chafed; replace as necessary.

7. Check that the throttle lever moves smoothly and returns to the closed position. If the lever does not operate smoothly, lubricate the throttle housing as described in this chapter.

Choke Inspection and Adjustment (4-wheeled Models)

1. Pull the choke knob (**Figure 66**) up, then push it all the way down. Check for smooth operation. If necessary, lubricate the choke cable as described in this chapter.

2. Pull the choke knob all the way up to the fully closed position. Move the choke lever at the carburetor and check that the choke valve is completely closed.

3. If adjustment is necessary, proceed to Step 4.

4. Loosen the choke cable clamp screw (A, **Figure 67**).

5. Move the choke cable and lever (B, **Figure 67**) until the choke valve is completely closed.

6. Hold the cable in this position and tighten the choke cable clamp screw securely.

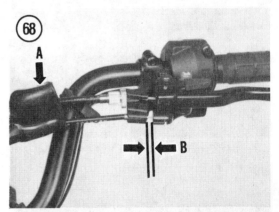

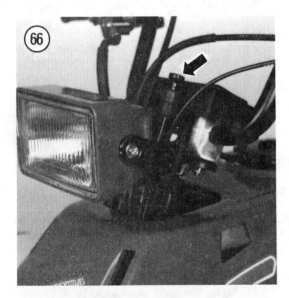

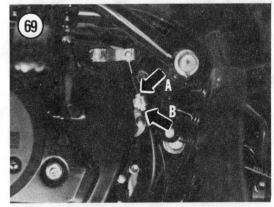

7. Again pull the choke knob all the way up to the fully closed position. Move the choke lever at the carburetor and check that the choke valve is now completely closed.

8. Push the choke knob all the way down to the fully open position. Move the choke lever at the carburetor and check that the choke valve is now completely open. Also check that there is free play in the cable between the lever on the carburetor and the cable sheath; readjust if necessary.

REVERSE Lock Mechanism (4-wheeled Models)

The REVERSE lock mechanism cable free play should be checked at the interval indicated in **Table 1**. The REVERSE lock cable should have 2-4 mm (1/16-1/8 in.) of free play measured at the cable end of the hand lever (rear brake lever).

1. At the rear brake lever, slide back the rubber boot (A, **Figure 68**).

2. Measure the free play (B, **Figure 68**) between the rear brake lever and the cable attachment point on the lever assembly.

3. At the lower end of the cable on the engine, loosen the locknut (A, **Figure 69**) and turn the adjusting nut (B, **Figure 69**) in either direction until the correct amount of free play is achieved.

4. Tighten the locknut securely.

5. Slide the rubber boot back onto the adjuster.

Starter Decompressor Adjustment (3-wheeled Models)

These models are equipped with a starter decompressor to make engine starting easier. The decompressor is cable operated and works automatically when the kickstarter is operated.

NOTE
*Valve clearance must be correctly adjusted before adjusting the starter decompressor. Refer to **Valve Clearance** in this chapter.*

1. Place the ATV on level ground and set the parking brake.

NOTE
Step 2 is not necessary, but it does give you additional working room.

2. Remove the fuel tank as described in Chapter Seven.

3. Remove the spark plug lead (A, **Figure 70**) and spark plug from the cylinder head.

4. Remove the bolts and clip (B, **Figure 70**) securing the valve adjuster cover and remove the cover (C, **Figure 70**).

5. Remove the timing hole cap (A, **Figure 71**) and the alternator rotor bolt cap (B, **Figure 71**).

6. Use a wrench on the alternator rotor bolt and rotate the engine *counterclockwise* until the "T" timing mark aligns with the index mark on the crankcase (**Figure 72**). The piston must be at top dead center (TDC) on the compression stroke.

NOTE
A cylinder at TDC on its compression stroke will have free play in both of its rocker arms, indicating that both the

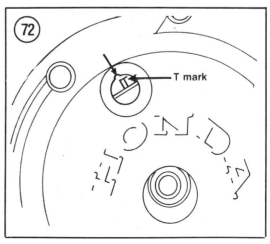

intake and exhaust valves are closed. On this engine the "T" timing mark must align with the index mark and the camshaft indicator must be visible.

7. Remove the timing hole cap (**Figure 73**) in the cylinder head. Make sure the indicator on the camshaft (**Figure 74**) is visible and is facing upward (**Figure 75**).

8. If the camshaft indicator is not visible, use a wrench on the alternator rotor bolt and rotate the engine *counterclockwise* an additional 360°. Check again that the "T" timing mark is aligned with the index mark on the crankcase (**Figure 72**).

9. Measure the free play at the end of the cam follower shaft arm (**Figure 76**). The specified free play is 0.5-1.5 mm (0.02-0.06 in.).

10. If adjustment is necessary, loosen the locknut (A, **Figure 77**) and turn the adjusting nut (B, **Figure 77**) in either direction until the correct amount of free play is achieved.

11. Install the timing hole cap and the valve adjuster cover. Tighten the screws securely.

12. Install the spark plug and tighten to the torque specification listed in **Table 4**.

13. Install the timing hole cap (A, **Figure 71**) and alternator rotor bolt cap (B, **Figure 71**).

14. If removed, install the fuel tank as described in Chapter Seven.

Air Filter Element Cleaning

The air filter element should be removed and cleaned at the interval indicated in **Table 1** and replaced whenever it is damaged or starts to deteriorate.

The air filter removes dust and abrasive particles before the air enters the carburetor and engine. Without the air filter, very fine particles could enter into the engine and cause rapid wear of the piston rings, cylinder and bearings. They also might clog small passages in the carburetor. Never run the ATV without the element installed.

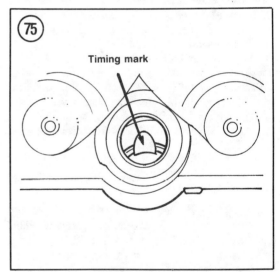

Timing mark

3

Proper air filter servicing can ensure long service from your engine.

1986 3-wheeled models

1. Remove the seat/rear fender assembly as described in Chapter Fifteen.
2. Release the clips (**Figure 78**) securing the air filter cover and remove the cover and gasket.
3. Loosen the screw on the clamping band (A, **Figure 79**) securing the front of the element assembly.
4. Remove the screw and element bracket (B, **Figure 79**) securing the rear of the element assembly.
5. Withdraw the air filter element assembly from the air box.
6. Carefully slide the foam element off of the metal holder (**Figure 80**).
7. Clean the element gently in cleaning solvent until all dirt is removed. Dry it thoroughly with a clean shop cloth until all solvent residue is removed. Let it dry for about one hour.

> *NOTE*
> *Inspect the element. If it is torn or broken in any area it should be replaced. Do not run with a damaged element as it may allow dirt to enter the engine.*

8. Pour a small amount of SAE 80 or SAE 90 gear oil or special foam air filter oil onto the element and work it into the porous foam material. Do not oversaturate the element as too much oil will restrict air flow. The element will be discolored by the oil and should have an even color indicating that the oil is distributed evenly. Let it dry for another hour before installation. If installed too soon, the chemical carrier in the special foam air filter oil will be drawn into the engine and may cause damage.
9. If the metal holder is dirty, clean it in cleaning solvent and dry thoroughly.

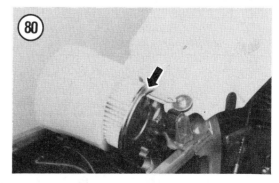

10. Wipe out the interior of the air box with a shop rag dampened with cleaning solvent. Remove any foreign matter that may be in the bottom of the air box.

11. Inspect the cover seal (**Figure 81**). If damaged or starting to deteriorate, replace it with a new one.

12. Carefully slide the foam element onto the metal holder.

13. Insert the element bracket into the rear of the element assembly.

14. Install the air filter assembly into the air box. Make sure the inlet end is seated correctly in the opening adjacent to the carburetor.

15. Install and tighten the screw securing the rear of the element assembly and tighten the clamping screw at the front of the element assembly.

16. Install the air filter cover and seal. Make sure the cover is properly seated on the air box. Flip up the clips and secure the cover in place.

17. Disconnect the air box drain tube (**Figure 82**) and drain out any residue. Perform this more often if riding in rain or under full throttle.

18. Install the seat/rear fender assembly as described in Chapter Fifteen.

1987 3-wheeled models

1. Remove the seat/rear fender assembly as described in Chapter Fifteen.

2. Release the clips (**Figure 78**) securing the air filter cover and remove the cover and gasket.

3. Loosen the screw on the clamping band (A, **Figure 79**) securing the front of the element assembly.

4. Remove the screw (B, **Figure 79**) securing the rear of the element assembly.

5. Withdraw the air filter element assembly from the air box.

6. Carefully slide the foam element off of the inner paper element and holder (**Figure 80**).

7. Clean the foam element gently in warm soapy water until all dirt is removed. Rinse a couple of times in clean water. Thoroughly dry in a clean shop cloth until all excess water is removed. Let it dry for about one hour.

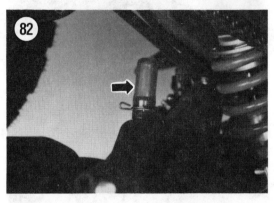

> *NOTE*
> *Inspect the foam element; if it is torn or broken in any area it should be replaced. Do not run with a damaged foam element as it may allow dirt to enter the engine.*

8. Gently tap the inner paper element to remove any loose dirt from the element. Use compressed air and direct the air from inside surface of the element and force the dirt off of the outer surface. If the compressed air is directed onto the outer

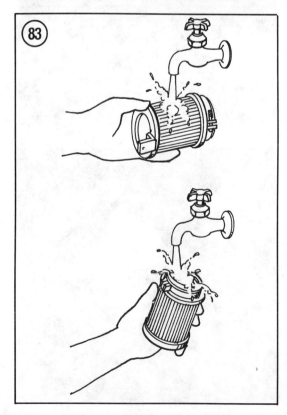

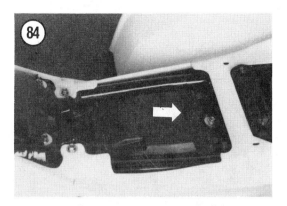

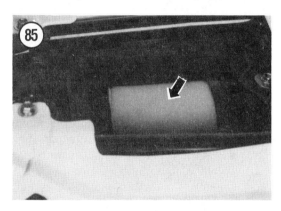

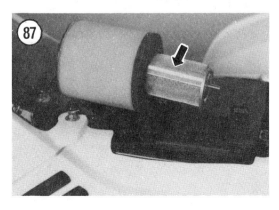

surface, the existing dirt will be forced into the element paper and cannot be removed.

9. If the paper element is excessively dirty or spattered with mud, carefully wash it with clean water. Apply the clean water to both the inner and outer surfaces of the element (**Figure 83**). Shake out all excess water and allow to dry for about one hour.

10. Wipe out the interior of the air box with a shop rag dampened with cleaning solvent. Remove any foreign matter that may be in the bottom of the air box.

11. Carefully slide the foam element onto the paper element. Make sure that both ends of the foam element seat completely against the outside ridges of the paper element.

12. Install the air filter assembly into the air box. Make sure the inlet end is seated correctly into the opening adjacent to the carburetor.

13. Install and tighten the screw securing the rear of the element assembly and tighten the clamping screw at the front of the element assembly.

14. Inspect the cover seal (**Figure 81**). If damaged or starting to deteriorate; replace it with a new one.

15. Install the air filter cover and seal. Make sure the cover is properly seated on the air box. Flip up the clips and secure the cover in place.

16. Disconnect the air box drain tube (**Figure 82**) and drain out any residue. Perform this more often if riding in rain or under full throttle.

17. Install the seat/rear fender assembly as described in Chapter Fifteen.

4-wheeled models

1. Remove the seat as described in Chapter Fifteen.

2. Release the clips securing the air filter cover (**Figure 84**) and remove the cover and gasket.

3. Loosen the screw on the clamping band securing the element assembly (**Figure 85**).

4. Withdraw the air filter element assembly from the air box.

5. Remove the nut (A, **Figure 86**) securing the element holder base (B, **Figure 86**) and remove the base.

6. Carefully slide the foam element off of the metal holder (**Figure 87**).

7. Clean the element gently in cleaning solvent until all dirt is removed. Thoroughly dry in a clean shop cloth until all solvent residue is removed. Let it dry for about one hour.

NOTE
Inspect the element. If it is torn or broken in any area it should be

replaced. Do not run with a damaged element as it may allow dirt to enter the engine.

8. Pour a small amount of SAE 80 or SAE 90 gear oil or special foam air filter oil onto the element and work it into the porous foam material. Do not oversaturate the element as too much oil will restrict air flow. The element will be discolored by the oil and should have an even color, indicating that the oil is distributed evenly. Let it dry for another hour before installation. If installed too soon, the chemical carrier in the special foam air filter oil will be drawn into the engine and may cause damage.

9. If the metal holder (**Figure 87**) is dirty, clean it in cleaning solvent and dry thoroughly.

10. Wipe out the interior of the air box with a shop rag dampened with cleaning solvent. Remove any foreign matter that may be in the bottom of the air box.

11. Carefully slide the foam element onto the metal holder.

12. Install the element holder base and nut. Tighten the nut securely.

13. Install the air filter assembly into the air box. Make sure the inlet end is seated correctly into the opening adjacent to the carburetor.

14. Tighten the clamping screw at the front of the element assembly.

15. Inspect the cover seal. If damaged or starting to deteriorate, replace it with a new one.

16. Install the air filter cover and seal. Make sure the cover is properly seated on the air box. Flip up the clips and secure the cover in place.

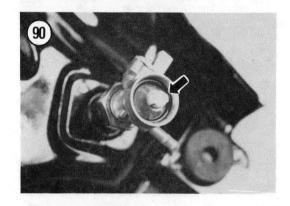

17. Install the seat/rear fender assembly as described in Chapter Fifteen.

Fuel Line Inspection

Inspect the fuel line (**Figure 88**) from the fuel tank to the carburetor. If it is cracked or starting to deteriorate it must be replaced. Make sure the small hose clamps are in place and holding securely.

> *WARNING*
> *A damaged or deteriorated fuel line presents a very dangerous fire hazard to both the rider and the vehicle if fuel should spill onto a hot engine or exhaust pipe.*

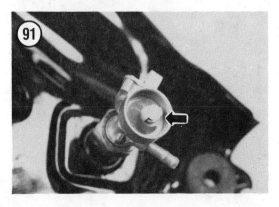

Fuel Strainer Cleaning

1. Turn the fuel shutoff valve to the OFF position.
2. Unscrew the fuel cup (**Figure 89**).

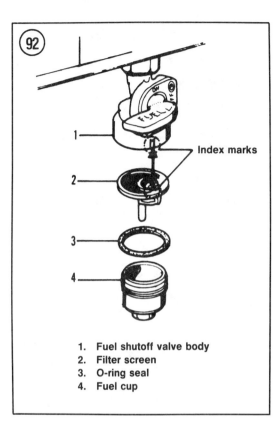

1. Fuel shutoff valve body
2. Filter screen
3. O-ring seal
4. Fuel cup

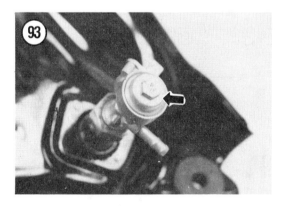

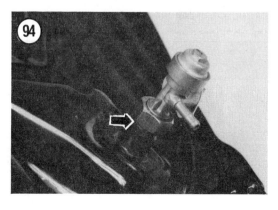

NOTE
The following steps are shown with the fuel tank removed for clarity. It is not necessary to remove the fuel tank for this procedure.

3. Remove the O-ring seal (**Figure 90**) and filter screen (**Figure 91**) from the base of the fuel shutoff valve. Dispose of fuel remaining in the cup properly.

4. Clean the filter screen with a medium soft toothbrush and blow out with compressed air. Replace the filter screen if it is broken in any area.

5. Wash the fuel cup in solvent to remove any residue or foreign matter. Dry thoroughly with compressed air.

6. On models so equipped, align the index marks on the filter screen and the fuel shutoff valve body (**Figure 92**).

7. Install the O-ring seal and screw on the fuel cup.

8. Hand tighten the fuel cup (**Figure 93**) by hand and then tighten to the torque specification listed in **Table 4**. Do not overtighten the cup as it may be damaged.

9. Turn the fuel shutoff valve to the ON position and check for fuel leakage.

Fuel Shutoff Valve and Filter
Removal/Installation

The integral fuel filter in the fuel shutoff valve removes particles in the fuel which might otherwise enter the carburetor. This could cause the float needle to stay in the open position or clog one of the jets.

1. Turn the fuel shutoff valve to the OFF position and remove the fuel line from the valve to the carburetor.

NOTE
The fuel tank can either be removed or left in place. Drain all fuel from the tank in either case.

2. Install a longer piece of clean fuel line to the valve and place the loose end into a clean, sealable metal container. If the fuel is kept clean, it can be reused.

WARNING
Do not drain the fuel into an open container.

3. Turn the fuel shutoff valve to the RES position and open the fuel filler cap. This will speed up the flow of fuel. Drain the tank completely.

4. Unscrew the locknut (**Figure 94**) securing the fuel shutoff valve to the fuel tank and remove the valve.

5. After removing the valve, insert a corner of a clean shop rag into the opening in the tank to stop the dribbling of fuel onto the engine and frame.

6. Remove the fuel filter from the shutoff valve. Clean it with a medium soft toothbrush and blow out with compressed air. Replace the filter if it is defective.

7. Install by reversing these removal steps. Do not forget to install the gasket between the valve and the tank. Check for fuel leakage after installation.

Spark Arrester Cleaning

The spark arrester should be cleaned at the interval indicated in **Table 1** or sooner if a considerable amount of slow riding is done.

> *WARNING*
> *To avoid burning your hands, do not perform this cleaning operation with the exhaust system hot. Work in a well-ventilated area (outside of your garage) that is free of any fire hazards. Be sure to protect your eyes with safety glasses or goggles.*

1. Remove the bolts securing the muffler plate (**Figure 95**) and remove the muffler plate and gasket.

2. Start the engine and rev it up about 20 times to blow out accumulated carbon in the tail section of the muffler. Continue until carbon stops coming out of the muffler opening.

3. Turn the engine off and let the muffler cool off.

4. Inspect the gasket on the muffler plate. If it is damaged or deteriorated, replace it before installing the muffler plate.

5. Install the muffler plate and gasket and tighten the bolts securely.

Wheel Bearings

There is no factory-recommended interval for cleaning and repacking the wheel bearings. They should be serviced whenever the wheel or drum is removed or whenever there is the likelihood of water contamination (especially salt water). The correct service procedures are covered in Chapter Nine or Chapter Ten.

Steering Head Adjustment Check
(3-wheeled Models)

The steering head is fitted with loose ball bearings. It should be checked every year of operation or after a serious spill.

Place wood block(s) under the frame so that the front wheel is off the ground.

Hold onto the front fork tubes and gently rock the fork assembly back and forth. If you can feel

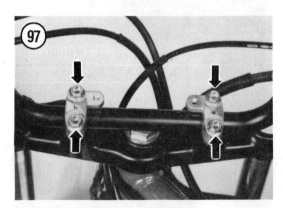

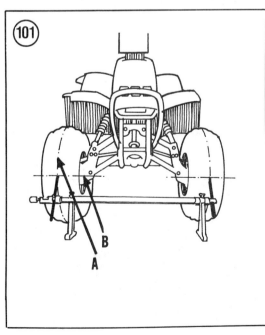

looseness refer to *Steering Stem Adjustment* in Chapter Nine.

**Steering System and
Front Suspension Inspection**

The steering system and front suspension should be checked at the interval indicated in **Table 1**.
1A. On 3-wheeled models, perform the following:
  a. Apply the front brake and pump the forks up and down as vigorously as possible. Check for smooth operation and check for any oil leaks.
  b. Make sure the upper and lower fork bridge bolts are tight (**Figure 96**).
1B. On 4-wheeled models, visually inspect all components of the steering system. Pay close attention to the tie-rods and steering shaft, especially after a hard spill or collision. If any signs of damage are apparent, the steering components must be repaired as described in Chapter Ten.
2. Check the tightness of the handlebar holder bolts (**Figure 97**) securing the handlebar.
3A. On 3-wheeled models, make sure the front axle (**Figure 98**) and front axle holder nuts (**Figure 99**) are tight.
3B. On 4-wheeled models, remove the rubber hub cover (A, **Figure 100**) and make sure the front axle nuts are tight and that the cotter pins are in place. Also make sure the wheel nuts are tight (B, **Figure 100**).

> *CAUTION*
> *If any of the previously mentioned bolts and nuts are loose, refer to Chapter Nine or Chapter Ten for correct procedures and torque specifications.*

**Front Wheel Toe-in Adjustment
(4-wheeled Models)**

The front wheel toe-in alignment should be checked at the interval indicated in **Table 1**.
1. Inflate the front tires to the recommended tire pressure. Refer to **Table 2**.
2. Place the ATV on level ground and set the parking brake. Block the rear wheels so the vehicle will not roll in either direction.
3. Place wood block(s) under the frame so the front wheels are off the ground.
4. Turn the handlebar so the wheels are at the straight ahead position.
5. Hold a scribe or toe-in gauge, white crayon or white tire marker against the center of the front tire (A, **Figure 101**) and spin the wheel slowly. Make sure the line is visible at both the front and rear of the tire. Repeat for the other tire.
6. Also mark the center line of the front axle (B, **Figure 101**) on the front tire.

7. Carefully measure the distance between the center line of both front tires at the front and rear (**Figure 102**). The front dimension "A" should be less than the rear dimension "B" by 10 ±10 mm (0.39 ±0.39 in.) as shown in **Figure 103**. This amount of toe-in is necessary for proper steering. Too much toe-in can cause excessive tire wear and hard steering. Too little toe-in will allow the front end to wander.

8. If the toe-in is incorrect, refer to Chapter Ten for the adjustment service procedure.

Rear Suspension Check

1. Place wood block(s) under the frame to support the ATV securely with the rear wheels off the ground.

2. Push hard on the rear wheels (sideways) to check for side play in the rear swing arm bearings.

3. Make sure the swing arm pivot bolt nut is tight. Refer to **Figure 104** for 3-wheeled models or **Figure 105** for 4-wheeled models.

4. Make sure the shock absorber bolts and nuts are tight.

5. On 4-wheeled models, remove the rubber hub covers and make sure the rear axle nuts are tight and that the cotter pin is in place on each side. Also make sure the wheel nuts are tight (**Figure 106**).

> *CAUTION*
> *If any of the previously mentioned bolts and nuts are loose, refer to Chapter Eleven or Chapter Twelve for correct procedures and torque specifications.*

Nuts, Bolts and Other Fasteners

Constant vibration can loosen many of the fasteners on the ATV. Check the tightness of all fasteners, especially those on:

    a. Engine mounting hardware.
    b. Engine crankcase covers.
    c. Handlebar and front steering components.
    d. Gearshift lever.
    e. Kickstarter lever (models so equipped).
    f. Brake pedal and lever.
    g. Exhaust system.

ENGINE TUNE-UP

A complete tune-up should be performed at the interval indicated in **Table 1** with normal riding. More frequent tune-ups may be required if the ATV is ridden primarily in dusty areas.

The number of definitions of the term "tune-up" is probably equal to the number of people defining it. For the purposes of this book, a tune-up is

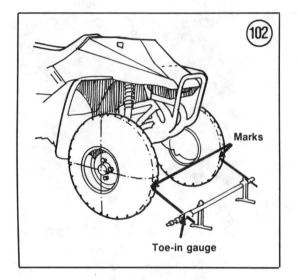

Marks

Toe-in gauge

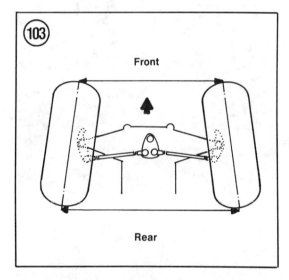

Front

Rear

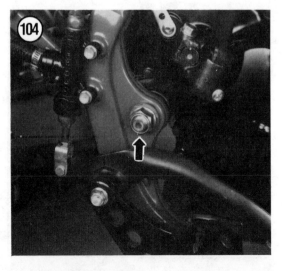

general adjustment and maintenance to ensure peak engine performance.

Table 8 summarizes tune-up specifications.

The spark plug should be routinely replaced at every other tune-up or if the electrodes show signs of erosion. Have new parts on hand before you begin.

The air filter element should be cleaned or replaced before doing other tune-up procedures as described in this chapter.

Because different systems in an engine interact, the procedures should be done in the following order.

    a. Clean or replace the air filter element.
    b. Adjust valve clearances.
    c. Run a compression test.
    d. Check or replace the spark plug.
    e. Check the ignition timing.
    f. Adjust the carburetor idle speed.

To perform a tune-up on your Honda, you will need the following tools and equipment.

    a. 18 mm spark plug wrench.
    b. Socket wrench and assorted sockets.
    c. Flat feeler gauge.
    d. Spark plug wire feeler gauge and gapper tool.
    e. Compression gauge.
    f. Ignition timing light.
    g. Portable tachometer.

Camshaft Chain Tensioner Adjustment

The cam chain tensioner on all models is non-adjustable and is designed with no means for adjustment, once the tensioner is installed in the engine.

Air Filter Element

Air filter element cleaning is described earlier in this chapter.

Valve Clearance Adjustment

Valve clearance adjustment must be made with the engine cool, at room temperature (below 35° C/95° F). The valve clearance procedure for this engine is unique and differs from most motorcycle and ATV engines.

The specified valve clearance for both the intake and exhaust valves is 0.08 mm (0.003 in.). The exhaust valve is located on the front of the engine and the intake valve is at the rear of the engine.

1. Place the ATV on level ground and set the parking brake.

NOTE
Step 2 is not necessary but it does give you additional working room.

2. Remove the fuel tank as described in Chapter Seven.
3. Remove the spark plug lead (A, **Figure 107**) and spark plug from the cylinder head. This will make it easier to rotate the engine.
4. Remove the bolts and clip (B, **Figure 107**) securing the valve adjuster cover and remove the cover (C, **Figure 107**).

5A. On 3-wheeled models, remove the timing hole cap (A, **Figure 108**) and alternator rotor bolt cap (B, **Figure 108**).

5B. On 4-wheeled models, remove the timing hole cap (**Figure 109**) on the left-hand side of the crankcase next to the top of the recoil starter housing.

6A. On 3-wheeled models, use a wrench on the alternator rotor bolt and rotate the engine *counterclockwise* until the "T" timing mark aligns with the index mark on the crankcase (**Figure 72**). The piston must be at top dead center (TDC) on the compression stroke. If the camshaft indicator is not visible, use a wrench on the alternator rotor bolt and rotate the engine *counterclockwise* an additional 360°. Check again that the "T" timing mark is aligned with the index mark on the crankcase (**Figure 72**).

6B. On 4-wheeled models, rotate the engine with the recoil starter until the "T" timing mark aligns with the index mark on the crankcase (**Figure 110**). The piston must be at top dead center (TDC) on the compression stroke. If the camshaft indicator is not visible, rotate the engine with the recoil starter an additional 360°. Check again that the "T" timing mark is aligned with the index mark on the crankcase (**Figure 110**).

> *NOTE*
> *A cylinder at TDC on its compression stroke will have free play in both of its rocker arms, indicating that both the intake and exhaust valves are closed. On this engine the "T" timing mark must align with the index mark and the camshaft indicator must be visible.*

7. Remove the timing hole cap (**Figure 111**) and make sure the indicator on the camshaft is visible (**Figure 112**) and is facing upward (**Figure 75**).

8. Loosen both intake and exhaust valve adjuster lockbolts fully (A, **Figure 113**).

9. Move each individual valve adjuster (B, **Figure 113**) to the left (counterclockwise) until resistance is felt, then *stop*.

10. Note the location of the adjuster in relation to the fixed reference mark on the cylinder head cover.

11. Move each valve adjuster to the right (clockwise) one-half of a graduation mark on the valve adjuster (**Figure 114**). One half of a graduation mark is equal to 0.08 mm (0.003 in.).

12. Tighten the valve adjuster lockbolt to the torque specification listed in **Table 4**.

13. Install the timing hole cap (**Figure 111**) and the valve adjuster cover. Tighten the screws securely.

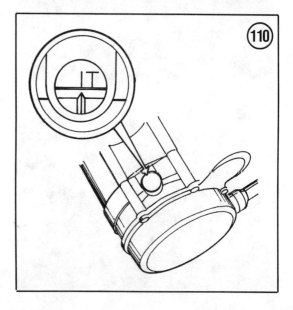

14. Install the spark plug and tighten to the torque specification listed in **Table 4**.

15A. On 3-wheeled models, install the timing hole cap (A, **Figure 108**) and rotor bolt cap (B, **Figure 108**).

15B. On 4-wheeled models, install the timing hole cap (**Figure 109**).

16. If removed, install the fuel tank as described in Chapter Seven.

17. On 3-wheeled models, adjust the starter decompressor as described under *Starter Decompressor Adjustment* in this chapter.

Compression Test

At the interval indicated in **Table 1**, check cylinder compression pressure. Record the results and compare them at the next interval. A running record will show trends in deterioration so that corrective action can be taken before complete failure occurs to a given set of parts.

The results, when properly interpreted, can indicate general cylinder, piston ring and valve condition.

1. Place the ATV on level ground and set the parking brake.

2. Run the engine and let it reach normal operating temperature.

3. Fully open the throttle lever and move the choke lever (or knob) all the way to the completely open position.

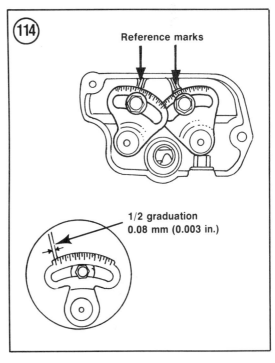

Reference marks

1/2 graduation
0.08 mm (0.003 in.)

4. Disconnect the spark plug wire and remove the spark plug (**Figure 115**).

5. Connect a compression gauge to the cylinder following manufacturer's instructions.

6. Have an assistant operate the recoil starter, kickstarter or starter motor several times.

> *NOTE*
> *If you perform this operation by yourself, make sure the compression gauge does not leak around the spark plug hole. This will give a false reading.*

> *CAUTION*
> *Do not turn the engine over more than absolutely necessary. When the spark plug lead is disconnected the electronic ignition will produce the highest voltage possible; the ignition coil may overheat and be damaged.*

7. Remove the compression gauge and record the reading. The readings should be as indicated in **Table 8**.

If the reading is higher than normal, there may be a buildup of carbon deposits in the combustion chamber or on the piston crown.

If a low reading (10 percent or more), is obtained it indicates a leaking cylinder head gasket, valve or piston ring trouble. To isolate the problem, pour about one teaspoon of engine oil through the spark plug hole onto the top of the piston.

Turn the engine over once to clear the oil, then take another compression reading. If the compression returns to normal, the valves are good but the piston rings are defective. If compression does not increase, the head gasket is defective or the valves require servicing. A valve could be hanging open or burned or a piece of carbon could be on a valve seat.

Spark Plug Selection

Spark plugs are available in various heat ranges, hotter or colder than the plugs originally installed at the factory.

Select a plug of the heat range designed for the loads and conditions under which the ATV will be run. Use of incorrect heat ranges can cause a seized piston, scored cylinder wall or damaged piston crown.

> *NOTE*
> *For NGK and ND spark plugs, higher plug numbers designate colder plugs; lower plug numbers designate hotter plugs. For example, an NGK DR8ES-L plug is colder than a DR9ES-L plug.*

In general, use a hot plug for low speeds and low temperatures. Use a cold plug for high speeds, high engine loads and high temperatures. The plug should operate hot enough to burn off unwanted deposits, but not so hot that it is damaged or causes preignition. A spark plug of the correct heat range will show a light tan color on the portion of the insulator within the cylinder after the plug has been in service.

The reach (length) of a plug is also important. A longer than normal plug could interfere with the piston, causing permanent and severe damage; refer to **Figure 116**.

Refer to **Table 8** for Honda factory recommended spark plug heat ranges.

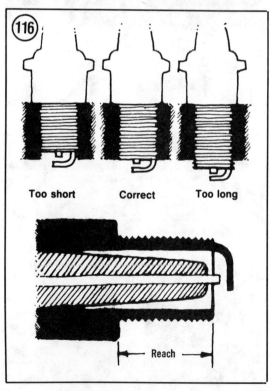

Too short   **Correct**   **Too long**

Reach

Spark Plug Removal/Cleaning

1. Grasp the spark plug lead (**Figure 115**) as near the plug as possible and pull it off the plug. If it is stuck to the plug, twist it slightly to break it loose.
2. Blow away any dirt that has accumulated in the spark plug well.

> *CAUTION*
> *The dirt could fall into the cylinder when the plug is removed, causing serious engine damage.*

3. Remove the spark plug with an 18 mm spark plug wrench.

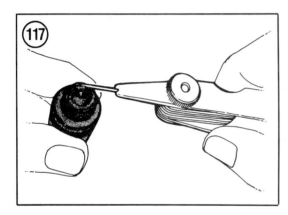

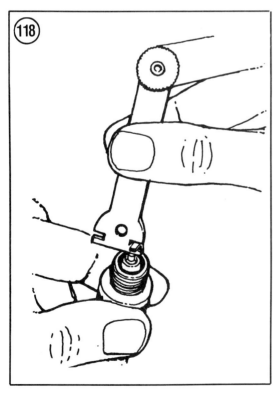

> *NOTE*
> *If the plug is difficult to remove, apply penetrating oil such as WD-40 or Liquid Wrench around the base of the plug and let it soak in about 10-20 minutes.*

4. Inspect the plug carefully. Look for a broken center porcelain, excessively eroded electrodes and excessive carbon or oil fouling. If present, replace the plug. If deposits are light, the plug may be cleaned in solvent with a wire brush or cleaned in a special spark plug sandblast cleaner. Regap the plug as explained in the following section.

Gapping and Installing the Plug

A spark plug should be carefully gapped to ensure a reliable, consistent spark. You must use a special spark plug gapping tool and a wire feeler gauge.

1. Remove the new spark plug from its box. Do *not* screw on the small piece that is loose in the box; it is not used.
2. Insert a wire feeler gauge between the center and side electrode of each plug (**Figure 117**). The correct gap is listed in **Table 7**. If the gap is correct, you will feel a slight drag as you pull the wire through. If there is no drag, or the gauge won't pass through, bend the side electrode with a gapping tool (**Figure 118**) to set the proper gap.
3. Put a small drop of oil on the threads of the spark plug.
4. Screw the spark plug in by hand until it seats. Very little effort is required. If force is necessary, you have the plug cross-threaded; unscrew it and try again.
5. Use a spark plug wrench and tighten the plug to the torque specification listed in **Table 4**.

> *CAUTION*
> *Do not overtighten. This will only squash the gasket and destroy its sealing ability.*

6. Install the spark plug lead. Rotate it slightly in both directions and make sure it is on tight.

Reading Spark Plugs

Much information about engine and spark plug performance can be determined by careful examination of the spark plug. This information is valid only after performing the following steps.

1. Ride the ATV a short distance at full throttle in any gear.
2. Turn the ignition switch to the OFF position before closing the throttle and simultaneously shift to NEUTRAL. Coast and brake to a stop.

SPARK PLUG CONDITION

NORMAL
- Identified by light tan or gray deposits on the firing tip.
- Can be cleaned.

GAP BRIDGED
- Identified by deposit buildup closing gap between electrodes.
- Caused by oil or carbon fouling. If deposits are not excessive, the plug can be cleaned.

OIL FOULED
- Identified by wet black deposits on the insulator shell bore and electrodes.
- Caused by excessive oil entering combustion chamber through worn rings and pistons, excessive clearance between valve guides and stems, or worn or loose bearings. Can be cleaned. If engine is not repaired, use a hotter plug.

CARBON FOULED
- Identified by black, dry fluffy carbon deposits on insulator tips, exposed shell surfaces and electrodes.
- Caused by too cold a plug, weak ignition, dirty air cleaner, too rich a fuel mixture, or excessive idling. Can be cleaned.

LEAD FOULED
- Identified by dark gray, black, yellow, or tan deposits or a fused glazed coating on the insulator tip.
- Caused by highly leaded gasoline. Can be cleaned.

WORN
- Identified by severely eroded or worn electrodes.
- Caused by normal wear. Should be replaced.

FUSED SPOT DEPOSIT
- Identified by melted or spotty deposits resembling bubbles or blisters.
- Caused by sudden acceleration. Can be cleaned.

OVERHEATING
- Identified by a white or light gray insulator with small black or gray brown spots and with bluish-burnt appearance of electrodes.
- Caused by engine overheating, wrong type of fuel, loose spark plugs, too hot a plug, or incorrect ignition timing. Replace the plug.

PREIGNITION
- Identified by melted electrodes and possibly blistered insulator. Metallic deposits on insulator indicate engine damage.
- Caused by wrong type of fuel, incorrect ignition timing or advance, too hot a plug, burned valves, or engine overheating. Replace the plug.

3. Remove the spark plug and examine it. Compare it to **Figure 119**.

If the insulator is white or burned, the plug is too hot and should be replaced with a colder one.

A too-cold plug will have sooty or oily deposits ranging in color from dark brown to black. Replace with a hotter plug and check for too-rich carburetion or evidence of oil blow-by at the piston rings.

If the plug has a light tan or gray colored deposit and no abnormal gap wear or electrode erosion is evident, the plug and the engine are running properly.

If the plug exhibits a black insulator tip, a damp and oily film over the firing end and a carbon layer over the entire nose, it is oil-fouled. An oil-fouled plug can be cleaned, but it is better to replace it.

Ignition Timing

All models are equipped with a capacitor discharge ignition system (CDI). This system uses no breaker points, but timing does have to be checked to make sure all components of the ignition system are functioning properly.

Incorrect ignition timing can cause a drastic loss of engine performance and efficiency. It may also cause overheating.

Before starting on this procedure, check all electrical connections related to the ignition system. Make sure all connections are tight and free from corrosion and that all ground connections are clean and tight.

1. Place the ATV on level ground and set the parking brake.
2. **Start the engine and let it reach normal operating temperature. Turn the engine off.**
3A. **On 3-wheeled models, remove the timing hole cap (Figure 120)** located on the alternator cover.
3B. **On 4-wheeled models, remove the timing hole cap (Figure 109)** on the left-hand side of the crankcase next to the top of the recoil starter housing.
4. Connect a portable tachometer following the manufacturer's instructions.
5. Connect a timing light following the manufacturer's instructions.

> *CAUTION*
> *The exhaust system is hot. Protect yourself accordingly.*

6. Restart the engine and let it idle at the idle speed indicated in **Table 8**.
7. Adjust the idle speed if necessary as described under *Idle Speed Adjustment* in this chapter.
8. Aim the timing light at the timing window and pull the trigger. The timing is correct if the "F" mark aligns with the fixed index mark. Refer to **Figure 121** for 3-wheeled models or **Figure 122** for 4-wheeled models.

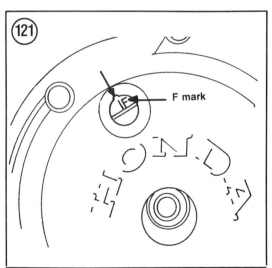

F mark

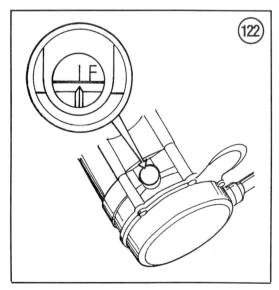

9. To check ignition advance, perform the following:

   a. Increase engine speed to 3,700 rpm.

   b. Aim the timing light at the timing window and pull the trigger.

   c. The timing is correct if fixed index mark falls between the advance marks. Refer to **Figure 123** for 3-wheeled models or **Figure 124** for 4-wheeled models.

10. If timing or ignition advance is incorrect, test the CDI unit and the pulse generator as described in Chapter Eight.

11. Disconnect the timing light and portable tachometer.

12. Install all items removed.

Carburetor Idle Mixture

The idle mixture (pilot screw) is preset at the factory and is *not* to be reset. Do not adjust the pilot screw unless the carburetor has been overhauled. If so, refer to *Pilot Screw Adjustment* in Chapter Seven.

Idle Speed Adjustment

Before making this adjustment, the air filter must be clean and the engine must have adequate compression. See *Compression Test* in this chapter.

1. Place the ATV on level ground and set the parking brake.

2. Connect a portable tachometer following the manufacturer's instructions.

3. Start the engine and let it reach normal operating temperature.

4. Set the idle speed by turning the idle speed stop screw. Refer to **Figure 125** for 3-wheeled models or **Figure 126** for 4-wheeled models.

5. The correct idle speed is listed in **Table 8**.

6. Open and close the throttle a couple of times. Check for variation in idle speed; readjust if necessary.

> *WARNING*
> *With the engine idling, move the handlebar from side to side. If idle speed increases during this movement, the throttle cable needs adjusting or may be incorrectly routed through the frame. Correct this problem immediately. Do not ride the vehicle in this unsafe condition.*

7. Turn the engine off and disconnect the portable tachometer.

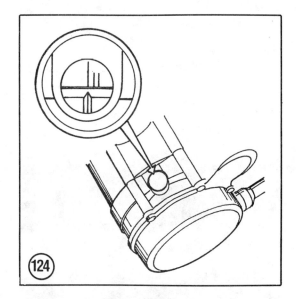

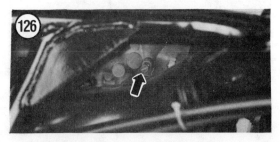

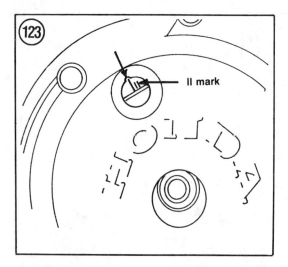

II mark

Table 1 MAINTENANCE SCHEDULE *

Before each ride	• Inspect tires and rims and check inflation pressure
Every 30 operating days	• Change engine oil • Clean engine oil screen and rotor • Clean engine oil filter screen • Clean air filter element (perform sooner if used in wet or dusty terrain) • Check and adjust the carburetor • Check ignition timing • Check cylinder head nuts and exhaust pipe nuts; tighten if necessary • Inspect valve clearance; adjust if necessary • Clean spark arrester • Inspect brake hoses for cracked or swollen ends; replace if necessary • Check brake fluid level in master cylinder(s); add fluid if necessary • Check throttle operation; adjust if necessary • Check and adjust clutch free play • Inspect REVERSE lock mechanism free play; adjust if necessary (4-wheeled models) • Inspect drive chain tension—adjust if necessary • Lubricate drive chain • Inspect drive chain slider and roller (3-wheeled models) • Check and adjust brakes • Check and adjust rear brake pedal free play • Lubricate rear brake pedal and shift lever • Lubricate control cables • Check tire and wheel condition • Check wheel bearings for smooth operation • Check engine mounting bolts for tightness • Check chassis bolts for tightness
Every year	• Inspect and clean spark plug, regap if necessary • Clean fuel filter or strainer • Inspect fuel line for deterioration, chafed, cracked or swollen ends; replace if necessary • Drain crankcase breather sediment from hose • Inspect front steering for looseness • Check front suspension toe-in (4-wheeled models) • Replace front fork oil (3-wheeled models) • Check brake lining wear indicator(s) or brake lining thickness
Every 2 years	• Replace hydraulic brake fluid
Every 4 years	• Replace fuel hoses • Replace flexible brake hoses

* This Honda factory maintenance schedule should be considered as a guide to general maintenance and lubrication intervals. Harder than normal use (racing) and exposure to mud, water, sand, high humidity, etc. will naturally dictate more frequent attention to most maintenance items.

3

Table 2 TIRE INFLATION PRESSURE (COLD) *

		Tire pressure					
		Standard		Minimum		Maximum	
Model	Tire size	kPa	psi	kPa	psi	kPa	psi
3-wheeled models							
Front	23.5×11.0-8	25	3.6	22	3.2	28	4.1
Rear	22×10-9	17	2.5	14	2.0	20	2.9
4-wheeled models							
Front	20×7.0-8	21	3.0	18	2.6	24	3.5
Rear	22×11-8	17	2.5	14	2.0	20	2.9

* Tire inflation pressure for factory equipped tires. Aftermarket tires may require different inflation pressure.

**Table 3 BATTERY CHARGING AMPERAGE AND
LENGTH OF CHARGING TIME (SEALED BATTERIES)**

Standard	1.2 amps	5 hours
Maximum	5.0 amps	1 hour

Table 4 MAINTENANCE TORQUE SPECIFICATIONS

Item	N•m	ft.-lb.
Oil drain plug		
1986-1987	35-40	25-29
1988	20-30	14-22
Front fork top cap bolt (3-wheeled)	15-30	11-22
Disc brake—parking brake adjuster		
locknut	15-20	11-15
Clutch mechanism adjust locknut	19-25	14-18
(4-wheeled)		
Fuel strainer cup	3-5	2-4
Rear axle holder or housing pinch bolts		
3-wheeled models	18-24	13-17
4-wheeled models	80-110	58-72
Valve adjuster lockbolt	10-14	7.2-10
Spark plug	12-19	9-14

Table 5 ENGINE OIL CAPACITY

	Draining		After engine disassembly	
Model	Liter	U.S. qt.	Liter	U.S. qt.
3-wheeled	1.5	1.6	1.8	1.9
4-wheeled	1.6	1.7	1.9	2.0

Table 6 FORK OIL CAPACITY (3-WHEELED MODELS)

| Year | Capacity | | Dimension from top | |
	cc	oz.	mm	in.
1986	216-221	7.3-7.5	178	7.0
1987	226-231	7.6-7.8	160	6.25

3

Table 7 DRIVE CHAIN REPLACEMENT NUMBERS

Model	Drive chain number	Number of links
3-wheeled		
1986	DID 520 V-S	86
	RK 520 HMO	86
1987	DID 520 V-6	86
	RK 520 SMOZ10	86
4-wheeled	DID 520 V-S	80
	RK 520 HMOX-LE	80

Table 8 TUNE-UP SPECIFICATIONS

Valve clearance (intake and exhaust)	0.08 mm (0.003 in.)
Spark plug	NGK DR8ES-L, ND X24ESR-U
Spark plug gap	0.6-0.7 mm (0.024-0.028 in.)
Compression pressure (at sea level)	1,200-1,400 kPa (170-198 psi)
Idle speed	1,300-1,500 rpm

CHAPTER FOUR

ENGINE

The engine is an air-cooled, 4-stroke, single cylinder design with a single overhead camshaft. The crankshaft is supported by 2 main ball bearings in a vertically split crankcase.

The camshaft is chain-driven from the timing sprocket on the right-hand side of the crankshaft and operates rocker arms that are individually adjustable.

Engine lubrication is by wet sump with the oil pump located on the right-hand side of the engine next to the clutch. The oil pump delivers oil under pressure throughout the engine and is chain-driven by a sprocket on the crankshaft.

This chapter contains removal, inspection, service and reassembly procedures for the engine. Although the clutch and transmission are located within the engine crankcase, they are covered in Chapter Five or Chapter Six to simplify this material.

Table 1 provides complete specifications for the engine and **Table 2** lists all of the engine torque specifications. **Table 1** and **Table 2** are located at the end of this chapter.

Before beginning work, re-read Chapter One of this book. You will do a better job with this information fresh in your mind.

Throughout the text there is frequent mention of the right-hand and left-hand side of the engine.

This refers to the engine as it sits in the ATV's frame, not as it sits on your workbench. The "right-" and "left-hand" sides refer to the sides of the ATV with a rider sitting on the seat facing forward.

ENGINE PRINCIPLES

Figure 1 explains how the engine works. This will be helpful when troubleshooting or repairing the engine.

ENGINE COOLING

Cooling is provided by air passing over the cooling fins on the engine cylinder head and cylinder. It is very important to keep these fins free from buildup of dirt, oil, grease and other foreign matter. Brush out the fins with a whisk broom or small stiff paint brush.

> *CAUTION*
> *Remember, these fins are thin in order*
> *to dissipate heat and may be damaged*
> *if struck too hard.*

SERVICING ENGINE IN FRAME

The following components can be serviced while the engine is mounted in the frame (the ATV's

4-STROKE PRINCIPLES

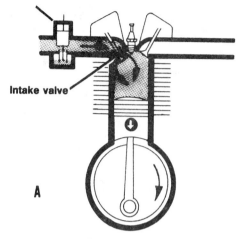

Carburetor

Intake valve

A

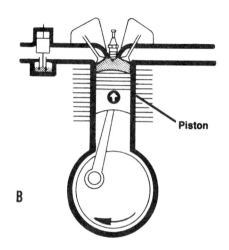

Piston

B

4

As the piston travels downward, the exhaust valve is closed and the intake valve opens, allowing the new air-fuel mixture from the carburetor to be drawn into the cylinder. When the piston reaches the bottom of its travel (BDC), the intake valve closes and remains closed for the next 1 1/2 revolutions of the crankshaft.

While the crankshaft continues to rotate, the piston moves upward, compressing the air-fuel mixture.

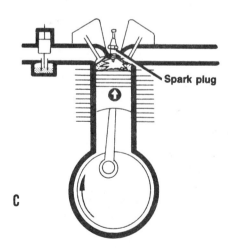

Spark plug

C

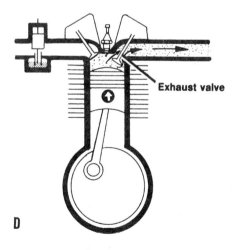

Exhaust valve

D

As the piston almost reaches the top of its travel, the spark plug fires, igniting the compressed air-fuel mixture. The piston continues to top dead center (TDC) and is pushed downward by the expanding gases.

When the piston almost reaches BDC, the exhaust valve opens and remains open until the piston is near TDC. The upward travel of the piston forces the exhaust gases out of the cylinder. After the piston has reached TDC, the exhaust valve closes and the cycle starts all over again.

frame is a great holding fixture for breaking loose stubborn bolts and nuts).

a. Cylinder head cover, camshaft and cylinder head.
b. Cylinder and piston.
c. Carburetor.
d. Kickstarter (models so equipped).
e. Alternator.
f. Clutch assembly(ies).
g. External shift mechanism.
h. Starter and starter gears (models so equipped).
i. Recoil starter (models so equipped).

ENGINE

Removal/Installation
(3-wheeled Models)

1. Drain the engine oil as described in Chapter Three.

2. Remove the seat/rear fender assembly as described in Chapter Fifteen.

3. Remove the fuel tank as described in Chapter Seven.

4. Remove the exhaust system as described in Chapter Seven.

5. Remove the carburetor as described in Chapter Seven.

6. Disconnect the crankcase breather hose from the cylinder head cover (**Figure 2**).

7. Disconnect the spark plug lead (**Figure 3**) and tie it up out of the way.

8. Disconnect the alternator/pulse generator (A, **Figure 4**) electrical connector.

9. Remove the bolts securing the engine guard and remove the guard (**Figure 5**).

10. Disconnect the clutch cable from the clutch actuating arm (A, **Figure 6**). Remove the clutch cable from the clamp (B, **Figure 6**) on the crankcase cover.

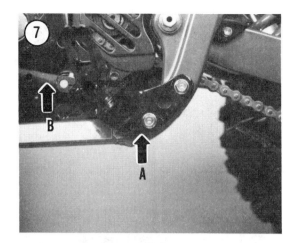

11. Remove the bolts securing the left-hand footpeg assembly and remove the assembly (A, **Figure 7**).

12. Remove the clamping bolt securing the gearshift lever and remove the gearshift lever (B, **Figure 7**).

13. Remove the clamping bolt (**Figure 8**) securing the kickstarter lever and remove the kickstarter lever.

14. Disconnect the decompression cable from the crankcase clip and the actuating arm (**Figure 9**).

15. Remove the bolts securing the drive sprocket cover and remove the cover (**Figure 10**).

16. To relieve drive chain tension perform the following:

    a. Loosen the swing arm pinch bolts (A, **Figure 11**) securing the axle holder.

    b. Insert a drift or round bar into one of the holes (B, **Figure 11**) in the axle holder.

    c. Push the drift toward the front of the vehicle, rotating the top of the axle holder toward the front.

    d. Rotate the axle holder until there is the maximum amount of drive chain slack.

4

17. Remove the bolts (**Figure 12**) securing the drive sprocket and set plate. Rotate the sprocket set plate in either direction to disengage it from the transmission shaft splines. Remove the set plate.

18. Disengage the drive chain (A, **Figure 13**) from the drive sprocket (B, **Figure 13**). Let the drive chain rest on the swing arm.

NOTE
If you are just removing the engine and are not planning to disassemble it, do not perform Step 19. The engine assembly is small enough that external components can be left on for engine removal. Proceed to Step 20.

19. If the engine is going to be disassembled, remove the following parts:

   a. Remove the cylinder head cover, camshaft and cylinder head as described in this chapter.

   b. Remove the cylinder and piston as described in this chapter.

   c. Remove the kickstarter as described in this chapter.

   d. Remove the alternator as described in Chapter Eight.

   e. Remove the starter gears as described in this chapter.

   f. Remove the clutch assembly as described in Chapter Five.

   g. Remove the external shift mechanism as described in Chapter Five.

20. Take a final look all over the engine to make sure everything has been disconnected.

CAUTION
The following steps require the aid of a helper to safely remove the engine assembly from the frame.

21. Place a suitable size jack, with a piece of wood to protect the engine crankcase, under the engine. Apply a slight amount of jack pressure up on the engine.

22. Remove the engine upper hanger bolts and nuts and remove the hanger plates (B, **Figure 4**).

23. Remove the bolts and nuts securing the engine front hanger plates (A, **Figure 14**) and remove the engine front hanger plates.

24. Remove the bolts and nuts securing the engine rear hanger plates (B, **Figure 14**) and remove the engine rear hanger plates.

25. Remove the rear lower mounting bolt and nut (C, **Figure 14**).

26. Pull the engine slightly forward and out of the right-hand side of the frame. Take it to a workbench for further disassembly.

27. Install by reversing these removal steps, noting the following.

28. Tighten the engine mounting bolts to the torque specifications in **Table 2**.

29. Fill the engine with the recommended type and quantity of oil as described in Chapter Three.

30. Adjust the clutch as described in Chapter Three.

31. Start the engine and check for fluid leaks.

**Removal/Installation
(4-wheeled Models)**

1. Drain the engine oil as described in Chapter Three.

2. Remove the seat, front fender and the rear fender as described in Chapter Fifteen.

3. Disconnect the battery negative lead (**Figure 15**).

4. Remove the fuel tank as described in Chapter Seven.

5. Remove the exhaust system as described in Chapter Seven.

6. Remove the carburetor as described in Chapter Seven.

7. Disconnect the spark plug lead (**Figure 16**) and tie it up out of the way.

8. Remove the engine ground strap from the starter motor mounting bolt (**Figure 17**).

9. Disconnect the crankcase breather hose from the cylinder head cover.

10. Remove the electrical junction box cover (**Figure 18**).

11. Disconnect the alternator/pulse generator (**Figure 19**) electrical connectors.

12. Remove the starter (**Figure 20**) as described under *Starter Removal/Installation* in Chapter Eight.

13. Remove the nut (A, **Figure 21**) securing the REVERSE selector arm and remove the selector arm.

14. Remove the REVERSE selector arm cable from the cable holder (B, **Figure 21**).

15. Remove the bolts securing the left-hand footpeg assembly and remove the assembly (**Figure 22**).

16. Remove the clamping bolt securing the gearshift lever and remove the gearshift lever (**Figure 23**).

17. Remove the bolts securing the right-hand footpeg assembly and remove the assembly (**Figure 24**).

18. To relieve drive chain tension perform the following:
   a. Loosen the axle housing lockbolts (**Figure 25**) on each side, securing the axle holder.
   b. Loosen the adjuster nuts (**Figure 26**) until there is sufficient slack in the drive chain.

19. Remove the bolts (**Figure 27**) securing the drive chain cover and remove the cover.

20. Remove the drive chain guide (**Figure 28**).

21. Remove the bolts (**Figure 29**) securing the drive sprocket and set plate.

22. Rotate the sprocket set plate (A, **Figure 30**) in either direction to disengage it from the

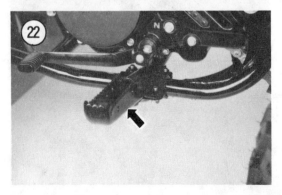

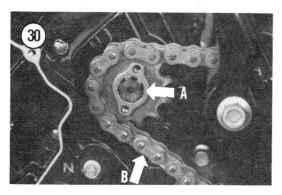

transmission shaft splines. Remove the drive sprocket and drive chain (B, **Figure 30**).

> *NOTE*
> *If you are just removing the engine and are not planning to disassemble it, do not perform Step 23. The engine assembly is small enough that external components can be left on for engine removal. Proceed to Step 24.*

23. If the engine is going to be disassembled, remove the following parts:
   a. Remove the cylinder head cover, camshaft and cylinder head as described in this chapter.
   b. Remove the cylinder and piston as described in this chapter.
   c. Remove the recoil starter as described in this chapter.
   d. Remove the alternator as described in Chapter Eight.
   e. Remove the starter gears as described in this chapter.
   f. Remove the clutch assemblies as described in Chapter Six.
   g. Remove the external shift mechanism as described in Chapter Six.

24. Take a final look all over the engine to make sure everything has been disconnected.

> *WARNING*
> *The following steps require the aid of a helper to safely remove the engine assembly from the frame.*

25. Remove the engine upper hanger bolt and nut (A, **Figure 31**) and remove the hanger plates.

26. Remove the bolts and nuts securing the engine front hanger plates (B, **Figure 31**) and remove the engine front hanger plates.

27. Remove the rear lower through-bolt and nut (C, **Figure 31**).

28. Remove the rear upper through-bolt and nut (D, **Figure 31**).

29. Pull the engine slightly forward and out of the right-hand side of the frame. Take it to a workbench for further disassembly.

30. Install by reversing these removal steps, noting the following.

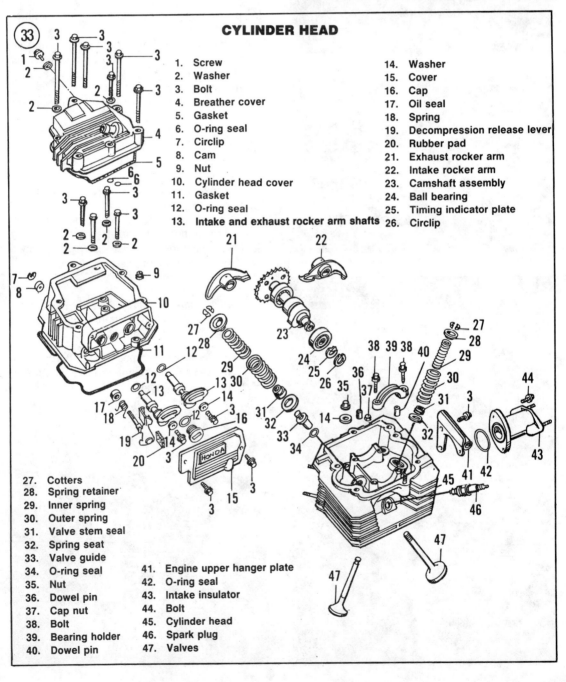

CYLINDER HEAD

1.	Screw	14.	Washer
2.	Washer	15.	Cover
3.	Bolt	16.	Cap
4.	Breather cover	17.	Oil seal
5.	Gasket	18.	Spring
6.	O-ring seal	19.	Decompression release lever
7.	Circlip	20.	Rubber pad
8.	Cam	21.	Exhaust rocker arm
9.	Nut	22.	Intake rocker arm
10.	Cylinder head cover	23.	Camshaft assembly
11.	Gasket	24.	Ball bearing
12.	O-ring seal	25.	Timing indicator plate
13.	Intake and exhaust rocker arm shafts	26.	Circlip

27.	Cotters		
28.	Spring retainer		
29.	Inner spring		
30.	Outer spring		
31.	Valve stem seal		
32.	Spring seat		
33.	Valve guide		
34.	O-ring seal	41.	Engine upper hanger plate
35.	Nut	42.	O-ring seal
36.	Dowel pin	43.	Intake insulator
37.	Cap nut	44.	Bolt
38.	Bolt	45.	Cylinder head
39.	Bearing holder	46.	Spark plug
40.	Dowel pin	47.	Valves

31. Tighten the engine mounting bolts to the torque specifications in **Table 2**.

32. Install the footpeg with the rubber stopper (**Figure 32**) on the left-hand side. The rear brake pedal comes to a stop against this rubber stopper.

33. Fill the engine with the recommended type and quantity of oil as described in Chapter Three.

34. Start the engine and check for fluid leaks.

CYLINDER HEAD COVER AND CAMSHAFT

Cylinder Head Cover and Camshaft Removal

CAUTION
To prevent any warpage and damage, remove the cylinder head cover only when the engine is at room temperature.

Refer to **Figure 33** for this procedure.

1. Remove the fuel tank as described in Chapter Seven.

2A. On 3-wheeled models, remove the seat/rear fender assembly as described in Chapter Fifteen.

2B. On 4-wheeled models, remove the seat and front fender as described in Chapter Fifteen.

3. Disconnect the crankcase breather hose (**Figure 2**) from the breather cover.

4. Remove the spark plug lead (A, **Figure 34**) and spark plug from the cylinder head.

5. Remove the bolts and clip (B, **Figure 34**) securing the valve adjuster cover and remove the cover (C, **Figure 34**).

6. Loosen the valve adjuster lockbolts (**Figure 35**). This is to relieve strain on the rocker arms and cylinder head cover.

7. Remove the bolts securing the breather cover and remove the cover (**Figure 36**) and dowel pins. Don't lose the copper washers under the two bolts. These copper washers must be installed under the correct bolts to avoid an oil leak.

8. Remove the bolts (**Figure 37**) securing the camshaft chain tensioner. Remove the tensioner assembly and gasket.

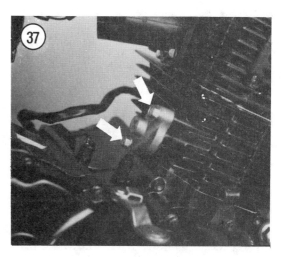

9. Remove the nut (**Figure 38**) on the left-hand side and the bolts (A, **Figure 39**) on the top securing the cylinder head cover. Remove the cylinder head cover and gasket.

10. Remove the bolts (**Figure 40**) securing the camshaft bearing holder and remove the holder.

11. Tie a piece of wire to the camshaft chain and tie it to an external portion of the engine to prevent the camshaft chain from falling down into the crankcase.

12. Disengage the camshaft from the chain (A, **Figure 41**) and remove the camshaft (B, **Figure 41**) from the cylinder head.

> *CAUTION*
> *If the crankshaft must be rotated with the camshaft removed, pull up on the camshaft chain and keep it taut, make certain that the camshaft chain is properly meshed onto the crankshaft timing sprocket, then rotate the crankshaft. If this step is not followed, the chain may become kinked and cause damage to the crankcases, the camshaft chain and the timing sprocket on the crankshaft.*

Camshaft Inspection

1. Check the camshaft ball bearings (**Figure 42**) for wear. Rotate each bearing by hand. Make sure the bearing turns smoothly with no evidence of wear or damage.

2. The camshaft right-hand bearing, next to the sprocket, cannot be replaced. If faulty, the camshaft must be replaced.

3. If necessary, refer to **Figure 43** and remove the camshaft left-hand bearing as follows:

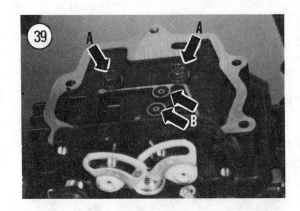

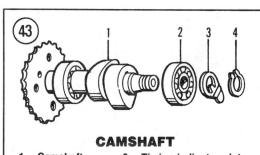

CAMSHAFT

1. Camshaft   3. Timing indicator plate
2. Ball bearing   4. Circlip

a. Remove the snap ring (**Figure 44**).

b. Remove the timing indicator plate (**Figure 45**).

c. Remove the left-hand bearing (**Figure 46**) with a bearing puller.

d. Install the new bearing onto the camshaft with Honda special tools—Driver Handle B (part No. 07749-0010000) and 15 mm attachment (part No. 07746-0020200 or M9360-277-91775). Drive the bearing on until it seats completely.

e. Align the tab on the timing indicator plate with the groove in the camshaft and install the indicator plate.

f. Install the circlip with the sharp side facing out, away from the camshaft. Make sure the circlip is correctly seated in the camshaft groove.

4. Check the camshaft lobes (**Figure 47**) for wear or scoring. The lobes should show no signs of wear or scoring and the edges should be square. Slight damage may be removed with a silicon carbide oilstone. Use a No. 100-120 grit stone initially, then polish with a No. 280-320 grit stone.

NOTE
The exhaust cam lobe is on the right-hand side (next to the camshaft sprocket) and the intake cam lobe is on the left-hand side.

5. Even though the lobe surface appears to be satisfactory, with no visible signs of wear, each camshaft lobe must be measured with a micrometer. Compare to dimensions listed in **Table 1**. If either dimension is worn to the service limit dimension or less, the camshaft must be replaced.

6. Inspect the camshaft sprocket (**Figure 48**) for wear or damage. The camshaft sprocket is an integral part of the camshaft. If it is worn or damaged, the camshaft must be replaced.

Cylinder Head Cover
Disassembly/Inspection/Assembly

Before removing the rocker arm assemblies, mark them in sets with "I" (intake—rear of engine) or "E" (exhaust—front of engine) so they will be reinstalled in the correct location in the cylinder head cover.

Refer to **Figure 33** for this procedure.

1. Remove the rubber gasket (**Figure 49**) from the cylinder head cover.

2. Remove the valve adjuster lockbolts and washers.

3. First withdraw the exhaust rocker arm shaft (A, **Figure 50**), then remove the rocker arm from the cylinder head cover.

4. Remove the intake rocker arm shaft (B, **Figure 50**) and rocker arm from the cylinder head cover.

5. Remove the circlip (**Figure 51**) securing the decompression cam and remove the cam.

6. Withdraw the decompression shaft (**Figure 52**) and return spring from the cylinder head cover.

7. Wash all parts in cleaning solvent and thoroughly dry.

8. Remove and discard the O-ring seal (**Figure 53**) on each rocker arm shaft. New ones must be installed prior to shaft installation.

9. Measure the inside diameter of the rocker arm bore (**Figure 54**) with an inside micrometer and check against the dimension listed in **Table 1**. Replace if worn to the service limit or greater.

10. Inspect the rocker arm pad where it rides on the camshaft (A, **Figure 55**) and the valve stem (B, **Figure 55**). Check for signs of wear or scoring, replace as necessary.

11. Inspect the rocker arm shaft for signs of wear or scoring. Measure the outside diameter with a

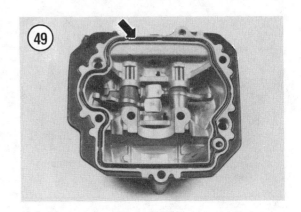

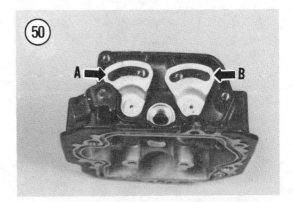

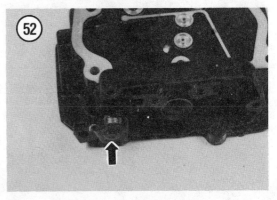

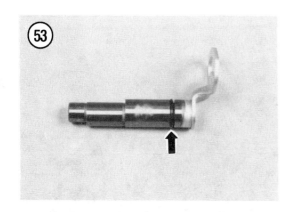

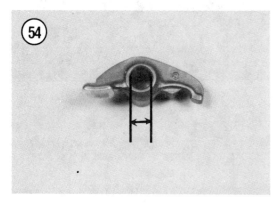

micrometer (**Figure 56**) and check against the dimension listed in **Table 1**. Replace if worn to the service limit or less.

12. Inspect the rocker arm bores (**Figure 57**) in the cylinder head cover for wear or damage. If worn or damaged, replace the cylinder head cover.

13. Position the return spring onto the decompression shaft and install the shaft into the cylinder head cover.

14. Install the cam and the circlip. Make sure the circlip is properly seated in the shaft groove.

15. Install a new O-ring seal onto each rocker arm shaft.

16. Coat the rocker arm shaft and rocker arm bore with assembly oil or fresh engine oil.

17. Apply molybdenum disulfide grease to the rocker arm pad where it makes contact with the camshaft.

> *CAUTION*
> *The rocker arms are **not** symmetrical.*
> *The exhaust rocker arm has a pad (C,*
> ***Figure 55**) for the decompression cam*
> *to ride against. The exhaust rocker arm*
> *must be installed in the front section of*
> *the cylinder head cover.*

18. First insert the intake valve rocker arm shaft (**Figure 58**) into the cylinder head cover and

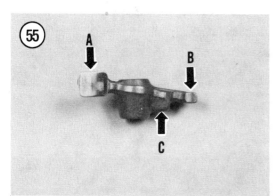

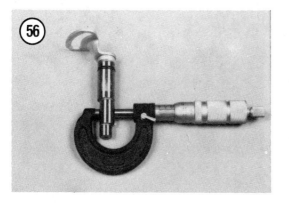

position the intake rocker arm (**Figure 59**) into the cylinder head cover. Push the rocker arm shaft all the way in until it stops (**Figure 60**).

> *CAUTION*
> *The exhaust rocker arm has a pad (A,* ***Figure 61****) for the decompression cam to ride against.*

19. Insert the exhaust valve rocker arm shaft (**Figure 62**) into the cylinder head cover and position the exhaust rocker arm (B, **Figure 61**) into the cylinder head cover. Push the rocker arm shaft all the way in until it stops.

20. Install the valve adjuster lockbolts and washers. Tighten only finger-tight at this time.

21. Install a new rubber gasket (**Figure 49**) into the cylinder head cover.

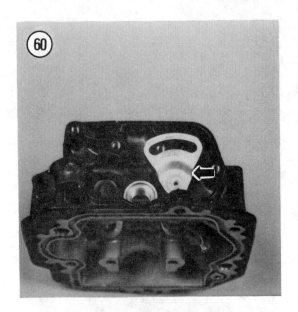

Camshaft and Cylinder Head Cover Installation

1. If the spark plug is still installed, remove it. This will make it easier to rotate the engine.

> *CAUTION*
> *In the following step the crankshaft will be rotated with the camshaft removed. Pull up on the camshaft chain and keep it taut, make certain that the camshaft chain is properly meshed onto the crankshaft timing sprocket, then rotate the crankshaft. If this step is not followed, the chain may become kinked and cause damage to the crankcases, the camshaft chain and the timing sprocket on the crankshaft.*

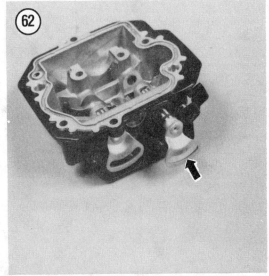

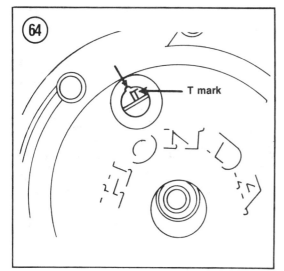

T mark

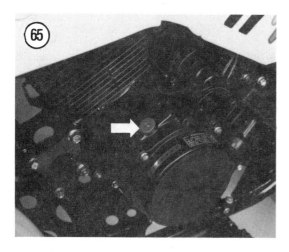

2A. On 3-wheeled models, perform the following:
  a. Remove the timing hole cap (A, **Figure 63**) and rotor bolt cap (B, **Figure 63**) located on the alternator cover.
  b. Use a wrench on the alternator rotor bolt and rotate the engine *counterclockwise* (as viewed from the left-hand side) until the "T" timing mark aligns with the index mark on the crankcase (**Figure 64**). The piston must be at top dead center (TDC) on the compression stroke.
2B. On 4-wheeled models, perform the following:
  a. Remove the timing hole cap (**Figure 65**) on the left-hand side of the crankcase next to the top of the recoil starter housing.
  b. Rotate the engine with the recoil starter until the "T" timing mark aligns with the index mark on the crankcase (**Figure 66**). The piston must be at top dead center (TDC) on the compression stroke.

3. Lubricate the camshaft bearings with assembly oil or fresh engine oil.

4. Apply molybdenum disulfide grease to the camshaft lobes before installation.

5. Position the camshaft so the index lines on the chain sprocket are horizontal so they will align with the top surface of the cylinder head. Also, the camshaft timing indicator plate arrow must point straight up.

6. Install the camshaft into the cylinder head.

4

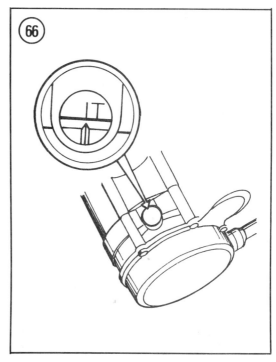

7. Make sure the camshaft chain is meshed properly with the crankshaft timing sprocket.

> *CAUTION*
> *Very expensive damage could result from improper camshaft and camshaft chain alignment. Recheck your work several times to make sure alignment is correct.*

8. Mesh the camshaft sprocket with the camshaft chain and install the camshaft in the cylinder head. The index lines must align with the top surface of the cylinder head (**Figure 67**). Make sure the timing marks in Step 2 are still correct. Refer to **Figure 64** and **Figure 66**. Also the camshaft timing indicator plate arrow must point straight up (**Figure 68**).

9. Install the camshaft bearing holder and bolts (**Figure 40**). Tighten the bolts to the torque specification listed in **Table 2**.

10A. On 3-wheeled models, use a wrench on the alternator rotor bolt and rotate the engine *counterclockwise* (as viewed from the left-hand side) 360° until the "T" timing mark aligns with the index mark on the crankcase (**Figure 64**).

10B. On 4-wheeled models, rotate the engine 360° with the recoil starter until the "T" timing mark aligns with the index mark on the crankcase (**Figure 66**).

11. Make sure the camshaft sprocket index lines (**Figure 67**) still align with the top surface of the cylinder head.

12. Remove the sealing bolt and washer (**Figure 69**) from the camshaft chain tensioner assembly.

13. Using a flat-bladed screwdriver, turn the tensioner shaft *clockwise* until the tensioner is fully retracted into the body (**Figure 70**).

14. Keep the screwdriver (A, **Figure 71**) in place to keep the tensioner shaft retracted in the body.

15. Install the camshaft chain tensioner and gasket into the cylinder (B, **Figure 71**). Install the bolts (C, **Figure 71**) and tighten securely.

16. Remove the screwdriver and install the sealing washer and bolt (**Figure 72**). Tighten the bolt securely.

17. Make sure the locating dowels are in place in the cylinder head cover.

18. Fill the pocket in the cylinder head with clean engine oil to provide lubrication for the initial start-up.

19. Install a new cylinder head cover gasket (**Figure 49**).

20. Install the cylinder head cover (**Figure 36**).

21. Install the cylinder head cover bolts and nut. Tighten the cylinder head cover bolts (A, **Figure**

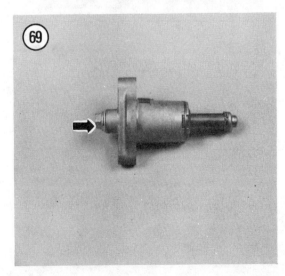

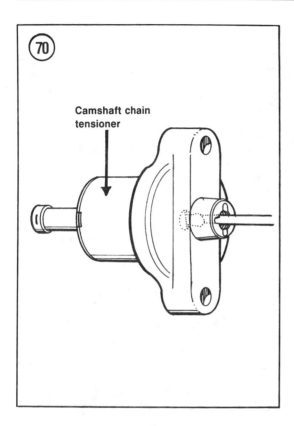

Camshaft chain tensioner

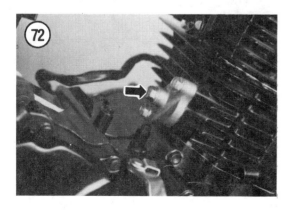

39) and nut (**Figure 38**) in 2-3 stages in a crisscross pattern. Tighten to the torque specifications listed in **Table 2**.

22. Install new O-ring seals (B, **Figure 39**) in the cylinder head cover.

23. Install a new gasket in the breather cover.

24. Install the breather cover (**Figure 36**).

25. Install the breather cover bolts. Be sure to install the washers under the bolts designated by raised arrows on the cover (**Figure 73**). This will prevent an oil leak. Tighten the breather cover bolts in 2-3 stages in a crisscross pattern. Tighten to the torque specifications listed in **Table 2**.

26. Attach the crankcase breather hose to the breather cover (**Figure 2**).

27. Adjust the valve clearance as described under *Valve Clearance Adjustment* in Chapter Three.

28A. On 3-wheeled models, install the seat/rear fender assembly as described in Chapter Fifteen.

28B. On 4-wheeled models, install the seat and front fender as described in Chapter Fifteen.

29. Install the fuel tank as described in Chapter Seven.

30. Refill the engine with the recommended type and quantity of engine oil as described in Chapter Three.

CYLINDER HEAD

Removal/Installation

> *CAUTION*
> *To prevent any warpage and damage, remove the cylinder head only when the engine is at room temperature.*

1. Remove the cylinder head cover and camshaft as described in this chapter.

2. Remove the exhaust pipe as described in Chapter Seven.

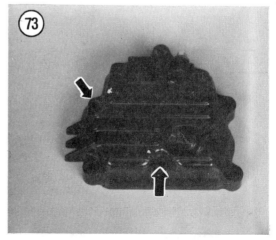

3. Remove the bolts and nuts securing the engine upper hanger plates and remove the plates. Refer to **Figure 74** for 3-wheeled models or **Figure 75** for 4-wheeled models.

4. Loosen in a crisscross pattern in 2-3 stages, the nuts and washers (**Figure 76**) and the cap nuts (**Figure 77**) securing the cylinder head.

5. Remove the nuts and washers loosened in Step 4.

6. Loosen the cylinder head by tapping around the perimeter with a rubber or soft-faced mallet. If necessary, *gently* pry the head loose with a broad-tipped screwdriver.

> *CAUTION*
> *Remember the cooling fins are fragile and may be damaged if tapped or pried too hard. Never use a metal hammer.*

7. Untie the wire securing the camshaft chain and retie the wire to the cylinder head.

8. Lift the cylinder head straight up and off the crankcase studs. Guide the cam chain through the opening in the cylinder head and retie the wire to the exterior of the engine. This will prevent the drive chain from falling down into the crankcase.

9. Remove the cylinder head gasket and discard it. Don't lose the locating dowels.

10. Place a clean shop cloth into the cam chain opening in the cylinder to prevent the entry of foreign matter.

11. Install by reversing these removal steps, noting the following.

12. If removed, install the locating dowels (A, **Figure 78**) in the cylinder.

13. Position a new head gasket with the UP mark upward (**Figure 79**). Install the new head gasket (B, **Figure 78**).

14. Install the cylinder head onto the crankcase studs. With your fingers, carefully insert the cam

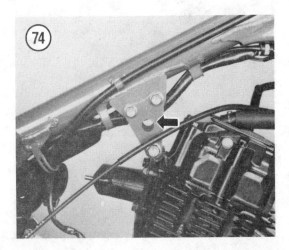

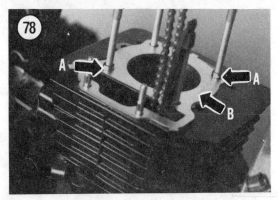

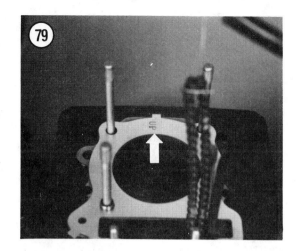

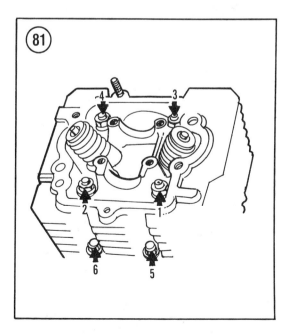

chain into the cam chain cavity on the side of the cylinder head while pushing the cylinder head down into position.

15. Tie the wire attached to the cam chain to the exterior of the engine (**Figure 80**).

16. Install the cap nuts (**Figure 77**).

17. Install the nuts and copper washers (**Figure 76**).

18. Tighten the nuts and cap nuts in the torque pattern shown in **Figure 81**. Tighten to the torque specifications listed in **Table 2**.

19. Install the exhaust pipe to the cylinder head as described in Chapter Seven.

20. Install the cylinder head cover and camshaft as described in this chapter.

21. Adjust the valves as described under *Valve Clearance Adjustment* in Chapter Three.

Disassembly/Inspection/Assembly

1. Remove all traces of gasket material from the cylinder head mating surfaces.

2. *Without removing the valves,* remove all carbon deposits from the combustion chamber (**Figure 82**) and valve ports with a wire brush. A blunt screwdriver or chisel may be used if care is taken not to damage the head, valves and spark plug threads.

3. After the carbon is removed from the combustion chamber and the valve intake and exhaust ports, clean the entire head in cleaning solvent. Blow dry with compressed air.

4. Clean away all carbon from the piston crown. Do not remove the carbon ridge at the top of the cylinder bore.

5. Check for cracks in the combustion chamber and exhaust ports. A cracked head must be replaced.

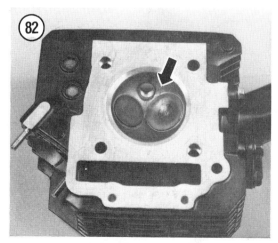

6. After the head has been thoroughly cleaned, place a straightedge across the cylinder head/cylinder gasket surface (**Figure 83**) at several points. Measure the warp by inserting a flat feeler gauge between the straightedge and the cylinder head at each location. There should be no warpage; if a small amount is present, the head can be resurfaced by a dealer or qualified machine shop. Replace the cylinder head and cylinder head cover as a set if the gasket surface is warped to or beyond the limit listed in **Table 1**.

7. Check the cylinder head cover mating surface using the procedure in Step 6. There should be no warpage.

8. Remove the bolts securing the engine hanger and the intake insulator (**Figure 84**) to the cylinder head. Remove the hanger and the intake insulator.

9. Check the valves and valve guides as described in this chapter.

VALVES AND VALVE COMPONENTS

General practice among those who do their own service is to remove the cylinder head and take it to a machine shop or dealer for inspection and service. Since the cost is low relative to the required effort and equipment, this is the best approach, even for the experienced mechanics.

This procedure is included for those who choose to do their own valve service.

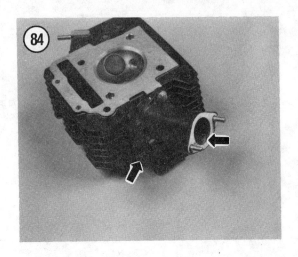

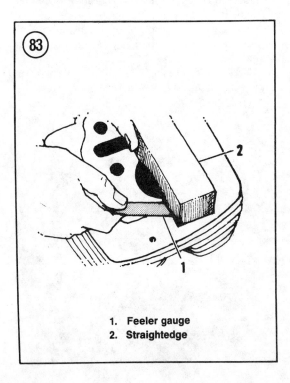

1. Feeler gauge
2. Straightedge

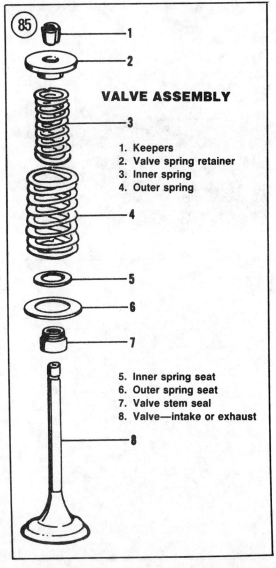

VALVE ASSEMBLY

1. Keepers
2. Valve spring retainer
3. Inner spring
4. Outer spring

5. Inner spring seat
6. Outer spring seat
7. Valve stem seal
8. Valve—intake or exhaust

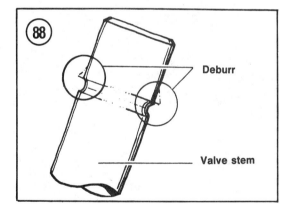

Deburr

Valve stem

Removal

Refer to **Figure 85** for this procedure.

1. Remove the cylinder head as described in this chapter.

CAUTION
To avoid loss of spring tension, do not compress the springs any more than necessary to remove the keepers.

2. Compress the valve springs with a valve compressor tool (**Figure 86**). Remove the valve keepers and release the compression. Remove the valve compressor tool.

3. Remove the valve spring retainer and valve springs (**Figure 87**).

NOTE
The valve spring seat and valve stem seal will stay in the cylinder head.

4. Remove the valve spring seat and the valve stem seal.

5. Before removing the valve, remove any burrs from the valve stem (**Figure 88**). Otherwise the valve guide will be damaged.

6. Mark all parts as they are disassembled so that they will be installed in their same locations (**Figure 89**).

Inspection

1. Clean valves with a wire brush and solvent.

2. Inspect the contact surface of each valve for burning or pitting (**Figure 90**). Unevenness of the contact surface is an indication that the valve is not serviceable. The valve contact surface can *not* be ground as it has a special coating. If defective, the valve(s) must be replaced.

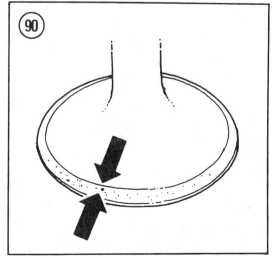

3. Measure the valve stem for wear (**Figure 91**). Compare with specifications given in **Table 1**.

4. Remove all carbon and varnish from the valve guide as described in this chapter.

5. Insert each valve in its guide. Hold the valve with the head just slightly off the valve seat and rock it sideways. If it rocks more than slightly, the guide is probably worn and should be replaced. As a final check, measure the valve guides.

6. Measure each valve spring free length with a vernier caliper (**Figure 92**). All should be within the length specified in **Table 1** with no signs of bends or distortion. Replace defective springs in pairs (inner and outer).

7. Check the valve spring retainer and valve keepers. If they are in good condition they may be reused; replace as necessary.

8. Inspect the valve seats. If worn or burned, they must be reconditioned. This should be performed by a dealer or qualified machine shop.

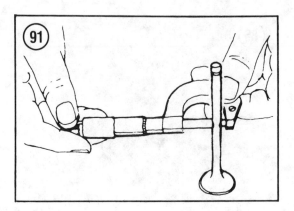

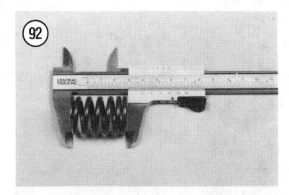

Installation

1. Install the valve stem seal (**Figure 93**).

2. Coat the valve stems with molybdenum disulfide grease. To avoid damage to the valve stem seal, turn the valve slowly while inserting the valve into the cylinder head (**Figure 94**).

3. Install the valve spring seat (**Figure 95**).

> *NOTE*
> *Install the valve springs with their closer wound coils facing the cylinder head.*

4. Install the inner spring (**Figure 96**) and the outer spring (**Figure 97**).

5. Install the valve spring retainer (**Figure 87**).

> *CAUTION*
> *To avoid loss of spring tension, do not compress the springs any more than necessary to install the keepers.*

6. Compress the valve springs with a compressor tool (**Figure 86**) and install the valve keepers. Remove the compressor tool.

7. After all springs have been installed, gently tap the end of the valve stems with a soft aluminum or brass drift and hammer. This will ensure that the keepers are properly seated.

Valve Guide Inspection

1. Remove the valves as described in this chapter.

2. Ream out each valve guide before measuring the guide. Use a valve guide reamer (Honda part No. 07984-200000A) or equivalent.

CAUTION
Always *rotate the valve guide reamer* ***clockwise***. *If the reamer is rotated counterclockwise, damage to a good valve guide will occur.*

3. Insert the valve guide reamer into the valve guide and rotate the reamer *clockwise* as shown in **Figure 98**. Continue to rotate the reamer and work it down through the entire length of the valve guide.

4. Rotate the reamer *clockwise* and remove all carbon buildup and varnish within the valve guide.

5. Rotate the reamer *clockwise* and withdraw the reamer from the valve guide. Remove the reamer.

6. Repeat Steps 3-5 for the other valve guide.

7. Thoroughly clean the cylinder head and valve guides with solvent and dry with compressed air.

8. Using a bore gauge, measure the inside diameter of each valve guide (**Figure 99**). Record the measurement for each valve guide.

9. Subtract the valve stem dimension from the valve guide dimension. This will give the clearance. Compare to the dimension listed in **Table 1**. If the valve stem-to-valve guide dimension exceeds the service limit, determine if a new guide with the standard dimension would bring the clearance within tolerance. If it will, replace the valve guides as described in this chapter.

10. If the valve stem-to-valve guide clearance exceeds the service limits with new guide, replace the valve also.

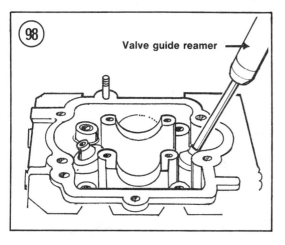

Valve guide reamer →

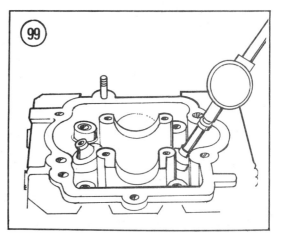

Valve Guide Replacement

When valve guides are worn so that there is excessive stem-to-guide clearance or valve tipping, the guides must be replaced. Replace both, even if only one is worn. This job should only be done by a dealer as special tools are required as well as considerable expertise. If the valve guides are replaced, also replace both valves.

The following procedure is provided in case you choose to perform this task yourself.

CAUTION
*There **may** be a residual oil or solvent odor left in the oven after heating the cylinder head. If you use a household oven first check with the person who uses the oven for food preparation to avoid getting into trouble.*

1. The valve guides are installed with a slight interference fit. The cylinder head must be heated in an oven (or on a hot plate) to a temperature between 100-150° C (212-300° F). An easy way to check the proper temperature is to drop tiny drops of water on the cylinder head; if they sizzle and evaporate immediately, the temperature is correct.

CAUTION
Do not heat the cylinder head with a torch (propane or acetylene). Never bring a flame into contact with the cylinder head or valve guide. The direct heat will destroy the case hardening of the valve guide and will likely cause warpage of the cylinder head.

2. Remove the cylinder head from the oven and hold onto it with kitchen pot holders, heavy gloves or heavy shop cloths—it is very *hot*.
3. Turn the cylinder head upside down on wood blocks. Make sure the cylinder is properly supported on the wood blocks.
4. From the combustion chamber side of the cylinder, drive out the old valve guide (**Figure 100**) with a hammer and Honda special tool (Valve Guide Remover, part No. 07942-3290100) or equivalent. Remove the special tool.
5. While heating up the cylinder head, place the new valve guides in a freezer if possible. Chilling them will slightly reduce their overall diameter while the hot cylinder head is slightly larger due to heat expansion. This will make valve guide installation much easier.
6. Install a new O-ring seal onto the valve guide.
7. While the cylinder head is still hot, drive the new valve guide into place in the cylinder head.

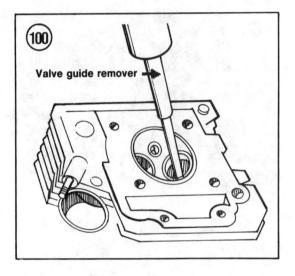
(100) Valve guide remover →

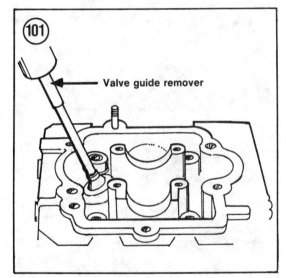
(101) ← Valve guide remover

(102)

The same Honda special tool is used for removal and installation of the valve guide.

8. From the top side (valve side) of the cylinder head, drive in the new valve guide (**Figure 101**) with a hammer and Honda special tool (Valve Guide Remover, part No. 07942-3290100) or equivalent. Drive the valve guide in until it completely seats in the cylinder head. Remove the special tool.

9. Ream the new valve guide as follows:
   a. Ream out the new valve guide with a valve guide reamer (Honda part No. 07984-200000A) or equivalent.

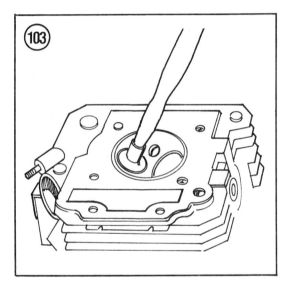

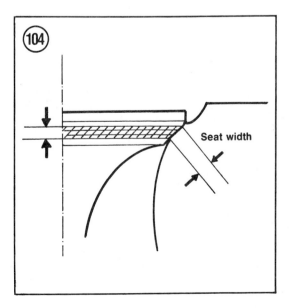

CAUTION
Always *rotate the valve guide reamer* ***clockwise***. *If the reamer is rotated counterclockwise, damage to a good valve guide will occur.*

   b. Apply cutting oil to both the new valve guide and the valve guide reamer.
   c. Insert the valve guide reamer into the valve guide and rotate the reamer *clockwise* as shown in **Figure 98**. Continue to rotate the reamer and work it down through the entire length of the valve guide. Apply additional cutting oil during this procedure.
   d. Rotate the reamer *clockwise* until the reamer has traveled all the way through the new valve guide.
   e. Rotate the reamer *clockwise* and withdraw the reamer from the valve guide. Remove the reamer.

10. Repeat Step 9 for the other valve guide.

11. Thoroughly clean the cylinder head and valve guides with solvent to wash out all metal particles. Dry with compressed air.

12. Reface the valve seats as described in this chapter.

Valve Seat Inspection

1. Remove the valves as described in this chapter.

2. The most accurate method for checking the valve seal is to use Prussian blue (machinist's) dye, available from auto parts stores or machine shops. To check the valve seal with Prussian blue, perform the following:
   a. Thoroughly clean off all carbon deposits from the valve face with solvent or detergent, then dry thoroughly.
   b. Spread a thin layer of Prussian blue evenly on the valve face.
   c. Moisten the end of a suction cup valve tool (**Figure 102**) and attach it to the valve. Insert the valve into the guide.
   d. Using the suction cup tool, tap the valve up and down in the cylinder head (**Figure 103**). Do *not* rotate the valve or a false indication will result.
   e. Remove the valve and examine the impression left by the Prussian blue. If the impression left in the dye (on the valve or in the cylinder head) is not even and continuous and the valve seat width (**Figure 104**) is not within specified tolerance listed in **Table 1**, the cylinder head valve seat must be reconditioned.

3. Closely examine the valve seat in the cylinder head. It should be smooth and even with a polished seating surface.

4. If the valve seat is okay, install the valves as described in this chapter.

5. If the valve seat is not correct, recondition the valve seat as described in this chapter.

Valve Seat Reconditioning

Special valve cutter tools and considerable expertise are required to properly recondition the valve seats in the cylinder head. You can save considerable money by removing the cylinder head and taking just the cylinder head to a dealer or machine shop to have the valve seats ground.

The following procedure is provided in case you choose to perform this task yourself.

Honda valve seat cutters and a grinder are available from Honda dealers or from machine shop supply outlets. Follow the manufacturer's instruction to operate the cutters and grinder. You will need 3 cutters—one 32°, one 45° and one 60° (**Figure 105**).

1. Use the 45° cutter and descale and clean the valve seat with one or two turns (**Figure 106**).

> *CAUTION*
> *Measure the valve seat contact area in the cylinder head after each cut to make sure the contact area is correct and to prevent removing too much material. If too much material is removed, the cylinder head must be replaced.*

2. Inspect the valve seat-to-valve face impression as follows:

    a. Spread a thin layer of Prussian blue evenly on the valve face.

    b. Moisten the end of a suction cup valve tool (**Figure 102**) and attach it to the valve. Insert the valve into the guide.

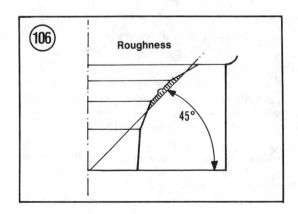

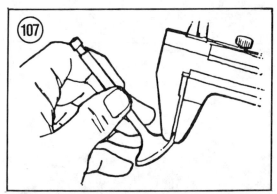

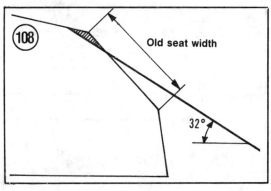

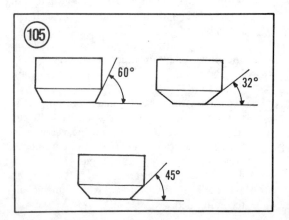

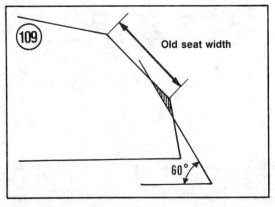

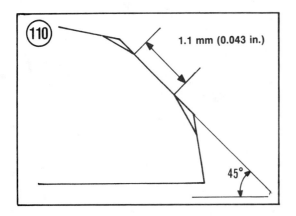

110

1.1 mm (0.043 in.)

45°

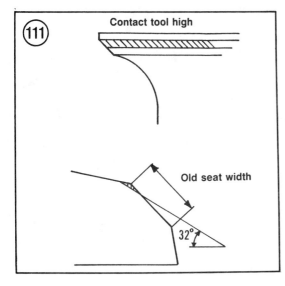

111

Contact tool high

Old seat width

32°

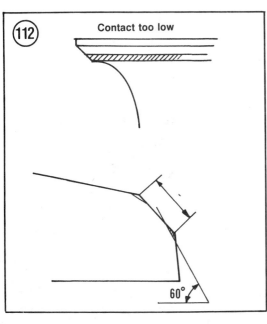

112

Contact too low

60°

c. Using the suction cup tool, tap the valve up and down in the cylinder head (**Figure 103**). Do *not* rotate the valve or a false indication will result.

d. Remove the valve and examine the impression left by the Prussian blue.

e. Measure the valve seat width as shown in **Figure 107**. The seat width should be 1.0-1.2 mm (0.039-0.047 in.). If the valve seat is burned or pitted, turn the 45 degree cutter an additional turn or two.

3. Use the 32° cutter and remove the top 1/4 of the existing valve seat material (**Figure 108**).

4. Use the 60° cutter and remove the bottom 1/4 of the existing valve seat material (**Figure 109**).

5. Install the 45° finish cutter and cut the valve seat to the proper width (**Figure 110**) listed in **Table 1**. Make sure all pitting and irregularities are removed. Repeat Steps 2-5 if necessary.

6. Spread a thin layer of Prussian blue evenly on the valve face.

7. Moisten the end of a suction cup valve tool (**Figure 102**) and attach it to the valve. Insert the valve into the guide.

8. Using the suction cup tool, tap the valve up and down in the cylinder head (**Figure 103**). Do *not* rotate the valve or a false indication will result.

9. Remove the valve and examine the impression left by the Prussian Blue or machinist's dye. If the contact area is too *high* on the valve, the seat must be lowered.

10. Use the 32° cutter and remove a portion of the top area of the valve seat material (**Figure 111**).

11. If the contact area is too *low* on the valve, the seat must be lowered.

12. Use the 60° cutter and remove a portion of the lower area of the valve seat material (**Figure 112**).

13. Install the 45° finish cutter and cut the valve seat to the proper width (**Figure 110**) listed in **Table 1**. Make sure all pitting and irregularities are removed.

14. After cutting the seat, apply a small amount of lapping compound to the valve face.

15. Moisten the end of a suction cup valve tool (**Figure 102**) and attach it to the valve. Insert the valve into the guide.

CAUTION
Do not allow any lapping compound to enter the valve guide area as it will damage the valve guide.

16. Lap the valve *lightly*. Do *not* apply heavy pressure or the valve facing material will be removed.

17. Check that the finish has a smooth and velvety surface. The final seating will take place when the engine is first run.

18. Thoroughly clean the cylinder head and all valve components in solvent or detergent and hot water.

19. Install the valve assemblies and fill the ports with solvent to check for leaks. If any leaks are present, the valve seats must be inspected for foreign matter or burrs that may be preventing a proper seal.

20. If the cylinder head and valve components were cleaned in detergent and hot water, apply a light coat of engine oil to all bare metal surfaces that can rust.

CYLINDER

Removal

1. Remove the cylinder head cover, camshaft and cylinder head as described in this chapter.

2. Remove the cylinder head locating dowels (A, **Figure 78**) and gasket (B, **Figure 78**).

3. Remove the camshaft chain guide (**Figure 113**).

4. Loosen the cylinder by tapping around the perimeter with a rubber or plastic mallet. If necessary, *gently* pry the cylinder loose with a broad-tipped screwdriver.

5. Pull the cylinder straight out and off of the crankcase studs. Work the cam chain wire through the opening in the cylinder and retie the wire to the crankcase so the chain will not fall into the crankcase.

6. Remove the cylinder base gasket and discard it. Remove the dowel pins from the crankcase studs.

7. Install a piston holding fixture under the piston to protect the piston skirt from damage. This fixture may be purchased or may be a homemade unit of wood. See **Figure 114** for dimensions.

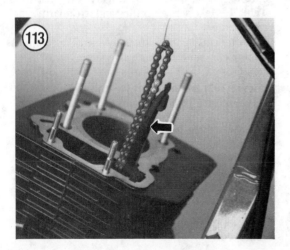

Inspection

The following procedure requires the use of highly specialized and expensive measuring instruments. If such equipment is not readily available, have the measurements performed by a dealer or qualified machine shop.

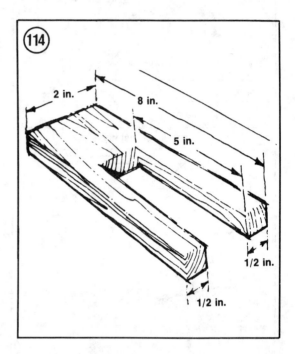

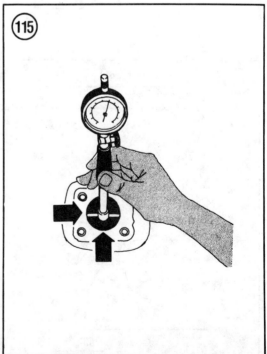

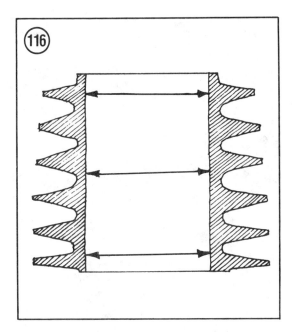

1. Soak with solvent any old cylinder head gasket material on the cylinder. Use a broad-tipped *dull* chisel and gently scrape off all gasket residue. Do not gouge the sealing surface as oil and air leaks will result.

2. Measure the cylinder bore with a cylinder gauge (**Figure 115**) or inside micrometer at the points shown in **Figure 116**.

3. Measure in 2 axes—in line with the piston pin and at 90° to the pin. If the taper or out-of-round is 0.10 mm (0.004 in.) or greater, the cylinder must be rebored to the next oversize and a new piston installed.

NOTE
*The new piston should be obtained before the cylinder is rebored so that the piston can be measured; slight manufacturing tolerances must be taken into account to determine the actual size and working clearance. Piston-to-cylinder wear limit is listed in **Table 1**.*

4. Check the cylinder wall (**Figure 117**) for scratches; if evident, the cylinder should be rebored.

NOTE
*The maximum wear limit on the cylinder is listed in **Table 1**. If the cylinder is worn to this limit, it must be replaced. Never rebore a cylinder if the finished rebore diameter will be this dimension or greater.*

NOTE
After having the cylinder rebored, wash it thoroughly in hot soapy water. This is the best way to clean the cylinder of all fine grit material left from the bore job. After washing the cylinder, run a clean white cloth through it; the cloth should show no traces of dirt or other debris. If the rag is dirty, the cylinder is not clean enough and must be rewashed. After the cylinder is thoroughly clean, dry the cylinder wall and lubricate it with clean engine oil to prevent rust.

Installation

1. Check that the top surface of the crankcase and the bottom surface of the cylinder are clean before installing a new base gasket.

2. Install a new cylinder base gasket (A, **Figure 118**).

3. Install the dowel pins (B, **Figure 118**) on the right-hand crankcase studs.

4. Install a piston holding fixture under the piston.

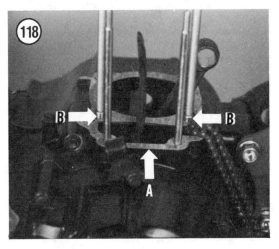

5. Make sure the end gaps of the piston rings are *not* lined up with each other—they must be staggered. Lightly oil the piston rings and the inside of the cylinder bores with assembly oil or fresh engine oil.

6. Carefully feed the cam chain and wire up through the opening in the cylinder and tie it to the engine.

7. Install the cylinder and slide it down onto the crankcase studs. Guide the camshaft chain and camshaft tensioner assembly into the camshaft chain slot in the cylinder.

8. Carefully feed the camshaft chain wire up through the opening in the cylinder and tie the wire to the exterior of the engine.

9. Start the cylinder down over the piston (**Figure 119**). Compress each piston ring with your fingers as it enters the cylinder.

10. Slide the cylinder down until it bottoms on the piston holding fixture.

11. Remove the piston holding fixture and slide the cylinder down into place on the crankcase (**Figure 120**).

12. Install the camshaft chain guide (**Figure 113**).

13. Install the cylinder head and cylinder head cover as described in this chapter.

14. Adjust the valves as described under *Valve Clearance Adjustment* in Chapter Three.

15. Follow the *Break-in Procedure* in this chapter if the cylinder was rebored or honed or a new piston or piston rings were installed.

CAMSHAFT CHAIN TENSIONER

Removal/Installation

The camshaft chain tensioner cannot be disassembled nor serviced. If faulty it must be replaced as a unit.

1. Remove the bolts (**Figure 121**) securing the camshaft chain tensioner to the cylinder and remove the tensioner.

2. Remove the gasket and discard it.

3. Remove the sealing bolt and washer from the center of the tensioner.

4. Install by reversing these removal steps, noting the following.

5. Install a new gasket on the cylinder.

6. Using a flat-bladed screwdriver, turn the tensioner shaft *clockwise* until the tensioner is fully retracted into the body (**Figure 70**).

7. Keep the screwdriver (A, **Figure 71**) in place to keep the tensioner shaft retracted in the body.

8. Install the camshaft chain tensioner and gasket into the cylinder (B, **Figure 71**). Install the bolts (C, **Figure 71**) and tighten securely.

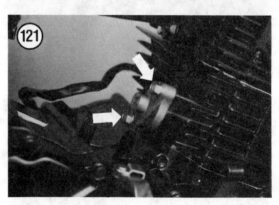

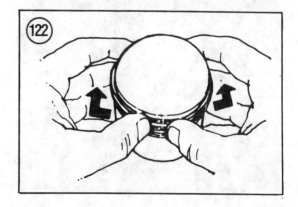

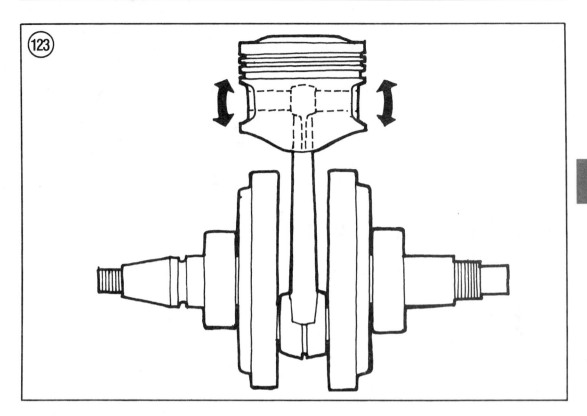

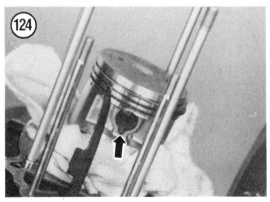

9. Remove the screwdriver and install the sealing washer and bolt (**Figure 72**). Tighten the bolt securely.

10. Install the camshaft chain tensioner into the cylinder. Install the bolts and tighten securely.

PISTON, PISTON PIN
AND PISTON RINGS

The piston is made of an aluminum alloy. The piston pin is made of steel and is a precision fit. The piston pin is held in place by a clip at each end.

Piston Removal

1. Remove the cylinder head cover, camshaft, cylinder head and cylinder as described in this chapter.

> *WARNING*
> *The edges of all piston rings are very sharp. Be careful when handling them to avoid cutting fingers.*

2. Remove the top ring with a ring expander tool or by spreading the ends with your thumbs just enough to slide the ring up over the piston (**Figure 122**). Repeat for the remaining rings.

3. Before removing the piston, hold the rod tightly and rock the piston as shown in **Figure 123**. Any rocking motion (do not confuse with the normal sliding motion) indicates wear on the piston pin, piston pin bore or connecting rod small-end bore (more likely a combination of these).

> *NOTE*
> *Wrap a clean shop cloth under the piston so that the piston pin clip will not fall into the crankcase.*

4. Remove the clip from each side of the piston pin bore (**Figure 124**) with a small screwdriver or

scribe. Hold your thumb over one edge of the clip when removing it to prevent the clip from springing out.

5. Use a proper size wooden dowel or socket extension and push out the piston pin.

> **CAUTION**
> *Be careful when removing the pin to avoid damaging the connecting rod. If it is necessary to gently tap the pin to remove it, be sure that the piston is properly supported so that lateral shock is not transmitted to the lower connecting rod bearing.*

6. If the piston pin is difficult to remove, heat the piston and pin with a butane torch. The pin will probably push right out. Heat the piston to only about 140° F (60° C), i.e., until it is too warm to touch, but not excessively hot. If the pin is still difficult to push out, use a homemade tool as shown in **Figure 125**.

7. Lift the piston off the connecting rod.

8. If the piston is going to be left off for some time, place a piece of foam insulation tube over the end of the rod to protect it.

Inspection

1. Carefully clean the carbon from the piston crown with a chemical remover or with a soft scraper (**Figure 126**). Do not remove or damage the carbon ridge around the circumference of the piston above the top ring. If the piston, rings and cylinder are found to be dimensionally correct and can be reused, removal of the carbon ring from the top of the piston or the carbon ridge from the top of the cylinder will promote excessive oil consumption.

> **CAUTION**
> *Do not wire brush the piston skirts.*

2. Examine each ring groove for burrs, dented edges and wide wear. Pay particular attention to the top compression ring groove as it usually wears more than the other grooves.

3. Make sure the oil holes (**Figure 127**) in the piston pin area of the piston are clear.

4. If damage or wear indicates piston replacement, select a new piston as described under *Piston Clearance* in this chapter.

5. Oil the piston pin and install it in the connecting rod. Slowly rotate the piston pin and check for play (**Figure 128**). If any play exists, the piston pin should be replaced, providing the rod bore is in good condition.

6. Measure the inside diameter of the piston pin bore with a snap gauge and measure the outside

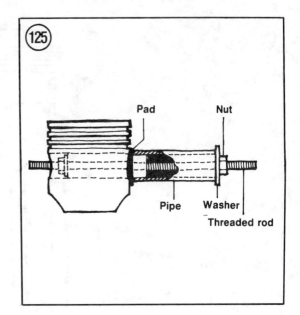

Pad   Nut

Pipe   Washer

Threaded rod

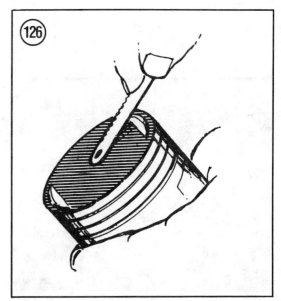

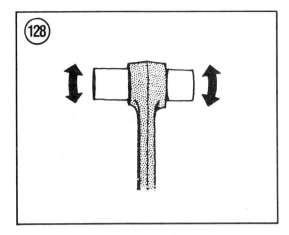

diameter of the piston pin with a micrometer (**Figure 129**). Compare with dimensions given in **Table 1**. Replace the piston and piston pin as a set if either or both are worn.

7. Check the piston skirt for galling and abrasion which may have been caused by piston seizure. If light galling is present, smooth the affected area with No. 400 emery paper and oil or a fine oilstone. However, if galling is severe or if the piston is deeply scored, replace it.

Piston Clearance

1. Make sure the piston and cylinder walls are clean and dry.

2. Measure the inside diameter of the cylinder bore at a point 13 mm (1/2 in.) from the upper edge with a bore gauge (**Figure 130**).

3. Measure the outside diameter of the piston across the skirt (**Figure 131**) at right angles to the piston pin. Measure at a distance 10 mm (0.40 in.) up from the bottom of the piston skirt.

4. Piston clearance is the difference between the maximum piston diameter and the minimum cylinder diameter. Subtract the dimension of the piston from the cylinder dimension and compare to the dimension listed in **Table 1**. If the clearance exceeds that specified, the cylinder should be rebored to the next oversize and a new piston installed.

5. To establish a final overbore dimension with a new piston, add the piston skirt measurement to the specified clearance. This will determine the dimension for the cylinder overbore size. Remember, do not exceed the cylinder maximum service limit inside diameter indicated in **Table 1**.

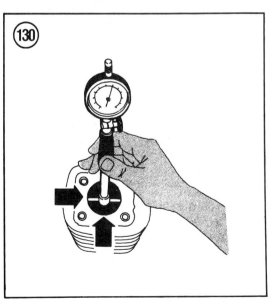

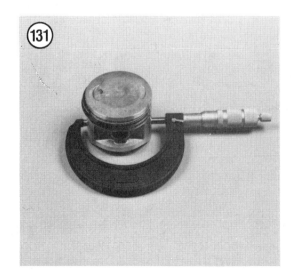

Piston Installation

1. Apply molybdenum disulfide grease to the inside surface of the connecting rod.
2. Oil the piston pin with assembly oil or fresh engine oil and install it in the piston until its end extends slightly beyond the inside of the boss (**Figure 132**).
3. Place the piston over the connecting rod with the IN mark (**Figure 133**) on the piston crown directed toward the intake port or the rear of the engine.
4. Line up the piston pin with the hole in the connecting rod. Push the piston pin through the connecting rod and into the other side of the piston until it is even with the piston pin clip grooves.

> *CAUTION*
> *If it is necessary to tap the piston pin into the connecting rod, do so gently with a block of wood or a soft-faced hammer. Make sure you support the piston to prevent the lateral shock from being transmitted to the connecting rod bearing.*

> *NOTE*
> *In the next step, install the clips with the gap away from the cutout in the piston (**Figure 134**).*

5. Install new piston pin clips in both ends of the pin boss. Make sure they are seated in the grooves in the piston.
6. Check the installation by rocking the piston back and forth around the pin axis and from side to side along the axis. It should rotate freely back and forth but not from side to side.
7. Install the piston rings as described in this chapter.
8. Install the cylinder, cylinder head, camshaft and cylinder head cover as described in this chapter.

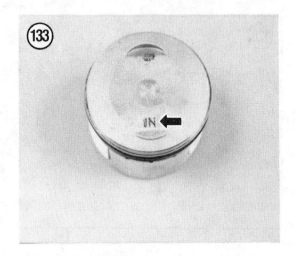

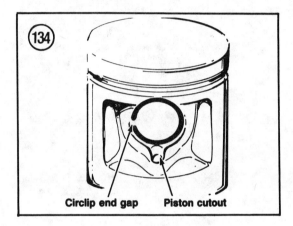

Circlip end gap   Piston cutout

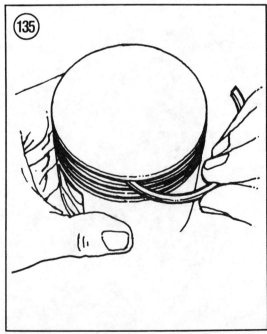

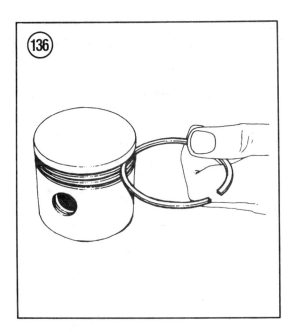

Piston Ring Replacement

WARNING
The edges of all piston rings are very sharp. Be careful when handling them to avoid cutting fingers.

1. Remove the top ring by spreading the ends with your thumbs just enough to slide the ring up over the piston (**Figure 122**). Repeat for the remaining rings.

2. Carefully remove all carbon buildup from the ring grooves with a broken piston ring (**Figure 135**). Inspect the grooves carefully for burrs, nicks or broken and cracked lands. Recondition or replace the piston if necessary.

3. Roll each ring around its piston groove as shown in **Figure 136** to check for binding. Minor binding may be cleaned up with a fine-cut file.

4. Measure the side clearance of each ring in its groove with a flat feeler gauge (**Figure 137**) and compare to dimensions given in **Table 1**. If the

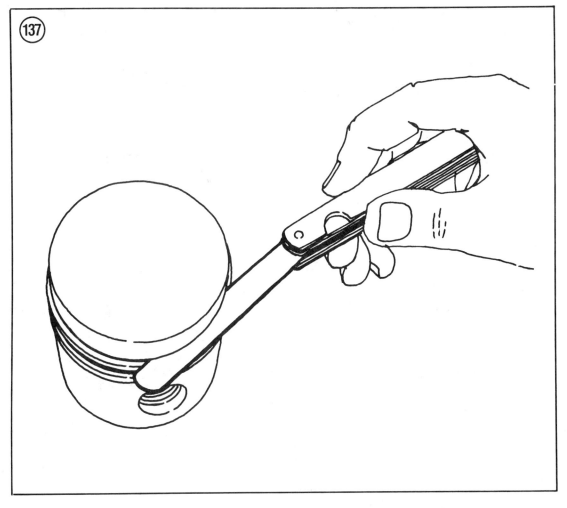

clearance is greater than specified, the rings must be replaced. If the clearance is still excessive with the new rings, the piston must also be replaced.

5. Measure each ring for wear. Place each ring, one at a time, into the cylinder and push it in about 20 mm (3/4 in.) with the crown of the piston to ensure that the ring is square in the cylinder bore. Measure the gap with a flat feeler gauge (**Figure 138**) and compare to dimensions in **Table 1**. If the gap is greater than specified, the rings should be replaced. When installing new rings, measure their end gap in the same manner as for old ones. If the

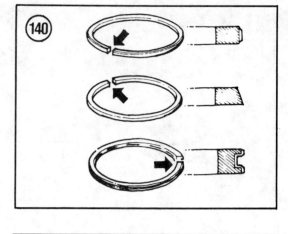

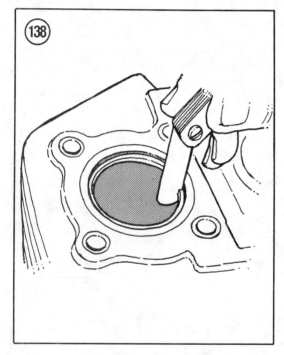

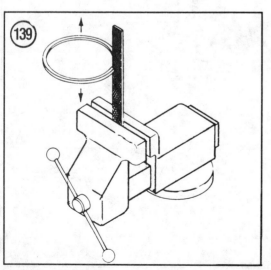

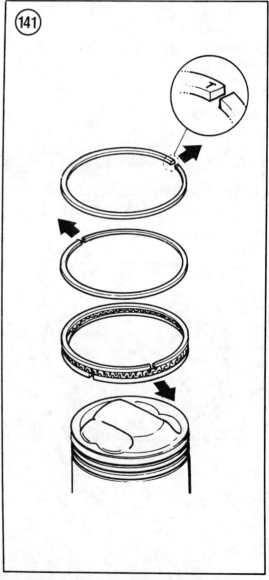

gap is less than specified, carefully file the ends (**Figure 139**) with a fine-cut file until the gap is correct.

6. Install the piston rings in the order shown in **Figure 140**.

NOTE
Install the compression rings with their markings facing up.

7. **Install the oil ring spacer first, then the side rails. Some new oil ring side rails do not have top and bottom designations. If reassembling used parts, install the side rails as they were removed.**

8. Install the second compression ring, then the top compression ring by carefully spreading the ends of the ring with your thumbs and slipping the ring over the top of the piston. Remember that the marks on the piston rings are toward the top of the piston.

9. Make sure the rings are seated completely in their grooves all the way around the piston and that the ends are distributed around the piston as shown in **Figure 141**. The important thing is that the ring gaps are not aligned with each other when installed.

10. If new rings were installed, measure the side clearance of each ring in its groove with a flat feeler gauge (**Figure 142**) and compare to dimensions given in **Table 1**.

11. Follow the *Break-in Procedure* in this chapter if a new piston or new piston rings have been installed or the cylinder was rebored or honed.

4

OIL PUMP

The oil pump is located on the right-hand side of the engine forward of the clutch assemblies. The oil pump can be removed with the engine in the frame.

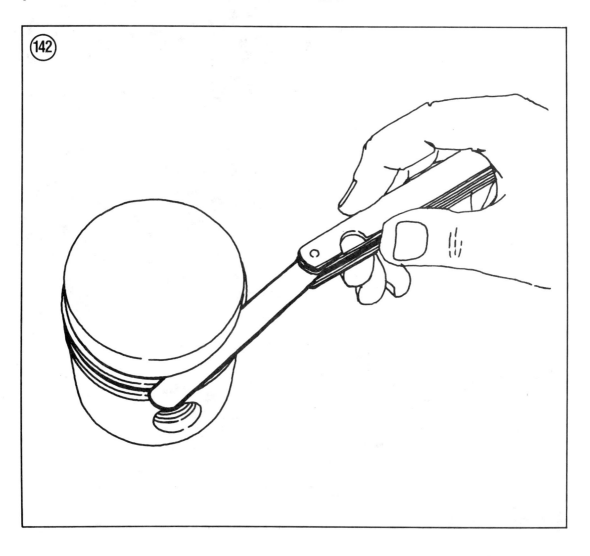

Removal

NOTE
This procedure is shown with the clutch assembly(ies) removed for clarity. It is not necessary to remove these items to perform this procedure.

1. Drain the engine oil as described under *Engine Oil Change* in Chapter Three.
2. Remove the right-hand crankcase cover as described under *Right-hand Crankcase Cover Removal* (for your specific model) in this chapter.
3. Remove the oil pump separator plate (**Figure 143**) from the crankcase.
4. Remove the circlip (**Figure 144**) securing the oil pump driven sprocket.
5. Withdraw the driven sprocket and drive chain (**Figure 145**) from the oil pump shaft. Remove the driven sprocket.
6. Remove the bolts (**Figure 146**) securing the oil pump and remove the oil pump assembly.
7. Don't lose the locating dowels. The locating dowels may either stick to the oil pump (A, **Figure 147**) or stay in the crankcase.
8. Inspect the oil pump as described in this chapter.

Installation

1. Make sure the locating dowels (A, **Figure 147**) are in place, then install the oil pump assembly. Tighten the bolts securely.
2. Make sure the oil pump drive chain is properly meshed with the drive sprocket on the crankshaft.
3. Mesh the drive chain with the driven sprocket.
4. Align the flat of the driven sprocket with the flat on the oil pump shaft and install the driven sprocket.
5. Position the circlip with the sharp side facing toward the outside. Install the circlip to secure the driven sprocket. Make sure the circlip is correctly seated in the shaft groove.
6. Install the oil pump separator plate.

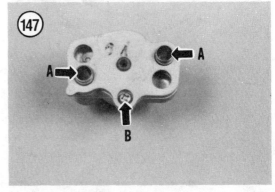

7. Install the right-hand crankcase cover as described under *Right-hand Crankcase Cover Installation* (for your specific model) in this chapter.

8. Refill the crankcase with the recommended type and quantity of engine oil, as described under *Engine Oil Change* in Chapter Three.

Disassembly/Inspection/Assembly

Refer to **Figure 148** for this procedure.

1. Remove the Phillips head screw (B, **Figure 147**) securing the pump cover to the body and remove the cover.

2. Remove the inner and outer rotors and the drive shaft. Inspect both rotors (**Figure 149**) for scratches and abrasions. Replace both parts if evidence of this is found.

3. Clean all parts in solvent and dry thoroughly. Coat all parts with fresh engine oil before assembly.

4. Inspect the oil pump body (**Figure 150**) and cover for cracks.

4

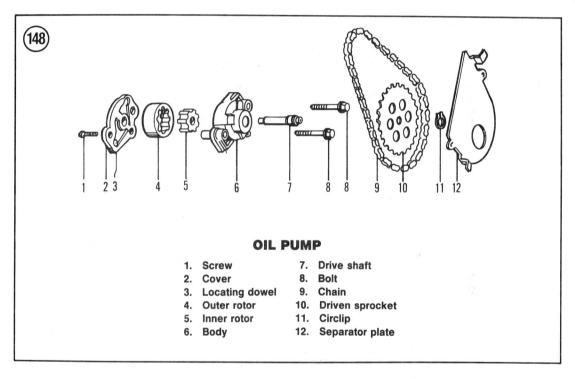

OIL PUMP

1.	Screw	7.	Drive shaft
2.	Cover	8.	Bolt
3.	Locating dowel	9.	Chain
4.	Outer rotor	10.	Driven sprocket
5.	Inner rotor	11.	Circlip
6.	Body	12.	Separator plate

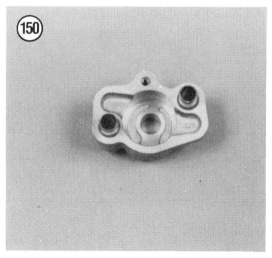

5. Inspect the teeth on the driven sprocket (**Figure 151**). Replace the driven sprocket if the teeth are damaged or any are missing.

6. Inspect the drive chain (**Figure 152**) for wear or damage; replace if necessary.

7. Install the drive shaft (**Figure 153**) into the oil pump body.

8. Install the inner rotor (**Figure 154**) and outer rotor (**Figure 155**) into the oil pump body.

9. Using a flat feeler gauge, measure the clearance between the outer rotor and the oil pump body (**Figure 156**). Compare to specifications listed in **Table 1**. If the clearance is worn to the service limit dimension or greater, replace the worn part.

10. Using a flat feeler gauge measure the clearance between the inner rotor tip and the outer rotor (**Figure 157**). Compare to specifications listed in **Table 1**. If the clearance is worn to the service limit dimension or greater, replace the worn part.

11. Remove the oil pump drive shaft. Place a straightedge across both rotors and the oil pump body. Insert a flat feeler gauge between the rotors and the body. Compare to specifications listed in **Table 1**. If the clearance is worn to the service limit dimension or greater, replace the worn part(s).

12. Install the oil pump drive shaft.

13. Install the cover and Phillips head screw. Tighten the screw securely.

STARTER REDUCTION GEARS (4-WHEELED MODELS)

Removal/Inspection/Installation

Refer to **Figure 158** for this procedure.

1. Remove the bolts securing the starter reduction gear cover (**Figure 159**). Remove the cover and O-ring seal.

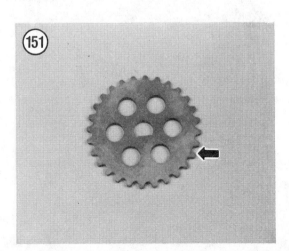

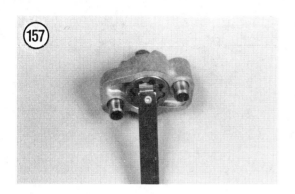

4

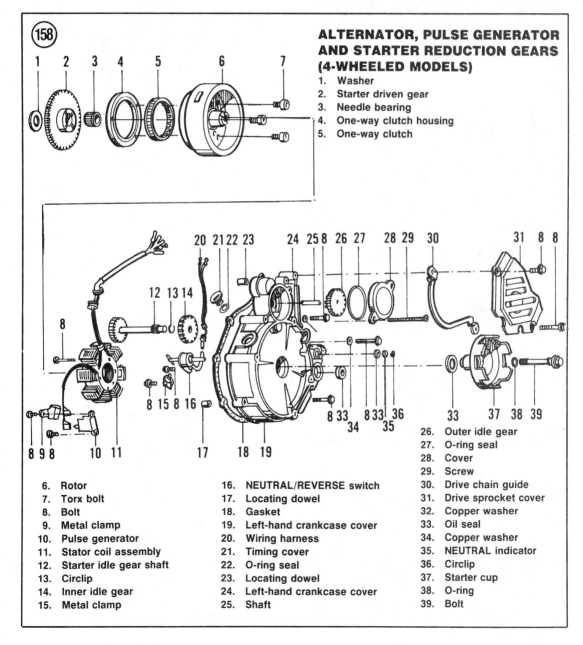

ALTERNATOR, PULSE GENERATOR AND STARTER REDUCTION GEARS (4-WHEELED MODELS)

1. Washer
2. Starter driven gear
3. Needle bearing
4. One-way clutch housing
5. One-way clutch

6. Rotor
7. Torx bolt
8. Bolt
9. Metal clamp
10. Pulse generator
11. Stator coil assembly
12. Starter idle gear shaft
13. Circlip
14. Inner idle gear
15. Metal clamp
16. NEUTRAL/REVERSE switch
17. Locating dowel
18. Gasket
19. Left-hand crankcase cover
20. Wiring harness
21. Timing cover
22. O-ring seal
23. Locating dowel
24. Left-hand crankcase cover
25. Shaft
26. Outer idle gear
27. O-ring seal
28. Cover
29. Screw
30. Drive chain guide
31. Drive sprocket cover
32. Copper washer
33. Oil seal
34. Copper washer
35. NEUTRAL indicator
36. Circlip
37. Starter cup
38. O-ring
39. Bolt

2. Slide off outer idle gear (**Figure 160**) and shaft (**Figure 161**).

3. Remove the left-hand crankcase cover as described under *Left-hand Crankcase Cover Removal (4-wheeled Models)* in this chapter.

4. Slide off inner idle gear (**Figure 162**).

5. Remove the alternator rotor as described under *Alternator, Pulse Generator and Starter Clutch Removal* in this chapter.

6. Withdraw the starter idle gear shaft (**Figure 163**) from the crankcase.

> *NOTE*
> *The starter driven gear will sometimes come off with the alternator rotor or it may stay on the crankshaft.*

7. If not already removed, remove the starter driven gear and needle bearing from the crankshaft.

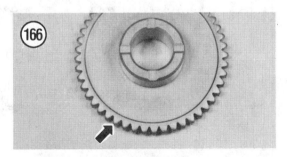

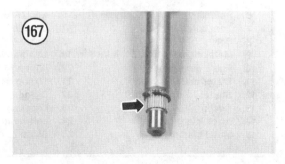

168

169

8. Check for chipped or missing teeth on the starter gears. Refer to **Figures 164-166**. Replace the gears if necessary.

9. Inspect the splines (**Figure 167**) on the starter idle gear shaft for wear or damage; replace the shaft if necessary.

10. Check for chipped or missing teeth on the starter idle gear (**Figure 168**). The gear is an integral part of the shaft and if damaged, the shaft must be replaced.

11. Install by reversing these removal steps, noting the following.

12. Install new gaskets and a new O-ring seal (**Figure 169**) on the reduction gear cover.

13. Tighten the cover bolts securely.

ALTERNATOR AND PULSE GENERATOR (3-WHEELED MODELS)

Removal

Refer to **Figure 170** for this procedure.

1. Place the ATV on level ground and set the parking brake.

4

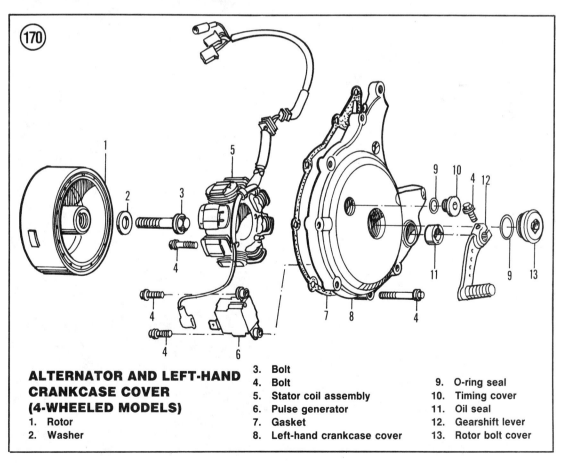

170

ALTERNATOR AND LEFT-HAND CRANKCASE COVER (4-WHEELED MODELS)
1. Rotor
2. Washer
3. Bolt
4. Bolt
5. Stator coil assembly
6. Pulse generator
7. Gasket
8. Left-hand crankcase cover
9. O-ring seal
10. Timing cover
11. Oil seal
12. Gearshift lever
13. Rotor bolt cover

2. Disconnect the alternator/pulse generator electrical connectors (**Figure 171**).

3. Remove the left-hand crankcase cover as described under *Left-hand Crankcase Cover Removal (3-wheeled Models)* in this chapter.

4. Remove the bolt and washer (**Figure 172**) securing the alternator rotor to the crankshaft.

NOTE
If necessary, use a strap wrench to keep the rotor from turning while removing the bolt.

5. Screw a flywheel puller into the alternator rotor (**Figure 173**).

6. Screw the puller in until it stops. Use the Honda flywheel puller (part No. 07733-0020001 or 07933-2160000), a K & N puller (part No. 82-0100) or equivalent.

CAUTION
Don't try to remove the rotor without a puller. Any attempt to do so will ultimately lead to some form of damage to the engine and/or the rotor. Many aftermarket pullers are available from motorcycle dealers or mail order houses. The cost of these pullers is relatively low and it makes an excellent addition to any mechanic's tool collection. If you can't buy or borrow one, have a dealer remove the rotor.

7. Carefully tap on the end of the puller with a metal hammer. Sometimes this is sufficient to disengage the rotor from the crankshaft.

8. If the rotor didn't disengage from the crankshaft, gradually tighten the puller with a wrench until the rotor disengages from the crankshaft.

NOTE
If the rotor is still difficult to remove, strike the puller with a metal hammer a few times. This will usually break it loose.

CAUTION
If normal rotor removal attempts fail, do not force the puller as the threads may be stripped out of the rotor, causing expensive damage. Take the vehicle to a dealer and have the rotor removed.

9. Remove the rotor and puller. Unscrew the puller from the rotor.

10. Don't lose the Woodruff key (**Figure 174**) on the crankshaft.

> *CAUTION*
> *Carefully inspect the inside of the rotor (**Figure 175**) for small bolts, washers or other metal debris that may have been picked up by the magnets. These small metal bits can cause severe damage to the alternator stator plate components.*

11. To remove the stator and pulse generator assembly, perform the following:

   a. Remove the bolts and metal plate securing the pulse generator assembly (A, **Figure 176**) to the left-hand crankcase cover.

   b. Disconnect the electrical connector (B, **Figure 176**) from the pulse generator and remove the pulse generator and metal plate.

   c. Remove the bolts securing the stator assembly (A, **Figure 177**) to the left-hand crankcase cover.

   d. Pull the rubber grommet (B, **Figure 177**) free from the cover. Remove the stator assembly.

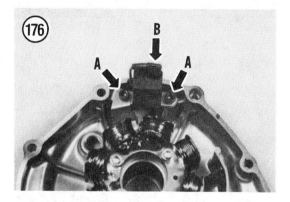

Inspection

Refer to Chapter Eight for electrical inspection of the alternator rotor and stator and the pulse generator.

Installation

1. If removed, install the stator assembly and the pulse generator in the left-hand crankcase cover. Make sure the rubber grommet (B, **Figure 177**) is positioned correctly in the cover and tighten the bolts to the torque specifications listed in **Table 2**.

2. Make sure the metal plate (**Figure 178**) is in position and that it secures the pulse generator electrical wire against the left-hand crankcase cover. If the wire is not secured, it can come in contact with the rotor and be damaged.

3. Make sure the Woodruff key (**Figure 174**) is in place on the crankshaft and align the keyway in the rotor with the key when installing the rotor. Push the rotor all the way on until it stops.

4. Install the bolt and washer securing the rotor.

5. Temporarily install the gearshift pedal and shift the transmission into 6th gear. Have a helper apply the rear brake. Tighten the rotor bolt to the torque specification listed in **Table 2**. Remove the gearshift pedal.

6. Install the left-hand crankcase cover as described under *Left-hand Crankcase Cover Installation (3-wheeled Models)* in this chapter.

7. Connect the alternator/pulse generator electrical connectors.

ALTERNATOR, PULSE GENERATOR
AND STARTER CLUTCH
(4-WHEELED MODELS)

The starter clutch is mounted on the backside of the alternator rotor and the ignition pulse generator is tied in with the alternator rotor assembly.

Removal

Refer to **Figure 158** for this procedure.

1. Place the ATV on level ground and set the parking brake.

2. Remove the recoil starter as described under *Recoil Starter Removal/Installation (4-wheeled Models)* in this chapter.

3. Remove the left-hand crankcase cover as described under *Left-hand Crankcase Cover (4-wheeled Models)* in this chapter.

4. Remove the electrical connector junction box cover (**Figure 179**).

5. Disconnect the alternator/pulse generator electrical connectors (**Figure 180**).

6. Remove the starter inner idle gear (**Figure 162**).

7. Screw a flywheel puller into the alternator rotor.

8. Screw the puller in until it stops. Use the Honda flywheel puller (part No. 07733-0010000 or equivalent.

9. Carefully tap on the end of the puller with a soft-faced mallet. Sometimes this is sufficient to disengage the rotor from the crankshaft.

10. If the rotor didn't disengage from the crankshaft, gradually tighten the puller with a wrench until the rotor disengages from the crankshaft.

NOTE
If the rotor is still difficult to remove, strike the puller with a metal hammer a few times. This will usually break it loose.

CAUTION
Don't try to remove the rotor without a puller; any attempt to do so will ultimately lead to some form of damage to the engine and/or the rotor. Many aftermarket pullers are available from motorcycle dealers or mail order houses. The cost of these pullers is relatively low and it makes an excellent addition to any mechanic's tool collection. If you can't buy or borrow one, have a dealer remove the rotor.

CAUTION
If normal rotor removal attempts fail, do not force the puller as the threads may be stripped out of the rotor, causing expensive damage. Take the vehicle to a dealer and have the rotor removed.

11. Remove the rotor/starter driven gear (**Figure 181**) and puller. Unscrew the puller from the rotor.

12. Remove the Woodruff key (**Figure 182**) on the crankshaft.

13. Remove the needle bearing (**Figure 183**) and washer (**Figure 184**) from the crankshaft.

14. Remove the starter driven gear assembly (**Figure 185**) from the backside of the alternator rotor.

CAUTION
*Carefully inspect the inside of the rotor (**Figure 186**) for small bolts, washers or other metal debris that may have been picked up by the magnets. These small metal bits can cause severe damage to the alternator stator plate components.*

15. To remove the stator assembly, perform the following:

   a. Remove the bolt (A, **Figure 187**) securing the NEUTRAL and REVERSE switch wiring harness to the crankcase cover.

b. Remove the bolt (B, **Figure 187**) securing the NEUTRAL and REVERSE switch to the crankcase cover.

c. Remove the bolts securing the alternator stator assembly (C, **Figure 187**) to the cover.

d. Pull the rubber grommet (D, **Figure 187**) free from the cover. Remove the stator assembly.

Inspection

1. Inspect the one-way clutch (A, **Figure 188**) on the backside of the rotor for wear or damage.

2. To replace the one-way clutch, perform the following:

a. Remove the one-way clutch (A, **Figure 188**) from the backside of the rotor.

b. Use an impact driver and a Torx socket and remove the Torx bolts (**Figure 189**) securing the one-way clutch housing to the backside of the rotor.

c. Remove the one-way clutch housing (B, **Figure 188**) from the backside of the rotor and remove the housing.

d. Inspect the inner surface (**Figure 190**) of the one-way clutch housing for scoring or damage. If damaged, replace the one-way clutch and housing as an assembly. The individual parts cannot be replaced separately.

e. Inspect the rollers (**Figure 191**) of the one-way clutch for scoring or damage. If damaged, replace the one way clutch and housing as an assembly. The individual parts cannot be replaced separately.

f. Position the one-way clutch housing with the flange side going on first, then install the housing (**Figure 192**).

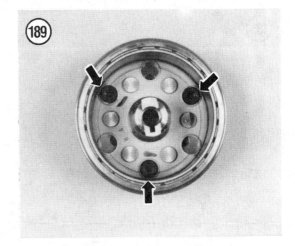

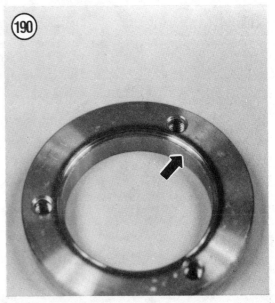

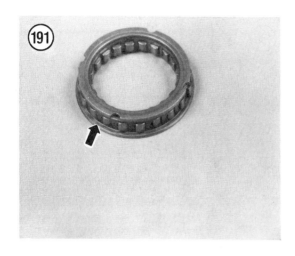

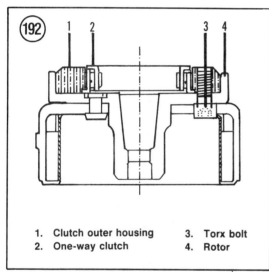

1. Clutch outer housing	3. Torx bolt
2. One-way clutch	4. Rotor

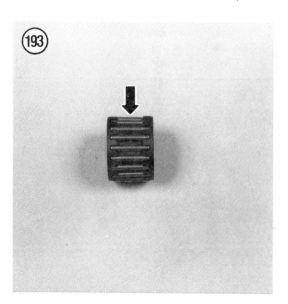

g. Apply Loctite Lock N' Seal to the Torx bolt threads before installation.

h. Install the Torx bolts and tighten to the torque specification listed in **Table 2**.

i. Position the one-way clutch with the notches (C, **Figure 188**) in the outer race, facing toward the outside. Install the one-way clutch.

3. Inspect the gear teeth (**Figure 166**) on the starter driven gear for wear or damage. Replace the starter driven gear if necessary.

4. Inspect the needles (**Figure 193**) in the needle bearing. The needles must rotate freely with no binding. Replace the needle bearing if necessary.

5. Inspect the outer surface (**Figure 194**) of the starter driven gear where the one-way clutch rides for scoring or damage. If damaged, replace the starter driven gear.

6. Refer to Chapter Eight for electrical inspection of the alternator rotor and stator and the pulse generator.

Installation

1. If removed, install the stator assembly and the pulse generator in the left-hand crankcase cover. Make sure the rubber grommet is positioned correctly in the cover and tighten the bolts to the torque specification listed in **Table 2**.

2. Make sure the electrical wire harness clamp and bolts are installed. If left off, the electrical wires will come in contact with the rotor and be damaged, causing a short circuit.

3. Install the washer (**Figure 184**) and the needle bearing (**Figure 183**) onto the crankshaft.

4. Install the Woodruff key (**Figure 182**) on the crankshaft.

5. If removed, install the starter idle gear shaft (**Figure 163**).

6. If removed, rotate the starter driven gear (**Figure 185**) *clockwise,* (viewed from the back of the rotor) and install the starter driven gear onto the backside of the rotor.

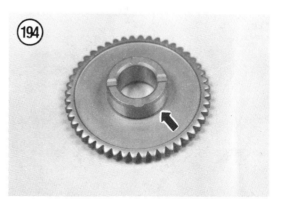

7. Align the keyway in the rotor with the Woodruff key when installing the rotor. Push the rotor all the way on until it stops (**Figure 181**).

8. Install the starter inner idle gear (**Figure 162**).

9. Install the left-hand crankcase cover as described under *Left-hand Crankcase Cover (4-wheel Drive Models)* in this chapter.

10. Install the recoil starter as described under *Recoil Starter Removal/Installation (4-wheeled Models)* in this chapter.

11. Connect the alternator/pulse generator electrical connectors.

KICKSTARTER
(3-WHEELED MODELS)

Removal

1. Drain the engine oil as described in Chapter Three.

2. Remove the right-hand crankcase cover as described under *Right-hand Crankcase Cover (3-wheeled Models)* in this chapter.

3. Remove the clutch assembly as described under *Manual Clutch Removal/Disassembly* in Chapter Five.

4. Temporarily install the kickstarter lever (**Figure 195**) onto the kickstarter shaft.

5. Rotate the kickstarter lever *clockwise* to free the ratchet pawl from the ratchet guide mounted on the crankcase and the return spring. Pull the assembly slightly outward.

6. Withdraw the kickstarter shaft assembly from the crankcase and remove the kickstarter lever from the assembly.

Disassembly

Refer to **Figure 196** for this procedure.

1. Slide off the return spring collar.

2. Remove the return spring, spring seat and ratchet spring.

3. Slide off the ratchet.

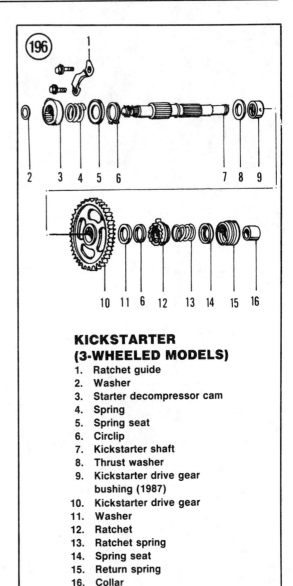

**KICKSTARTER
(3-WHEELED MODELS)**

1. Ratchet guide
2. Washer
3. Starter decompressor cam
4. Spring
5. Spring seat
6. Circlip
7. Kickstarter shaft
8. Thrust washer
9. Kickstarter drive gear bushing (1987)
10. Kickstarter drive gear
11. Washer
12. Ratchet
13. Ratchet spring
14. Spring seat
15. Return spring
16. Collar

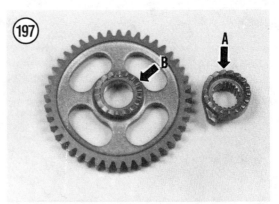

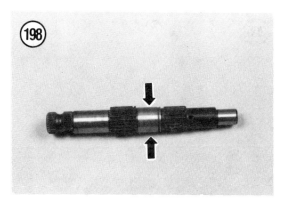

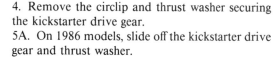

4. Remove the circlip and thrust washer securing the kickstarter drive gear.

5A. On 1986 models, slide off the kickstarter drive gear and thrust washer.

5B. On 1987 models, slide off the kickstarter drive gear and bushing and the thrust washer.

6. From the other end of the shaft, remove the thrust washer, starter decompressor cam, spring and spring seat.

7. If necessary, remove the circlip from the kickstarter shaft.

8. Inspect all parts as described in this chapter.

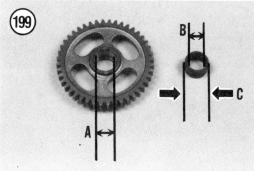

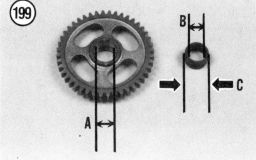

Inspection

1. Check for chipped or missing teeth on all gears.

2. Check all parts for uneven wear; replace as necessary.

3. Inspect the splines on the kickstarter shaft for wear or damage. Replace the shaft if necessary.

4. Check the ratchet surfaces on both the kickstarter ratchet (A, **Figure 197**) and the kickstarter drive gear (B, **Figure 197**) for wear; replace if necessary.

5. On 1987 models, measure the outside diameter of the kickstarter shaft (**Figure 198**) where the kickstarter drive gear rides. Compare to specifications listed in **Table 1**. If worn to the service limit dimension or less, replace the shaft.

6. On 1987 models, measure the inside diameter of the kickstarter drive gear (A, **Figure 199**). Compare to specifications listed in **Table 1**. If worn to the service limit dimension or greater, replace the gear.

7. On 1987 models, measure the inside diameter (B, **Figure 199**) and the outside diameter (C, **Figure 199**) of the kickstarter drive gear bushing. Compare to specifications listed in **Table 1**. If worn to the service limit dimension or beyond, replace the drive gear bushing.

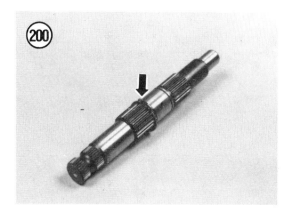

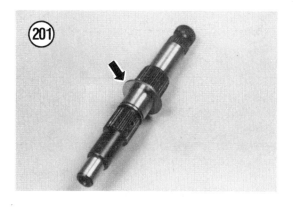

Assembly

1. Apply clean engine oil to all sliding surfaces of all parts before assembly and installation.

2. If removed, install the circlip (**Figure 200**).

3. Slide the thrust washer (**Figure 201**) onto the kickstarter shaft.

4A. On 1986 models, slide on the kickstarter drive gear and thrust washer.

4B. On 1987 models, slide on the kickstarter drive gear bushing (**Figure 202**), drive gear (**Figure 203**) and thrust washer (**Figure 204**).

5. Install the circlip (**Figure 205**).

6. Align the interrupted spline (**Figure 206**) in the kickstarter ratchet with the flattened portion of the kickstarter shaft spline (**Figure 207**).

7. Slide the kickstarter ratchet (**Figure 208**) onto the kickstarter shaft.

8. Slide on the ratchet spring (**Figure 209**) and spring seat (**Figure 210**).

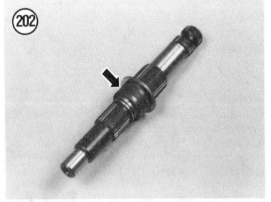

9. Slide on the return spring (**Figure 211**) and insert the spring end into the hole in the kickstarter shaft.

10. Slide the plastic collar (**Figure 212**) into the return spring. Push the collar all the way in until it seats.

11. Onto the right-hand end of the shaft, perform the following:

    a. Install the spring seat (**Figure 213**) and spring (**Figure 214**).

    b. Align the interrupted spline (**Figure 215**) in the starter decompressor cam with the index mark on the kickstarter shaft spline.

4

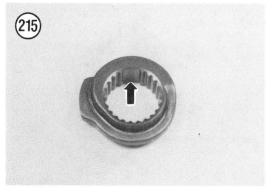

c. Install the starter decompressor cam (**Figure 216**).

d. Slide on the thrust washer (**Figure 217**).

12. Before installation, check the placement of all parts on the shaft (**Figure 218**).

Installation

1. Temporarily install the kickstarter lever onto the kickstarter shaft assembly.

2. Install the kickstarter assembly into the crankcase.

3. Rotate the kickstarter assembly *clockwise* and hook the end of the return spring onto the opening in the crankcase. You will usually hear a click when the return spring hooks on correctly.

4. Continue to rotate the kickstarter assembly *clockwise* (**Figure 219**) and hook the ratchet pawl onto the ratchet guide on the crankcase.

5. After installation is complete, make sure the punch mark on the kickstarter shaft is pointing straight UP (**Figure 220**). If the punch mark is pointing straight down, the ratchet was incorrectly aligned onto the kickstarter shaft during the assembly procedure. Refer to Step 6, *Assembly* in this chapter.

6. Check the operation of the kickstarter drive gear at this point as follows:

a. With the kickstarter lever in the relaxed position spin the gear—it should spin freely.

b. Move the kickstarter *clockwise* about 90°. Try to spin the kickstarter gear. It should not spin since the ratchet is now meshed with the backside of the drive gear.

7. Remove the kickstarter lever.

8. Install the clutch assembly as described under *Manual Clutch Assembly/Installation* in Chapter Five.

9. Install the right-hand crankcase cover as described under *Right-hand Crankcase Cover (3-wheeled Models)* in this chapter.

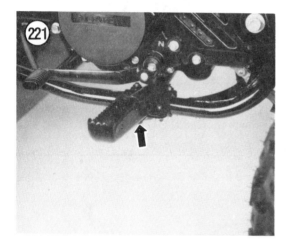

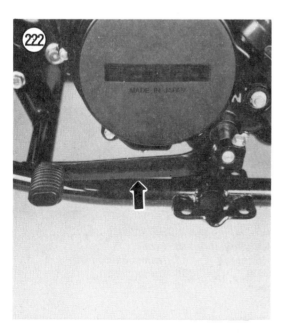

RECOIL STARTER
(4-WHEELED MODELS)

Removal/Installation

1. Place the ATV on level ground and set the parking brake.

2. Remove the bolts securing the left-hand footpeg assembly (**Figure 221**) and remove the assembly.

3. Shift the transmission into NEUTRAL and remove the clamping bolt securing the gearshift lever (**Figure 222**). Remove the gearshift lever.

4. Remove the bolts securing the recoil starter assembly (**Figure 223**) and remove the assembly. On 1986-1987 models, remove the gasket. 1988 models do not use a gasket.

5. Install by reversing these removal steps. Make sure to install a new gasket (1986-1987 models) on the assembly before installation.

Disassembly and
Starter Rope Removal

> *NOTE*
> *If you have been stranded with a broken starter rope, consider replacing the Honda nylon starter rope with an aftermarket vinyl coated flexible wire cable. These cables are available from many dealers and mail order houses and will outlast the original equipment rope.*

Refer to **Figure 224** for this procedure.

> *WARNING*
> *The return spring is under pressure and may jump out during the disassembly procedure. It is a very strong spring and may cut fingers or cause eye damage. Wear safety glasses and gloves when disassembling and assembling.*

1. Remove the cover from the starter handle and untie the knot in the starter rope or cut the rope.

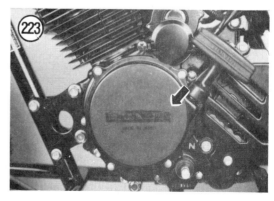

2. Hold the starter rope with Vise Grips (A, **Figure 225**) and remove the starter handle from the rope.

3. On 1986-1987 models, remove and discard the gasket.

4. Remove the nut (B, **Figure 225**) and ratchet cover (C, **Figure 225**).

5. Remove the ratchet guide (**Figure 226**).

6. Remove the ratchet (A, **Figure 227**) and the friction spring and cup (B, **Figure 227**).

7. Remove the Vise Grips and release the starter rope slowly into the housing.

> *WARNING*
> *The recoil spring may jump out at this time; protect yourself accordingly.*

8. Remove the drive pulley (C, **Figure 227**).

9. Untie and remove the starter rope from the drive pulley.

> *NOTE*
> *If the stock Honda nylon starter rope is used, it is a good idea to replace it every time the recoil starter is disassembled.*

10. Clean all parts in solvent and thoroughly dry.

11. Inspect all moving parts (**Figure 228**) for wear or damage and replace as necessary.

**Assembly and
Starter Rope Installation**

1. Install a new starter rope in the drive pulley (A, **Figure 229**). If a stock Honda nylon rope is used, tie a special knot at the end (**Figure 230**). Apply heat to the knot (a match is sufficient) and *slightly* melt the nylon rope. This will hold the knot securely.

2. Apply multipurpose grease to the housing shaft (A, **Figure 231**).

> *WARNING*
> *This step requires an assistant as it is very **dangerous**, and almost impossible, to try to install the spring by yourself. Both of you must wear eye and hand protection as the recoil spring could jump out at any time—protect yourself accordingly.*

3. Install the recoil spring into the housing as follows:

  a. Have the assistant hold onto the cover so it will not rotate.

  b. Hook the end of the spring onto the outer hook (B, **Figure 231**) in the cover.

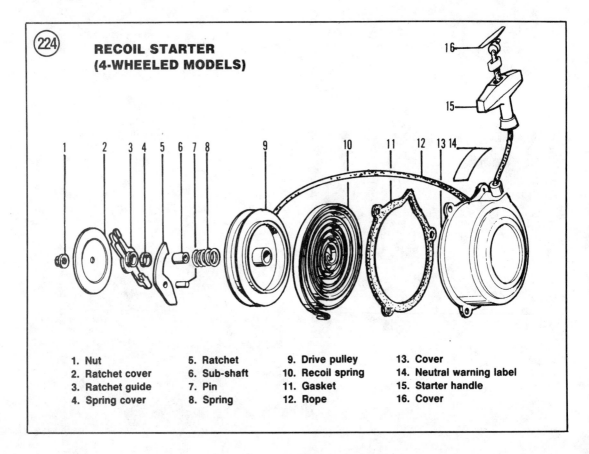

(224)

**RECOIL STARTER
(4-WHEELED MODELS)**

1. Nut	5. Ratchet	9. Drive pulley	13. Cover
2. Ratchet cover	6. Sub-shaft	10. Recoil spring	14. Neutral warning label
3. Ratchet guide	7. Pin	11. Gasket	15. Starter handle
4. Spring cover	8. Spring	12. Rope	16. Cover

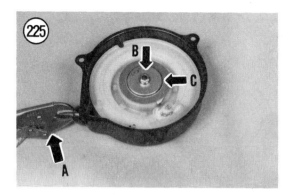

c. Hold the end of the spring in place and start feeding the spring into the housing in a clockwise direction.

d. As you feed the spring into the housing, have the assistant hold the spring down after each loop is installed. The spring must be continuously held in place or it will jump out.

e. Continue to feed the spring in and hold it down until the entire spring is installed.

f. After the spring is completely installed, do not move the cover and spring assembly as at this point the spring is under a lot of pressure and could jump out at any time. Protect yourself and your assistant accordingly.

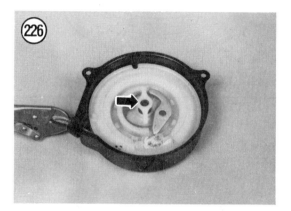

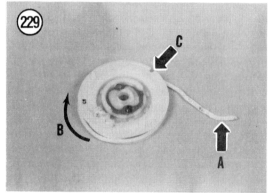

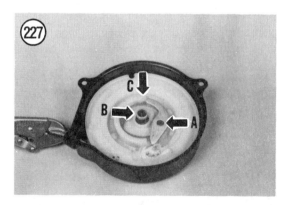

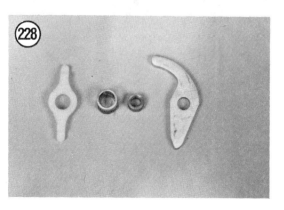

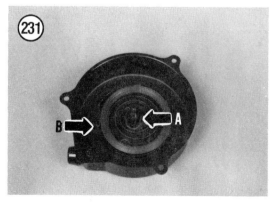

4. Coil the rope onto the drive pulley in a *clockwise* direction (B, **Figure 229**).

5. Position the end of the rope in the drive pulley so the starter grip end is located within the notch (C, **Figure 229**) in the drive pulley.

6. Install the drive pulley into the cover and spring assembly while rotating it in a *clockwise* direction. Make sure the rope is positioned up through the notch in the drive pulley. The tab (A, **Figure 232**) on the bottom of the drive pulley must engage with the hook (B, **Figure 232**) in the end of the recoil spring. If they engage, proceed to Step 9. If the 2 will not engage, *carefully* remove the drive pulley as the spring could jump out at this point. Use the procedure in Step 7 and Step 8.

7. Make a *soft* wire hook (do not use stiff wire) and hook it onto the inner end of the recoil spring as shown in **Figure 233**. The other end of the hook must lie flat on top of the spring coils to allow the drive pulley to drop into position. The wire must be long enough so it can be pulled on.

8. Reinstall the drive pulley into the cover while rotating it in a *clockwise* direction. Make sure the rope is positioned up through the notch in the drive pulley. When the drive pulley comes into contact with the recoil spring, pull sideways on the hook to bring the inner end of the recoil spring away from the shaft in the cover. Continue to rotate the drive pulley and push it the rest of the way down until it seats and engages with the spring hook. Hold the drive pulley down and pull the soft wire hook out from between the drive pulley and the spring.

9. Feed the rope out through the hole in the cover and make sure there is at least 12 in. of rope remaining outside of the opening in the cover.

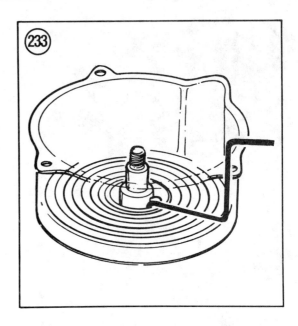

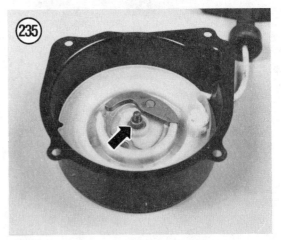

4

10. Install the rope through the starter handle and if a stock Honda nylon rope is used, tie the end using the same special knot as shown in **Figure 230**. Apply heat to the knot (a match is usually sufficient) and *slightly* melt the nylon rope. This will hold the knot securely. Install the cover in the starter handle.

11. Apply a light coat of multipurpose grease to the ratchet and install the ratchet (**Figure 234**).

12. Install the collar (**Figure 235**) onto the threaded stud.

13. Install the spring, spring cover and ratchet guide (**Figure 236**).

14. Install the ratchet cover (**Figure 237**) and secure with the nut (**Figure 238**).

15. After the recoil starter is assembled, the spring tension must be set as follows:

   a. Rotate the drive pulley until the notch is aligned with the area in the cover where the rope exits.

   b. Pull the handle end of the rope up out of the drive pulley and into the notch (**Figure 239**) in the drive pulley.

   c. Within the cover, hold the rope up and make sure it stays in the notch. The rope must stay in the notch during the next step or all rope slack (out past the cover) will be taken up.

   d. **Rotate the reel** *clockwise* **3 to 4 complete revolutions to wind up the spring.**

   e. Move the rope out of the notch in the drive pulley and down into the drive pulley.

16. After assembly is complete, check the operation of the recoil starter by pulling on the starter handle. Make sure the drive pulley rotates freely and returns completely. Also make sure the ratchet moves out and in correctly. If either does not operate correctly, disassemble and correct the problem.

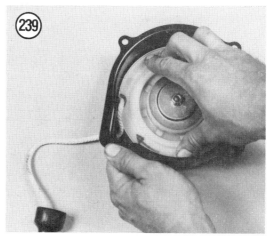

17. Inspect the slots (**Figure 240**) in the starter cup. If they are damaged the starter cup should be replaced as follows:

   a. Remove the bolt and O-ring seal (A, **Figure 241**) securing the starter cup and remove the starter cup (B, **Figure 241**).

   b. Inspect the O-ring seal (**Figure 242**) on the bolt for wear or deterioration; replace if necessary.

   c. Install the starter cup, O-ring and bolt. Tighten the bolt securely.

18. On 1986-1987 models, install a new cover gasket.

RIGHT-HAND CRANKCASE COVER
(3-WHEELED MODELS)

Removal

1. Place the ATV on level ground and set the parking brake.

2. Drain the engine oil as described under *Engine Oil Change* in Chapter Three.

3. Remove the seat/rear fender assembly as described in Chapter Fifteen.

> *NOTE*
> *It is not necessary to remove the exhaust pipe but it allows more working room.*

4. Remove the exhaust pipe as described in Chapter Seven.

5. Remove the pinch bolt securing the kickstarter lever and remove the lever (A, **Figure 243**).

6. Disconnect the clutch cable from the clutch actuating arm and clip on the crankcase cover (B, **Figure 243**).

7. Disconnect the decompressor cable from the cam follower shaft arm and the bracket on the crankcase cover bolt (**Figure 244**).

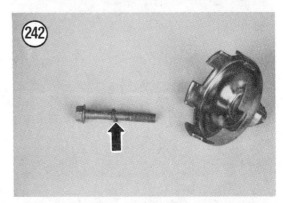

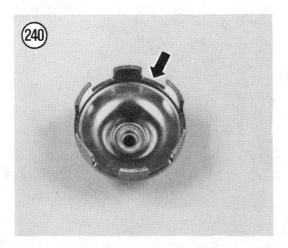

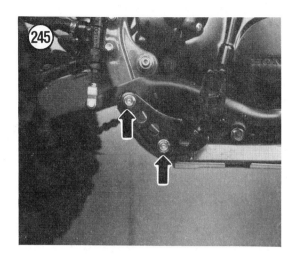

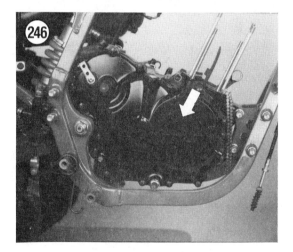

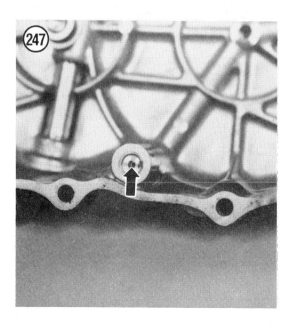

8. Remove the bolts (**Figure 245**) securing the right-hand rear footpeg assembly and remove the assembly.

9. Remove the rear brake pedal as described under *Rear Brake Pedal Removal/Installation* in Chapter Fourteen.

10. Remove the bolts securing the right-hand crankcase cover (**Figure 246**) and remove the cover and gasket. Don't lose the locating dowels. Discard the gasket.

Inspection

1. Clean the right-hand crankcase cover in solvent and dry thoroughly.

2. Inspect the case for cracks or fractures. Repair or replace the crankcase cover.

3. Make sure the oil control orifice (**Figure 247**) is clean. Clean out the orifice if necessary.

4. Make sure that the starter decompressor lever operates smoothly with no binding. If necessary, replace as follows:

    a. Remove the circlip (A, **Figure 248**) securing the cam follower (B, **Figure 248**).

    b. Remove the cam follower and the return spring (C, **Figure 248**).

    c. Withdraw the shaft and lever assembly (**Figure 249**) from the right-hand crankcase cover.

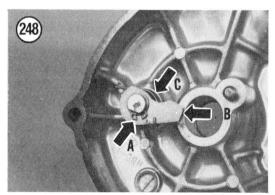

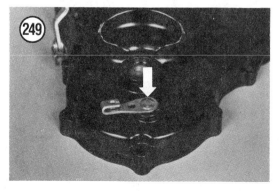

d. Inspect the shaft oil seal in the right-hand crankcase cover; replace if necessary.

e. Install the shaft and lever assembly into the right-hand crankcase.

f. Install the return spring onto the cam follower.

g. Align the flat on the cam follower with the flat on the shaft and install the cam follower onto the shaft.

h. Hook the spring onto the cam follower (A, **Figure 250**) and the raised rib (B, **Figure 250**) on the right-hand crankcase cover.

i. Install the circlip (C, **Figure 250**) securing the cam follower. Make sure the circlip is properly seated in the groove in the shaft.

Installation

1. If removed, install the locating dowels (A, **Figure 251**). Install a new gasket (B, **Figure 251**).

2. Rotate the decompressor arm *clockwise* to align it with the cam on the end of the kickstarter shaft. Hold the arm in this position during the next step.

> *NOTE*
> *Be sure to install the starter decompressor cable bracket (**Figure 252**) under the crankcase cover bolt.*

3. Install the right-hand crankcase cover and bolts. Tighten the bolts securely in a crisscross pattern.

4. Install the right-hand footpeg assembly and rear brake pedal as described under *Rear Brake Pedal Removal/Installation* in Chapter Fourteen.

5. Attach the clutch cable to the clutch actuating arm.

6. Connect the decompressor cable to the cam follower shaft arm.

7. Align the punch mark of the kickstarter arm with the shaft (**Figure 253**) and install the kickstarter arm. Tighten the pinch bolt to the torque specification listed in **Table 2**.

8. Install the exhaust pipe as described in Chapter Seven.

9. Install the seat/rear fender assembly as described in Chapter Fourteen.

10. Fill the engine with the recommended type and quantity of engine oil as described under *Engine Oil Change* in Chapter Three.

11. Adjust the clutch and decompressor cables as described in Chapter Three.

RIGHT-HAND CRANKCASE COVER (4-WHEELED MODELS)

Removal

1. Place the ATV on level ground and set the parking brake.

2. Drain the engine oil as described under *Engine Oil Change* in Chapter Three.

3. Remove the seat and rear fenders as described in Chapter Fourteen.

NOTE
It is not necessary to remove the exhaust pipe but it allows more working room.

4. Remove the exhaust pipe as described in Chapter Seven.

5. Shift the transmission into NEUTRAL.

6. Remove the nut (A, **Figure 254**) securing the REVERSE cable selector arm to the shaft and remove the selector arm.

7. Loosen the locknut on the REVERSE selector cable and unhook the cable (B, **Figure 254**) from the cable holder.

8. Remove the screws (A, **Figure 255**) securing the plastic heat shield and remove the heat shield.

9. Remove the bolts securing the right-hand crankcase cover (**Figure 256**) and remove the cover and gasket. Don't lose the locating dowels or the cable holder. Discard the gasket.

Inspection

1. Wash the right-hand crankcase cover in solvent and dry thoroughly.

2. Inspect the cover for cracks or fractures. Repair or replace the crankcase cover if necessary.

3. Inspect the crankshaft end bearing in the right-hand crankcase cover. Make sure it rotates freely with no binding. If necessary, replace as follows:

   a. Remove the screws (A, **Figure 257**) securing the bearing retainer and remove the retainer (B, **Figure 257**).

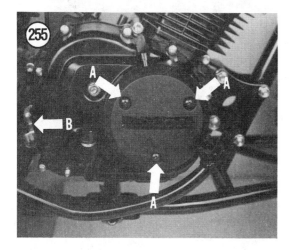

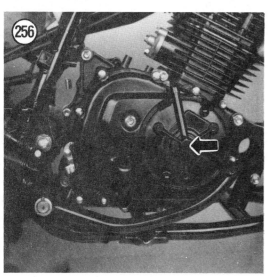

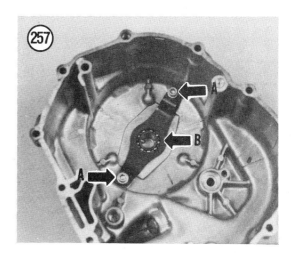

b. Remove the bearing (**Figure 258**) from the right-hand crankcase cover.

c. Install the bearing into the right-hand crankcase cover.

d. Install the bearing retainer and screws. Tighten the screws securely.

Installation

1. If removed, install the locating dowels (A, **Figure 259**). Install a new gasket (B, **Figure 259**).

2. Make sure the thrust washer (C, **Figure 259**) is on the REVERSE lock shaft.

3. Install the right-hand crankcase cover and bolts. Be sure to attach the cable holder with one of the bolts as shown in B, **Figure 255**. Tighten the bolts in a crisscross pattern, tighten them securely.

4. Install the REVERSE selector arm and nut. Tighten the nut securely.

5. Hook the cable onto the REVERSE cable selector arm.

6. Hook the cable into the cable holder on the right-hand crankcase cover.

7. Install the exhaust pipe as described in Chapter Seven.

8. Install the seat and rear fenders as described in Chapter Fifteen.

9. Fill the engine with the recommended type and quantity of engine oil as described under *Engine Oil Change* in Chapter Three.

10. Adjust the REVERSE lock system as described under *Reverse Lock Mechanism (4-wheeled Models)* in Chapter Three.

LEFT-HAND CRANKCASE COVER (3-WHEELED MODELS)

Removal

1. Drain the engine oil as described under *Engine Oil Change* in Chapter Three.

2. Remove the bolts (**Figure 260**) securing the left-hand footpeg assembly and remove the assembly.

3. Remove the clamping bolt (**Figure 261**) on the gearshift lever and remove the lever.

4. Remove the bolts securing the drive sprocket cover and remove the cover (**Figure 262**).

5. Disconnect the alternator and pulse generator electrical connectors (**Figure 263**). Remove the electrical wires from the clips on the frame.

6. Remove the bolts securing the left-hand crankcase cover (**Figure 264**) and gasket. Don't lose the locating dowels or the copper washers under 2 of the bolts.

Installation

1. Inspect the gearshift shaft oil seal in the left-hand crankcase half; replace if necessary.

2. If removed, install the locating dowels (A, **Figure 265**). Install a new gasket (B, **Figure 265**).

3. Install the left-hand crankcase cover.

4. Install a copper washer under the bolts with a raised arrow on the crankcase cover (**Figure 266**). These washers are necessary to prevent an oil leak.

5. Tighten the bolts in a crisscross pattern and tighten them securely.

6. Install the drive sprocket cover and bolts. Tighten the bolts securely.

7. Align the punch mark on the gearshift lever and shaft and install the lever. Tighten the bolt to the torque specification listed in **Table 2**.

8. Install the left-hand footpeg assembly and tighten the bolts to the torque specification listed in **Table 2**.

9. Connect the alternator and pulse generator electrical connectors. Make sure all electrical connections are free of corrosion and are tight. Reconnect the electrical wires under the clips on the frame.

10. Fill the engine with the recommended type and quantity of engine oil as described under *Engine Oil Change* in Chapter Three.

LEFT-HAND CRANKCASE COVER (4-WHEELED MODELS)

Removal

1. Drain the engine oil as described under *Engine Oil Change* in Chapter Three.
2. Remove the seat and the rear fenders as described in Chapter Fifteen.
3. Remove the screws securing the starter reduction gear cover and remove the cover and O-ring seal (**Figure 267**).
4. Withdraw the starter reduction gear and shaft (**Figure 268**).

5. Shift the transmission into NEUTRAL.

6. Remove the bolts securing the left-hand footpeg assembly (**Figure 221**) and remove the assembly.

7. Remove the clamping bolt on the gearshift lever (**Figure 222**) and remove the lever.

8. Remove the recoil starter (**Figure 223**) as described under *Recoil Starter Removal/ Installation* in this chapter.

9. Secure the recoil starter cup and loosen the alternator rotor bolt (A, **Figure 241**). Remove the bolt and O-ring seal (**Figure 242**), then remove the recoil starter cup.

10. Remove the circlip securing the NEUTRAL switch indicator (**Figure 269**) and remove the indicator.

11. Remove the junction box cover (**Figure 270**).

12. Disconnect the alternator, pulse generator and the NEUTRAL/REVERSE switch electrical connectors (**Figure 271**). Remove the electrical wires from the clips on the frame.

13. Remove the bolts securing the left-hand crankcase cover (**Figure 272**) and gasket. Don't lose the locating dowels nor the copper washers under 2 of the bolts. Remove and discard the gasket.

Inspection

1. Clean the left-hand crankcase cover in solvent and dry thoroughly.

2. Inspect the case for cracks or fractures. Repair or replace the crankcase cover.

3. Inspect the recoil starter cup oil seal (**Figure 273**) in the right-hand crankcase cover for wear or damage; replace if necessary.

4. Inspect the gearshift lever shaft oil seal (A, **Figure 274**) and the NEUTRAL/REVERSE switch oil seal (B, **Figure 274**) in the right-hand crankcase cover for wear or damage; replace if necessary.

5. Inspect the starter reduction gear shaft receptacle (**Figure 275**) for wear or damage. Install

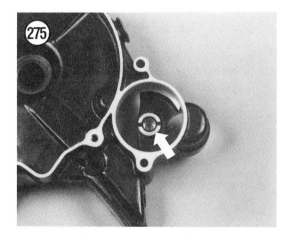

the shaft and spin it around. The shaft should have a tight fit, but still rotate freely. If the receptacle is damaged, replace the right-hand crankcase cover.

Installation

1. If removed, install the locating dowels (A, **Figure 276**). Install a new gasket (B, **Figure 276**).

> *NOTE*
> *The painted portion of the switch pin must face UP when the transmission is in NEUTRAL.*

2. Align the NEUTRAL/REVERSE switch pin (**Figure 277**) with the groove in the end of the shift drum (**Figure 278**).
3. Install the left-hand crankcase cover.
4. Install a copper washer under the bolts with a raised arrow on the crankcase cover (**Figure 279**). These washers are necessary to prevent an oil leak.
5. Tighten the bolts in a crisscross pattern. Tighten them securely.
6. Install the NEUTRAL switch indicator (**Figure 269**) and circlip.
7. Align the punch mark on the gearshift lever and shaft and install the lever. Tighten the bolt securely.
8. Connect the alternator, pulse generator and the NEUTRAL/REVERSE switch electrical connectors (**Figure 271**). Install the electrical wires onto the clips on the frame.
9. Make sure all electrical connections are free of corrosion and are tight.
10. Install the junction box cover (**Figure 270**).
11. Install the drive sprocket guide (**Figure 280**), cover and bolts (**Figure 281**). Tighten the bolts securely.
12. Align the flats on the backside of the starter cup (**Figure 282**) with the groove in the alternator rotor and install the recoil starter cup.
13. Make sure the O-ring seal (**Figure 242**) is on the bolt and install the alternator rotor bolt (A, **Figure 241**). Tighten to the torque specification listed in **Table 2**.
14. Install the recoil starter as described under *Recoil Starter Removal/Installation* in this chapter.
15. Install the starter reduction gear and shaft (**Figure 268**).
16. Make sure the O-ring seal (**Figure 283**) is in place on the cover. Install the starter reduction gear cover (**Figure 267**) and screws. Tighten the screws securely.
17. Install the gearshift lever (**Figure 222**) and clamping bolt. Tighten the bolt securely.
18. Install the left-hand footpeg assembly (**Figure 221**) and bolts. Tighten the bolts securely.

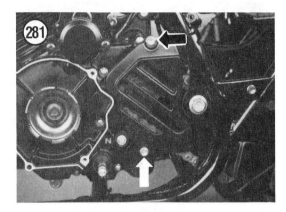

19. Install the seat and the rear fenders as described in Chapter Fifteen.

20. Fill the engine with the recommended type and quantity of engine oil as described under *Engine Oil Change* in Chapter Three.

CRANKCASE AND CRANKSHAFT

Disassembly of the crankcase—splitting the cases—and removal of the crankshaft assembly require that the engine be removed from the frame.

The crankcase is made in 2 halves of precision diecast aluminum alloy and is of the "thin-walled" type. The cases are split vertically down the centerline of the connecting rod. The cases are assembled with a gasket between the 2 halves. Dowel pins align the halves when they are bolted together. To avoid damage, do not hammer or pry on any of the interior or exterior projected walls. These areas are easily damaged.

The crankshaft assembly is made up of 2 flywheels pressed together on a hollow crankpin. The connecting rod big end bearing on the crankpin is a needle bearing assembly. The crankshaft assembly is supported in 2 ball bearings in the crankcase. Service to the crankshaft assembly must be performed by a dealer.

The procedure which follows is presented as a complete, step-by-step, major lower end rebuild that should be followed if an engine is to be completely reconditioned. However, if you're replacing a part that you know is defective, the disassembly should be carried out only until the failed part is accessible; there is no need to disassemble the engine beyond that point so long as you know the remaining components are in good condition and that they were not affected by the failed part.

Crankcase Disassembly

1. Remove the engine as described in this chapter.
2. Remove all exterior engine assemblies as described in this chapter and other related chapters:
    a. Cylinder head cover, camshaft and cylinder head.
    b. Cylinder and piston.
    c. Clutch assembly(ies).
    d. Clutch release mechanism.
    e. Kickstarter (models so equipped).
    f. Recoil starter (models so equipped).
    g. Alternator.
    h. External shift mechanism.
    i. Oil pump.
    j. Starter motor and starter reduction gears (models so equipped).

3. If not already removed, remove the camshaft drive chain tensioner as follows:

   a. Remove the nut (**Figure 284**) and collar (**Figure 285**) securing the camshaft drive chain tensioner arm to the threaded stud in the crankcase.

   b. Pivot the lower end of the tensioner arm out and away from the threaded stud (**Figure 286**).

   c. Withdraw the tensioner arm up and out of the camshaft drive chain channel in the right-hand crankcase.

   d. Remove the washer (**Figure 287**) from the threaded stud.

4. Remove the camshaft drive chain (**Figure 288**).

5. Before removing the crankcase bolts, cut a cardboard template approximately the size of the crankcase and punch holes in the template for each bolt location. Place each bolt in the template hole as it is removed. This will speed up the assembly time by eliminating the search for the correct length bolt.

6. Remove the bolts in 2-3 stages from the left-hand crankcase side that secure the crankcase halves together. Refer to **Figure 289** for 3-wheeled models or **Figure 290** for 4-wheeled models. To prevent warpage, loosen them in a crisscross

pattern. Refer to the "C" arrows in **Figure 289** or **Figure 290** for electrical wire clip locations.

NOTE
Set the engine on 4×4 inch wood blocks or fabricate a holding fixture of 2×4 inch wood as shown in **Figure 291**.

NOTE
*On 3-wheeled models, in the next step, don't forget the bolt (**Figure 292**) within the crankcase next to the kickstarter ratchet guide.*

7. Turn the crankcase over and remove the bolts from the right-hand side. Refer to **Figure 293** for 3-wheeled models or **Figure 294** for 4-wheeled models.

CAUTION
*Perform the next step directly over and close to the workbench as the crankcase halves may separate easily. Do **not** hammer on the crankcase halves or they will be damaged.*

8. Hold onto the right-hand crankcase and studs and tap on the right-hand end of the crankshaft and transmission shafts with a plastic or rubber mallet until the crankshaft and crankcase separate.

9. Remove the right-hand crankcase half.

10. If the crankcase and crankshaft will not separate using this method, check to make sure that all bolts are removed. If you still have a problem, take the crankcase assembly to a dealer and have it separated. Do not risk expensive crankcase damage with improper tools or techniques.

CAUTION
Never pry between case halves. Doing so may result in oil leaks, requiring replacement of the case halves.

11. Don't lose the locating dowels if they came out of the case. They do not have to be removed from the case if they are secure.

12. Disassemble the transmission, shift drum and shift fork shaft assemblies as described in Chapter Five or Chapter Six.

13. The crankshaft (**Figure 295**) may or may not come out of the left-hand crankcase half easily. If the crankshaft assembly is loose, carefully pull it out of the left-hand crankcase half. If the crankshaft will not come out easily, the crankshaft must be pressed out and in of the left-hand crankcase half. This job should be entrusted to a dealer as special tools and a hydraulic press are required.

14. Inspect the crankcase halves and crankshaft as described in this chapter.

Crankcase Assembly

1. Apply assembly oil to the inner race of all bearings in both crankcase halves.

> *NOTE*
> *Set the left-hand crankcase half assembly (including the crankshaft) on wood blocks or the wood holding fixture shown in the disassembly procedure.*

2. Install the transmission assemblies, shift shafts and shift drum as described in Chapter Five or Chapter Six.

> *NOTE*
> *Make sure the crankcase mating surfaces are clean and free of all old gasket material. Spray both surfaces with electrical contact cleaner and wipe clean with a lint-free cloth. Make sure you get a leak-free seal.*

3A. On 3-wheeled models, perform the following:
  a. If removed, install the locating dowels (A, **Figure 296**).
  b. Install a new crankcase gasket (B, **Figure 296**).

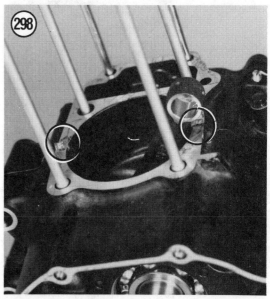

3B. On 4-wheeled models, perform the following:
  a. If removed, install the locating dowels (A, **Figure 297**).
  b. Install a new crankcase gasket (B, **Figure 297**).
4. Set the right-hand crankcase half over the left-hand side assembly on the wood blocks. Push it down squarely into place until it reaches the crankshaft bearing. There is usually about 1/2 inch left to go.
5. Lightly tap the case halves together with a plastic or rubber mallet until they seat.

CAUTION
Crankcase halves should fit together without force. If the crankcase halves do not fit together completely, do not attempt to pull them together with the crankcase screws. Separate the crankcase halves and investigate the cause of the interference. If the transmission shafts were disassembled, recheck to make sure that a gear is not installed backwards. Do not risk damage by trying to force the cases together.

6. After the crankcase halves are completely assembled, rotate the crankshaft and transmission

shafts to make sure there is no binding. If any is present, disassemble the crankcase and correct the problem.
7. Install the bolts on the right-hand side that secure the crankcase halves together. Refer to **Figure 293** for 3-wheeled models or **Figure 294** for 4-wheeled models. Be sure to install all electrical wire clips at the location shown with a "C" on these two figures.
8. Securely tighten the screws in 2 stages in a crisscross pattern until they are firmly hand-tight.
9. Turn the crankcase over and install the bolts on the left-hand side. Refer to **Figure 289** for 3-wheeled models or **Figure 290** for 4-wheeled models. Be sure to install the electrical wire clips at locations marked "C."
10. After the crankcase halves are completely assembled, again rotate the crankshaft and transmission shafts to make sure there is no binding. If any is present, disassemble the crankcase and correct the problem. Tighten the bolts on the right- and left-hand side to the torque specification listed in **Table 2**.

NOTE
*After a new crankcase gasket has been installed, it must be trimmed. Carefully trim off all gasket material where the cylinder base gasket comes in contact with the crankcase. Refer to **Figure 298** for 3-wheeled models or **Figure 299** for 4-wheeled models. If the gasket is not trimmed the cylinder base gasket will not seal properly.*

11. Feed the camshaft drive chain down through the top of the chain opening in the crankcase and install the camshaft chain onto the timing sprocket on the crankshaft. Make sure it is correctly engaged onto the timing sprocket.
12. Install the camshaft tensioner slipper assembly as follows:
  a. Install the washer (**Figure 300**) onto the threaded stud.
  b. Pivot the lower end of the tensioner arm out and away from the crankcase.
  c. Install the tensioner arm down into the camshaft drive chain channel in the right-hand crankcase.
  d. Pivot the lower end of the tensioner arm in and onto the threaded stud (**Figure 286**).
  e. Install the collar (**Figure 285**) and the nut (**Figure 284**) securing the camshaft drive chain tensioner arm onto the threaded stud in the crankcase. Tighten the nut to the torque specification listed in **Table 2**.

13. Install all exterior engine assemblies as described in this chapter and other related chapters.

   a. Starter motor and starter reduction gears (models so equipped).
   b. Oil pump.
   c. External shift mechanism.
   d. Alternator.
   e. Kickstarter (models so equipped).
   f. Recoil starter (models so equipped).
   g. Clutch release mechanism.
   h. Clutch assembly(ies).
   i. Cylinder and piston.
   j. Cylinder head cover, camshaft and cylinder head.

Crankcase and Crankshaft Inspection

1. Clean both crankcase halves inside and out with cleaning solvent. Thoroughly dry with compressed air and wipe off with a clean shop cloth. Be sure to remove all traces of old gasket material from all mating surfaces.

2. Check the crankshaft, transmission and shift drum bearings for roughness, pitting, galling and play by rotating them slowly by hand. Refer to **Figure 301** and **Figure 302** for 3-wheeled models or **Figure 303** and **Figure 304** for 4-wheeled models. If any roughness or play can be felt in the bearing, it must be replaced as described in this chapter.

3. Carefully inspect the cases for cracks and fractures, especially in the lower areas; they are vulnerable to rock damage. Also check the areas around the stiffening ribs, around bearing bosses and threaded holes. If damage is found, have them repaired by a shop specializing in the repair of precision aluminum castings or replace them.

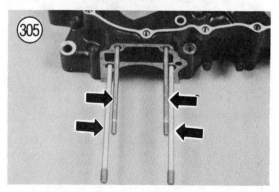

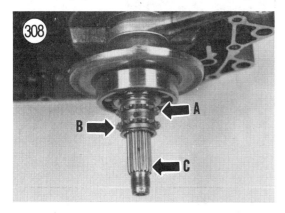

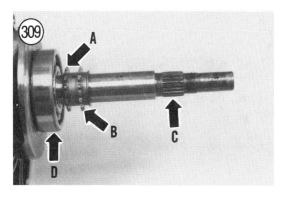

4. Make sure the crankcase studs (**Figure 305**) are tight in each case half; retighten if necessary.

5. Inspect the oil control orifice (**Figure 306**) in the left-hand crankcase half. Remove the orifice and install a new O-ring seal (**Figure 307**), then reinstall the orifice. Make sure it is completely seated in its receptacle.

6A. On 3-wheeled models, inspect the camshaft drive chain sprocket (A, **Figure 308**) and oil pump drive chain sprocket (B, **Figure 308**). If either sprocket is damaged, the sprocket assembly for both drive chains must be replaced by a dealer.

6B. On 4-wheeled models, inspect the camshaft drive chain sprocket (A, **Figure 309**) and oil pump drive chain sprocket (B, **Figure 309**). If either sprocket is damaged, the sprocket assembly for both drive chains may be replaced by a dealer.

7A. On 3-wheeled models, inspect the oil filter rotor splines (C, **Figure 308**) on the crankshaft. If the splines are damaged, the crankshaft must be replaced.

7B. On 4-wheeled models, inspect the centrifugal clutch splines (C, **Figure 309**) on the crankshaft. If the splines are damaged, the crankshaft must be replaced.

8. Measure the inside diameter of the connecting rod small end (**Figure 310**) with a snap gauge and an inside micrometer. Compare to dimensions given in **Table 1**. If worn to the service limit or greater, the crankshaft assembly must be replaced.

9. Check the connecting rod big end bearing by grasping the rod in one hand and lifting up on it. With the heel of your other hand, rap sharply on the top of the rod. A sharp metallic sound, such as a click, is an indication that the bearing or crankpin or both are worn and the crankshaft assembly should be replaced.

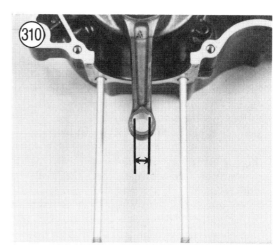

10. Check the connecting rod-to-crankshaft side clearance with a flat feeler gauge (**Figure 311**). Compare to dimensions given in **Table 1**. If the clearance is greater than specified, the crankshaft assembly must be replaced.

11. Inspect the crankshaft ball bearings for roughness, pitting, galling and play by rotating them slowly by hand. Refer to **Figure 312** for 3-wheeled models or D, **Figure 309** for 4-wheeled models. If any roughness or play can be felt in the bearing, it must be replaced. Bearing replacement must be entrusted to a dealer.

12. Other inspections of the crankshaft assembly involve accurate measuring equipment and should be entrusted to a dealer or competent machine shop. The crankshaft assembly operates under severe stress and dimensional tolerances are critical. These dimensions are given in **Table 1**. If any are off by the slightest amount it may cause a considerable amount of damage or destruction of the engine. The crankshaft assembly must be replaced as a unit as it cannot be serviced without the aid of a 9,000-11,000 kilogram (10-12 ton) capacity press, holding fixtures and crankshaft jig.

13. Inspect the oil seals. They should be replaced every other time the crankcase is disassembled. Refer to *Bearing and Oil Seal Replacement* in this chapter.

14. Inspect the sliding surface of camshaft chain guide and the tensioner (**Figure 313**). If either is worn or starting to disintegrate, it must be replaced. This may indicate a worn camshaft drive chain or faulty camshaft chain tensioner assembly.

15. Inspect the camshaft drive chain (**Figure 314**) for wear or damage. Honda does not provide service length limit dimension for the chain. If the chain seems to be noisy and the tensioner is at its limit for applied tension, the chain has stretched to the point where it must be replaced.

Bearing and Oil Seal Replacement

Crankshaft bearing removal and installation is the same on both models. The location of the bearing in the crankcase may vary slightly but the service procedure is still the same.

1. Remove the screws securing the transmission bearing set plate and remove the set plate.

2. On 3-wheeled models, remove the circlip (**Figure 315**) securing the oil seal for the transmission countershaft in the left-hand crankcase half.

3. Pry out the oil seals with a small screwdriver, taking care not to damage the crankcase bore. If the seals are old and difficult to remove, heat the cases

as described in Step 4 and use an awl to punch a small hole in the steel backing of the seal. Install a small sheet metal screw part way into the seal and pull the seal out with a pair of pliers.

CAUTION
Do not install the screw too deep or it may contact and damage the bearing behind it.

CAUTION
*There **may** be a residual oil or solvent odor left in the oven after heating the crankcases. If you use a household oven first check with the person who uses the oven for food preparation to avoid getting into trouble.*

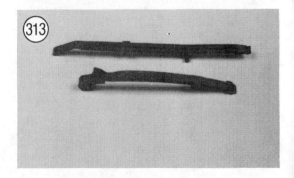

4. The bearings are installed with a slight interference fit. The crankcase must be heated in an oven to a temperature of about 100°C (212°F). An easy way to check the proper temperature is to drop tiny drops of water on the case; if they sizzle and evaporate immediately, the temperature is correct. Heat only one case at a time.

CAUTION
Do not heat the cases with a torch (propane or acetylene); never bring a flame into contact with the bearing or case. The direct heat will destroy the case hardening of the bearing and will likely cause warpage of the case.

5. Remove the case from the oven and hold onto the 2 crankcase studs with a kitchen pot holder, heavy gloves or heavy shop cloths—it is *hot*.
6. Remove the oil seals if not already removed (see Step 3).

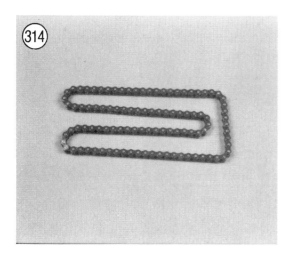

7. Hold the crankcase with the bearing side down and tap it squarely on a piece of soft wood. Continue to tap until the bearing(s) fall out. Repeat for the other half.

CAUTION
Be sure to tap the crankcase squarely on the piece of wood. Avoid damaging the sealing surface of the crankcase.

8. If the bearings are difficult to remove, they can be gently tapped out with a socket or piece of pipe the same size as the bearing outer race.

NOTE
If the bearings or seals are difficult to remove or install, don't take a chance on expensive damage. Have the work performed by a dealer or competent machine shop.

9. While heating up the crankcase halves, place the new bearings in a freezer if possible. Chilling them will slightly reduce their overall diameter while the hot crankcase is slightly larger due to heat expansion. This will make bearing installation much easier.

NOTE
On 3-wheeled models, install the transmission mainshaft bearing into the left-hand crankcase half with the sealed side facing down into the crankcase half.

10. While the crankcase is still hot, press each new bearing(s) into place in the crankcase by hand until it seats completely. Do not hammer it in. If the bearing will not seat, remove it and cool it again. Reheat the crankcase and install the bearing again.
11. Oil seals are best installed with a special tool available at a dealer or motorcycle supply store. However, a proper size socket or piece of pipe can be substituted. Make sure that the bearings and seals are not cocked in the crankcase hole and that they are seated properly.

BREAK-IN PROCEDURE

If the rings were replaced, a new piston installed, the cylinder rebored or honed or major lower end work performed, the engine should be broken in just as though it were new. The performance and service life of the engine depends greatly on a careful and sensible break-in.

For the first 5-10 hours of operation, no more than one-third throttle should be used and speed should be varied as much as possible within the one-third throttle limit. Prolonged steady running at one speed, no matter how moderate, is to be avoided as well as hard acceleration.

Following the first 5-10 hours of operation more throttle should not be used until the ATV has run for 100 hours and then it should be limited to short bursts of speed until 150 hours have been logged.

The mono-grade oils recommended for break-in and normal use provide a better bedding pattern for rings and cylinder than do multi-grade oils. As a result, piston ring and cylinder bore life are greatly increased. During this period, oil consumption will be higher than normal. It is therefore important to frequently check and correct oil level. At no time, during the break-in or later, should the oil level be allowed to drop below the bottom line on the dipstick; if the oil level is low, the oil will become overheated resulting in insufficient lubrication and increased wear.

Service After 10 Hours of Operation

It is essential that the oil be changed and the oil filter rotor and filter screen be cleaned after the first 10 hours of operation. In addition, it is a good idea to change the oil and clean the oil filter rotor and filter screen at the completion of the first 100 hours of operation to ensure that all of the particles produced during break-in are removed from the lubrication system. The small added expense may be considered a smart investment that will pay off in increased engine life.

SERVICE AND ADJUSTMENT

When the engine has been assembled and installed in the ATV, walk around the vehicle and double check all work. Do not be in a hurry for the first ride. You have invested a lot of time, energy and money so don't waste it by forgetting some little item. *Thoroughly* check and recheck all components, systems and controls. Make sure all cables are correctly routed, adjusted and secured and all bolts and nuts are properly tightened. Position all electrical wires and connectors away from the exhaust system and control levers.

Refer to Chapter Three and perform all maintenance and lubrication procedures including all adjustments. Do *not* forget to add oil to the engine.

This little time spent will prevent a lot of frustration and save not only time but money as well.

Table 1 ENGINE SPECIFICATIONS

Item	Specifications	Wear limit
General		
Type	4-stroke, air-cooled, SOHC	
Number of cylinders	1	
Bore and stroke	65.0×60.0 mm (2.55×2.36 in.)	
Displacement	199 cc (12.15 cu. in.)	
Compression ratio		
3-wheeled models	9.5 to 1	
4-wheeled models	9.0 to 1	
Compression pressure		
(at sea level)	1,200-1,400 kPa (170-198 psi)	
Lubrication	Wet sump	
Cylinder		
Bore	65.000-65.010 mm	65.01 mm (2.563 in.)
	(2.5590-2.5594 in.)	
Out of round	—	0.10 mm (0.004 in.)
Piston/cylinder	0.018-0.048 mm	0.10 mm (0.004 in.)
clearance	(0.0007-0.0019 in.)	
Piston		
Diameter	64.962-64.982 mm	64.90 mm (2.555 in.)
	(2.5576-2.5583 in.)	
Piston pin bore	15.002-15.008 mm	15.04 mm (0.592 in.)
	(0.5906-0.5909 in.)	
Piston pin outer	14.994-15.000 in.	14.96 mm (0.589 in.)
diameter	(0.5903-0.5906 in.)	
Piston-to piston	0.002-0.014 mm	0.02 mm (0.001 in.)
pin clearance	(0.0001-0.0006 in.)	
Piston rings		
Number of rings		
Compression	2	
Oil control	1	
Ring end gap		
Top and second	0.20-0.40 mm	0.50 mm (0.020 in.)
	(0.008-0.016 in.)	
Oil	0.20-0.80 mm	—
	(0.008-0.031 in.)	
Ring side clearance		
Top	0.005-0.045 mm	0.09 mm (0.004 in.)
	(0.0002-0.0018 in.)	
Second	0.015-0.045 mm	0.09 mm (0.004 in.)
	(0.0006-0.0018 in.)	

4

(continued)

Table 1 ENGINE SPECIFICATIONS (cont.)

Item	Specifications	Wear limit
Connecting rod		
Small end inner diameter	15.010-15.028 mm (0.5909-0.5917 in.)	15.06 mm (0.593 in.)
Connecting rod-to-piston pin clearance	0.010-0.034 mm (0.0004-0.0013 in.)	0.05 mm (0.002 in.)
Crankshaft		
Runout	—	0.08 mm (0.003 in.)
Connecting rod big end side clearance	0.05-0.50 mm (0.002-0.020 in.)	0.80 mm (0.032 in.)
Camshaft lobe height (3-wheeled models)		
Intake	34.683 mm (1.3655 in.)	34.503 mm (1.3584 in.)
Exhaust	34.557 mm (1.3605 in.)	34.377 mm (1.3534 in.)
Camshaft lobe height (4-wheeled models)		
Intake	34.371 mm (1.3532 in.)	34.191 mm (1.3461 in.)
Exhaust	34.242 mm (1.3481 in.)	34.062 mm (1.3410 in.)
Valve stem outer diameter		
Intake	5.475-5.490 mm (0.2156-0.2161 in.)	5.45 mm (0.215 in.)
Exhaust	5.455-5.470 mm (0.2148-0.2154 in.)	5.43 mm (0.214 in.)
Valve guide inner diameter		
Intake and exhaust	5.500-5.512 mm (0.2165-0.2170 in.)	5.52 mm (0.217 in.)
Stem to guide clearance		
Intake	0.010-0.037 in. (0.0004-0.0015 in.)	0.12 mm (0.005 in.)
Exhaust	0.030-0.057 in. (0.0012-0.0022 in.)	0.14 mm (0.006 in.)
Valve seat width		
Intake and exhaust	1.1 mm (0.04 in.)	1.4 mm (0.06 in.)
Valve springs free length (intake and exhaust)		
Inner spring		
Yellow	31.69 mm (1.248 in.)	29.5 mm (1.16 in.)
White	32.50 mm (1.280 in.)	30.5 mm (1.20 in.)
Outer spring		
Yellow	38.54 mm (1.517 in.)	36.5 mm (1.44 in.)
White	36.90 mm (1.453 in.)	35.0 mm (1.38 in.)
Rocker arm bore I.D.	12.000-12.018 mm (0.4724-0.4730 in.)	12.05 mm (0.474 in.)
Rocker arm shaft O.D.	11.966-11.984 mm (0.4711-0.4718 in.)	11.93 mm (0.470 in.)
Kickstarter (1987 3-wheeled models)		
Shaft OD	21.995-22.018 mm (0.8660-0.8668 in.)	21.95 mm (0.864 in.)
Drive gear ID	27.976-27.989 mm (1.1014-1.1019 in.)	28.03 mm (1.104 in.)

(continued)

Table 1 ENGINE SPECIFICATIONS (cont.)

Item	Specifications	Wear limit
Drive gear bushing		
ID	22.035-22.065 mm (0.8675-0.8687 in.)	22.10 mm (0.870 in.)
OD	27.934-27.955 mm (1.1000-1.1006 in.)	27.89 mm (1.098 in.)
Cylinder		
Warpage		0.10 mm (0.004 in)
Oil pump		
Outer rotor-to-oil pump body		0.40 mm (0.02 in.)
Inner rotor tip-to outer rotor		0.20 mm (0.008 in.)

4

Table 2 ENGINE TORQUE SPECIFICATIONS

Item	N•m	ft.-lb.
Engine mounting hardware (3-wheeled models)		
Top hanger plate		
8 mm	24-30	17-22
10 mm	60-70	43-51
Front and rear hanger plates		
8 mm	30-36	22-26
10 mm	60-70	43-51
Rear lower mounting		
bolt and nut	60-70	43-51
Engine mounting hardware (4-wheeled models)		
Front hanger plate	39-40	22-29
Rear through-bolt		
Upper and lower	60-80	43-58
Camshaft bearing holder bolts	10-14	7-10
Cylinder head and cover		
bolts and nut	10-14	7-10
Cylinder head breather cover	10-14	7-10
Cylinder		
6 mm cap nuts	10-14	7-10
8 mm nuts	28-30	20-22
Alternator rotor bolt		
3-wheeled models	45-55	33-40
4-wheeled models	30-34	22-25
Pulse generator mounting bolts	8-12	5.8-9
Starter clutch Torx bolts	26-30	19-22
Kickstarter pinch bolt	30-35	22-25
Gearshift pedal pinch bolt		
3-wheeled models	14-18	10-13
4-wheeled models	10-12	7-9
Left-hand footpeg bolts		
3-wheeled models	40-50	29-33
4-wheeled models	24-30	17-22
Crankcase bolts	10-14	7-10
Cam chain tensioner slipper nut	10-14	7-10

CLUTCH AND TRANSMISSION
(3-WHEELED MODELS)

This chapter contains service procedures for the manual clutch assembly, external and internal shift mechanisms and the transmission.

Tables 1-4 are at the end of this chapter.

CLUTCH OPERATION

The 3-wheeled models are equipped with a manual clutch mechanism that transmits power from the engine to the transmission. The clutch is a wet multi-plate type which operates immersed in the oil supply it shares with the engine and transmission. It is mounted on the end of the transmission shaft. The inner clutch hub is splined to the mainshaft and the outer clutch housing can rotate freely on the mainshaft. The outer clutch housing is geared to the crankshaft.

The clutch release mechanism is mounted within the crankcase and is operated by the clutch cable and hand lever mounted on the handlebar.

CLUTCH

Removal/Disassembly

Refer to **Figure 1** for this procedure.

1. Remove the right-hand crankcase cover as described under *Right-hand Crankcase Cover (3-wheeled models)* in Chapter Four.

2. Remove the screws securing the oil filter rotor cover and remove the cover and gasket (**Figure 2**).

3. Using a crisscross pattern, remove the clutch bolts (**Figure 3**) securing the clutch lifter plate and bearing. Remove the lifter plate assembly.

4. Remove the clutch springs (**Figure 4**).

5. Lift up and straighten out the depressed section of the locknut that has been staked down into the recess in the crankshaft.

6. Place a soft copper washer (or copper penny) (**Figure 5**) between the primary drive gear on the backside of the oil filter rotor and the drive gear on the clutch outer housing. This is to keep the oil filter rotor from rotating while loosening the locknut.

> *CAUTION*
> *The locknut has **left-hand** threads.*
> *Loosen it by turning it clockwise.*

7. Loosen, then remove the locknut (A, **Figure 6**)—remember to turn the wrench *clockwise*. Remove the copper washer or penny from the gears.

8. Remove the washer.

9. Remove the oil filter rotor (B, **Figure 6**) from the crankshaft.

10. Lift up and straighten out the depressed section of the clutch locknut that has been staked down into the recess in the transmission shaft.

11A. To loosen the locknut with the special tool, perform the following:

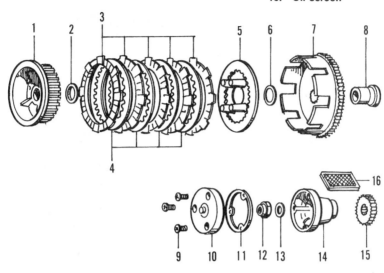

MANUAL CLUTCH ASSEMBLY

1. Clutch center
2. Washer
3. Clutch friction discs
4. Clutch plates
5. Pressure plate
6. Washer
7. Outer housing
8. Outer housing guide
9. Screw
10. Cover
11. Gasket
12. Locknut
13. Washer
14. Oil filter rotor
15. Primary drive gear
16. Oil screen

5

a. Hold the clutch pressure plate with the special tool (**Figure 7**) available from a Honda dealer (Universal Clutch Holder part No. 07HGB-001000A).

b. Correctly position the 4 holders over the posts of the clutch pressure plate. Tighten the nuts securing the holders to the holder plate and install the tool onto the clutch (**Figure 8**).

c. Loosen the clutch locknut.

11B. To loosen the locknut without the special tool, perform the following:

a. Place a soft copper washer (or copper penny) (**Figure 9**) between the primary drive gear and the drive gear on the clutch outer housing. This is to keep the clutch outer housing from rotating while loosening the locknut.

b. Loosen the clutch locknut (**Figure 10**). Remove the copper washer or penny from the gears.

12. Remove the clutch locknut (**Figure 10**) and washer (**Figure 11**).

13. Remove the clutch center, plates, discs, thrust washer and pressure plate (**Figure 12**).

14. Remove the thrust washer (**Figure 13**).

15. Remove the clutch outer housing (**Figure 14**) and clutch outer guide (**Figure 15**).

16. Slide the primary drive gear (**Figure 16**) off of the crankshaft.

17. Inspect the clutch parts as described under *Manual Clutch Inspection* in this chapter.

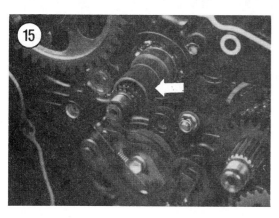

Assembly/Installation

NOTE
If new friction discs and clutch plates are being installed, apply new engine oil to all surfaces to avoid having the clutch lock up when used for the first time.

1. Working at your workbench, install the following onto the clutch center.

   a. Install a friction disc (**Figure 17**) and then a clutch plate (**Figure 18**).

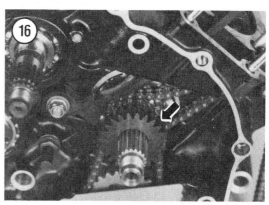

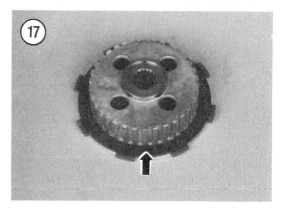

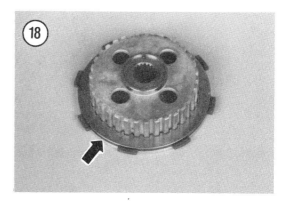

5

   b. Continue to install a friction disc, then a clutch plate, and alternate them until all are installed.

   c. The last item installed is a friction disc (**Figure 19**).

   d. Install the pressure plate (**Figure 20**).

2. Align the tabs of the friction discs to make installation easier.

3. Slide the primary drive gear (**Figure 16**) onto the crankshaft.

4. Position the clutch outer guide with the shoulder side going on first. Install the clutch outer guide (**Figure 15**) onto the transmission mainshaft.

5. Install the clutch outer housing (**Figure 14**) and the thrust washer (**Figure 13**).

6. Slide on the clutch parts (clutch center, friction discs, clutch plates and pressure plate) assembled in Step 1. See **Figure 12**. Push the assembly on slowly, carefully aligning the tabs of the friction discs into the slots in the clutch outer housing.

7. Install the washer (**Figure 11**).

8. Install the locknut (**Figure 10**). Use the same tool setup as used in Step 11, *Removal*. Tighten the locknut to the torque specification listed in **Table 2**.

9. Use a drift and hammer and stake a portion of the locknut down into the recess in the transmission mainshaft (**Figure 21**). If possible, use a portion of the locknut not previously staked.

10. Install the oil filter rotor (**Figure 22**).

11. Position the washer with the raised boss (**Figure 23**) toward the outside and install the washer.

12. Install a new locknut.

13. Place a copper washer (or copper penny) (**Figure 5**) between the primary drive gear and the clutch outer housing. This is to keep the oil filter rotor from turning in the next step.

14. Tighten the locknut to the torque specification listed in **Table 2**. Remove the copper washer or penny.

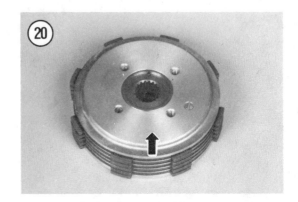

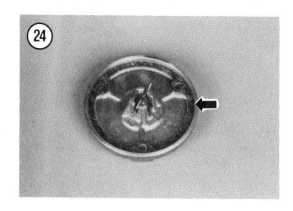

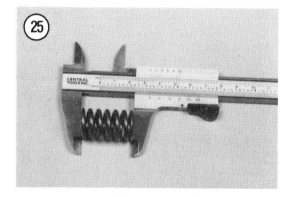

15. Use a drift and hammer and stake a portion of the locknut down into the recess in the crankshaft (A, **Figure 6**).

16. Install a new gasket (**Figure 24**) onto the oil filter rotor cover and gasket. Install the cover and screws. Tighten the screws securely.

17. Install the clutch springs (**Figure 4**).

18. Install the clutch lifter plate and the clutch bolts (**Figure 3**). Tighten the bolts securely in a crisscross pattern in 2 or 3 stages.

19. Install the right-hand crankcase cover as described under *Right-hand Crankcase Cover Installation (3-wheeled Models)* in Chapter Four.

20. Refill the engine with the recommended type and quantity of oil as described under *Engine Oil Change* in Chapter Three.

21. Adjust the clutch as described under *Clutch Adjustment* in Chapter Three.

Inspection

1. Clean all parts in a petroleum-based solvent such as kerosene and dry thoroughly with compressed air.

2. Measure the free length of each clutch spring as shown in **Figure 25**. Refer to **Table 1**. If any of the springs are worn to the service limit or less, replace all springs as a set.

3. Measure the thickness of each friction disc at several places around the disc as shown in **Figure 26**. Refer to **Table 1**. Replace any disc that is worn to the service limit or less. For optimum performance, replace all discs as a set even if only a few need replacement.

4. Check the clutch plates for warpage with a flat feeler gauge and a surface plate such as a piece of plate glass (**Figure 27**). Refer to **Table 1**. Replace any that are warped to the service limit or more. For optimum performance, replace all plates as a set even if only a few need replacement.

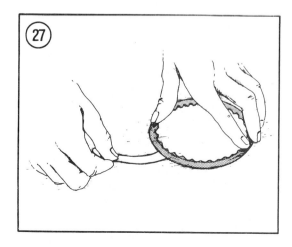

5. Inspect the grooves and studs in the pressure plate (**Figure 28**). If any show signs of wear or galling, the plate should be replaced.

6. Inspect the grooves and inner splines (**Figure 29**) in the clutch center for wear or damage. If any severe damage is evident, the clutch center must be replaced.

7. Inspect the teeth on the clutch outer housing (**Figure 30**). Remove any small nicks on the gear teeth with an oilstone. If damage is severe, the clutch housing should be replaced.

8. Inspect the slots in the clutch outer housing for cracks, nicks or galling where they come in contact with the friction disc tabs (**Figure 31**). If any severe damage is evident, the clutch housing must be replaced.

9. Measure the inside diameter (**Figure 32**) and outside diameter (**Figure 33**) of the clutch outer housing guide with a micrometer or vernier caliper. Refer to **Table 1** and replace the guide spacer if worn to the service limit dimension or beyond.

10. Measure the overall length (**Figure 34**) of the clutch outer housing guide with a micrometer or vernier caliper. Refer to **Table 1** and replace the guide spacer if worn to the service limit dimension or less.

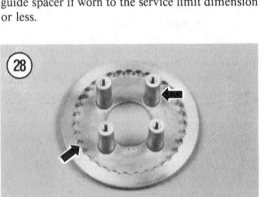

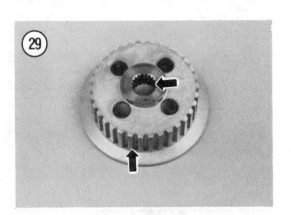

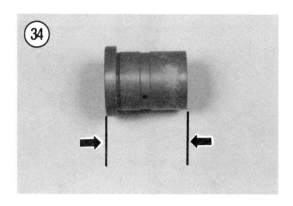

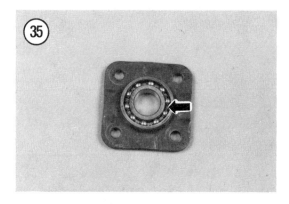

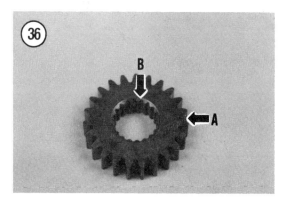

11. Measure the inside diameter of the clutch outer housing with a micrometer or vernier caliper. Refer to **Table 1** and replace the guide spacer if worn to the service limit dimension or greater.

12. Inspect the lifter guide bearing (**Figure 35**). Make sure it rotates smoothly with no signs of wear or damage; replace as necessary.

13. Inspect the teeth (A, **Figure 36**) and inner splines (B, **Figure 36**) on the primary drive gear. Remove any small nicks on the gear teeth with an oilstone. If damage is severe, the gear should be replaced.

CLUTCH LIFTER MECHANISM

The clutch lifter mechanism is located within the right-hand crankcase cover. The clutch lifter mechanism can be removed with the engine in the frame.

Removal/Installation

1. Remove the right-hand crankcase cover as described under *Right-hand Crankcase Cover Removal (3-wheeled Models)* in Chapter Four.

2. Within the right-hand crankcase cover, remove the clutch lifter piece (A, **Figure 37**).

3. Using a small diameter drift, tap the spring pin (B, **Figure 37**) in until it is flush with the lifter shaft surface.

4. Withdraw the lifter shaft (**Figure 38**) from the right-hand crankcase cover and remove the return spring (C, **Figure 37**).

5. Using a 3 mm drift (0.12 in.) drift, tap the spring pin out of the lifter shaft and discard it. Do not reuse the spring pin.

6. Apply a light coat of clean engine oil to the lifter shaft and partially install the lifter shaft into the right-hand crankcase cover.

7. Install the return spring and push the lifter shaft the rest of the way in until it stops.

8. Install a new spring pin into the lifter shaft. Do not drive the pin in all the way as the return spring

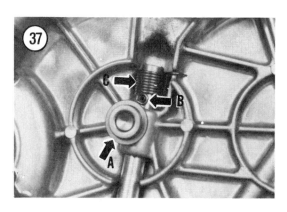

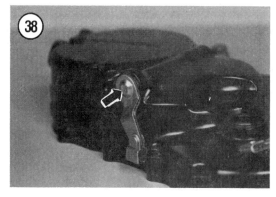

must hook onto the portion sticking out of the lifter shaft.

9. Hook the return spring onto the spring pin.

10. Align the cutout in the lifter arm shaft with the lifter piece hole in the right-hand crankcase cover and install the lifter piece.

11. Install the right-hand crankcase cover as described under *Right-hand Crankcase Cover Installation (3-wheeled Models)* in Chapter Four.

EXTERNAL SHIFT MECHANISM

The external shift mechanism is located on the same side of the crankcase as the clutch assemblies and can be removed with the engine in the frame.

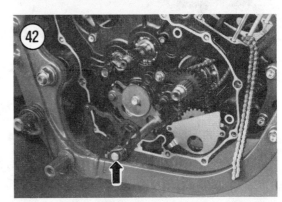

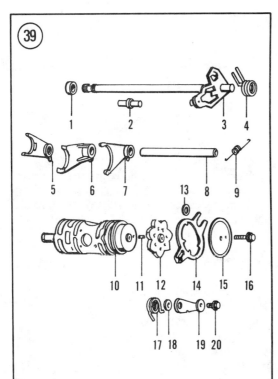

EXTERNAL SHIFT MECHANISM

1. Collar	11. Pin
2. Return spring pin	12. Drum shifter
3. Gearshift shaft	13. Thrust washer
4. Return spring	14. Gearshift plate
5. Left-hand shift fork	15. Shift guide plate
6. Center shift fork	16. Bolt
7. Right-hand shift fork	17. Spring
8. Shift fork shaft	18. Washer
9. Shift arm spring	19. Shift drum stopper
10. Gearshift drum	20. Bolt

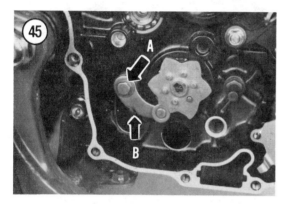

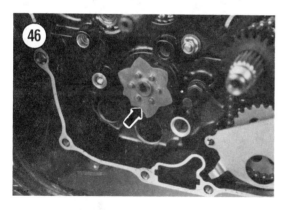

To remove the shift drum and shift forks it is necessary to remove the engine and split the crankcase. This procedure is covered under *Shift Drum and Shift Forks* in this chapter.

NOTE
The gearshift lever is subject to a lot of abuse. If the ATV has been in a hard spill, the gearshift lever may have been hit and the shift shaft bent. It is very hard to straighten the shaft without subjecting the crankcase to abnormal stress where the shaft enters the case. If the shaft is bent enough to prevent it from being withdrawn from the crankcase, there is little recourse but to cut the shaft off with a hacksaw very close to the crankcase. It is much cheaper in the long run to replace the shaft than risk damaging a very expensive crankcase.

Removal

Refer to **Figure 39** for this procedure.
1. Place the ATV on level ground and set the parking brake.
2. Drain the engine oil as described under *Engine Oil Change* in Chapter Three.
3. Remove the right-hand crankcase cover as described under *Right-hand Crankcase Cover Removal (3-wheeled Models)* in Chapter Four.
4. Remove the clutch assembly as described under *Manual Clutch Removal/Disassembly* in this chapter.
5. Shift the transmission into NEUTRAL and remove the bolt securing the gearshift lever (**Figure 40**). Remove the gearshift lever.

NOTE
See the NOTE in the introduction to this procedure regarding a bent shaft if the assembly is difficult to remove.

6. Unhook the spring from the gearshift plate (**Figure 41**) and withdraw the gearshift spindle assembly (**Figure 42**). Don't lose the thrust washer on the backside of the gearshift spindle assembly.
7. Remove the bolt (A, **Figure 43**) securing the gearshift guide plate.
8. Remove the guide plate (B, **Figure 43**) and the gearshift plate (**Figure 44**).
9. Loosen the bolt (A, **Figure 45**) securing the shift drum stopper arm. Unhook the return spring (B, **Figure 45**) and remove the shift drum stopper arm, washer and return spring.
10. Remove the drum shifter (**Figure 46**) and the dowel pin (**Figure 47**).

Inspection

1. Inspect the return springs on the gearshift spindle assembly. If broken or weak, they must be replaced.

2. Inspect the gearshift lever assembly shaft (**Figure 48**) for bending, wear or other damage; replace if necessary.

3. Inspect the ramps on the drum shifter (**Figure 49**). They must be smooth and free of burrs or cracks. Make sure the locating pin fits snugly into the drum shifter and the shift drum; replace if necessary.

4. Inspect the gearshift plate (**Figure 50**) for wear or damage. Replace if necessary.

5. Inspect the roller (**Figure 51**) on the shift drum stopper arm. The roller must rotate smoothly with no binding. Replace the shift drum stopper assembly if necessary.

Installation

1. Make sure the locating pin (**Figure 47**) is installed in the gearshift drum.

2. Align the locating pin with the hole in the drum shifter and install the drum shifter (**Figure 46**).

3. Install the spring, drum stopper arm and bolt (**Figure 52**). Tighten the bolt only finger-tight at this time.

4. Using a small flat-bladed screwdriver, locate the drum stopper arm correctly onto the drum shifter (**Figure 53**).

5. Tighten the drum stopper arm bolt to the torque specification listed in **Table 2**.

6. Install the gearshift plate (**Figure 44**).

7. Align the locating tab on the backside of the gearshift guide plate with the notch in the drum shifter and install the guide plate and the bolt. Tighten the bolt to the torque specification listed in **Table 2**.

8. Apply a heavy coat of multipurpose grease to the gearshift shaft thrust washer and place it on the opening in the crankcase (**Figure 54**).

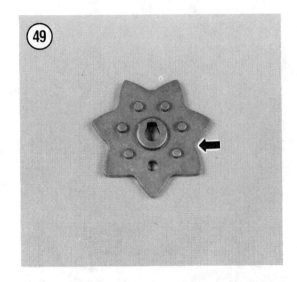

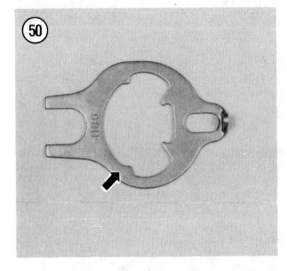

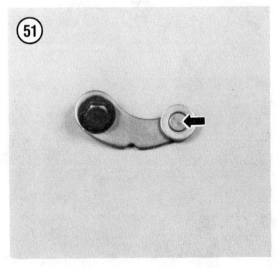

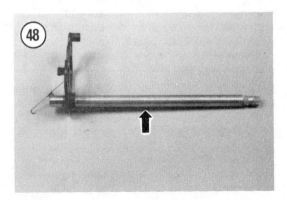

9. Install the gearshift spindle assembly (**Figure 42**). Make sure the gearshift spindle assembly goes through the thrust washer installed in Step 8.

10. Make sure the gearshift spindle assembly return spring is correctly positioned onto the stopper plate (**Figure 55**).

11. Hook the spring onto the gearshift plate (**Figure 41**).

12. Align the punch mark on the gearshift lever with the shaft and install the gearshift lever (**Figure 40**). Install and tighten the pinch bolt to the torque specification listed in **Table 2**.

13. Install the clutch assembly as described under *Manual Clutch Assembly/Installation* in this chapter.

14. Install the right-hand crankcase cover as described under *Right-hand Crankcase Cover Installation (3-wheeled Models)* in Chapter Four.

15. Refill the engine with the correct type and quantity oil as described under *Engine Oil Change* in Chapter Three.

16. Adjust the clutch as described under *Clutch Adjustment (3-wheeled Models)* in Chapter Three.

6-SPEED TRANSMISSION AND INTERNAL SHIFT MECHANISM

To gain access to the transmission and internal shift mechanism it is necessary to remove the engine and split the crankcase. After the crankcase has been split, removal of the transmission assemblies is a simple task of pulling the transmission shaft assemblies up and out of the crankcase. Installation is more complicated and is covered in greater detail than the removal sequence.

Refer to **Table 3** for transmission specifications and **Table 4** for specifications on the internal shift mechanism.

NOTE
If disassembling a used, well run-in engine for the first time by yourself, pay particular attention to any additional shims that may have been added by a previous owner. These may have been added to take up the tolerance of worn components and must be reinstalled in the same position since the shims have developed a wear pattern. If new parts are going to be installed these shims may be eliminated. This is something you will have to determine upon reassembly.

Transmission Removal

1. Remove the engine and split the crankcase as described under *Crankcase Disassembly* in Chapter Four.
2. Remove the shift fork shaft (**Figure 56**).
3. Swing the shift forks out of mesh with the gearshift drum. Remove the gearshift drum (**Figure 57**).
4. Remove all 3 shift forks (**Figure 58**).
5. Remove both transmission assemblies (**Figure 59**).
6. Disassemble and inspect the shift forks and transmission assemblies as described in this chapter.

Transmission Installation

1. Install the 2 transmission assemblies by meshing them together in their proper relationship to each other.
2. Install the transmission shaft assemblies into the left-hand crankcase (**Figure 59**). After both assemblies are installed, tap on the end of both shafts with a plastic or rubber mallet to make sure they are completely seated.

NOTE
*Install the shift forks with their marking facing **down**.*

3. Install the left-hand shift fork (**Figure 60**), the center shift fork (**Figure 61**) and the right-hand shift fork (**Figure 62**) into position in their respective gears, but do not insert the shift fork shaft at this time.
4. Coat all bearing and sliding surfaces of the shift drum with assembly oil or clean engine oil. Install the shift drum (**Figure 57**).
5. Rotate the shift drum to the NEUTRAL position.

6. Make sure all 3 cam pin followers are in mesh with the shift drum grooves and install the shift fork shaft (**Figure 56**).

NOTE
This procedure is best done with the aid of a helper as the assemblies are loose and won't spin very easily. Have the helper spin the transmission shaft while you turn the shift drum through all the gears.

7. Turn the crankcase to the nearly vertical position. Do not try this step with the crankcase horizontal as the gears are loaded, by their own weight, in an abnormal way. When loaded this way the gears will not shift easily, or in some cases will not shift at all. If done horizontally, you may get the false impression that a gear is installed incorrectly.

8. Spin the transmission shaft and shift through the gears using the shift drum. Make sure you can shift into all gears. This is the time to find that something may be installed incorrectly—not after the crankcase is completely assembled.

9. Assemble the crankcase and install the engine as described in Chapter Four.

Transmission Preliminary Inspection

After the transmission shaft assemblies have been removed from the crankcase, clean and inspect the assemblies before disassembling them. Place the assembled shaft into a large can or plastic bucket and thoroughly clean with a petroleum based solvent such as kerosene and a stiff brush. Dry with compressed air or let it sit on rags to drip dry. Repeat for the other shaft assembly.

1. After they have been cleaned, visually inspect the components of the assemblies for excessive wear. Any burrs, pitting or roughness on the teeth of a gear will cause wear on the mating gear. Minor roughness can be cleaned up with an oilstone but there's little point in attempting to remove deep scars.

NOTE
Defective gears should be replaced. It's a good idea to replace the mating gear on the other shaft even though it may not show as much wear or damage.

2. Carefully check the engagement dogs. If any are chipped, worn, rounded or missing, the affected gear must be replaced.

3. Rotate the transmission bearings in both crankcase halves by hand. Refer to **Figure 63** or **Figure 64**. Check for roughness, noise and radial

play. Any bearing that is suspect should be replaced as described in Chapter Four.

4. If the transmission shafts are satisfactory and are not going to be disassembled, apply assembly oil or fresh engine oil to all components and reinstall them in the crankcase as described in this chapter.

Mainshaft Disassembly

Refer to **Figure 65** for this procedure.

NOTE
A helpful "tool" that should be used for transmission disassembly is a large egg flat (the type that restaurants get their

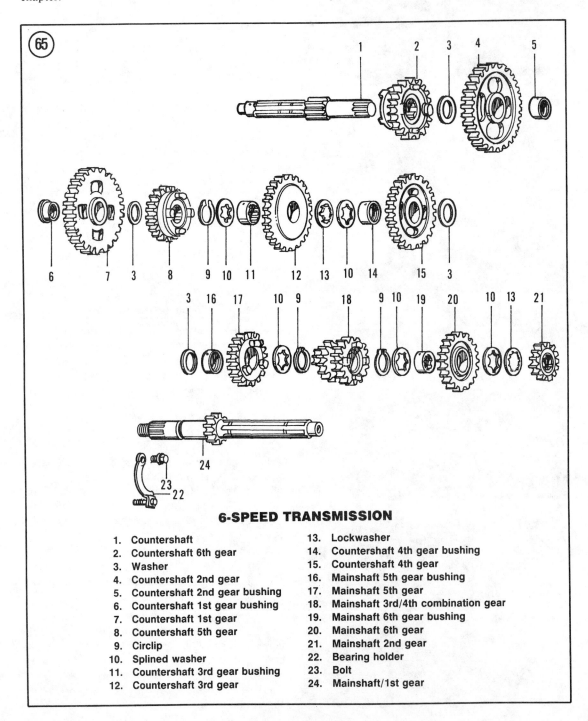

6-SPEED TRANSMISSION

1. Countershaft
2. Countershaft 6th gear
3. Washer
4. Countershaft 2nd gear
5. Countershaft 2nd gear bushing
6. Countershaft 1st gear bushing
7. Countershaft 1st gear
8. Countershaft 5th gear
9. Circlip
10. Splined washer
11. Countershaft 3rd gear bushing
12. Countershaft 3rd gear
13. Lockwasher
14. Countershaft 4th gear bushing
15. Countershaft 4th gear
16. Mainshaft 5th gear bushing
17. Mainshaft 5th gear
18. Mainshaft 3rd/4th combination gear
19. Mainshaft 6th gear bushing
20. Mainshaft 6th gear
21. Mainshaft 2nd gear
22. Bearing holder
23. Bolt
24. Mainshaft/1st gear

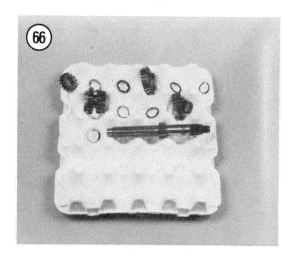

eggs in). As you remove a part from the shaft, set it in one of the depressions in the same position from which it was removed (Figure 66). This is an easy way to remember the correct relationship of all parts.

1. Clean and inspect the assembled shaft as described under *Preliminary Inspection* in this chapter.
2. Slide off the 2nd gear.
3. Slide off the lockwasher.
4. Rotate the splined washer in either direction so its tangs clear the transmission spline grooves and slide it off the shaft.
5. Slide off the 6th gear and 6th gear bushing.
6. Slide off the splined washer and remove the circlip.
7. Slide off the 3rd/4th combination gear.
8. Remove the circlip and splined washer.
9. Slide off the 5th gear and 5th gear bushing.
10. Slide off the thrust washer.

Mainshaft Inspection

> *NOTE*
> *Honda suggests that all circlips be replaced every time the transmission is disassembled to ensure proper gear alignment. Do not expand a circlip more than necessary to slide it over the shaft.*

> *NOTE*
> *Install the circlips with the sharp side going on last.*

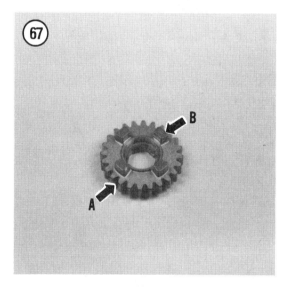

1. Check each gear for excessive wear, burrs, pitting, or chipped or missing teeth (A, **Figure 67**). Make sure the lugs (B, **Figure 67**) on the gears are in good condition.

> *NOTE*
> *The 1st gear is part of the mainshaft. If the gear is defective, the shaft must be replaced.*

> *NOTE*
> *Defective gears should be replaced. It is a good idea to replace the mating gear on the countershaft even though it may not show as much wear or damage.*

2. Make sure that all gears and the 6th gear bushing slide smoothly on the mainshaft.
3. On the mainshaft, make the following measurements:

  a. Measure the outside diameter of the raised portion of the splines on the mainshaft as shown in A, **Figure 68** at the 5th gear location. Refer to mainshaft dimension A in **Table 3**. If

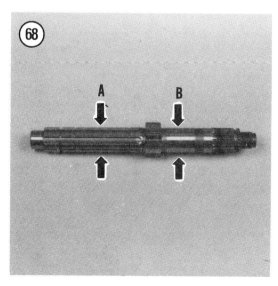

the shaft is worn to the service limit or less,. the shaft must be replaced.

    b. Measure the outside diameter of the mainshaft as shown in B, **Figure 68** at the clutch outer housing guide location. Refer to mainshaft dimension B in **Table 3**. If the shaft is worn to the service limit or less, the shaft must be replaced.

4. Measure the inside diameter (**Figure 69**) of the 5th and 6th gears. Refer to the dimensions in **Table 3**. If the gear(s) are worn to the service limit or greater, the gear(s) must be replaced.

5. Measure the *inside* diameter (A, **Figure 70**) of the 5th gear bushing. Refer to the dimensions in **Table 3**. If the gear bushing is worn to the service limit or greater the gear bushing must be replaced.

6. Measure the *outside* diameter (B, **Figure 70**) of 5th and 6th gear bushings. Refer to the dimensions in **Table 3**. If the gear bushing(s) are worn to the service limit or less the gear bushing(s) must be replaced.

7. Calculate the gear-to-bushing clearance. Subtract the outer diameter of the bushing from the inner diameter of the gear. If the clearance is greater than service limit dimension listed in **Table 3**, replace the worn part(s).

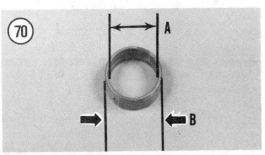

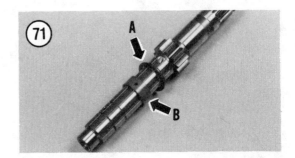

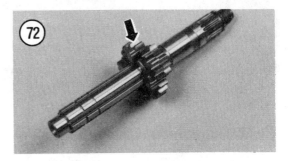

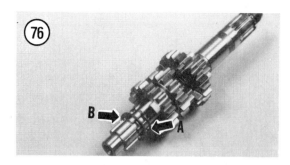

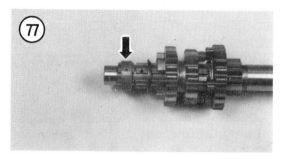

Mainshaft Assembly

Refer to **Figure 65** for this procedure.

1. Slide on the thrust washer (A, **Figure 71**).
2. Slide on the 5th gear bushing (B, **Figure 71**).
3. Slide on the 5th gear (**Figure 72**).
4. Slide on the thrust washer and install the circlip (**Figure 73**).
5. Position the 3rd/4th combination gear with the smaller diameter 3rd gear (**Figure 74**) on first and slide on the 3rd/4th combination gear (**Figure 75**).
6. Install the circlip (A, **Figure 76**).
7. Slide on the splined washer (B, **Figure 76**).
8. Align the oil hole in the 6th gear bushing (**Figure 77**) with the oil hole in the shaft and slide the bushing into place.
9. Slide on the 6th gear (**Figure 78**).
10. Slide on the splined washer (**Figure 79**). Rotate the splined washer in either direction so its tangs are engaged in the groove in the transmission shaft.
11. Slide on the lockwasher (**Figure 80**) with the tang side going on first.
12. Slide the lockwasher on until the tangs go into the open areas of the splined washer and lock the washer in place (**Figure 81**).
13. Slide on the 2nd gear (**Figure 82**).

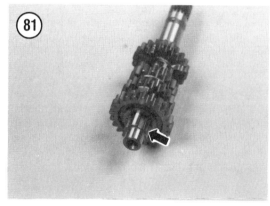

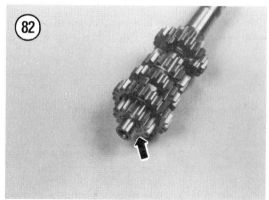

5

14. After assembly is complete, check for correct placement of all gears (**Figure 83**).

15. Make sure all circlips are seated correctly in the mainshaft grooves.

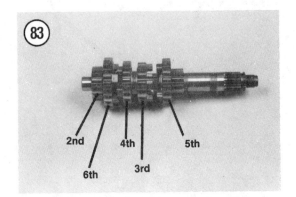

Countershaft Disassembly

Refer to **Figure 65** for this procedure.

> *NOTE*
> *Use the same large egg flat used for mainshaft disassembly. This is an easy way to remember the correct relationship of all parts (**Figure 84**).*

1. Clean the assembled shaft as described under *Preliminary Inspection* in this chapter.

2. Slide off the 2nd gear and 2nd gear bushing.

3. Slide off the thrust washer and the 6th gear.

4. From the other side of the shaft, slide off the 1st gear and 1st gear bushing.

5. Slide off the thrust washer and the 5th gear.

6. Remove the circlip and splined washer.

7. Slide off the 3rd gear and 3rd gear bushing.

8. Slide off the lockwasher.

9. Rotate the splined washer in either direction to disengage the tangs from the grooves on the transmission shaft. Slide off the splined washer.

10. Slide off the 4th gear, 4th gear bushing and thrust washer.

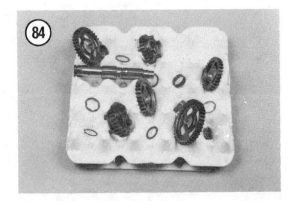

Countershaft Inspection

1. Check each gear for excessive wear, burrs, pitting or chipped or missing teeth (A, **Figure 85**). Make sure the lugs (B, **Figure 85**) on the gears are in good condition.

> *NOTE*
> *Honda suggests that all circlips be replaced every time the transmission is disassembled to ensure proper gear alignment. Do not expand a circlip more than necessary to slide it over the shaft.*

> *NOTE*
> *Install the circlips with the sharp side going on last.*

> *NOTE*
> *Defective gears should be replaced. It is a good idea to replace the mating gear on the mainshaft even though it may not show as much wear or damage.*

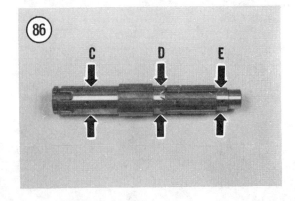

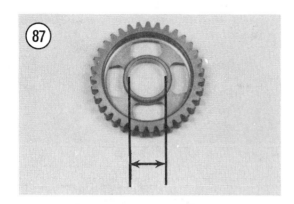

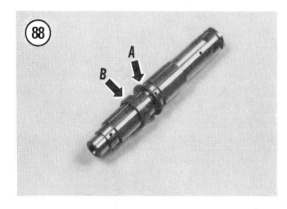

2. On the countershaft, make the following measurements:

   a. Measure the outside diameter of the countershaft as shown in C, **Figure 86** at the 2nd gear bushing location. Refer to countershaft dimension C in **Table 3**. If the shaft is worn to the service limit or less the shaft must be replaced.

   b. Measure the outside diameter of the raised portion of the splines on the mainshaft as shown in D, **Figure 86** at the 4th gear location. Refer to countershaft dimension D in **Table 3**. If the shaft is worn to the service limit or less the shaft must be replaced.

   c. Measure the outside diameter of the countershaft as shown in E, **Figure 86** at the countershaft 1st bushing location. Refer to countershaft dimension E in **Table 3**. If the shaft is worn to the service limit or less the shaft must be replaced.

3. Measure the inside diameter (**Figure 87**) of the 1st, 2nd, 3rd and 4th gears. Refer to the dimensions in **Table 3**. If the gear(s) are worn to the service limit or greater, the gear(s) must be replaced.

4. Measure the *inside* diameter (A, **Figure 70**) of the 1st, 2nd and 4th gear bushings. Refer to the dimensions in **Table 3**. If the gear bushing(s) is worn to the service limit or greater, the gear bushing(s) must be replaced.

5. Measure the *outside* diameter (B, **Figure 70**) of 1st, 2nd, 3rd and 4th gear bushings. Refer to the dimensions in **Table 3**. If the gear bushing(s) are worn to the service limit or less the gear bushing(s) must be replaced.

6. Calculate the gear-to-bushing clearance. Subtract the outer diameter of the bushing from the inner diameter of the gear. If the clearance is greater than service limit dimension listed in **Table 3**, replace the worn part(s).

7. Make sure that all gears and gear bushings slide smoothly on the countershaft.

Countershaft Assembly

1. Slide on the thrust washer (A, **Figure 88**).
2. Slide on the 4th gear bushing (B, **Figure 88**). There is no oil hole alignment on this bushing.
3. Slide on the 4th gear (**Figure 89**).
4. Slide on the splined washer (**Figure 90**). Rotate the splined washer in either direction to engage the

tangs into the grooves on the transmission shaft (**Figure 91**).

5. Slide on the lockwasher (**Figure 92**) with the tang side going on first.

6. Slide the lockwasher on until the tangs go into the open areas of the splined washer and lock the washer in place.

7. Align the oil hole in the 3rd gear bushing (**Figure 93**) with the oil hole in the shaft and slide the bushing into the shaft.

8. Slide on the 3rd gear (**Figure 94**) with the flush side on first.

9. Slide on the splined washer and install the circlip (**Figure 95**).

10. Slide on the 5th gear (**Figure 96**) and thrust washer (**Figure 97**).

11. Slide on the 1st gear (A, **Figure 98**), flush side on last, and insert the 1st gear bushing (B, **Figure 98**) into the 1st gear.

12. Onto the other end of the shaft, slide on the 6th gear (**Figure 99**).

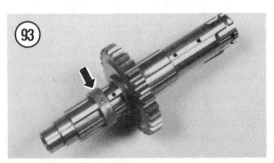

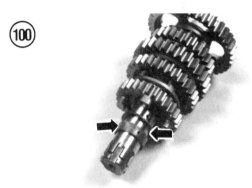

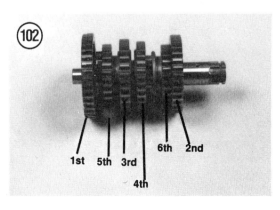

13. Slide on the thrust washer and the 2nd gear bushing (**Figure 100**).

14. Slide on the 2nd gear (**Figure 101**).

15. After assembly is complete check for correct placement of all gears (**Figure 102**).

16. Make sure all circlips are seated correctly in the countershaft grooves.

17. After both transmission shafts have been assembled, mesh the 2 assemblies together in the correct position (**Figure 103**). This is your last check before installing the assemblies into the crankcase; make sure they are correctly assembled.

Internal Shift Mechanism Inspection

Refer to **Figure 104** for this procedure.

1. Inspect each shift fork for signs of wear or cracking. Check for bending and make sure each

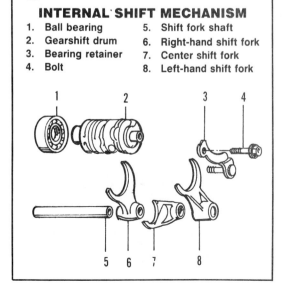

INTERNAL SHIFT MECHANISM

1. Ball bearing	5. Shift fork shaft
2. Gearshift drum	6. Right-hand shift fork
3. Bearing retainer	7. Center shift fork
4. Bolt	8. Left-hand shift fork

fork slides smoothly on the shaft. Replace any worn or damaged forks.

2. Check for any arc-shaped wear or burned marks on the shift forks (**Figure 105**). This indicates that the shift fork has come in contact with the gear. The fork fingers have become excessively worn and the fork must be replaced.

3. Check the shift cam dowel pins (**Figure 106**) for wear or damage; replace as necessary.

4. Roll the shift fork shaft on a flat surface such as a piece of plate glass and check for any bends. If the shaft is bent, it must be replaced.

5. Measure the width of the gearshift fork fingers with a micrometer (**Figure 107**). Replace the ones worn to the service limit listed in **Table 4** or less.

> *CAUTION*
> *Marginal shift forks should be replaced. Worn shift forks can cause the transmission to slip out of gear, leading to more serious and expensive problems.*

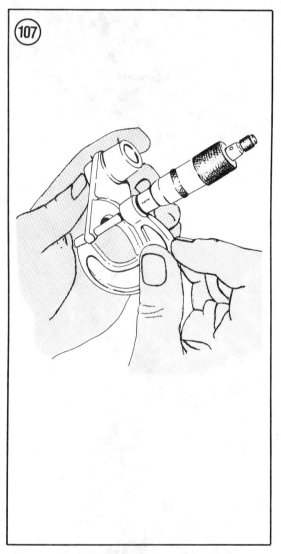

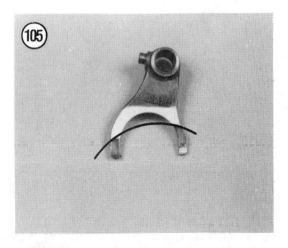

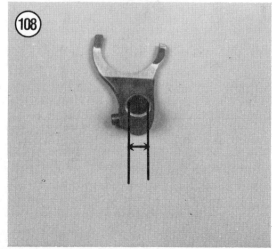

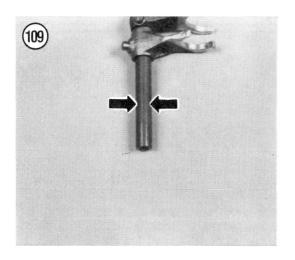

6. Measure the inside diameter of the each shift fork with a micrometer (**Figure 108**). Replace the ones worn to the service limit listed in **Table 4** or greater.

7. Measure the outside diameter of the shift fork shaft with a micrometer (**Figure 109**). Replace if worn to the service limit listed in **Table 4** or less.

8. Check the grooves in the shift drum (**Figure 110**) for wear or roughness. If any of the groove profiles have excessive wear or damage, replace the shift drum.

9. Inspect the shift drum bearing (**Figure 111**) for wear or damage. Replace the bearing if wear is evident.

10. Apply a light coat of oil to the shift fork shafts and the inside bores of the shift forks before installation.

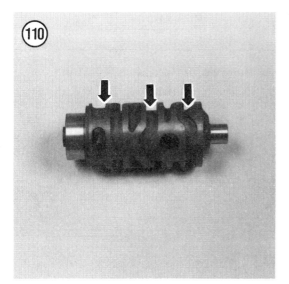

Tables are on following pages.

Table 1 CLUTCH SPECIFICATIONS

Item	Standard	Wear limit
Friction disc thickness	2.9-3.0 mm (0.11-0.12 in.)	2.6 mm (0.10 in.)
Clutch plate warpage	—	0.2 mm (0.008 in.)
Clutch disc warpage	—	0.2 mm (0.00 8 in.)
Clutch springs free length		
1986	37.2 mm (1.45 in.)	35.0 mm (1.38 in.)
1987	32.7 mm (1.29 in.)	31.0 mm (1.22 in.)
Clutch outer housing guide O.D.	24.959-24.980 mm (0.9826-0.9835 in.)	24.900 mm (0.9803 in.)
Clutch outer housing guide I.D.	20.00-20.020 mm (0.7874-0.7882 in.)	20.070 mm (0.7902 in.)
Clutch outer housing guide length	30.05-30.15 mm (1.183-1.187 in.)	30.00 mm (1.181 in.)
Clutch outer housing I.D.	25.000-25.021 mm (0.9842-0.9851 in.)	25.070 mm (0.9870 in.)

Table 2 CLUTCH AND EXTERNAL SHIFT MECHANISM TORQUE SPECIFICATIONS

Item	N•m	ft.-lb.
Oil filter rotor locknut	50-60	36-43
Clutch locknut	50-60	36-43
Gearshift drum stopper bolt	10-14	7-10
Gearshift plate and guide plate bolt	10-14	7-10
Gearshift pedal pinch bolt	14-18	10-13

Table 3 6-SPEED TRANSMISSION SPECIFICATIONS

Item	Specification	Wear limit
Transmission gears ID		
Mainshaft		
5th & 6th gears	23.000-23.021 mm (0.9055-0.9063 in.)	23.04 mm (0.907 in.)
Countershaft		
1st gear	20.500-20.521 mm (0.8071-0.8079 in.)	20.54 mm (0.809 in.)
2nd, 3rd & 4th gears	26.000-26.021 mm (1.0236-1.0244 in.)	26.04 mm (1.025 in.)
Transmission shaft OD		
Mainshaft		
Location A & B	19.959-19.980 mm (0.7858-0.7866 in.)	19.94 mm (0.785 in.)
Countershaft		
Location C & D	21.959-21.980 mm (0.8645-0.8654 in.)	21.94 mm (0.864 in.)
Location E	17.966-17.984 mm (0.7073-0.7080 in.)	17.94 mm (0.706 in.)

(continued)

Table 3 6-SPEED TRANSMISSION SPECIFICATIONS (cont.)

Item	Specification	Wear limit
Transmission gear bushing OD		
Mainshaft		
5th & 6th gears	22.959-22.980 mm (0.9039-0.9047 in.)	22.94 mm (0.903 in.)
Countershaft		
1st gear	20.459-20.480 mm (0.8055-0.8063 in.)	20.44 mm (0.805 in.)
2nd, 3rd & 4th gears	25.959-25.980 mm (1.0220-1.0228 in.)	25.94 mm (1.021 in.)
Transmission gear bushing ID		
Mainshaft		
5th gear	20.000-20.021 mm (0.7874-0.7882 in.)	20.04 mm (0.789 in.)
Countershaft		
1st gear	18.000-18.018 mm (0.7087-0.7094 in.)	18.04 mm (0.710 in.)
2nd & 4th gears	22.000-22.021 mm (0.8661-0.8670 in.)	22.04 mm (0.868 in.)
Transmission gear-to-bushing clearance		
All bushings	0.020-0.062 mm (0.0008-0.0024 in.)	0.10 mm (0.004 in.)
Transmission bushing-to-shaft clearance		
All gears	0.020-0.062 mm (0.0008-0.0024 in.)	0.10 mm (0.004 in.)

5

Table 4 INTERNAL SHIFT MECHANISM SPECIFICATIONS

Item	Specifications	Wear limit
Shift fork finger thickness	4.93-5.00 mm (0.194-0.197 in.)	4.88 mm (0.192 in.)
Shift fork shaft OD	12.966-12.984 mm (0.5105-0.5112 in.)	12.94 mm (0.509 in.)
Shift fork ID	13.00-13.02 mm (0.5118-0.5126 in.)	13.05 mm (0.514 in.)

CHAPTER SIX

CLUTCH AND TRANSMISSION
(4-WHEELED MODELS)

This chapter contains service procedures for the centrifugal and manual clutch assemblies, external and internal shift mechanisms and the transmission.

Tables 1-4 are at the end of this chapter.

CLUTCH OPERATION

The 4-wheeled models are equipped with both a centrifugal and manual clutch mechanism to transmit power from the engine to the transmission. Both clutch types are immersed in the oil supply they share with the engine and transmission.

The centrifugal clutch is mounted on the right-hand end of the crankshaft. The main components of this clutch are the outer drum, centrifugal clutch weights and a one-way sprag which allows the clutch outer housing to rotate in one direction only. The outer housing is not driven directly by the crankshaft, but by the centrifugal clutch weights attached to a hub that is splined to the crankshaft. As the engine rpm increases, the centrifugal weights are forced out against the outer drum, thus driving and rotating the outer drum. Complete engagement is achieved when engine speed reaches about 2,800 rpm. When engine speed decreases, springs retract the weights to disengage the weights from the outer drum. On the backside

of the outer drum is the primary drive gear that is geared directly to the manual clutch outer housing. The one-way sprag not only allows the outer housing to rotate in one direction, but also allows engine compression to be used to slow down the vehicle when the centrifugal clutch weights are not engaged (when coasting).

The manual clutch is a wet multiplate type and is activated by the gearshift linkage. The clutch outer housing is driven by the centrifugal clutch while the clutch center is splined to the transmission mainshaft. When the gearshift lever is moved to shift gears it also activates the clutch lifting mechanism, releasing the clutch.

Both clutch assemblies can be removed with the engine in the frame.

CENTRIFUGAL CLUTCH

Removal

Refer to **Figure 1** for this procedure.
1. Place the ATV on level ground and set the parking brake.
2. **Drain the engine oil as described under** *Engine Oil Change* in Chapter Three.
3. Remove the seat and the rear fenders as described in Chapter Fifteen.

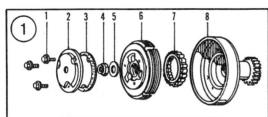

CENTRIFUGAL CLUTCH

1. Bolt
2. Oil filter cover
3. Gasket
4. Locknut
5. Washer
6. Clutch weight
7. Clutch sprag
8. Clutch outer housing

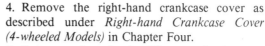

4. Remove the right-hand crankcase cover as described under *Right-hand Crankcase Cover (4-wheeled Models)* in Chapter Four.

5. Remove the clutch lifter mechanism as described in this chapter.

6. Remove the bolts (**Figure 2**) securing the oil filter cover. Remove the oil filter cover and large gasket.

7. Lift up and straighten out the depressed section of the locknut (**Figure 3**) that has been staked down into the recess in the crankshaft.

8. Place a soft copper washer (or copper penny) between the primary drive gear, on the backside of the outer drum, and the drive gear on the manual clutch outer housing. This is to keep the outer drum from rotating while removing the locknut.

> *CAUTION*
> *The locknut has **left-hand** threads. Loosen it by turning it clockwise.*

9. Use a 24 mm (15/16 in.) deep socket and remove the locknut (**Figure 4**)—remember to turn the wrench *clockwise*.

10. Remove the lockwasher (**Figure 5**).

11. Screw a special tool into the clutch weight assembly (**Figure 6**). Use Honda Clutch Puller (part No. 07933-HB3000A). Tighten the puller

with a wrench until the clutch weight assembly disengages from the crankshaft.

12. Remove the clutch weight assembly and unscrew the puller.

13. Rotate the manual clutch assembly until the relief in the outer housing aligns with the centrifugal clutch outer drum gear (**Figure 7**). This alignment is necessary in order for the centrifugal clutch outer drum to slide past the clutch outer housing during removal.

NOTE
Proceed to Step 17 unless the manual clutch is going to be removed also.

14. If the manual clutch is going to be removed, loosen the locknut at this time as you will need the outer drum to aid in removal. If not, proceed to Step 17.

15. Place a soft copper washer (or copper penny) between the primary drive gear, on the backside of the outer drum, and the drive gear on the manual clutch outer housing. This is to keep the manual clutch outer housing from rotating while removing the locknut.

16 Remove the copper washer (or copper penny).

17. Slide off the outer drum (**Figure 8**).

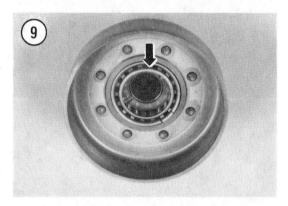

Inspection

1. Clean all parts in petroleum-based solvent such as kerosene and dry thoroughly with compressed air.

2. Rotate the clutch sprag (**Figure 9**). It should only rotate *clockwise*. If it will rotate counterclockwise, even the slightest amount, it is defective and must be replaced.

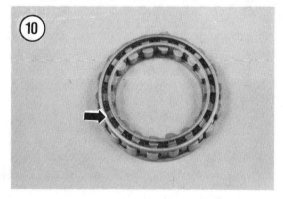

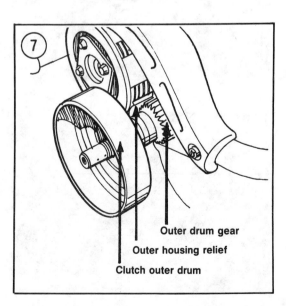

Outer drum gear
Outer housing relief
Clutch outer drum

3. Remove the clutch sprag from the clutch drum. Inspect the clutch sprag (**Figure 10**) for wear or damage; replace if necessary.

4. Measure the inside diameter (**Figure 11**) of the outer drum with a vernier caliper. Refer to **Table 1** for specifications. Replace if it is worn to the service limit or greater.

5. Inspect the teeth (**Figure 12**) on the outer drum primary drive gear. Remove any small nicks on the gear teeth with an oilstone. If damage is severe, the outer drum must be replaced. Also check the primary drive gear teeth on the manual clutch outer housing. Replace the housing if the teeth are worn or damaged.

6. Inspect the inside contact surface of the outer drum (**Figure 13**) where the centrifugal weights ride, for scratches, scoring or heat damage (bluish tint). If there are deep grooves, deep enough to catch a fingernail, the outer drum should be replaced. If there are indications of heat damage, the outer drum may be distorted and must be replaced.

7. Inspect the inside contact surface of the outer drum (**Figure 14**) where the clutch sprag rides, for scratches, scoring or heat damage (bluish tint). If there are deep grooves, deep enough to catch a fingernail, the outer drum should be replaced. If there are indications of heat damage, the outer drum may be distorted and must be replaced.

8. Inspect the clutch weight lining (**Figure 15**) for wear or damage. If damaged, replace the clutch weight assembly.

9. Measure the thickness of the weight lining with a vernier caliper (**Figure 16**). If worn to the service limit dimension listed in **Table 1** or less, replace the clutch weight assembly.

10. Inspect the splines (**Figure 17**) in the clutch weight. If worn or damaged, replace the clutch weight assembly.

11. Inspect the clutch lifting mechanism in the right-hand crankcase cover as described under *Clutch Lifting Mechanism—Centrifugal Clutch* in this chapter.

Installation

1. Rotate the manual clutch outer housing so the relief (**Figure 7**) aligns with the crankshaft. This is necessary to enable the centrifugal clutch outer drum primary drive gear to slide past it.
2. Slide on the outer drum (**Figure 8**).
3. Install the clutch sprag with the flange side (**Figure 18**) going in first and install it into the clutch drum (**Figure 19**).

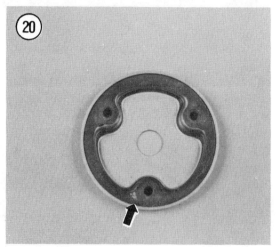

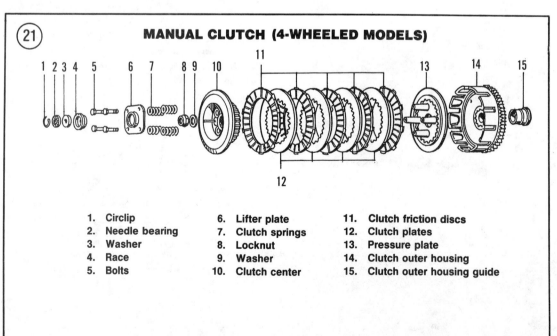

MANUAL CLUTCH (4-WHEELED MODELS)

1. Circlip
2. Needle bearing
3. Washer
4. Race
5. Bolts
6. Lifter plate
7. Clutch springs
8. Locknut
9. Washer
10. Clutch center
11. Clutch friction discs
12. Clutch plates
13. Pressure plate
14. Clutch outer housing
15. Clutch outer housing guide

NOTE
Proceed to Step 6 if the manual clutch was not removed.

4. If the manual clutch was removed tighten the locknut at this time as you will need the outer drum to aid in tightening the locknut. If not proceed to Step 6.

5. Place a soft copper washer (or copper penny) between the primary drive gear, on the backside of the outer drum, and the drive gear on the manual clutch outer housing. This is to keep the manual clutch outer housing from rotating while tightening the locknut.

6. Tighten the locknut to the torque specification listed in **Table 2**.

NOTE
If the centrifugal clutch weight assembly was replaced, apply new engine oil to all surfaces to avoid having the clutch lock up when used for the first time.

7. Slide on the centrifugal weight assembly.

NOTE
It is a good idea to install a new locknut every time it is removed.

8. Install the lockwasher (**Figure 5**) and the locknut (**Figure 4**).

9. Place a soft copper washer (or copper penny) between the primary drive gear, on the backside of the outer drum, and the drive gear on the manual clutch outer housing. This is to keep the outer drum from rotating while tightening the locknut.

CAUTION
*The locknut has **left-hand** threads. Tighten it by turning it **counter-clockwise**.*

10. Use a 24 mm, or 15/16 in. deep socket and tighten the locknut. The locknut has left-hand threads—*remember to turn the wrench counterclockwise.*

11. Tighten the locknut to the torque specification listed in **Table 2**.

12. Use a drift and hammer and stake portion of the locknut down into the recess in the crankshaft (**Figure 3**). If possible use a portion of the locknut not previously staked.

13. Install the oil filter cover and new gasket (**Figure 20**). Install the bolts (**Figure 2**) and tighten securely.

14. Install the clutch lifter mechanism as described in this chapter.

15. Install the right-hand crankcase cover as described under *Right-hand Crankcase Cover (4-wheeled Models)* in Chapter Four.

16. Install the seat and rear fenders as described in Chapter Fifteen.

17. Refill the engine with the correct type and quantity oil as described under *Engine Oil Change* in Chapter Three.

18. Start the engine and check for oil leaks.

19. Adjust the clutch as described under *Clutch Mechanism Adjustment (4-wheeled Models)* in Chapter Three.

MANUAL CLUTCH

Removal/Disassembly

Refer to **Figure 21** for this procedure.

1. Remove the centrifugal clutch assembly as described under *Centrifugal Clutch Removal* in this chapter.

2. Remove the manual clutch lifter mechanism as described under *Manual Clutch Lifter Mechanism* in this chapter.

3. Using a crisscross pattern, remove the clutch bolts securing the clutch lifter plate and remove the lifter plate (**Figure 22**).

4. Remove the clutch springs (**Figure 23**).

5. Lift up and straighten out the depressed section of the locknut that has been staked down into the recess in the transmission mainshaft (**Figure 24**).

6. Hold the clutch pressure plate with the special tool available from a Honda dealer (Universal Clutch Holder part No. 07HGB-001000A). Refer to **Figure 25**.

7. Correctly position the 4 holders over the posts of the clutch pressure plate. Tighten the nuts securing the holders to the holder plate and install the tool onto the clutch (**Figure 26**).

8. Loosen the clutch locknut.

9. Remove the clutch locknut (**Figure 27**) and washer (**Figure 28**).

10. Remove the clutch center, plates, discs and pressure plate (**Figure 29**).

11. Remove the clutch outer housing (**Figure 30**) and guide (**Figure 31**).

12. Inspect the clutch parts as described under *Manual Clutch Inspection* in this chapter.

Assembly/Installation

> *NOTE*
> *If new friction discs and clutch plates*
> *are being installed, apply new engine*

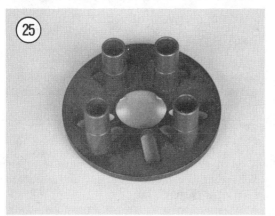

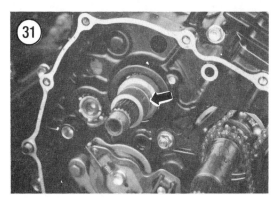

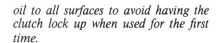
oil to all surfaces to avoid having the clutch lock up when used for the first time.

1. Working at your workbench, install the following parts onto the clutch center:
   a. Install a friction disc (**Figure 32**) and then a clutch plate (**Figure 33**).
   b. Continue to install a friction disc, then a clutch plate, and alternate them until all are installed.
   c. The last item installed is a friction disc (**Figure 34**).
   d. Install the pressure plate (**Figure 35**).
2. Align the tabs of the friction discs to make installation easier.
3. Position the clutch outer guide with the flange side going on first and install the clutch outer guide (**Figure 31**) onto the transmission mainshaft.
4. Install the clutch outer housing (**Figure 30**).
5. Slide on the clutch parts (clutch center, friction discs, clutch plates and pressure plate) assembled in Step 1. Push the assembly on slowly, carefully aligning the tabs of the friction discs into the slots in the clutch outer housing.
6. Install the washer (**Figure 28**).

6

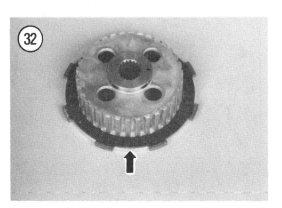

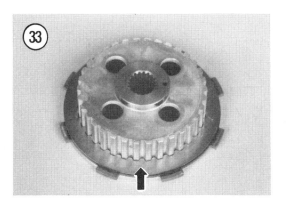

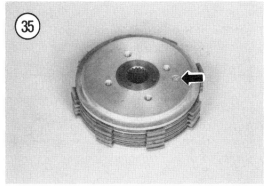

NOTE
It is a good idea to install a new locknut
every time it is removed.

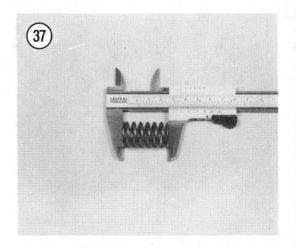

7. Install a new locknut (**Figure 27**). Use the same tool setup as used in Step 6, *Removal.* Tighten the locknut to the torque specification listed in **Table 2.**

8. Use a drift and hammer and stake a portion of the locknut down into the recess in the transmission mainshaft (**Figure 24**).

9. Instal` the clutch springs (**Figure 23**).

10. Position the lifter plate with the raised shoulder facing toward the outside (**Figure 36**) and install the clutch lifter plate and the clutch bolts (**Figure 22**). Tighten the bolts securely in a crisscross pattern in 2 or 3 stages.

11. Install the centrifugal clutch as described under *Centrifugal Clutch Installation* in this chapter.

12. Install the manual clutch lifter mechanism as described under *Manual Clutch Lifter Mechanism Installation* in this chapter.

13. Install the right-hand crankcase cover as described under *Right-hand Crankcase Cover Installation (4-wheeled Models)* in Chapter Four.

14. Refill the engine with the recommended type and quantity oil as described under *Engine Oil Change* in Chapter Three.

15. Adjust the clutch as described under *Clutch Mechanism Adjustment (4-wheeled Models)* in Chapter Three.

Inspection

1. Clean all parts in a petroleum-based solvent such as kerosene and dry thoroughly with compressed air.

2. Measure the free length of each clutch spring as shown in **Figure 37**. Refer to **Table 1**. If any of the springs are worn to the service limit or less, replace all springs as a set.

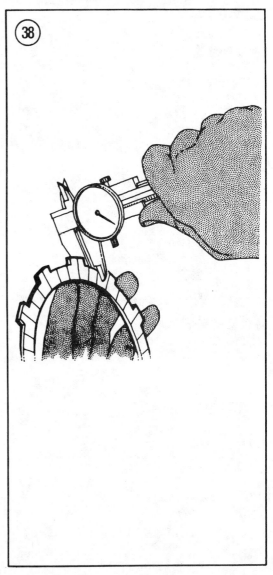

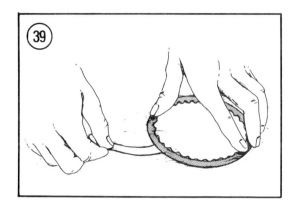

3. Measure the thickness of each friction disc at several places around the disc as shown in **Figure 38**. Refer to **Table 1**. Replace any disc that is worn to the service limit or less. For optimum performance, replace all discs as a set even if only a few need replacement.

4. **Check the clutch plates and discs for warpage with a flat feeler gauge and a surface plate such as a piece of plate glass (Figure 39). Refer to Table 1. Replace any that are warped to the service limit or more. For optimum performance, replace all plates as a set even if only a few need replacement.**

5. Inspect the grooves and studs in the pressure plate (**Figure 40**). If either shows signs of wear or galling, the plate should be replaced.

6. Inspect the grooves (**Figure 41**) and inner splines (**Figure 42**) in the clutch center. If either shows signs of wear or galling, the clutch center should be replaced.

7. Inspect the teeth on the clutch outer housing (**Figure 43**). Remove any small nicks on the gear teeth with an oilstone. If damage is severe the clutch housing should be replaced.

8. Inspect the bushing (**Figure 44**) in the clutch outer housing for wear or damage. If worn or damaged, replace the clutch outer housing and the outer housing guide spacer as a set.

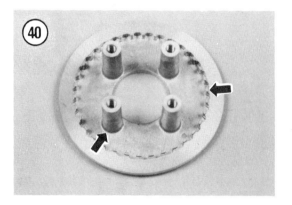

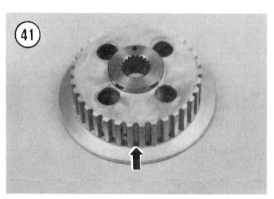

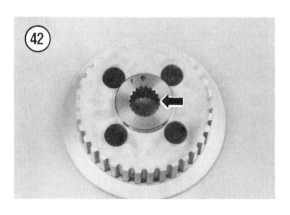

6

9. Inspect the slots in the clutch outer housing for cracks, nicks or galling where it comes in contact with the friction disc tabs (**Figure 45**). If any severe damage is evident, the clutch housing must be replaced.

10. Measure the outside diameter of the clutch outer housing guide spacer (**Figure 46**) with a micrometer or vernier caliper. Refer to **Table 1** and replace the guide spacer if worn to the service limit dimension or less.

11. Inspect the lifter guide bearing (**Figure 47**). Make sure it rotates smoothly with no signs of wear or damage. Replace as necessary.

CLUTCH LIFTER MECHANISM

The clutch lifter mechanism is located both within the right-hand crankcase cover and on the external shift mechanism. When the gearshift lever is moved to shift gears it also activates the clutch lifting mechanism releasing the clutch.

The clutch lifter mechanism can be removed with the engine in the frame.

Removal

Refer to **Figure 48** and **Figure 49** for this procedure.

1. Place the ATV on level ground and set the parking brake.

2. Remove the right-hand crankcase cover as described under *Right-hand Crankcase Cover Removal (4-wheeled Models)* in Chapter Four.

3. Remove the clutch adjusting bolt locknut (A, **Figure 50**) and adjusting bolt (B, **Figure 50**) from the right-hand crankcase cover.

4. Remove the clutch lifter plate (**Figure 51**).

5. Remove the ball retainer (**Figure 52**) and spring (**Figure 53**).

6. Remove the lifter sub-lever (**Figure 54**).

7. Remove the lifter cam (**Figure 55**).

8. Remove the release bearing assembly (**Figure 56**).

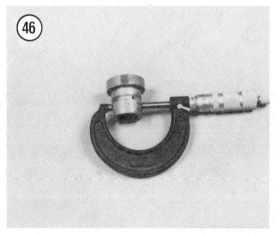

Installation

1. Install the release bearing assembly (**Figure 56**).

2. Install the lifter cam (**Figure 55**).

NOTE
*Do **not** oil the end of the lifter sub-lever or its receptacle in the crankcase. Oil on either part will trap air behind the shaft during installation. These 2 parts have such a tight fit that the trapped air will not allow the shaft to seat completely in the crankcase. If there is oil on either part, clean with electrical contact cleaner to remove all oil residue. After*

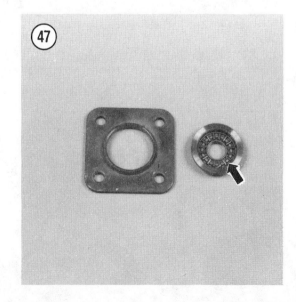

48 CLUTCH LIFTER MECHANISM

1. Screw
2. Heat shield
3. Bolt
4. Electrical cable strap
5. Nut
6. Oil seal
7. Washer
8. REVERSE stopper lever
9. O-ring seal
10. Oil filler/dipstick
11. Right-hand crankcase cover
12. Gasket
13. Oil control orifice
14. Clutch adjusting screw
15. Clutch lifter plate
16. Ball retainer
17. Spring
18. Clutch lifter cam
19. Locating dowel
20. Oil seal
21. Circlip
22. Spring
23. REVERSE stopper shaft

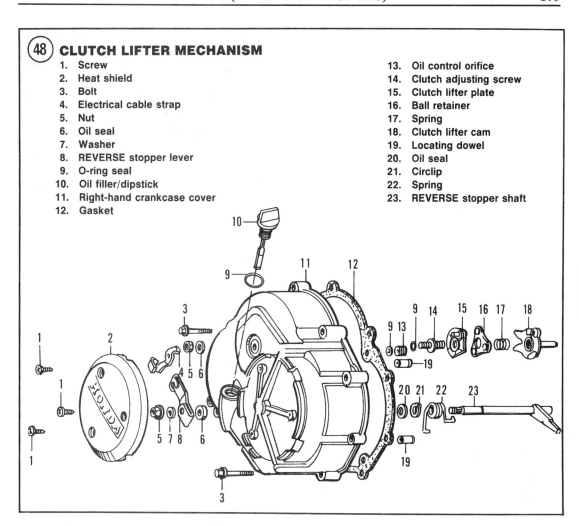

6

EXTERNAL SHIFT MECHANISM

1. Collar
2. Return spring pin
3. Gearshift shaft
4. Return spring
5. Left-hand shift fork
6. Center shift fork
7. Right-hand shift fork
8. Shift fork shaft
9. Shift arm spring
10. Gearshift drum
11. Pin
12. Drum shifter
13. Thrust washer
14. Gearshift plate
15. Shift guide plate
16. Bolt
17. Spring
18. Washer
19. Shift drum stopper
20. Bolt

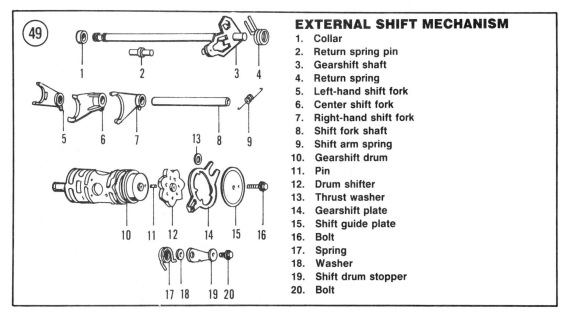

*the shaft is installed and completely
seated, then apply oil to the shaft where
it meets the crankcase.*

3. Install the lifter sub-lever (**Figure 54**) into the
crankcase. Make sure the lifter sub-lever is
correctly indexed with the lifter cam (A, **Figure 57**)
and the boss on the gearshift lever shaft (B, **Figure
57**).

4. Slide on the spring (**Figure 53**) and ball retainer
(**Figure 52**).

5. Install the clutch lifter plate, adjusting bolt and
locknut into the right-hand crankcase cover.

6. Install the right-hand crankcase cover as
described under *Right-hand Crankcase Cover
Installation (4-wheeled Models)* in Chapter Four.

7. Refill the engine with the correct type and
quantity oil as described under *Engine Oil Change*
in Chapter Three.

8. Adjust the clutch as described under *Clutch
Mechanism Adjustment (4-wheeled Models)* in
Chapter Three.

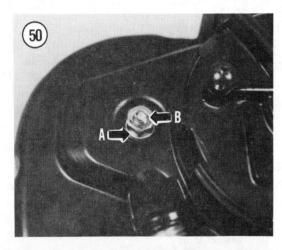

Inspection

1. Clean all parts in solvent and dry thoroughly with compressed air.

2. Inspect the balls (**Figure 58**) in the ball retainer. They must rotate freely in the ball retainer but not be so loose that they would fall out. Check the balls for evidence of wear, pitting or excessive heat (bluish tint); replace if necessary.

3. Inspect the grooves and inside surface of both the lifter cam (**Figure 59**) and the clutch lifter plate (**Figure 60**) where the balls ride. All surfaces must be smooth and free of burrs or scoring; replace as necessary.

> *NOTE*
> *For optimum performance replace all 3 of these parts if any one of them requires replacement.*

4. Inspect the pivot joint (**Figure 61**) of the lifter cam for wear or damage; replace if necessary.

6

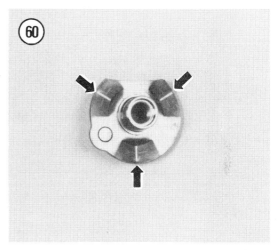

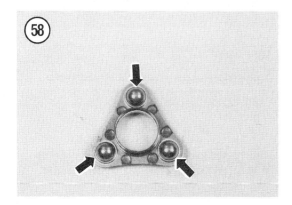

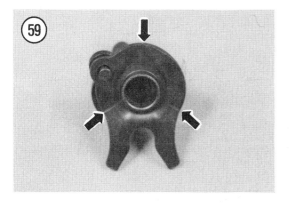

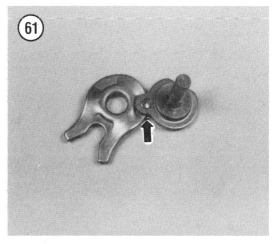

5. Inspect the threads (**Figure 62**) in the lifter plate for wear or damage; replace if necessary.

6. Inspect the threads on the adjusting bolt (A, **Figure 63**) and nut (B, **Figure 63**) for wear or damage. Replace as a set if either is damaged.

7. Install a new O-ring seal (C, **Figure 63**) on the adjusting bolt.

EXTERNAL SHIFT MECHANISM

The external shift mechanism is located on the same side of the crankcase as the clutch assemblies and can be removed with the engine in the frame. To remove the shift drum and shift forks it is necessary to remove the engine and split the crankcase. This procedure is covered under *Shift Drum and Shift Forks* in this chapter.

> *NOTE*
> *The gearshift lever is subject to a lot of abuse. If the ATV has been in a hard spill, the gearshift lever may have been hit and the shift shaft bent. It is very hard to straighten the shaft without subjecting the crankcase to abnormal stress where the shaft enters the case. If the shaft is bent enough to prevent it from being withdrawn from the crankcase, there is little recourse but to cut the shaft off with a hacksaw very close to the crankcase. It is much cheaper in the long run to replace the shaft than risk damaging a very expensive crankcase.*

Removal

Refer to **Figure 64** for this procedure.

1. Place the ATV on level ground and set the parking brake.

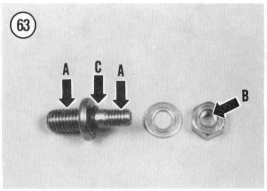

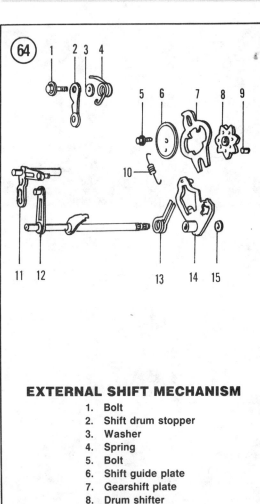

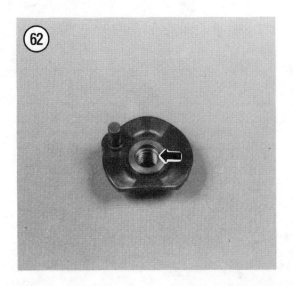

EXTERNAL SHIFT MECHANISM

1. Bolt
2. Shift drum stopper
3. Washer
4. Spring
5. Bolt
6. Shift guide plate
7. Gearshift plate
8. Drum shifter
9. Pin
10. Spring
11. Lifter sub-lever
12. Gearshift shaft
13. Return spring
14. Gearshift arm
15. Thrust washer

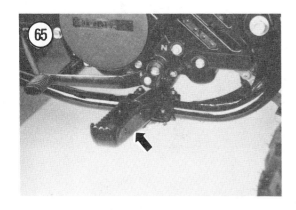

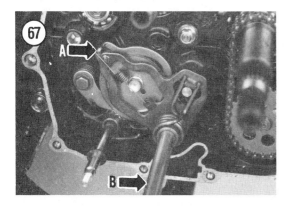

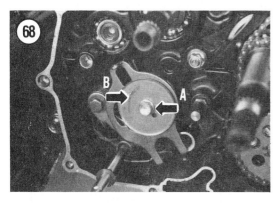

2. Drain the engine oil as described under *Engine Oil Change* in Chapter Three.

3. Remove the right-hand crankcase cover as described under *Right-hand Crankcase Cover Removal (4-wheeled Models)* in Chapter Four.

4. Remove the centrifugal clutch assembly as described under *Centrifugal Clutch Removal/ Disassembly* in this chapter.

5. Remove the manual clutch assembly as described under *Manual Clutch Removal/ Disassembly* in this chapter.

6. Remove the bolts securing the left-hand footpeg (**Figure 65**) and remove the footpeg assembly.

7. Shift the transmission into NEUTRAL and remove the bolt securing the gearshift lever (**Figure 66**). Remove the gearshift lever.

> *NOTE*
> *See the NOTE in the introduction to this procedure regarding a bent shaft if the assembly is difficult to remove.*

8. Unhook the spring (A, **Figure 67**) from the gearshift plate and withdraw the gearshift spindle assembly (B, **Figure 67**). Don't lose the small thrust washer on the backside of the gearshift spindle assembly.

9. Remove the bolt (A, **Figure 68**) securing the gearshift guide plate.

10. Remove the guide plate (B, **Figure 68**) and the gearshift plate (**Figure 69**). Don't lose the locating pin on the backside of the stopper plate.

11. Loosen the bolt (A, **Figure 70**) securing the stopper arm.

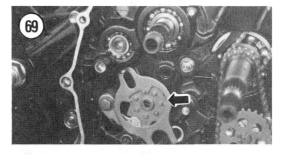

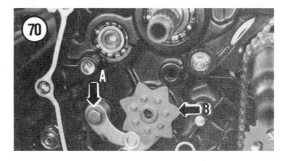

12. Remove the drum shifter (B, **Figure 70**) and dowel pin (**Figure 71**).

13. Remove the stopper bolt, stopper arm, washer and spring (**Figure 72**).

14. Withdraw the reverse stopper shaft (**Figure 73**) from the crankcase.

15. Inspect all components as described in this chapter.

Inspection

1. Inspect the return springs (**Figure 74**) on the gearshift spindle arm. If broken or weak they must be replaced.

2. Inspect the gearshift lever assembly shaft (**Figure 75**) for bending, wear or other damage; replace if necessary.

3. Inspect the lifter sub-lever assembly shaft (**Figure 76**) for bending, wear or other damage; replace if necessary.

4. Check the roller (**Figure 77**) on the lifter sub-lever shaft for wear or other damage. It must rotate freely; replace the shaft if necessary.

5. Inspect the gearshift plate (**Figure 78**) for wear or damage; replace if necessary.

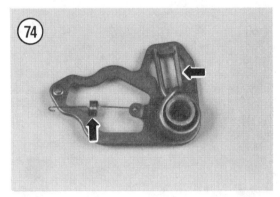

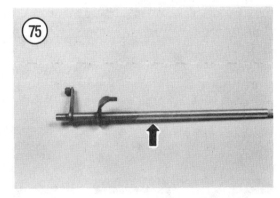

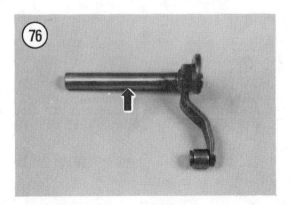

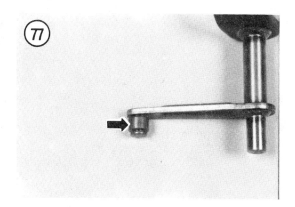

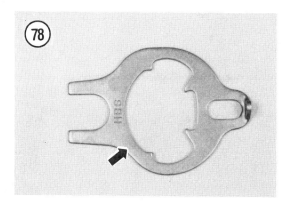

6. Inspect the ramps on the drum shifter (**Figure 79**). They must be smooth and free of burrs or cracks. Make sure the locating pin fits snugly into the drum shifter and the shift drum; replace if necessary.

7. Inspect the reverse stopper shaft (A, **Figure 80**) for bending, wear or other damage; replace if necessary.

8. Inspect the return spring (B, **Figure 80**) on the reverse stopper shaft. If broken or weak, it must be replaced.

9. Inspect the roller (**Figure 81**) on the shift drum stopper arm. The roller must rotate smoothly with no binding. Replace the shift drum stopper assembly if necessary.

Installation

1. Install the reverse stopper shaft (**Figure 73**) into the crankcase.

2. Install the spring, drum stopper arm and bolt (**Figure 72**). Tighten the bolt only finger-tight at this time.

3. Install the locating pin (**Figure 71**) into the gearshift drum.

4. Align the hole in the drum shifter with the locating pin in the gearshift drum and install the drum shifter (A, **Figure 82**).

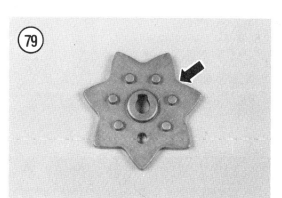

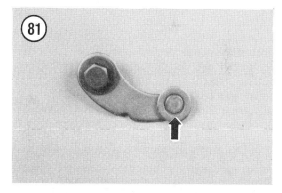

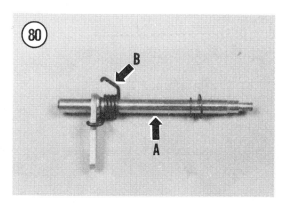

5. Using a small flat-bladed screwdriver, locate the drum stopper arm (B, **Figure 82**) correctly onto the drum shifter. Tighten the shift drum stopper arm bolt to the torque specification listed in **Table 2**.

6. Install the gearshift plate onto the drum shifter as shown in **Figure 69**.

7. Align the raised tab (A, **Figure 83**) on the backside of the shift guide plate with the notch in the drum shifter (B, **Figure 83**). Install the shift guide plate.

8. Install the shift guide plate bolt (A, **Figure 68**). Tighten the bolt to the torque specification listed in **Table 2**.

9. Pull up on the gearshift plate (A, **Figure 84**), partially install the gearshift shaft (B, **Figure 84**) and install the thrust washer (C, **Figure 84**) onto the gearshift shaft behind the gearshift plate.

10. Push the gearshift shaft (**Figure 85**) the rest of the way into the crankcase.

11. Make sure the gearshift spindle assembly is correctly positioned onto the stopper bolt (A, **Figure 86**).

12. Hook the spring onto the gearshift plate (B, **Figure 86**).

13. Install the gearshift lever and bolt. Tighten the pinch bolt to the torque specification listed in **Table 2**.

14. Install the left-hand footpeg assembly and tighten the bolts securely.

15. Install the manual clutch assembly as described under *Manual Clutch Assembly Installation* in this chapter.

16. Install the centrifugal clutch assembly as described under *Centrifugal Clutch Assembly Installation* in this chapter.

17. Install the right-hand crankcase cover as described under *Right-hand Crankcase Cover Installation* in Chapter Four.

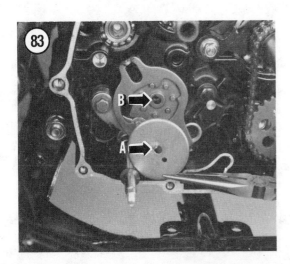

18. Refill the engine with the correct type and quantity oil as described under *Engine Oil Change* in Chapter Three.

19. Adjust the clutch as described under *Clutch Mechanism Adjustment (4-wheeled Models)* in Chapter Three.

5-SPEED TRANSMISSION AND INTERNAL SHIFT MECHANISM

To gain access to the transmission and internal shift mechanism it is necessary to remove the engine and split the crankcase. After the crankcase has been split, removal of the transmission assemblies is a simple task of pulling the transmission shaft assemblies up and out of the crankcase. Installation is more complicated and is covered in more detail than the removal sequence.

Refer to **Table 3** for transmission specifications and **Table 4** for internal shift mechanism specifications.

> *NOTE*
> *If disassembling a used, well run-in transmission for the first time, pay particular attention to any additional shims that may have been added by a previous owner. These may have been added to take up the tolerance of worn components and must be reinstalled in the same position since the shims have developed a wear pattern. If new parts are going to be installed these shims may be eliminated. This is something you will have to determine upon reassembly.*

5-SPEED TRANSMISSION

Removal

1. Remove the engine and split the crankcase as described under *Crankcase Disassembly* in Chapter Four.

2. Remove the countershaft thrust washer, 1st gear and 1st gear bushing (**Figure 87**).

3. Remove the outer thrust washer (**Figure 88**) and the REVERSE idler gear (**Figure 89**).

4. Remove the REVERSE idler gear shaft and inner thrust washer (**Figure 90**).

5. Remove the shift fork shaft (A, **Figure 91**).

6. Swing the shift forks out of mesh with the gearshift drum. Remove the gearshift drum (B, **Figure 91**).

7. Remove all 3 shift forks (**Figure 92**).

8. Remove both transmission assemblies (**Figure 93**). Don't lose the thrust washer (**Figure 94**) on the end of the mainshaft.

9. Disassemble and inspect the shift forks and transmission assemblies as described in this chapter.

Installation

1. Apply a light coat of cold grease to the thrust washer and install the washer (**Figure 94**) onto the left-hand end of the mainshaft next to the 5th gear.

2. Hold the washer in place with your finger during the next step.

3. Install the 2 transmission assemblies by meshing them together in their proper relationship to each other.

4. Install the transmission shaft assemblies into the left-hand crankcase (**Figure 93**). After both assemblies are installed, tap on the end of both shafts with a plastic or rubber mallet to make sure they are completely seated (**Figure 95**).

> *NOTE*
> *Install the shift forks with their marking facing* **up** *(**Figure 96**).*

5. Install the left-hand shift fork (**Figure 97**), the center shift fork (**Figure 98**) and the right-hand shift fork (**Figure 99**) into position in the their respective gears. Do not insert the shift fork shaft at this time.

6. Coat all bearing and sliding surfaces of the shift drum with assembly oil and install the shift drum (B, **Figure 91**).

7. Mesh the shift fork cam pin followers into the correct shift drum grooves.

8. Make sure all 3 cam pin followers are in mesh with the shift drum grooves and install the shift fork shaft (A, **Figure 91**).

9. Install the REVERSE idler shaft and inner thrust washer (**Figure 90**).

10. Install the REVERSE idler (**Figure 89**) gear and outer thrust washer (**Figure 88**).

11. Install the 1st gear and thrust washer (**Figure 87**).

> *NOTE*
> *The next procedure is best done with the aid of a helper as the assemblies are loose and won't spin very easily. Have the helper spin the transmission shaft while you turn the shift drum through all the gears.*

12. Turn the crankcase to the nearly vertical position. Do not try this step with the crankcase horizontal as the gears are loaded, by their own

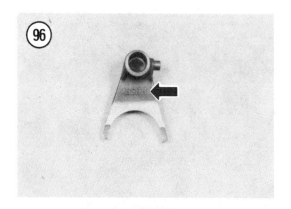

weight, in an abnormal way. Loaded this way the gears will not shift easily, or in some cases will not shift at all. If done horizontally, you may get the false impression that a gear is installed incorrectly.

13. Spin the transmission shaft and shift through the gears using the shift drum. Make sure you can shift into all gears. This is the time to find that something may be installed incorrectly—not after the crankcase is completely assembled.

14. Assemble the crankcase and install the engine as described under *Crankcase Assembly* in Chapter Four.

Transmission
Preliminary Inspection

After the transmission shaft assemblies have been removed from the crankcase, clean and inspect the assemblies before disassembling them. Place the assembled shaft into a large can or plastic bucket and thoroughly clean with a petroleum based solvent such as kerosene and a stiff brush. Dry with compressed air or let it sit on rags to drip dry. Repeat for the other shaft assembly.

1. After they have been cleaned, visually inspect the components of the assemblies for excessive wear. Any burrs, pitting or roughness on the teeth of a gear will cause wear on the mating gear. Minor roughness can be cleaned up with an oilstone but there's little point in attempting to remove deep scars.

NOTE
Defective gears should be replaced. It's a good idea to replace the mating gear on the other shaft even though it may not show as much wear or damage.

2. Carefully check the engagement dogs. If any are chipped, worn, rounded or missing, the affected gear must be replaced.

3. Rotate the transmission bearings in both crankcase halves by hand. Refer to **Figure 100** and

Figure 101. Check for roughness, noise and radial play. Any bearing that is suspect should be replaced as described in Chapter Four.

4. If the transmission shafts are satisfactory and are not going to be disassembled, apply assembly oil or fresh engine oil to all components and reinstall them in the crankcase as described in this chapter.

Mainshaft Disassembly

Refer to **Figure 102** for this procedure.

NOTE
If disassembling a used, well run-in (high mileage) transmission for the first

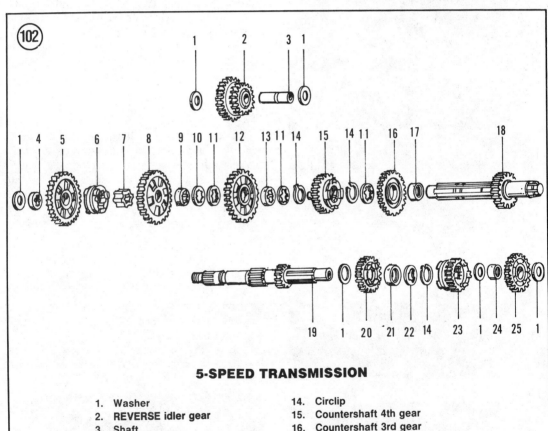

5-SPEED TRANSMISSION

1. Washer
2. REVERSE idler gear
3. Shaft
4. Countershaft 1st gear bushing
5. Countershaft 1st gear
6. REVERSE shifter
7. Splined collar
8. REVERSE gear
9. REVERSE gear bushing
10. Lockwasher
11. Splined washer
12. Countershaft 2nd gear
13. Countershaft 2nd gear bushing

14. Circlip
15. Countershaft 4th gear
16. Countershaft 3rd gear
17. Countershaft 3rd gear bushing
18. Countershaft/5th gear
19. Mainshaft/1st/REVERSE gear
20. Mainshaft 4th gear
21. Mainshaft 4th gear bushing
22. Splined washer
23. Mainshaft 3rd gear
24. Mainshaft 5th gear bushing
25. Mainshaft 5th gear

time, pay particular attention to any additional shims that may have been added by a previous owner. These may have been added to take up the tolerance of worn components and must be reinstalled in the same position since the shims have developed a wear pattern. If new parts are going to be installed, these shims may be eliminated. This is something you will have to determine upon reassembly.

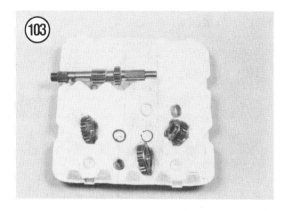

NOTE
A helpful "tool" that should be used for transmission disassembly is a large egg flat (the type that restaurants get their eggs in). As you remove a part from the shaft,. set it in one of the depressions in the same position from which it was removed (Figure 103). This is an easy way to remember the correct relationship of all parts.

1. Clean the assembled shaft as described under *Preliminary Inspection* in this chapter.
2. Slide off the thrust washer.
3. Slide off the 5th gear, 5th gear bushing and washer.
4. Slide off the 3rd gear.
5. Remove the circlip and slide off the splined washer.
6. Slide off the 4th gear and 4th gear bushing.
7. Slide off the thrust washer.

Mainshaft and REVERSE Idler Shaft Inspection

NOTE
Honda suggests that all circlips be replaced every time the transmission shaft is disassembled to ensure proper gear alignment. Do not expand a circlip more than necessary to slide it over the shaft.

NOTE
Install the circlips with the sharp side going on last.

1. Check each gear for excessive wear, burrs, pitting or chipped or missing teeth (A, **Figure 104**). Make sure the lugs (B, **Figure 104**) on the gears are in good condition.

NOTE
The 1st gear, the 2nd gear and the REVERSE gears are part of the mainshaft (Figure 105). If any of the gears are defective, the shaft must be replaced.

NOTE
Defective gears should be replaced. It is a good idea to replace the mating gear on the countershaft even though it may not show as much wear or damage.

2. Make sure that all gears and gear bushings slide smoothly on the mainshaft.
3. On the mainshaft, make the following measurements:
   a. Measure the outside diameter of the raised portion of the splines on the mainshaft as

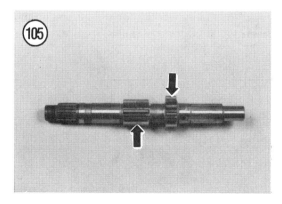

shown in A, **Figure 106** at the 4th gear location. Refer to mainshaft dimension A in **Table 3**. If the shaft is worn to the service limit or less, the shaft must be replaced.

b. Measure the outside diameter of the raised portion of the splines on the mainshaft as shown in B, **Figure 106** at the 5th gear location. Refer to mainshaft dimension B in **Table 3**. If the shaft is worn to the service limit or less, the shaft must be replaced.

4. Measure the outside diameter of the REVERSE idler shaft (**Figure 107**). Refer to REVERSE idler shaft dimension in **Table 3**. If the shaft is worn to the service limit or less, the shaft must be replaced.

5. Measure the inside diameter of the following gears:

a. Mainshaft gears: 4th gear, 5th gear (**Figure 108**).

b. REVERSE idler gear (**Figure 109**).

Refer to the dimensions in **Table 3**. If the gear(s) are worn to the service limit or greater, the gear(s) must be replaced.

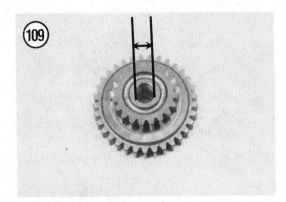

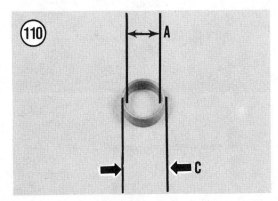

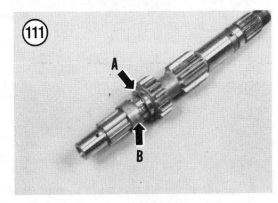

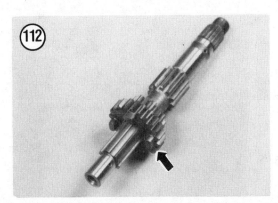

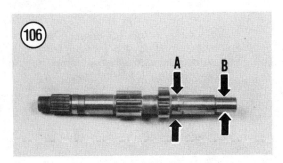

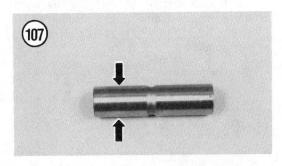

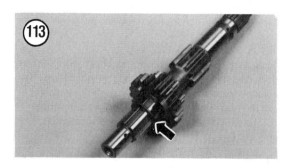

6. Measure the *inside* diameter (A, **Figure 110**) of the 4th and 5th gear bushings. Refer to the dimensions in **Table 3**. If the gear bushing(s) are worn to the service limit or greater, the gear bushing(s) must be replaced.

7. Measure the *outside* diameter (C, **Figure 110**) of the 5th gear bushing. Refer to the dimensions in **Table 3**. If the gear bushing is worn to the service limit or less, the gear bushing must be replaced.

8. Calculate the gear-to-bushing clearance. Subtract the outer diameter of the bushing from the inner diameter of the gear. If the clearance is greater than service limit dimension listed in **Table 3**, replace the worn part(s).

9. Make sure that all gears and gear bushings slide smoothly on the mainshaft.

Mainshaft Assembly

Refer to **Figure 102** for this procedure.

1. Slide on the thrust washer (A, **Figure 111**).
2. Slide the 4th gear bushing into place (B, **Figure 111**).
3. Slide on the 4th gear (**Figure 112**).
4. Slide on the splined washer (**Figure 113**) and install the circlip (**Figure 114**).
5. Slide on the 3rd gear (**Figure 115**).
6. Slide on the thrust washer (**Figure 116**) and the 5th gear bushing (**Figure 117**).
7. Slide on the 5th gear (**Figure 118**) and the thrust washer (**Figure 119**).

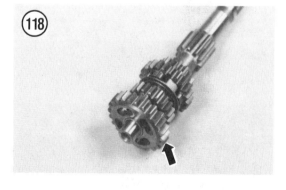

8. After assembly is complete, check for correct placement of all gears (**Figure 120**).

9. Make sure all circlips are seated correctly in the mainshaft grooves.

Countershaft Disassembly

Refer to **Figure 102** for this procedure.

NOTE
*Use the same large egg flat used for mainshaft disassembly. This is an easy way to remember the correct relationship of all parts (**Figure 121**).*

NOTE
The thrust washer, 1st gear and 1st gear bushing were removed from the end of the countershaft during the transmission shaft removal procedure.

1. Clean the assembled shaft as described under *Preliminary Inspection* in this chapter.

2. Slide off the REVERSE shifter and splined collar.

3. Slide off the REVERSE gear and REVERSE gear bushing.

4. Slide off the lockwasher.

5. Rotate the splined washer in either direction to disengage the tangs from the grooves on the transmission shaft. Slide off the splined washer.

6. Slide off the 2nd gear and 2nd gear bushing.

7. Slide off the splined washer and remove the circlip.

8. Slide off the 4th gear.

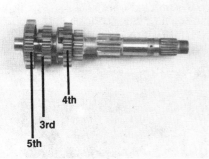

4th
3rd
5th

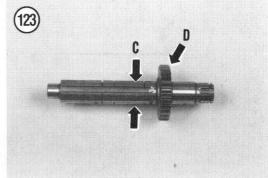

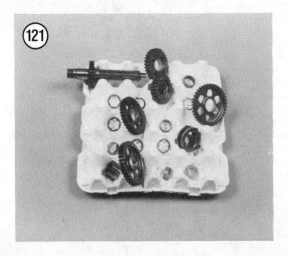

9. Remove the circlip and slide off the splined washer.

10. Slide off the 3rd gear and 3rd gear bushing.

Countershaft Inspection

1. Check each gear for excessive wear, burrs, pitting or chipped or missing teeth (A, **Figure 122**). Make sure the lugs (B, **Figure 122**) on the gears are in good condition.

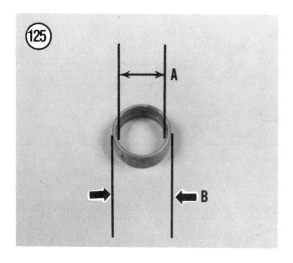

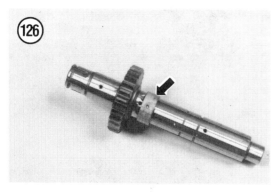

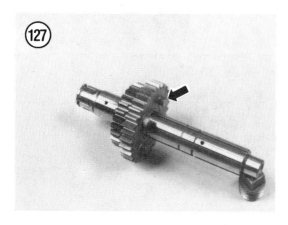

NOTE
Honda suggests that all circlips be replaced every time the transmission shaft is disassembled to ensure proper gear alignment. Do not expand a circlip more than necessary to slide it over the shaft.

NOTE
Install the circlips with the sharp side going on last.

NOTE
Defective gears should be replaced. It is a good idea to replace the mating gear on the mainshaft even though it may not show as much wear or damage.

2. On the countershaft, measure the outside diameter of the raised portion of the splines on the countershaft as shown in C, **Figure 123** at the 3rd gear location. Refer to countershaft dimension C in **Table 3**. If the shaft is worn to the service limit or less, the shaft must be replaced.

NOTE
*The 5th gear is part of the countershaft (D, **Figure 123**). If the gear is defective, the shaft must be replaced.*

3. Measure the inside diameter (**Figure 124**) of the 1st, 2nd, 3rd and REVERSE gears. Refer to the dimensions in **Table 3**. If the gear(s) are worn to the service limit or greater, the gear(s) must be replaced.

4. Measure the *inside* diameter (A, **Figure 125**) of the 3rd gear bushing. Refer to the dimensions in **Table 3**. If the gear bushing is worn to the service limit or greater, the gear bushing must be replaced.

5. Measure the *outside* diameter (B, **Figure 125**) of the 1st, 2nd, 3rd and REVERSE gear bushings. Refer to the dimensions in **Table 3**. If the gear bushing is worn to the service limit or less, the gear bushing(s) must be replaced.

6. Calculate the gear-to-bushing clearance. Subtract the outer diameter of the bushing from the inner diameter of the gear. If the clearance is greater than service limit dimension listed in **Table 3**, replace the worn part(s).

7. Make sure that all gears and gear bushings slide smoothly on the countershaft.

Countershaft Assembly

1. Slide on the 3rd gear bushing (**Figure 126**). There is no oil hole alignment on this bushing.

2. Slide on the 3rd gear (**Figure 127**) with the engagement lug side going on last.

3. Slide on the splined washer (**Figure 128**) and install the circlip (**Figure 129**).
4. Slide on the 4th gear (**Figure 130**).
5. Install the circlip (**Figure 131**) and slide on the splined washer (**Figure 132**).
6. Align the oil hole in the 2nd gear bushing (**Figure 133**) with the oil hole in the shaft and slide the bushing into the shaft.
7. Slide on the 2nd gear (**Figure 134**).
8. Slide on the splined washer (**Figure 135**). Rotate the splined washer in either direction to engage the tangs into the grooves on the transmission shaft (**Figure 136**).

9. Slide on the lockwasher (**Figure 137**) with the tang side going on first.

10. Slide the lockwasher on until the tangs go into the open areas of the splined washer and lock the washer in place (**Figure 138**).

11. Align the oil hole in the REVERSE gear bushing (**Figure 139**) with the oil hole in the shaft and slide the bushing onto the shaft.

12. Slide on the REVERSE gear (**Figure 140**).

13. Slide on the splined collar (**Figure 141**).

14. Slide the REVERSE shifter onto the splined collar (**Figure 142**) with the engagement lug side going on last.

6

15. Align the oil hole in the countershaft 1st gear bushing with the oil hole in the shaft (**Figure 143**) and install the bushing.

> *NOTE*
> *Do **not** install the 1st gear and thrust washer onto the end of the countershaft at this time. They will be installed during the transmission shaft installation procedure. These components are shown installed on the transmission shaft in **Figure 144** in order to show a complete shaft assembly.*

16. After assembly is complete, check for correct placement of all gears (**Figure 144**).
17. Make sure all circlips are seated correctly in the countershaft grooves.
18. After both transmission shafts have been assembled, mesh the 2 assemblies together in the correct position (**Figure 145**). This is your last check before installing the assemblies into the crankcase; make sure they are correctly assembled.

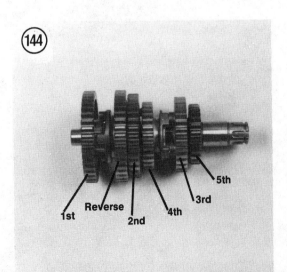

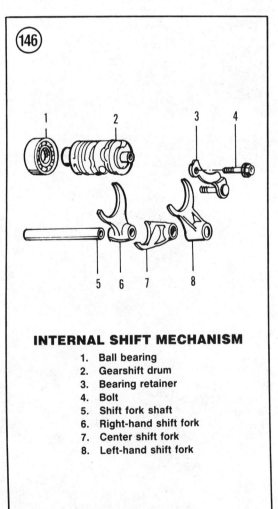

INTERNAL SHIFT MECHANISM

1. Ball bearing
2. Gearshift drum
3. Bearing retainer
4. Bolt
5. Shift fork shaft
6. Right-hand shift fork
7. Center shift fork
8. Left-hand shift fork

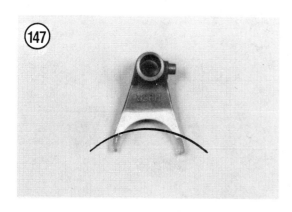

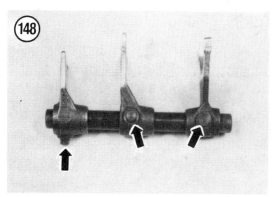

INTERNAL SHIFT MECHANISM

Inspection

Refer to **Figure 146** for this procedure.

1. Inspect each shift fork for signs of wear or cracking. Check for bending and make sure each fork slides smoothly on the shaft. Replace any worn or damaged forks.

2. Check for any arc-shaped wear or burn marks on the shift forks (**Figure 147**). This indicates that the shift fork has come in contact with the gear. The fork fingers have become excessively worn and the fork must be replaced.

3. Check the shift cam dowel pins (**Figure 148**) for wear or damage; replace as necessary.

4. Roll the shift fork shaft on a flat surface such as a piece of plate glass and check for any bends. If the shaft is bent, it must be replaced.

5. Measure the width of the gearshift fork fingers with a micrometer (**Figure 149**). Replace the ones worn to the service limit listed in **Table 4** or less.

CAUTION
Marginal shift forks should be replaced. Worn shift forks can cause the transmission to slip out of gear, leading to more serious and expensive problems.

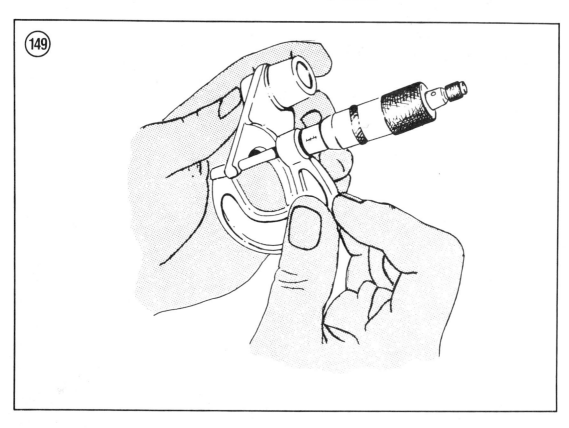

6. Measure the inside diameter of each shift fork with a micrometer (**Figure 150**). Replace the ones worn to the service limit listed in **Table 4** or greater.

7. Measure the outside diameter of the shift fork shaft with a micrometer (**Figure 151**). Replace if worn to the service limit listed in **Table 4** or less.

8. Check the grooves in the shift drum (**Figure 152**) for wear or roughness. If any of the groove profiles have excessive wear or damage, replace the shift drum.

9. Inspect the shift drum bearing (**Figure 153**) for wear or damage. Replace the bearing if wear is evident.

10. Apply a light coat of oil to the shift fork shafts and the inside bores of the shift forks before installation.

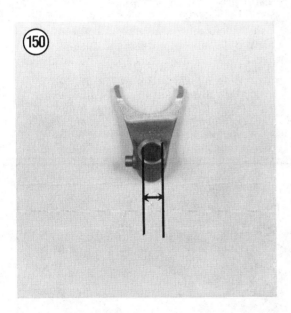

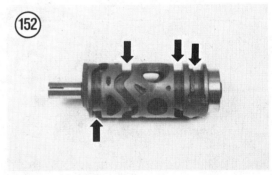

Table 1 CLUTCH SPECIFICATIONS

Item	Standard	Wear limit
MANUAL CLUTCH		
Friction disc thickness	2.9-3.0 mm (0.11-0.12 in.)	2.6 mm (0.10 in.)
Clutch plate warpage	—	0.2 mm (0.008 in.)
Clutch disc warpage	—	0.2 mm (0.00 8 in.)
Clutch springs free length	35.2 mm (1.39 in.)	34.5 mm (1.36 in.)
Clutch outer guide O.D.	27.959-27.979 mm (1.1007-1.1015 in.)	27.920 mm (1.099 in.)
Clutch outer guide I.D.	20.000-20.020 mm (0.7874-0.7882 in.)	20.070 mm (0.7902 in.)
Clutch outer guide length	30.05-30.15 mm (1.183-1.187 in.)	30.00 mm (1.181 in.)
CENTRIFUGAL CLUTCH		
Drum bushing ID	24.000-24.021 mm (0.9449-0.9457 in.)	24.05 mm (0.947 in.)
Clutch drum ID	116.0-116.2 mm (4.567-4.575 in.)	116.5 mm (4.59 in.)
Weight lining thickness	1.5 mm (0.06 in.)	1.2 mm (0.05 in.)

Table 2 CLUTCH AND EXTERNAL SHIFT MECHANISM TORQUE SPECIFICATIONS

Item	N•m	ft.-lb.
Manual clutch locknut	76-94	55-61
Centrifugal clutch locknut	86-94	62-68
Gearshift pedal pinch bolt	10-12	7-9
Shift drum arm stopper bolt	10-14	7-10
Shift guide plate bolt	10-14	7-10

Table 3 5-SPEED TRANSMISSION SPECIFICATIONS

Item	Specification	Wear limit
Transmission gears ID		
Mainshaft		
4th gear	23.000-23.021 mm (0.9055-0.9063 in.)	23.04 mm (0.907 in.)
5th gear	18.000-18.021 (0.7087-0.7095 in.)	18.04 mm (0.710 in.)
Countershaft		
1st, 2nd 3rd and REVERSE gears	25.000-25.021 mm (0.9843-0.9851 in.)	25.04 mm (0.986 in.)
REVERSE idle gear	13.000-13.018 mm (0.5118-0.5125 in.)	13.04 mm (0.513 in.)
	(continued)	

Table 3 5-SPEED TRANSMISSION SPECIFICATIONS (cont.)

Item	Specification	Wear limit
Transmission shaft O.D.		
Mainshaft		
Location A	19.959-19.980 mm (0.7858-0.7866)	19.94 mm (0.785 in.)
Location B	14.966-14.984 mm (0.5892-0.5899 in.)	14.94 mm (0.588 in.)
Location C	21.959-21.980 mm (0.8645-0.8654 in.)	21.94 mm (0.864 in.)
Transmission gear bushing OD		
Mainshaft		
4th gear	22.595-22.980 mm (0.9039-0.9047 in.)	22.94 mm (0.903 in.)
5th gear	17.959-17.980 mm (0.7070-0.7079 in.)	17.94 mm (0.706 in.)
Countershaft		
1st, 2nd, 3rd and REVERSE Gears	24.959-24.980 mm (0.9826-0.9835 in.)	24.94 mm (0.982 in.)
Transmission gear bushing ID		
Mainshaft		
4th gear	20.000-20.021 mm (0.7874-0.7882 in.)	20.04 mm (0.789 in.)
5th gear	15.000-15.018 mm (0.5906-0.5913 in.)	15.04 mm (0.592 in.)
Countershaft		
3rd gear	22.000-22.021 mm (0.8661-0.8670 in.)	22.04 mm (0.868 in.)
Transmission gear-to-bushing shaft clearance		
All bushings	0.020-0.062 mm (0.0008-0.0024 in.)	0.10 mm (0.004 in.)
Transmission bushing-to-shaft clearance		
Mainshaft		
4th gear	0.020-0.062 mm (0.0008-0.0024 in.)	0.10 mm (0.004 in.)
5th gear	0.016-0.052 mm (0.0006-0.0020 in.)	0.10 mm (0.004 in.)
Countershaft		
3rd gear	0.020-0.062	0.10 mm (0.004 in.)
Transmission gear-to-shaft clearance		
REVERSE idler gear	0.016-0.052 mm (0.006-0.0020 in.)	0.10 mm (0.004 in.)

Table 4 INTERNAL SHIFT MECHANISM SPECIFICATIONS

Item	Specifications	Wear limit
Shift fork finger thickness	4.93-5.00 mm (0.194-0.197 in.)	4.88 mm (0.192 in.)
Shift fork shaft OD	12.966-12.984 mm (0.5105-0.5112 in.)	12.94 mm (0.509 in.)
Shift fork ID	13.00-13.02 mm (0.5118-0.5126 in.)	13.05 mm (0.514 in.)

CHAPTER SEVEN

FUEL AND EXHAUST SYSTEMS

The fuel system consists of the fuel tank, the shutoff valve, a single carburetor and an air filter.

The exhaust system consists of an exhaust pipe and a muffler.

This chapter includes service procedures for all parts of the fuel system and exhaust system. Air filter service is covered in Chapter Three.

Carburetor specifications are covered in **Table 1**. **Tables 1-3** are at the end of this chapter.

CARBURETOR OPERATION

For proper operation a gasoline engine must be supplied with fuel and air mixed in proper proportions by weight. A mixture in which there is an excess of fuel is said to be rich. A lean mixture is one which contains insufficient fuel. A properly adjusted carburetor supplies the proper mixture to the engine under all operating conditions.

The carburetor consists of several major systems. A float and float valve mechanism maintain a constant fuel level in the float bowl. The pilot system supplies fuel at low speeds. The main fuel system supplies fuel at medium and high speeds. A starter (choke) system supplies the very rich mixture needed to start a cold engine.

CARBURETOR SERVICE

Major carburetor service (removal and cleaning) should be performed at the intervals indicated in

Table 1 in Chapter Three or when poor engine performance, hesitation and little or no response to mixture adjustment is observed. Alterations in jet size, throttle slide cutaway, and changes in jet needle position, etc., should be attempted only if you're experienced in this type of "tuning" work; a bad guess could result in costly engine damage or, at best, poor performance. If, after servicing the carburetor and making the adjustments described in this chapter, the ATV does not perform correctly (and assuming that other factors affecting performance are correct, such as ignition timing and condition, etc.), the vehicle should be checked by a dealer or a qualified performance tuning specialist.

CARBURETOR

Removal/Installation

1. Place the vehicle on level ground and set the parking brake or block the rear wheels so the vehicle will not roll in either direction.

2A. On 3-wheeled models, remove the seat/rear fender assembly as described in Chapter Fifteen.

2B. On 4-wheeled models, remove the seat and the rear fenders as described in Chapter Fifteen.

3. Remove the fuel tank as described in this chapter.

4. On 4-wheeled models, loosen the screw (A, **Figure 1**) on the choke cable clamp and disconnect the choke cable (B, **Figure 1**) from the choke linkage on the carburetor.

5. Loosen the bolt securing the air filter air box.

6. Remove the nuts (**Figure 2**) securing the carburetor to the rubber insulator.

7. Pull the carburetor and air box toward the rear far enough to disengage the carburetor from the threaded studs on the rubber insulator.

8. Loosen the screw on the clamping band (A, **Figure 3**) on the carburetor-to-air filter tube.

9. Slide the clamping bands away from the carburetor.

10. Note the routing of the carburetor drain tube through the frame. Carefully pull the tube free from the frame and leave it attached to the carburetor.

11. Partially remove the carburetor from the engine and frame.

NOTE
Before removing the top cap, thoroughly clean the area around it so no dirt will fall into the carburetor.

12. Unscrew the carburetor top cap (B, **Figure 3**) and pull the throttle valve assembly up and out of the carburetor (**Figure 4**).

NOTE
If the top cap and throttle valve assembly are not going to be removed from the throttle cable for cleaning, wrap them in a clean shop cloth or place them in a plastic bag to help keep them clean.

13. Take the carburetor to a workbench for disassembly and cleaning.

14. Install by reversing these removal steps, noting the following.

15. Align the groove in the throttle slide with the pin in the carburetor body (**Figure 5**).

16. Make sure the screw on the clamping band and the nuts securing the carburetor to the rubber insulator are tight to avoid a vacuum leak and possible valve damage.

17. After the carburetor is installed, refer to this chapter or Chapter Three and perform the following:
   a. Idle speed adjustment.
   b. Throttle lever adjustment.
   c. Choke adjustment (4-wheeled models).

Disassembly/Assembly

Refer to **Figure 6** for this procedure and to **Table 1** for carburetor specifications.

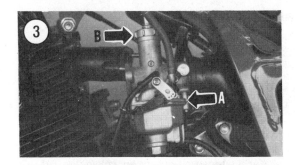

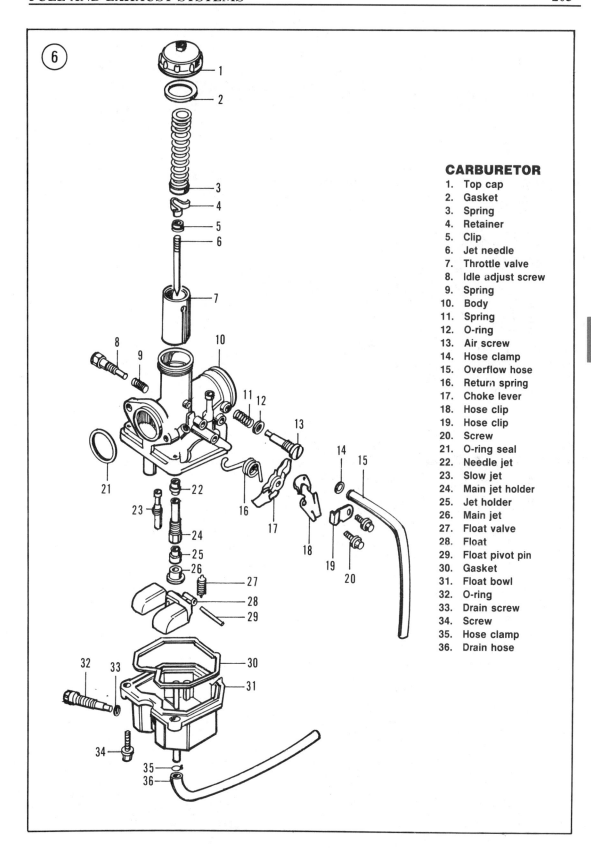

⑥

CARBURETOR

1. Top cap
2. Gasket
3. Spring
4. Retainer
5. Clip
6. Jet needle
7. Throttle valve
8. Idle adjust screw
9. Spring
10. Body
11. Spring
12. O-ring
13. Air screw
14. Hose clamp
15. Overflow hose
16. Return spring
17. Choke lever
18. Hose clip
19. Hose clip
20. Screw
21. O-ring seal
22. Needle jet
23. Slow jet
24. Main jet holder
25. Jet holder
26. Main jet
27. Float valve
28. Float
29. Float pivot pin
30. Gasket
31. Float bowl
32. O-ring
33. Drain screw
34. Screw
35. Hose clamp
36. Drain hose

7

1. Remove the O-ring seal (**Figure 7**) from the carburetor body.

2. Remove the screws (**Figure 8**) securing the float bowl and remove the float bowl.

3. On models so equipped, remove the main jet holder (**Figure 9**).

NOTE
*Before removing the pilot screw, carefully screw it in until it **lightly** seats. Count and record the number of turns so it can be installed in the same position.*

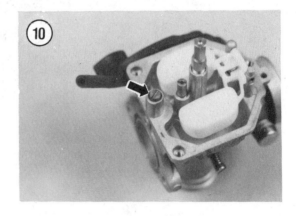

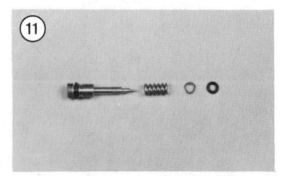

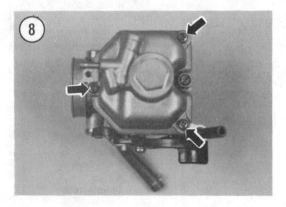

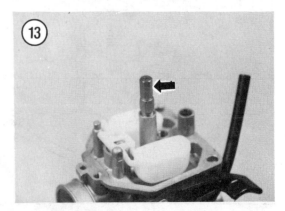

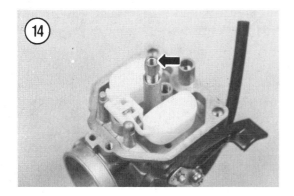

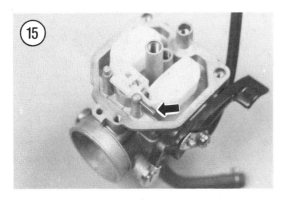

4. On 3-wheeled models, unscrew the pilot screw (**Figure 10**) and remove the screw, spring, washer and O-ring seal (**Figure 11**).

5. Remove the slow jet (**Figure 12**).

6. Remove the main jet (**Figure 13**).

7. Remove the needle jet holder (**Figure 14**).

8. Turn the carburetor over and gently tap the side of the body. Catch the needle jet as it falls out into your hand. If the needle jet does not fall out, use a plastic or fiber tool and gently push the needle jet out. Do not use any metal tool for this purpose.

9. Remove the float pivot pin (**Figure 15**) and remove the float valve assembly (**Figure 16**).

NOTE
*Before removing the air screw, carefully screw it in until it **lightly** seats. Count and record the number of turns so it can be installed in the same position.*

10. Remove the air screw (**Figure 17**) and remove the screw, O-ring and spring (**Figure 18**).

11. Remove the float bowl gasket (**Figure 19**) from the float bowl.

7

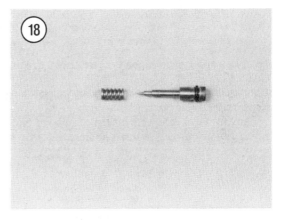

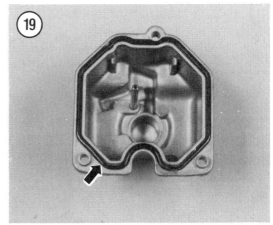

12. Unscrew the main jet cover and O-ring seal (**Figure 20**) from the float bowl.

13. Remove the O-ring seal (**Figure 21**) from the carburetor body.

14. Remove the choke lever from the carburetor body. Refer to **Figure 22** for 3-wheeled models or **Figure 23** for 4-wheeled models.

15. To remove the throttle valve from the throttle cable, perform the following:

   a. Depress the throttle spring away from the throttle valve.

   b. Push the throttle cable end down and out along the groove in the side of the throttle valve (**Figure 24**) and remove the throttle valve and needle jet assembly.

   c. Remove the needle clip retainer and remove the jet needle and needle clip (**Figure 25**).

NOTE
If the needle clip is going to be removed, record the clip position before removal.

NOTE
*Further disassembly is neither necessary nor recommended. If throttle or choke shafts or butterflies (**Figure 26**) are damaged, take the carburetor body to a dealer for replacement.*

16. Clean and inspect all parts as described in this chapter.

17. Assembly is the reverse of these disassembly steps, noting the following.

18. Install the needle jet with the chamfered end facing *up* toward the needle jet holder.

CAUTION
On 1986 3-wheeled models, be sure to refer to the correct model number for your specific vehicle. There were 2 different carburetor model numbers used during this year and the needle jet clip position is unique for each model.

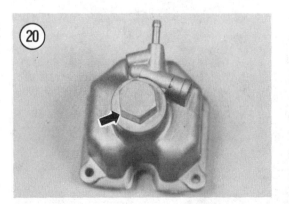

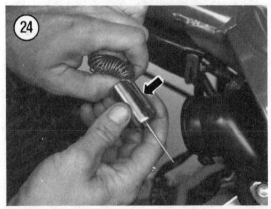

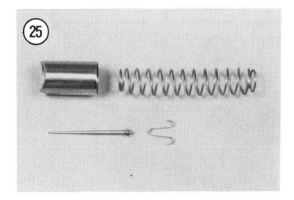

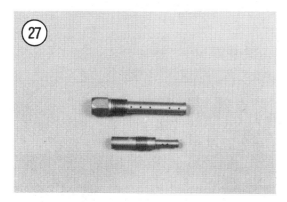

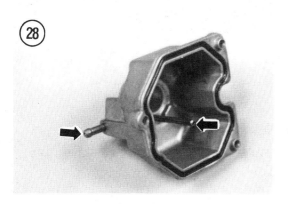

19. Install the needle jet clip in the correct groove; refer to **Table 1** at the end of this chapter.

20. Check the float height and adjust if necessary as described in this chapter.

21. After the carburetor has been disassembled, the pilot screw (or air screw) and the idle speed should be adjusted as described in this chapter.

Cleaning/Inspection

1. Clean all parts, except rubber or plastic parts, in a good grade of carburetor cleaner. This solution is available at most automotive or motorcycle supply stores in a small, resealable tank with a dip basket for just a few dollars. If it is tightly sealed when not in use, the solution will last for several cleanings. Follow the manufacturer's instructions for correct soak time (usually about 1/2 hour).

2. Remove all parts from the cleaner and blow dry with compressed air. Blow out the jets and needle jet holder (**Figure 27**) with compressed air.

> *CAUTION*
> *If compressed air is not available, allow the parts to air dry or use a clean lint-free cloth. Do **not** use a paper towel to dry carburetor parts, as small paper particles may plug openings in the carburetor body or jets.*

> *CAUTION*
> *Do **not** use a piece of wire to clean parts as minor gouges in the jet can alter flow rate and upset the fuel/air mixture.*

3. Be sure to clean out the overflow tube in the float bowl from both ends (**Figure 28**).

4. Inspect the end of the float valve needle (**Figure 29**) for wear or damage. Also check the inside of the needle valve body (**Figure 21**). If either part is damaged, replace as a set. A damaged needle valve or a particle of dirt or grit in the needle valve assembly will cause the carburetor to flood and overflow fuel.

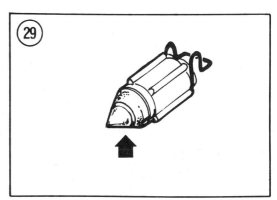

5. Inspect all O-ring seals. O-ring seals tend to become hardened after prolonged use and heat and therefore lose their ability to seal properly.

6. Examine the end of the pilot screw (or air screw) and the throttle adjust screw. If either screw is grooved or rough, replace it. A damaged end will prevent smooth low-speed engine operation.

7. Make sure the air openings (A, **Figure 30**) are open and that the choke butterfly screws (B, **Figure 30**) are tight.

CARBURETOR ADJUSTMENTS

Idle Speed Adjustment

Before making this adjustment, the air filter element must be clean and the engine must have adequate compression as described under *Compression Test* in Chapter Three.

1. Place the ATV on level ground and set the parking brake.

2. Connect a portable tachometer following the manufacturer's instructions.

3. Start the engine and let it reach normal operating temperature.

4. Set the idle speed by turning the idle speed screw. Refer to A, **Figure 31** for 3-wheeled models or **Figure 32** for 4-wheeled models.

5. The correct idle speed is listed in **Table 1**.

6. Open and close the throttle a couple of times. Check for variation in idle speed; readjust if necessary.

> *WARNING*
> *With the engine idling, move the handlebar from side to side. If idle speed increases during this movement, the throttle cable needs adjusting or may be incorrectly routed through the frame. Correct this problem immediately. Do not ride the vehicle in this unsafe condition.*

7. Turn the engine off and disconnect the portable tachometer.

Pilot Screw Adjustment (3-wheeled Models)

The air filter element must be cleaned before starting this procedure or the results will be inaccurate. Refer to *Air Filter Element Cleaning* in Chapter Three.

> *NOTE*
> *The pilot screw is pre-set at the factory and adjustment is not necessary unless the carburetor has been overhauled or someone has misadjusted it.*

1. For the preliminary adjustment, carefully turn the pilot screw (B, **Figure 31**) in until it seats *lightly* and then back it out the number of turns listed in **Table 1**.

> *CAUTION*
> *The pilot screw seat can be damaged if the pilot screw is tightened too hard against the seat.*

2. Start the engine and let it reach normal operating temperature. Approximately 5-10 minutes of stop and go riding is usually sufficient. Shut the engine off.

3. Connect a portable tachometer following the manufacturer's instructions.

4. Turn the idle speed screw (A, **Figure 31**) in or out to obtain the idle speed listed in **Table 1**.

5. Turn the pilot screw *clockwise* until the engine stops running. Back the pilot screw out 1 full turn. Restart the engine and proceed to Step 6.

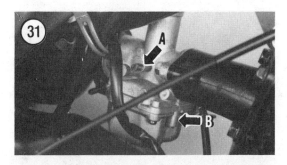

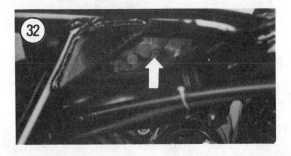

6. Reset the idle speed; refer to Step 4. Open and close the throttle a couple of times. Check for variation in idle speed; readjust if necessary.

WARNING
With the engine idling, move the handlebar from side to side. If idle speed increases during this movement, the throttle cable needs adjustment or it may be incorrectly routed through the frame. Correct this problem immediately. Do not ride the bike in this unsafe condition.

7. If necessary, repeat Step 5 and Step 6 until the engine runs smoothly at the correct idle speed.
8. Disconnect the portable tachometer.

Air Screw Adjustment
(4-wheeled Models)

The air filter element must be cleaned before starting this procedure or the results will be inaccurate. Refer to *Air Filter Element Cleaning* in Chapter Three.

NOTE
Figure 33 shows the carburetor removed for clarity. It is not necessary to remove the carburetor for this procedure.

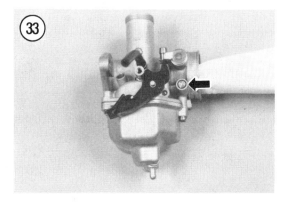

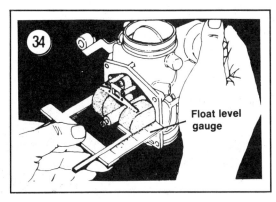

Float level gauge

1. For the preliminary adjustment, carefully turn the air screw (**Figure 33**) in until it seats *lightly* and then back it out the number of turns listed in **Table 1**.

CAUTION
The air screw seat can be damaged if the air screw is tightened too hard against the seat.

2. Start the engine and let it reach normal operating temperature. Approximately 5-10 minutes of stop and go riding is usually sufficient. Shut the engine off.
3. Connect a portable tachometer following the manufacturer's instructions.
4. Turn the idle speed screw (**Figure 32**) in or out to obtain the idle speed listed in **Table 1**.
5. Turn the air screw (**Figure 33**) *clockwise* until the engine misses or decreases in speed. Note this position.
6. Turn the air screw (**Figure 33**) *counterclockwise* until the engine misses or decreases in speed. Note this position.
7. Turn the air screw so it is centered between the 2 extreme positions noted in Step 5 and Step 6.
8. Turn the idle adjust screw in or out to obtain the idle speed listed in **Table 1**.

WARNING
With the engine idling, move the handlebar from side to side. If idle speed increases during this movement, the throttle cable needs adjustment or it may be incorrectly routed through the frame. Correct this problem immediately. Do not ride the ATV in this unsafe condition.

9. Turn the engine off and disconnect the portable tachometer.
10. After this adjustment is completed, test ride the vehicle. Throttle response from idle should be rapid and without any hesitation.

Float Adjustment

The carburetor assembly has to be removed and partially disassembled for this adjustment.
1. Remove the carburetor as described in this chapter.
2. Remove the screws (**Figure 8**) securing the float bowl and remove float bowl.
3. Hold the carburetor so the float arm is just touching the float needle—not pushing it down. Use a float level gauge, vernier caliper or small ruler (**Figure 34**) and measure the distance from the carburetor body to the float. The correct height is listed in **Table 1**.

4. The float assembly is all plastic and cannot be adjusted. If the float level is incorrect, the float assembly must be replaced.

> *NOTE*
> *If the float level is set too high, fuel will run from the float bowl overflow tube and cause the engine to flood. It will also cause a rich fuel/air mixture. If it is set too low, the mixture will be too lean and the engine will stumble on acceleration and run too lean to develop peak efficiency and power.*

5. Reassemble and install the carburetor as described in this chapter.

Needle Jet Adjustment

The position of the needle jet can be adjusted to affect the fuel/air mixture for medium throttle openings. It is not necessary to remove the carburetor but the top of the carburetor must be removed for this adjustment.

1. Place the vehicle on level ground and set the parking brake or block the rear wheels so the vehicle will not roll in either direction.
2A. On 3-wheeled models, remove the seat/rear fender assembly as described in Chapter Fifteen.
2B. On 4-wheeled models, remove the seat and the rear fenders as described in Chapter Fifteen.
3. Remove the fuel tank as described in this chapter.

> *NOTE*
> *Before removing the top cap, thoroughly clean the area around it so no dirt will fall into the carburetor.*

4. Unscrew the carburetor top cap (**Figure 35**) and pull the throttle valve assembly up and out of the carburetor.
5. To remove the throttle valve from the throttle cable, perform the following:
  a. Depress the throttle spring away from the throttle valve.
  b. Push the throttle cable end down and out along the groove (**Figure 24**) in the side of the throttle valve and remove the throttle valve and needle jet assembly.

> *NOTE*
> *Record the clip position before removal.*

  c. Remove the needle clip retainer and remove the jet needle and needle clip (**Figure 25**).
6. Raising the needle (lowering the clip) will enrich the mixture during mid-throttle opening, while lowering the needle (raising the clip) will lean the mixture. Refer to **Figure 36**.
7. Refer to **Table 1** for standard clip position.
8. Reassemble and install the carburetor top cap.

High Altitude Adjustment

Make sure the pilot jet (or air screw) is adjusted properly before performing this procedure.

If the ATV is going to be ridden for any sustained period of time at high altitudes (1,500 m/5,000 ft.) the carburetor must be readjusted to improve performance and decrease exhaust emissions.

The carburetor is set with a standard main jet for normal sea level conditions. If the vehicle is run at higher altitudes or under heavy load—deep sand or mud—the main jet should be replaced with a one-step smaller size to prevent the engine from running too rich and carboning up quickly.

1. Place the ATV on level ground and set the parking brake or block the wheels so the vehicle will not roll in either direction.
2. Remove the carburetor as described in this chapter.
3. Remove the screws (**Figure 8**) securing the float bowl and remove the float bowl.
4. Remove the main jet and replace it with the factory recommended high altitude size (**Table 2**).
5. Install the float bowl and install the carburetor as described in this chapter.
6. Turn the pilot screw (or air screw) in from the factory pre-set position as indicated in **Table 2**.
7. When the ATV is returned to lower altitudes (near sea level), the main jet must be replaced with the original size, the pilot screw (or air screw) must be returned to its original position and the idle speed readjusted to idle speed listed in **Table 1**.

THROTTLE CABLE
REPLACEMENT

Removal

1. Place the vehicle on level ground and set the parking brake or block the rear wheels so the vehicle will not roll in either direction.

2A. On 3-wheeled models, perform the following:
    a. Remove the seat/rear fender assembly as described in Chapter Fifteen.
    b. Remove the headlight case as described under *Headlight Replacement and Headlight Case Removal/Installation* in Chapter Eight.

2B. On 4-wheeled models, remove the seat and the rear fenders as described in Chapter Fifteen.

3. Remove the fuel tank as described in this chapter.

NOTE
Before removing the top cap, thoroughly clean the area around it so no dirt will fall into the carburetor.

4. Unscrew the carburetor top cap (**Figure 35**) and pull the throttle valve assembly up and out of the carburetor.

5. To remove the throttle valve from the throttle cable, perform the following:
    a. Depress the throttle spring away from the throttle valve.
    b. Push the throttle cable end down and out along the groove (**Figure 24**) in the side of the throttle valve and remove the throttle valve and needle jet assembly.

NOTE
Place a clean shop rag over the top of the carburetor to keep any foreign matter from falling into the throttle slide area.

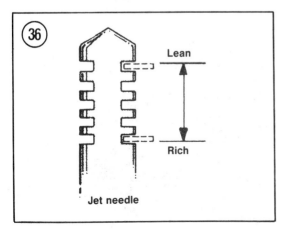

Lean

Rich

Jet needle

6. Disassemble the throttle housing as described in this chapter and disconnect the throttle cable from the throttle arm.

7. Disconnect the throttle cable from any clips holding the cable to the frame.

NOTE
The piece of string attached in the next step will be used to pull the new throttle cable back through the frame so it will be routed in the exact same position as the old one.

8. Tie a piece of heavy string or cord (approximately 2 m/7 ft.) to the carburetor end of the throttle cable. Wrap this end with masking or duct tape. Do not use an excessive amount of tape as it will be pulled through the frame. Tie the other end of the string to the frame.

9. At the throttle lever end of the cable, carefully pull the cable and attached string out through the frame. Make sure the attached string follows the same path as the cable through the frame.

10. Remove the tape and untie the string from the old cable.

Installation

1. Tie the string (used during removal) to the new throttle cable and wrap it with tape.

2. Carefully pull the string back through the frame, routing the new cable through the same path as the old cable.

3. Remove the tape and untie the string from the cable and the frame.

4. Reverse Steps 2-5 of *Removal*, noting the following.

5. Assemble the throttle housing and reconnect the throttle cable as described in this chapter.

6. Operate the throttle lever and make sure the carburetor throttle linkage is operating correctly and with no binding. If operation is incorrect or there is binding, carefully check that the cable is attached correctly and there are no tight bends in the cable.

7. Adjust the throttle cable as described under *Throttle Lever Adjustment* in Chapter Three.

8. Test ride the ATV and make sure the throttle is operating correctly.

CHOKE CABLE REPLACEMENT
(4-WHEELED MODELS)

Removal

1. Place the vehicle on level ground and set the parking brake or block the rear wheels so the vehicle will not roll in either direction.

2. Remove the fuel tank as described in this chapter.

3. Remove the seat, the front fender and the rear fenders as described in Chapter Fifteen.

4. Loosen the screw on the cable clamp (A, **Figure 37**) and disconnect the cable from the carburetor (B, **Figure 37**).

5. Loosen the locknut (**Figure 38**) and remove the choke cable from the bracket on the upper fork bridge.

> *NOTE*
> *The piece of string attached in the next step will be used to pull the new choke cable back through the frame so it will be routed in the same position as the old cable.*

6. Tie a piece of heavy string or cord (approximately 2 m/7 ft. long) to the carburetor end of the choke cable. Wrap this end with masking or duct tape. Do not use an excessive amount of tape as it must be pulled through the frame loop during removal. Tie the other end of the string to the frame or air box.

7. At the choke lever end of the cable, carefully pull the cable and attached string out through the frame. Make sure the attached string follows the same path as the cable through the frame.

8. Remove the tape and untie the string from the old cable.

Installation

1. Lubricate the new cable as described in Chapter Three.

2. Tie the string to the new choke cable and wrap it with tape.

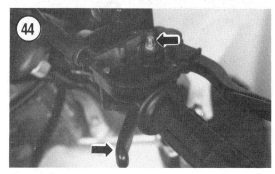

3. Carefully pull the string back through the frame, routing the new cable through the same path as the old cable.

4. Remove the tape and untie the string from the cable and the frame.

5. Install the cable into the bracket on the upper fork bridge. Tighten the locknut.

6. Connect the cable onto the carburetor. Tighten the screw on the cable clamp screw (A, **Figure 37**).

7. Operate the choke lever and make sure the carburetor choke linkage is operating correctly, with no binding. If operation is incorrect or there is binding carefully check that the cable is attached correctly and there are no tight bends in the cable.

8. Install the seat, the front fender and the rear fenders as described in Chapter Fifteen.

9. Install the fuel tank as described in this chapter.

10. Adjust the choke cable as described under *Choke Adjustment (4-wheeled Models)* in Chapter Three.

THROTTLE HOUSING

Disassembly/Assembly

1. Remove the screws (**Figure 39**) securing the throttle housing cover and remove the cover and gasket.

2. Straighten the tab (**Figure 40**) on the lockwasher.

3. Remove the nut (**Figure 41**) securing the throttle arm.

4. Remove the lockwasher, the throttle arm (**Figure 42**) and spring from the throttle lever shaft.

5. Disconnect the throttle cable from the throttle arm (**Figure 43**).

6. Connect the cable onto the carburetor. Tighten the screw on the cable clamp (A, **Figure 37**).

7. Lubricate the throttle cable as described under *Control Cables* in Chapter Three.

8. Apply a light coat of multipurpose grease to all pivoting areas of the throttle housing and to the throttle arm shaft.

9. Attach the throttle cable to the throttle arm (**Figure 43**).

10. Install the throttle arm return spring onto the throttle housing post.

11. Align the flats of the throttle arm with the flats on the throttle shaft. Hold the throttle shaft in place and install the throttle arm.

12. Hook the spring onto the throttle arm as shown in **Figure 45**.

13. Install the lockwasher (**Figure 46**) onto the throttle shaft.

14. Install the nut (**Figure 41**) securing the throttle arm. Tighten the nut securely.

15. Operate the throttle lever several times to make sure it is operating correctly. Correct any problems that may exist at this time.

16. Bend the locking tab up against one of the flats on the nut (**Figure 40**).

17. Install a new gasket (**Figure 47**) onto the housing or cover.

18. Align the holes in the cover with the locating dowels in the housing and install the cover. Tighten the cover screws (**Figure 39**) securely.

FUEL SHUTOFF VALVE

Removal/Installation

1. Place the ATV on level ground and set the parking brake or block the rear wheels so the vehicle will not roll in either direction.

2. Remove the fuel tank as described in this chapter.

3A. On 3-wheeled models, unscrew the locknut (**Figure 48**) securing the fuel shutoff valve to the base of the fuel tank and remove the shutoff valve assembly.

3B. On 4-wheeled models, unscrew the locknut (**Figure 49**) securing the fuel shutoff valve to the base of the fuel tank and remove the shutoff valve assembly.

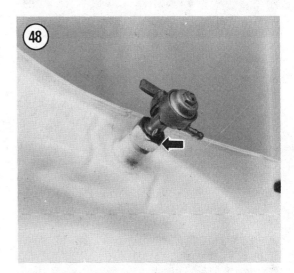

4. Remove the fuel filter from the shutoff valve. Clean with a medium soft toothbrush and blow out with compressed air. Replace the filter if it is defective.

5. Install by reversing these removal steps, noting the following.

6. Install a new gasket between the shutoff valve and the fuel tank. Tighten the screws securely.

7. Check for fuel leakage after installation is completed.

FUEL TANK

Removal/Installation
(3-wheeled Models)

Refer to **Figure 50** for this procedure.

1. Place the ATV on level ground and set the parking brake or block the rear wheels so the vehicle will not roll in either direction.

2. Remove the seat/rear fender assembly as described in Chapter Fifteen.

3. Disconnect the fuel filler cap vent tube from the handlebar cover (**Figure 51**).

4. Remove the screws securing the side covers and remove both side covers (**Figure 52**).

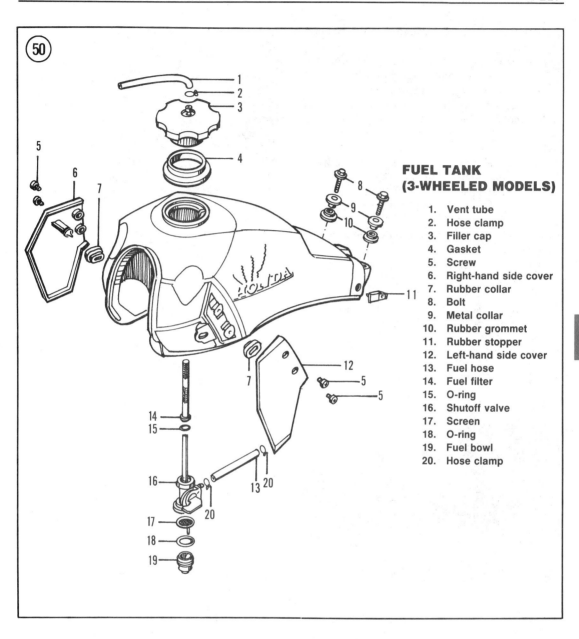

50

**FUEL TANK
(3-WHEELED MODELS)**

1. Vent tube
2. Hose clamp
3. Filler cap
4. Gasket
5. Screw
6. Right-hand side cover
7. Rubber collar
8. Bolt
9. Metal collar
10. Rubber grommet
11. Rubber stopper
12. Left-hand side cover
13. Fuel hose
14. Fuel filter
15. O-ring
16. Shutoff valve
17. Screen
18. O-ring
19. Fuel bowl
20. Hose clamp

7

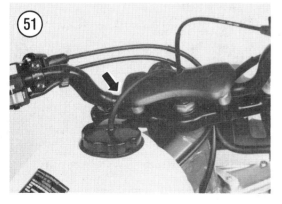

51

52

5. Turn the fuel shutoff valve to the OFF position (A, **Figure 53**).

6. Disconnect the fuel line (B, **Figure 53**) from the fuel tank to the carburetor. Plug the end with a golf tee to prevent fuel from dribbling onto the frame.

7. Remove the bolts (**Figure 54**) securing the fuel tank at the rear. Don't lose the washer or the metal plate and rubber cushion between each of the bolts and the fuel tank.

8. Pull the fuel tank to the rear and remove it.

9. Inspect the rubber cushions (**Figure 55**) on the frame where the fuel tank is held in place. Replace as a set if either is damaged or starting to deteriorate.

10. Install by reversing these removal steps, noting the following.

11. Check for fuel leakage after installation is completed.

12. On 1987 models, insert the loose end of the fuel filler cap breather tube into the hole in the handlebar cover until the white mark on the tube is no longer visible.

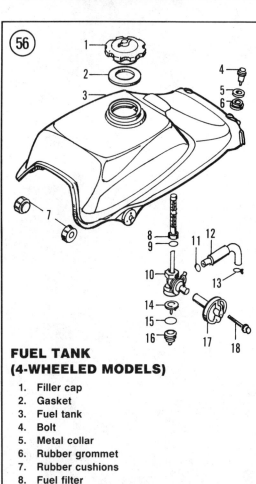

FUEL TANK (4-WHEELED MODELS)

1. Filler cap
2. Gasket
3. Fuel tank
4. Bolt
5. Metal collar
6. Rubber grommet
7. Rubber cushions
8. Fuel filter
9. O-ring
10. Shutoff valve
11. Hose clamp
12. Fuel hose
13. Hose clamp
14. Screen
15. O-ring
16. Fuel bowl
17. Shutoff valve knob
18. Screw

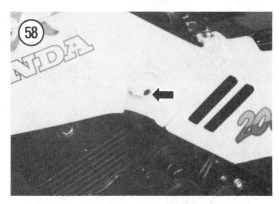

Removal/Installation
(4-wheeled Models)

Refer to **Figure 56** for this procedure.
1. Place the ATV on level ground and set the parking brake or block the rear wheels so the vehicle will not roll in either direction.
2. Remove the seat as described in Chapter Fifteen.
3. Disconnect the battery negative lead (**Figure 57**).
4. Turn the fuel shutoff valve to the OFF position.
5. Remove the screw securing the shutoff valve knob (**Figure 58**) to the fuel shutoff valve and remove the knob.

NOTE
In the following step, both the front fender and rear fender assemblies are removed for clarity. It is not necessary to remove the entire fender assemblies—only the items indicated.

6. Remove the air scoop grille, fuel tank center cover and cover stay of the front fender assembly as described in Chapter Fifteen.
7. Disconnect the fuel line (**Figure 59**) going to the carburetor. Plug the fuel line with a golf tee to prevent fuel spillage.
8. Remove the bolts securing the rear portion of the front fender.
9. Remove the bolts (**Figure 60**) securing the fuel tank at the rear. Don't lose the washer or the metal plate and rubber cushion between each of the bolts and the fuel tank.
10. Have an assistant carefully pull the rear portion of the front fender outward so the fuel tank will clear it.
11. Carefully pull the fuel tank toward the rear and remove it.
12. Install by reversing these removal steps, noting the following.
13. Inspect the rubber cushions on the mounting tabs on the fuel tank. Replace as a set if either is damaged or starting to deteriorate.
14. Check for fuel leakage after installation is completed.

AFTERMARKET FUEL FILTER

The ATV is equipped with a small fuel filter screen in the fuel shutoff valve. Considering the dirt and residue that is often found in today's gasoline, it is a good idea to install an inline fuel filter to help keep the carburetor clean. A good quality inline fuel filter (A.C. part No. GF453 or equivalent) is available at most auto and motorcycle supply stores. Just cut the fuel line

7

from the fuel tank to the carburetor and install the filter. Cut out a section of the fuel line the length of the filter so the fuel line does not kink and restrict fuel flow. Insert the fuel filter and make sure the fuel line is secured to the filter at each end.

GASOLINE/ALCOHOL BLEND TEST

Gasoline blended with alcohol is available in many areas. Most states and most fuel suppliers require labeling of gasoline pumps that dispense gasoline containing a certain percentage of alcohol (methyl or wood). If in doubt, ask the service station operator if their fuel contains any alcohol. A gasoline/alcohol blend, even if it contains co-solvents and corrosion inhibitors for methanol, may be damaging to the fuel system. It may also cause poor performance, hot engine restart or hot-engine running problems.

If you are not sure if the fuel you purchased contains alcohol, run this simple and effective test.

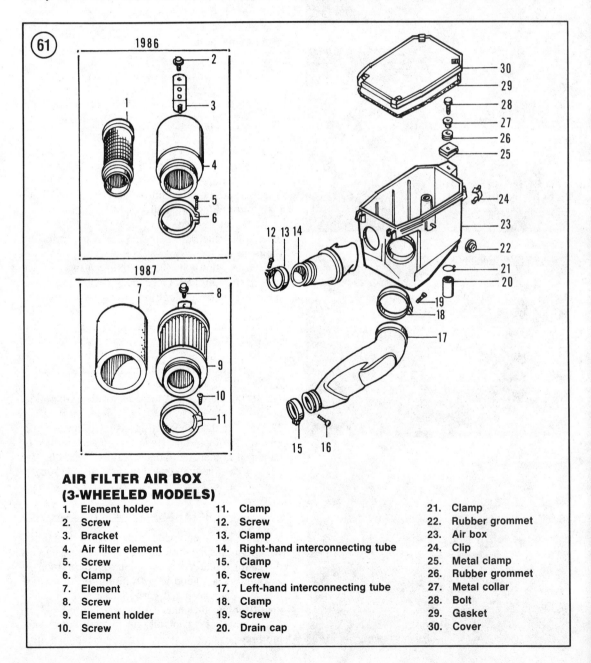

AIR FILTER AIR BOX (3-WHEELED MODELS)

1. Element holder
2. Screw
3. Bracket
4. Air filter element
5. Screw
6. Clamp
7. Element
8. Screw
9. Element holder
10. Screw
11. Clamp
12. Screw
13. Clamp
14. Right-hand interconnecting tube
15. Clamp
16. Screw
17. Left-hand interconnecting tube
18. Clamp
19. Screw
20. Drain cap
21. Clamp
22. Rubber grommet
23. Air box
24. Clip
25. Metal clamp
26. Rubber grommet
27. Metal collar
28. Bolt
29. Gasket
30. Cover

A blended fuel doesn't look any different from straight gasoline so it must be tested.

WARNING
Gasoline is very volatile and presents an extreme fire hazard. Be sure to work in a well-ventilated area away from any open flames (including pilot lights on household appliances). Do not allow anyone to smoke in the area and have a fire extinguisher rated for gasoline fires handy.

During this test keep the following facts in mind:
a. Alcohol and gasoline mix together.
b. Alcohol mixes *easier* with water.
c. Gasoline and water do *not* mix.

NOTE
If cosolvents have been used in the gasoline, this test may not work with water. Repeat this test using automotive antifreeze instead of water.

Use an 8 oz. transparent baby bottle with a sealable cap.
1. Set the baby bottle on a level surface and add water up to the 1.5 oz mark. Mark this line on the bottle with a fine-line permanent marking pen. This will be the reference line used later in this test.
2. Add the suspect fuel into the baby bottle up to the 8 oz. mark.
3. Install the sealable cap and shake the bottle vigorously for about 10 seconds.
4. Set the baby bottle upright on the level surface used in Step 1 and wait for a few minutes for the mixture to settle down.
5. If there is *no* alcohol in the fuel the gasoline/water separation line will be exactly on the 1.5 oz reference line made in Step 1.
6. If there *is* alcohol in the fuel the gasoline/water separation line will be *above* the 1.5 oz. reference line made in Step 1. The alcohol has separated from the gasoline and mixed in with the water (remember it is easier for the alcohol to mix with water than gasoline).

WARNING
*After the test, discard the baby bottle or place it out of reach of small children. There will always be a gasoline and alcohol residue in it and it should **not** be used to drink out of.*

AIR FILTER AIR BOX

Removal/Installation
(3-wheeled Models)

Refer to **Figure 61** for this procedure.
1. Remove the seat/rear fender assembly as described in Chapter Fifteen.
2. Loosen the screws on the clamping bands on each end of the left-hand interconnecting tube. Remove the left-hand interconnecting tube (**Figure 62**).
3. Disconnect the right-hand interconnecting tube from the air box and the inlet on the frame. Remove the right-hand interconnecting tube.
4. Remove the bolt (A, **Figure 63**) securing the air box to the frame. Don't lose the collar and rubber grommet on the bolt.
5. Withdraw the air box (B, **Figure 63**) up and out of the frame.
6. Install by reversing these removal steps, noting the following.
7. Make sure that all clamping bands are seated correctly and that the screws are tight.

Removal/Installation
(4-wheeled Models)

Refer to **Figure 64** for this procedure.
1. Remove the seat as described in Chapter Fifteen.
2. Loosen the screws on the clamping bands on each end of the interconnecting tube.
3. Disconnect the left-hand interconnecting tube from the air box and the inlet on the frame. Remove the left-hand interconnecting tube.
4. Loosen the screws on the clamping band on inlet tube at the carburetor and air filter air box. Slide the clamping band away from the carburetor and the air box. Remove the inlet tube.
5. Remove the bolt (A, **Figure 65**) securing the air box to the frame. Don't lose the collar and rubber grommet on the bolt.

6. Carefully slide the air box toward the rear and withdraw the air box (B, **Figure 65**) up and out of the frame.
7. Install by reversing these removal steps, noting the following.
8. Make sure all clamping bands are seated correctly and that the screws are tight.

EXHAUST SYSTEM

The exhaust system is a vital performance component and frequently, because of its design, it is a vulnerable piece of equipment.

If the exhaust system is damaged or if the muffler becomes clogged with carbon, the performance of the engine can be greatly affected.

Check the exhaust system for deep dents and fractures and repair them or replace parts

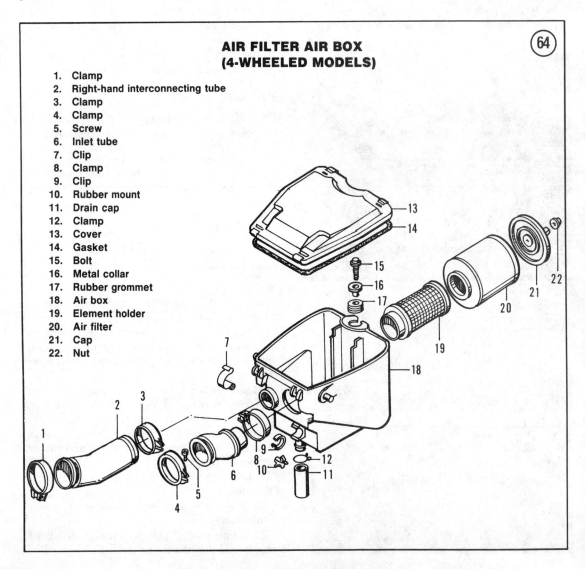

**AIR FILTER AIR BOX
(4-WHEELED MODELS)** (64)

1. Clamp
2. Right-hand interconnecting tube
3. Clamp
4. Clamp
5. Screw
6. Inlet tube
7. Clip
8. Clamp
9. Clip
10. Rubber mount
11. Drain cap
12. Clamp
13. Cover
14. Gasket
15. Bolt
16. Metal collar
17. Rubber grommet
18. Air box
19. Element holder
20. Air filter
21. Cap
22. Nut

immediately. Check the muffler frame mounting flanges for fractures and loose bolts. Check the cylinder head mounting flange for tightness. A loose exhaust pipe connection will cause excessive exhaust noise and rob the engine of power.

The exhaust system is a 2-piece system that consists of an exhaust pipe and a one-piece tailpipe and muffler assembly. Refer to **Figure 66** for 3-wheeled models or **Figure 67** for 4-wheeled models.

7

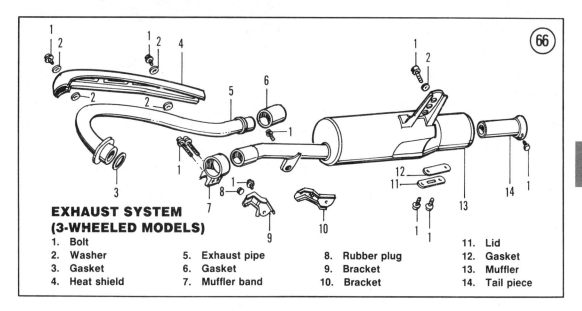

EXHAUST SYSTEM (3-WHEELED MODELS)

1. Bolt		11. Lid
2. Washer	5. Exhaust pipe	8. Rubber plug	12. Gasket
3. Gasket	6. Gasket	9. Bracket	13. Muffler
4. Heat shield	7. Muffler band	10. Bracket	14. Tail piece

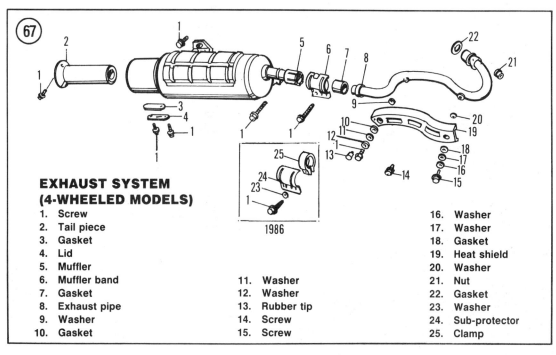

EXHAUST SYSTEM (4-WHEELED MODELS)

1986

1. Screw		16. Washer
2. Tail piece		17. Washer
3. Gasket		18. Gasket
4. Lid		19. Heat shield
5. Muffler		20. Washer
6. Muffler band	11. Washer	21. Nut
7. Gasket	12. Washer	22. Gasket
8. Exhaust pipe	13. Rubber tip	23. Washer
9. Washer	14. Screw	24. Sub-protector
10. Gasket	15. Screw	25. Clamp

Removal/Installation

1. Place the ATV on level ground and set the parking brake or block the rear wheels so the vehicle will not roll in either direction.

NOTE
Removal of the rear fender is not necessary, but it does allow additional work room.

2. Remove the seat and the rear fenders as described in Chapter Fifteen.

3. Remove the nuts securing the exhaust pipe to the cylinder head. Refer to **Figure 68** for 3-wheeled models or **Figure 69** for 4-wheeled models.

4. On 1986 3-wheeled models, remove the bolts securing the exhaust pipe sub-protector and remove the sub-protector.

5. On all other models, loosen the bolts at the clamping band securing the tailpipe and muffler assembly to the exhaust pipe. Refer to **Figure 70** for 3-wheeled models or **Figure 71** for 4-wheeled models.

6. Remove the exhaust pipe.

7. Remove the bolts securing the tailpipe and muffler assembly to the frame and remove the assembly. Refer to **Figure 72** for 3-wheeled models or **Figure 73** for 4-wheeled models.

8. Install by reversing these removal steps, noting the following.

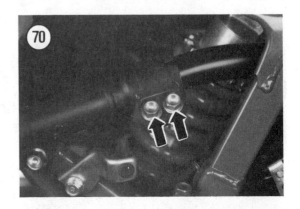

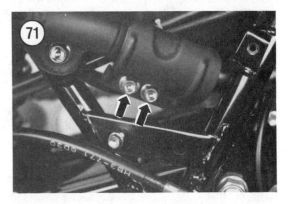

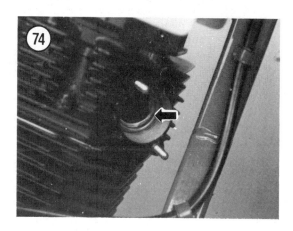

9. Inspect the gasket at the front of the tailpipe where the exhaust pipe joins; replace if necessary.

10. Make sure the cylinder head exhaust port gasket (**Figure 74**) is in place. Replace the gasket if necessary.

11. Tighten the nuts on the cylinder head first, then the bolts securing the tailpipe and muffler assembly to the frame. Tighten the clamping bolts last. This will minimize the chances of an exhaust leak at the cylinder head.

12. Tighten all nuts and bolts to the torque specifications listed in **Table 3**.

13. After installation is complete, start the engine and make sure there are no exhaust leaks.

Tables are on the following pages.

Table 1 CARBURETOR SPECIFICATIONS

Item	Fourtrax 200SX	ATC200X (1986)
Model No.	PD 63A	PD 64A
Main jet No.	98	122
Slow jet No.	35	35
Initial air (pilot)		
screw opening	1 1/2 turns out	2 turns out
Needle jet clip position	4th groove	Early, 2nd groove; Late, 3rd groove
Float level	14 mm (0.55 in.)	14 mm (0.55 in.)
Idle speed	1,400 ±100 rpm	1,400 ±100 rpm

	ATC200X (1987)
Model No.	PD 33AA
Main jet No.	122
Slow jet No.	35
Initial pilot screw opening	2 turns out
Needle jet clip position	2nd groove
Float level	14 mm (0.55 in.)
Idle speed	1,400 ±100 rpm

Table 2 HIGH ALTITUDE ADJUSTMENT

Model	Main jet size	Pilot screw setting from factory setting
TRX200SX	92	1/4 turn out
ATC200X		
1986	115	1/4 turn in
1987	108	1/4 turn in

Table 3 EXHAUST SYSTEM TORQUE SPECIFICATIONS

Item	N·m	ft.-lb.
Exhaust pipe-to-cylinder		
head nuts	10-14	7-10
Exhaust pipe clamp bolt		
1987 3-wheeled, all 4-wheeled	18-28	13-20
Muffler mounting bolts		
1986		
8 mm bolt	40-45	29-33
10 mm bolt	60-70	43-51
1987-on	60-70	43-51

CHAPTER EIGHT

ELECTRICAL SYSTEM

This chapter contains operating principles and service and test procedures for all electrical and ignition components. The battery and spark plugs are covered in Chapter Three.

The electrical system includes the following systems:

    a. Charging system (4-wheeled models).
    b. Ignition system.
    c. Lighting system.

Tables 1-4 are at the end of this chapter.

CHARGING SYSTEM (4-WHEELED MODELS)

The charging system consists of the battery, alternator and a solid-state voltage regulator (**Figure 1**).

Alternating current generated by the alternator is rectified to direct current. The voltage regulator maintains the voltage to the electrical load (lights, ignition, etc.) at a constant voltage regardless of variations in engine speed and load.

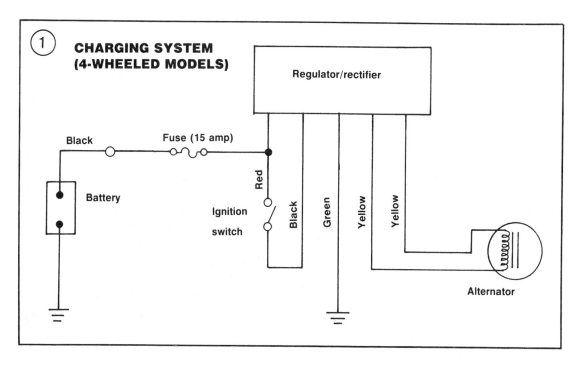

① CHARGING SYSTEM (4-WHEELED MODELS)

Regulator/rectifier

Black   Fuse (15 amp)

Red   Black   Green   Yellow   Yellow

Battery

Ignition switch

Alternator

Leak Test

1. Remove the seat as described in Chapter Fifteen.
2. Turn the ignition switch to the OFF position.
3. Disconnect the battery negative lead (**Figure 2**).
4. Connect a voltmeter between the battery negative terminal and the negative cable (**Figure 3**).
5. The voltmeter should read zero.
6. If there is a voltage reading, this indicates a voltage drain in the system that will drain the battery. Test the charging system as described in this chapter.
7. Disconnect the voltmeter and reconnect the battery negative lead.
8. Install the seat as described in Chapter Fifteen.

Charging System Test

Whenever charging system trouble is suspected, make sure the battery is fully charged and in good condition before going any further. Clean and test the battery as described under *Battery* in Chapter Three. Make sure all electrical connectors are tight and free of corrosion.

1. Start the engine and let it reach normal operating temperature; shut off the engine.
2. Connect a 0-15 volt DC voltmeter between the battery terminals. Do *not* disconnect the battery cables from the battery. With the engine off, there should be 12.4 volts present.
3. Start the engine and let it idle. Turn the headlight on.
4. Gradually increase engine speed and check voltage output at various engine speeds.
5. The voltage should be between 13.0-15.0 volts.
6. Shut the engine off.
7. If the charging voltage is greater than specified, perform the following:
   a. Turn the ignition switch on.
   b. Use a voltmeter and check the voltage between the black and the green terminals of the voltage regulator/rectifier. There should be battery voltage (12 volts).
   c. If there is no battery voltage, check for an open circuit (break or bad connection) in the black and the green wires in the wiring harness.
   d. If battery voltage is present, replace the voltage regulator/rectifier as described in this chapter.
8. If the charging voltage does not reach that specified even though engine speed increases, perform the following:
   a. Check the voltage regulator/rectifier electrical connector for loose or disconnected terminals.

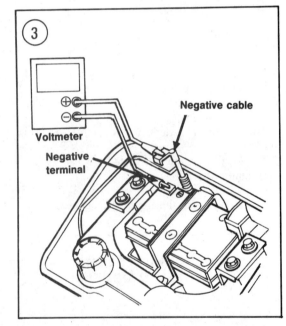

Voltmeter

Negative cable

Negative terminal

b. Use a voltmeter and check the voltage between the red (+) and green (–) terminals of the voltage regulator/rectifier. There should be battery voltage (12 volts).

c. If there is no battery voltage, check for an open circuit in the red and green wires in the wiring harness.

d. If battery voltage is present, inspect the charging coil of the alternator rotor as described in this chapter.

9. Disconnect the voltmeter from the battery.

VOLTAGE REGULATOR

Testing

1. Remove the seat and rear fender as described in Chapter Fifteen.

2. Remove the electrical junction box cover (**Figure 4**).

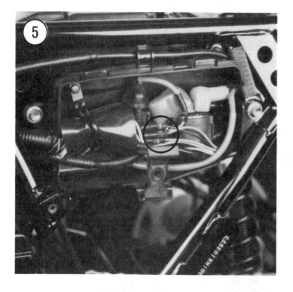

3. Disconnect the electrical connectors (2 yellow, one green, one red, and one black) going to the voltage regulator (**Figure 5**).

CAUTION
Tests may be performed on the voltage regulator unit but a good one may be damaged by someone unfamiliar with the test equipment. If you feel unqualified to perform the test, have the test made by a Honda dealer or substitute a known good unit for a suspected one.

NOTE
Tests must be made with a good quality ohmmeter (Kowa Tester TH-5H or equivalent) or the test readings may be false.

4. Make measurements using a good quality ohmmeter. Refer to **Table 1** for ohmmeter positive (+) and negative (–) test lead placement, wire color and specified resistance values.

5. If the voltage regulator fails any of these tests the unit is faulty and must be replaced.

Removal/Installation

1. Place the ATV on level ground and set the parking brake.

2. Remove the seat and the rear fenders as described in Chapter Fifteen.

3. Disconnect the battery negative lead (**Figure 2**).

4. Remove the junction box cover (**Figure 4**).

5. Disconnect the electrical connectors (**Figure 5**) going to the voltage regulator from the wiring harness.

6. Remove the nuts (**Figure 6**) securing the voltage regulator to the frame and remove the voltage regulator.

7. Install by reversing these removal steps, noting the following.

8. Make sure all electrical connectors are free of corrosion and are tight.

ALTERNATOR

Alternator rotor and stator assembly removal and installation procedures are covered in Chapter Four.

Stator Coil Testing
(3-wheeled Models)

It is not necessary to remove the stator plate to perform the following tests. Disconnect the electrical connector from the alternator and make the following checks on the alternator side of the electrical connector.

8

In order to get accurate resistance measurements the stator assembly and coil must be warm (minimum temperature is 20° C−68° F). If necessary, start the engine and let it warm up to normal operating temperature.

Exciter coil resistance check

The exciter coil is used in the ignition system.
1. Remove the seat as described in Chapter Fifteen.
2. Disconnect the multi-pin electrical connectors from the CDI unit (**Figure 7**).
3. Use an ohmmeter set at R×10 and check resistance between the black/red wire terminal in the electrical connector and ground. The specified resistance is 50-200 ohms.
4. If the indicated resistance is not within specifications, perform the following:
   a. Disconnect the individual black/red electrical connector from the multi-pin electrical connector going to the CDI unit.
   b. Use an ohmmeter set at R×10 and check resistance between the end of the black/red wire and ground. The specified resistance is 50-200 ohms.
5. If there is continuity (indicated resistance) and it is within the specified resistance, the exciter coil is good. If there is no continuity (infinite resistance) or the resistance is less than specified, the coil is bad and the stator assembly must be replaced (the individual coil cannot be replaced).

Lighting coil resistance check

1. Disconnect the lighting coil white electrical connector containing 2 wires (1 white/yellow and 1 green) (**Figure 7**).
2. Use an ohmmeter set at R×10 and check resistance between the white/yellow wire and the green wire terminals in the electrical connector. The specified resistance is 0.1-1.0 ohms.
3. If there is continuity (indicated resistance) and it is within the specified resistance, the coil is good.
4. If there is no continuity (infinite resistance) or the resistance is less than specified, check the following:
   a. Use an ohmmeter and check for an open circuit in the 2 wires between the lighting switch and the AC regulator.
   b. Use an ohmmeter and check for an open circuit in the 2 wires between the AC regulator and the alternator.
   c. If there is no continuity (infinite resistance) repair or replace the circuit wires.
5. If the wire harness is in good condition and the resistance is still not within specifications, the coil

is bad and the stator assembly must be replaced (the individual coil cannot be replaced).

Stator Coil Testing
(4-wheeled Models)

It is not necessary to remove the stator plate to perform the following tests. Disconnect the electrical connector from the alternator and make the following checks on the alternator side of the electrical connector.

In order to get accurate resistance measurements the stator assembly and coil must be warm (minimum temperature is 20° C−68° F). If necessary, start the engine and let it warm up to normal operating temperature.

Exciter coil resistance check

The exciter coil is used in the ignition system.
1. Remove the seat and the rear fender as described in Chapter Fifteen.
2. Remove the junction box cover (**Figure 4**).
3. Disconnect the exciter coil electrical connectors, one black/red and one green/white (**Figure 5**).
4. Use an ohmmeter set at R×100 and check resistance between the black/red wire and the green/white wire on the alternator side of the wire harness. The specified resistance is 100-300 ohms.
5. If there is continuity (indicated resistance) and it is within specifications the coil is good. If there is no continuity (infinite resistance) or the resistance is less than specified, the coil is bad and the stator assembly must be replaced (the individual coil cannot be replaced).

Charging coil resistance check

1. Remove the seat and the rear fender as described in Chapter Fifteen.
2. Remove the junction box cover (**Figure 4**).
3. Disconnect the charging coil yellow electrical connectors (**Figure 5**).

4. Use an ohmmeter set at R×10 and check resistance between the 2 yellow wires on the alternator side of the wire harness. The specified resistance is 0.1-1.0 ohms.

5. If there is continuity (indicated resistance) and it is within specifications, the coil is good. If there is no continuity (infinite resistance) or the resistance is less than specified, the coil is bad and the stator assembly must be replaced (the individual coil cannot be replaced).

6. Use an ohmmeter set at R×10 and check resistance between each yellow wire and ground. If there is continuity (indicated resistance) between any yellow wire and ground, the coil is shorted and the stator assembly must be replaced (the individual coil cannot be replaced).

Lighting coil resistance check

Honda does not provide service information for the lighting coil on this model.

CAPACITOR DISCHARGE IGNITION

All models are equipped with a capacitor discharge ignition (CDI) system, a solid-state system that uses no breaker points.

Alternating current from the alternator is rectified to direct current and is used to charge the capacitor. As the piston approaches the firing position, a pulse from the exciter coil is used to trigger the silicon controlled rectifier. The rectifier in turn allows the capacitor to discharge quickly into the primary circuit of the ignition coil, where the voltage is stepped up in the secondary circuit to a value sufficient to fire the spark plug.

The ignition systems used among the different models are shown in the following diagrams:

  a. 3-wheeled models: **Figure 8**.
  b. 4-wheeled models: **Figure 9**.

CDI Precautions

Certain measures must be taken to protect the capacitor discharge system. Instantaneous damage to the semiconductors in the system will occur if the following precautions are not observed.

1. Never disconnect any of the electrical connections while the engine is running.

2. Keep all connections between the various units clean and tight. Be sure that the wiring connectors are pushed together firmly to help keep out moisture.

8

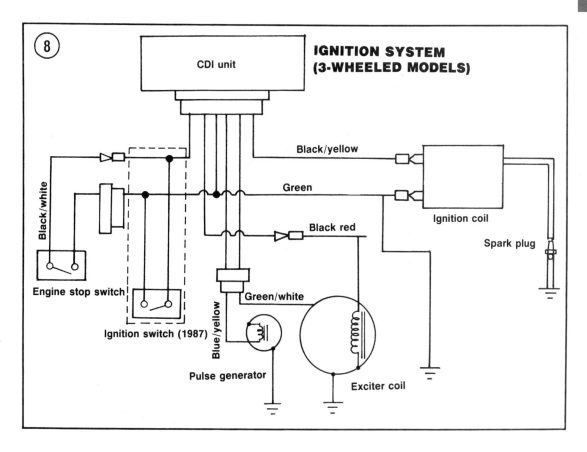

⑧ IGNITION SYSTEM (3-WHEELED MODELS)

CDI unit — Black/yellow — Green — Black red — Ignition coil — Spark plug — Black/white — Engine stop switch — Ignition switch (1987) — Blue/yellow — Green/white — Pulse generator — Exciter coil

3. Do not substitute another type of ignition coil.

4. The CDI unit is mounted within a rubber vibration isolator. Always be sure that the isolator is in place when installing the unit.

CDI Troubleshooting

Problems with the capacitor discharge system fall into one of the following categories. See **Table 2.**

    a. Weak spark.

    b. No spark.

CDI Testing
(3-wheeled Models)

NOTE
This procedure covers only 3-wheeled models. Honda does not provide information test procedures for the 4-wheeled models. If you suspect a faulty CDI unit, take your vehicle to a dealer and have them test it. Chances are they will perform a "remove and replace" test (substitute a known good unit) to see if the CDI unit is faulty. This type of test is expensive if performed by individual owners.

*Remember, if you purchase a new CDI unit and it does **not** solve your particular ignition system problem, you cannot return the CDI unit for refund. Most motorcycle dealers will **not** accept returns on any electrical component since the component could be damaged internally even though it looks okay externally.*

Honda does not recommend the CDI test procedures previously used by the factory. This test procedure was to measure the resistance values between the various connector pins on the CDI unit. This inspection method has been determined to be unreliable because of the following:

    a. The wrong type of multimeter was used and would give incorrect resistance value readings.

    b. The multimeter's battery voltage was low and would result in an incorrect resistance value reading.

    c. Human error in performing the test and/or misreading the specifications in the resistance value reading table.

    d. Varying manufacturing tolerances among the different CDI units of the same type for the same model.

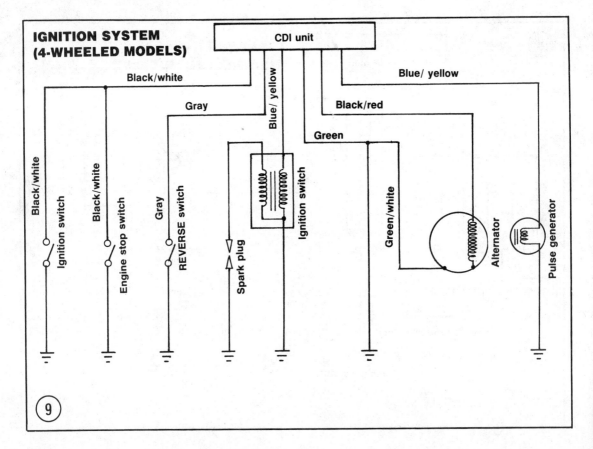

IGNITION SYSTEM (4-WHEELED MODELS)

1. Test the CDI's unit ability to produce a spark. Perform the following:

   a. Disconnect the high voltage lead from the spark plug. Remove the spark plug from the cylinder head.

   b. Connect a new or known good spark plug to the high voltage lead. Place the spark plug base on a good ground like the engine cylinder head (**Figure 10**). Position the spark plug so you can see the electrodes.

   WARNING
   If it is necessary to hold the high voltage lead, do so with an insulated pair of pliers. The high voltage generated by the CDI could produce serious or fatal shocks.

   NOTE
   *The engine must be kicked over **rapidly** since the ignition system does not produce a spark at a low rpm.*

   c. Kick the engine over rapidly with the kickstarter and check for a spark. If there is a fat blue spark, the CDI is okay.

   d. If a weak spark or no spark is produced, continue this procedure.

   e. Reinstall the spark plug and connect the high voltage lead to the spark plug.

2. Remove the seat as described in Chapter Fifteen.

3. Remove the fuel tank as described in Chapter Seven.

4. Carefully pull the CDI unit and its rubber isolator (**Figure 11**) from the tab on the frame.

5. Disconnect the electrical connector(s) (**Figure 12**) from the backside of the CDI unit.

   NOTE
   For best results, in the following step use a quality digital multimeter (Honda part No. KS-AHM-32-003) or equivalent. Install a fresh battery in the multimeter before performing these tests.

   NOTE
   *Make the resistance check between the electrical connector terminals on the **wire harness side** of the electrical connector. Do **not** perform these tests on the terminals of the CDI unit.*

6. Use an ohmmeter and check for continuity between the black/white and green wires as follows:.

   a. Turn the ignition switch and engine kill switch to the OFF position. There should be continuity (low resistance).

   b. Leave the ignition switch in the OFF position and turn the engine kill switch to the RUN position. There should be continuity (low resistance).

   c. Turn the ignition switch to the ON position and engine kill switch to the OFF position. There should be continuity (low resistance).

   d. Turn the ignition switch to the ON position and engine kill switch to the RUN position. There should be no continuity (infinite resistance).

7. If any of the continuity checks failed in Step 6, then check the following:

   a. Check for an open or short in the wire harness between each component.

   b. Make sure all connections between the various components are clean and tight. Be sure that the wiring connectors are pushed together firmly to help keep out moisture.

8

8. If the wiring harness checks out okay, then test and inspect the following ignition system components as described in this chapter.

    a. Ignition switch.

    b. Engine stop switch.

> *NOTE*
> *For best results, in the following step use a quality digital multimeter (Honda part No. KS-AHM-32-003) or equivalent. Install a fresh battery in the multimeter before performing these tests.*

> *NOTE*
> *Make the resistance check between the electrical connector terminals on the **wire harness side** of the electrical connector. Do **not** perform these tests on the terminals of the CDI unit.*

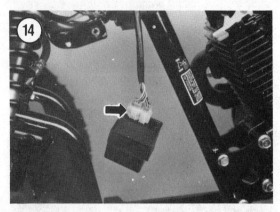

9. Use an ohmmeter and check the resistance value between the black/yellow and green wire terminals. The specified resistance is 0.1-0.3 ohms. If the resistance value is not within these specifications, inspect the ignition coil as described in this chapter.

10. Use an ohmmeter and check the resistance value between the blue/yellow and green/white wire terminals. The specified resistance is 290-360 ohms. If the resistance value is not within these specifications, inspect the pulse generator as described in this chapter.

11. Use an ohmmeter and check the resistance value between the black/red wire terminal and ground. The specified resistance is 50-200 ohms. If the resistance value is not within these specifications, inspect the alternator exciter coil as described in this chapter.

12. If the CDI unit passes all tests in Steps 1-11, it is faulty and must be replaced as described in this chapter.

Replacement

1. Remove the fuel tank as described in Chapter Seven.

2. Remove the CDI unit and the rubber isolator attached to the frame. Refer to **Figure 11** for 3-wheeled models or **Figure 13** for 4-wheeled models.

3. Disconnect the electrical wires from the CDI unit. Refer to **Figure 12** for 3-wheeled models or **Figure 14** for 4-wheeled models.

4. Install a new CDI unit into the rubber isolator and attach the electrical wires to it.

5. Reinstall all items removed.

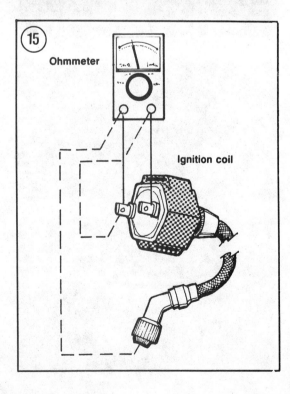

Ohmmeter

Ignition coil

IGNITION COIL

Testing

The ignition coil is a form of transformer which develops the high voltage required to jump the spark plug gap. The only maintenance required is that of keeping the electrical connections clean and tight and occasionally checking to see that the coil is mounted securely.

If the condition of the coil is doubtful, there are several checks which may be made.

As a quick check of coil condition, disconnect the high voltage lead from the spark plug. Remove the spark plug from the cylinder head. Connect a new or known good spark plug to the high voltage lead and place the spark plug base on a good ground like the engine cylinder head (**Figure 10**). Position the spark plug so you can see the electrode.

> *WARNING*
> *If it is necessary to hold the high voltage lead, do so with an insulated pair of pliers. The high voltage generated by the CDI could produce serious or fatal shocks.*

Turn the engine over with the recoil starter or kickstarter. If a fat blue spark occurs the coil is in good condition; if not, proceed as follows. Make sure that you are using a known good spark plug for this test. If the spark plug used is defective the test results will be incorrect.

Reinstall the spark plug in the cylinder head. Refer to **Figure 15** for this procedure.

> *NOTE*
> *In order to get accurate resistance measurements the coil must be warm (minimum temperature is 20° C—68° F). If necessary, start the engine and let it warm up to normal operating temperature. If the engine won't start and air temperature is below the minimum, warm the ignition coil with a hair drier.*

1. Measure the coil primary resistance using an ohmmeter set at R×1. Measure the resistance between the 2 primary terminals. The value should be as follows:

 a. 3-wheeled models: 0.10-0.30 ohms.

 b. 4-wheeled models: 0.16-0.20 ohms.

2. Disconnect the high voltage lead (spark plug lead) from the spark plug.
3. With the spark plug cap still installed to the high voltage lead (spark plug lead), measure the secondary resistance using an ohmmeter set at R×1,000. Measure the resistance between the secondary lead (spark plug lead) and the green terminal on the ignition coil. The value should be as follows:

 a. 3-wheeled models: 7.4-11.1 k (7,400-11,100) ohms.

 b. 4-wheeled models: Information not available from Honda.

4. Remove the spark plug cap from the secondary lead. Measure the secondary resistance using an ohmmeter set at R×1,000. Measure the resistance between the secondary lead (spark plug cap) and the black terminal on the ignition coil. The value should be 3.7-4.5 k (3,700-4,500) ohms for all models.
5. On 4-wheeled models, perform the following:

 a. Remove the spark plug cap from the secondary lead.

 b. Measure the resistance of the spark plug cap from end-to-end.

 c. The value should be 3.75-6.25 k (3,750-6,250) ohms.

6. Install the spark plug cap onto the secondary lead. Make sure it is on tight.
7. If the coil resistance does not meet specifications, the coil must be replaced. If the coil exhibits visible damage, it should be replaced.
8. Reconnect all ignition coil wires to the ignition coil.

Removal/Installation (3-wheeled Models)

1. Place the ATV on level ground and set the parking brake.
2. Remove the fuel tank as described in Chapter Seven.
3. Carefully pull the ignition coil out of the rubber isolator on the frame (**Figure 16**).

4. Disconnect the electrical wires (**Figure 17**) from the ignition coil and remove the coil.

5. Disconnect the high voltage lead from the spark plug (**Figure 18**).

6. Install by reversing these removal steps, noting the following.

7. Make sure all electrical connections are tight and free of corrosion.

Removal/Installation (4-wheeled Models)

1. Place the ATV on level ground and set the parking brake.

2. Remove the fuel tank as described in Chapter Seven.

3. Carefully pull the ignition coil out of the rubber isolator on the frame (**Figure 19**).

4. Disconnect the electrical wires (A, **Figure 20**) from the ignition coil and remove the coil.

5. Remove the high voltage lead from the clip (B, **Figure 20**) on the cylinder head cover.

6. Disconnect the high voltage lead from the spark plug (C, **Figure 20**).

7. Install by reversing these removal steps, noting the following.

8. Make sure all electrical connections are tight and free of corrosion.

IGNITION PULSE GENERATOR

Inspection

> *NOTE*
> *In order to get accurate resistance measurements the unit must be warm (minimum temperature is 20°–68° F). If necessary, start the engine and let it warm up to normal operating temperature. If the engine won't run and air temperature is below the minimum, warm the unit with a hair drier.*

1. Place the ATV on level ground and set the parking brake.

2A. On 3-wheeled models, perform the following:

   a. Remove the seat/rear fender assembly as described in Chapter Fifteen.

   b. Disconnect the electrical connector from the ignition pulse generator (**Figure 7**).

   c. Use an ohmmeter set at R×100 and measure the resistance between the blue/yellow and green/white wire terminals in the electrical connector. The specified resistance is 290-360 ohms. If the coil resistance does not meet this specification or there is no continuity (infinite resistance) the unit is bad and must be replaced.

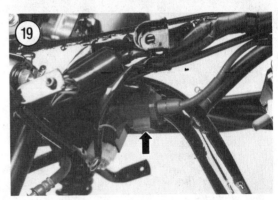

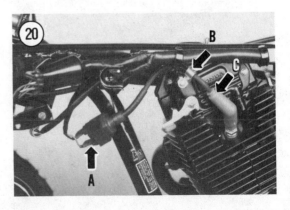

2B. On 4-wheeled models, perform the following:
a. Remove the rear fenders as described in Chapter Fifteen.
b. Remove the junction box cover (**Figure 4**).
c. Disconnect the electrical connector from the ignition pulse generator.
d. Use an ohmmeter set at $R \times 100$ and measure the resistance between the blue/yellow and green wire terminals in the electrical connector. The specified resistance is 357-393 ohms. If the coil resistance does not meet this specification or there is no continuity (infinite resistance) the unit is bad and must be replaced.

3. Reconnect the pulse generator electrical connector and the junction box cover on 4-wheeled models.

4. Install the seat/rear fender assembly (3-wheeled models) or rear fenders (4-wheeled models) as described in Chapter Fifteen.

STARTING SYSTEM (4-WHEELED MODELS)

The starting system consists of the starter motor, starter gears, solenoid and the starter button.

The layout of the starting system is shown in **Figure 21**. When the starter button is pressed, it engages the starter solenoid switch that completes the circuit allowing electricity to flow from the battery to the starter motor.

> *CAUTION*
> *Do not operate the starter for more than 5 seconds at a time. Let it rest approximately 10 seconds, then use it again.*

The starter gears are covered in Chapter Four. **Table 3**, at the end of the chapter, lists possible starter problems, probable causes and the most common remedies.

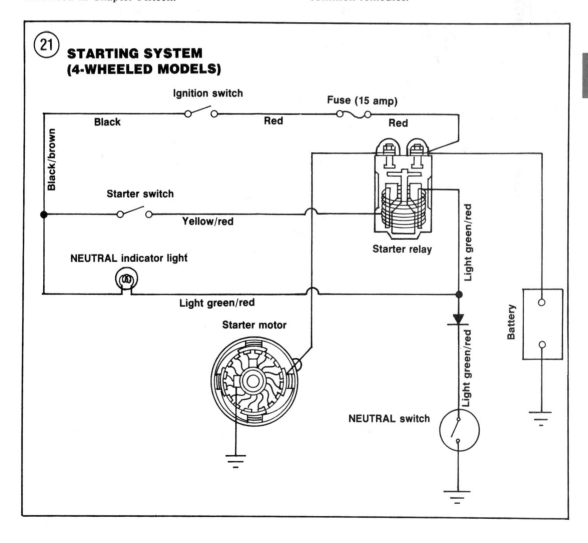

STARTING SYSTEM (4-WHEELED MODELS)

Starter Removal/Installation

1. Place the ATV on level ground and set the parking brake.
2. Remove the seat as described in Chapter Fifteen.
3. Remove the fuel tank as described in Chapter Seven.
4. Disconnect the battery negative lead (**Figure 2**).
5. Remove the left-hand crankcase cover as described under *Left-hand Crankcase Cover Removal (4-wheeled Models)* in Chapter Four.

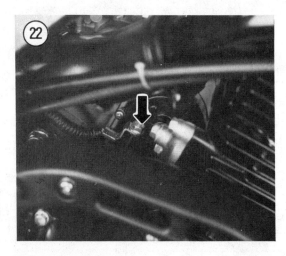

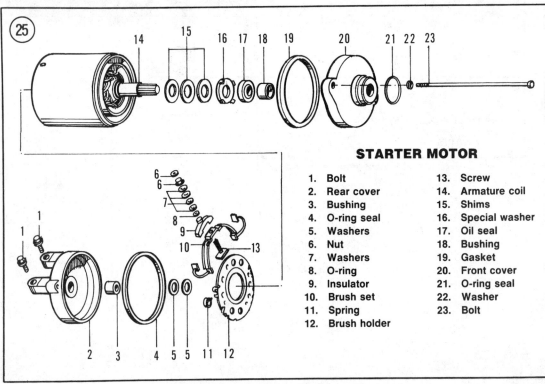

STARTER MOTOR

1.	Bolt	13. Screw
2.	Rear cover	14. Armature coil
3.	Bushing	15. Shims
4.	O-ring seal	16. Special washer
5.	Washers	17. Oil seal
6.	Nut	18. Bushing
7.	Washers	19. Gasket
8.	O-ring	20. Front cover
9.	Insulator	21. O-ring seal
10.	Brush set	22. Washer
11.	Spring	23. Bolt
12.	Brush holder	

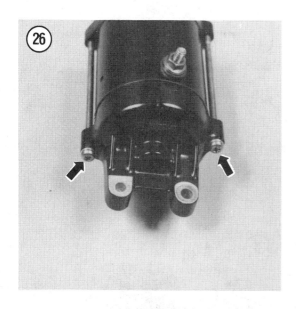

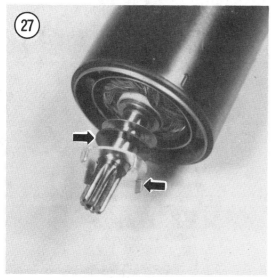

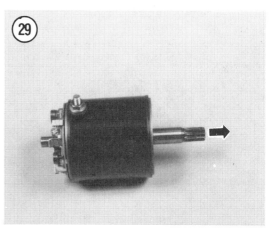

6. Remove the bolts securing the starter to the crankcase. The ground cable is attached to one of the rear mounting bolts (**Figure 22**).

7. Disconnect the starter electrical cable from the starter (A, **Figure 23**).

8. Lift up and remove the starter (B, **Figure 23**) from the top of the crankcase.

9. Install by reversing these removal steps.

Starter Preliminary Inspection

The overhaul of a starter motor is best left to an expert. This procedure shows how to detect a defective starter.

Inspect the O-ring seal (A, **Figure 24**). O-ring seals tend to harden after prolonged use and heat and therefore lose their ability to seal properly; replace as necessary.

Inspect the gear (B, **Figure 24**) for chipped or missing teeth. If damaged, the starter assembly must be replaced.

Starter Disassembly

Refer to **Figure 25** for this procedure.

1. Remove the case screws and washers (**Figure 26**), then separate the front and rear covers from the case.

NOTE
Write down the number of shims used on the shaft next to the commutator and next to the rear cover. Be sure to install the same number when reassembling the starter.

2. Remove the special washer and shims (**Figure 27**) from the front cover end of the shaft.

3. Remove the washers (**Figure 28**) from the armature end of the shaft.

4. Withdraw the armature coil assembly (**Figure 29**) from the front end of the case.

8

5. Remove the brush holder assembly (**Figure 30**) from the end of the case.

> *NOTE*
> *Before removing the nuts and washers, write down their description and order. They must be reinstalled in the same order to insulate this set of brushes from the case.*

6. Remove the nuts, washers and O-ring (A, **Figure 31**) securing the brush terminal set. Remove the brush terminal set (B, **Figure 31**).

> *CAUTION*
> *Do not immerse the wire windings in the case or the armature coil in solvent as the insulation may be damaged. Wipe the windings with a cloth lightly moistened with solvent and dry thoroughly.*

7. Clean all grease, dirt and carbon from all components.

Starter Assembly

1. Install the brush holder assembly (**Figure 32**).

> *NOTE*
> *In the next step, reinstall all parts in the same order as noted during removal. This is essential in order to insulate this set of brushes from the case.*

2. Install the O-ring, washers and nuts (A, **Figure 31**) securing the brush terminal set to the case.
3. Install the brush holder assembly (**Figure 30**) onto the end of the case. Align the holder locating tab with the case notch (**Figure 33**).
4. Install the brushes into their receptacles (**Figure 34**).
5. Install the brush springs (**Figure 35**), but do not place them against the brushes at this time.

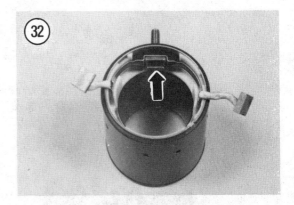

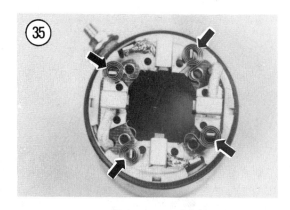

6. Insert the armature coil assembly (**Figure 29**) into the front end of the case. Do not damage the brushes during this step.

7. Bring the end of the spring up and onto the backside of the brush. Refer to **Figure 36** and **Figure 37** for correct spring-to-brush installation. Repeat for all remaining brushes.

8. Install the washers (**Figure 28**) onto the armature end of the shaft.

9. Align the raised tab on the brush holder with the locating notch (**Figure 38**) in the rear cover and install the rear cover.

10. Align the raised marks (**Figure 39**) on the rear cover with the case.

11. Install the shims and special washer (**Figure 27**) onto the front cover end of the shaft.

12. Install the front cover (A, **Figure 40**), then the case screws and washers (B, **Figure 40**). Tighten the screws securely.

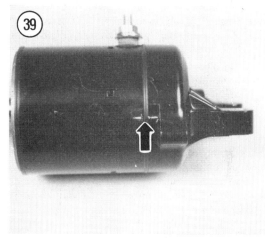

8

Starter Inspection

1. Measure the length of each brush (**Figure 41**) with a vernier caliper. If the length is 6.5 mm (0.26 in.) or less for any one of the brushes, the brush holder assembly and brush terminal set must be replaced. The brushes cannot be replaced individually.

2. Inspect the commutator (**Figure 42**). The mica in a good commutator is below the surface of the copper bars. On a worn commutator the mica and copper bars may be worn to the same level (**Figure 43**). If necessary, have the commutator serviced by a dealer or electrical repair shop.

3. Inspect the commutator copper bars for discoloration. If a pair of bars are discolored, grounded armature coils are indicated.

4. Use an ohmmeter and perform the following:
   a. Check for continuity between the commutator bars (**Figure 44**); there should be continuity (indicated resistance) between pairs of bars.
   b. Check for continuity between the commutator bars and the shaft (**Figure 45**); there should be *no* continuity (infinite resistance).
   c. If the unit fails either of these tests, the starter assembly must be replaced. The armature cannot be replaced individually.

5. Use an ohmmeter and perform the following:
   a. Check for continuity between the starter cable terminal and the starter case; there should be continuity (indicated resistance).
   b. Check for continuity between the starter cable terminal and the brush wire terminal; there should be *no* continuity (infinite resistance).
   c. If the unit fails either of these tests, the starter assembly must be replaced. The case/field coil assembly cannot be replaced individually.

6. Inspect the oil seal and bushing (**Figure 46**) in the front cover for wear or damage. If either is damaged, replace the starter assembly as these parts are not available separately.

7. Inspect the bushing (**Figure 47**) in the rear cover for wear or damage. If it is damaged, replace the starter assembly as this part is not available separately.

STARTER SOLENOID
(4-WHEELED MODELS)

Testing

1. Remove the seat and rear fenders as described in Chapter Fifteen.
2. Remove the junction box cover (**Figure 48**).
3. Shift the transmission into NEUTRAL.

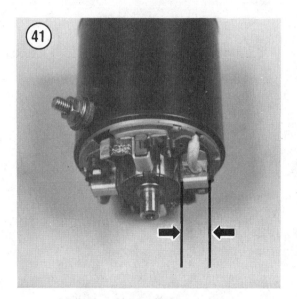

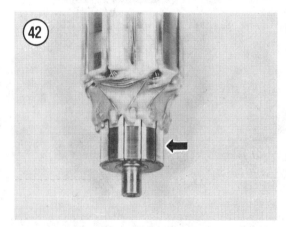

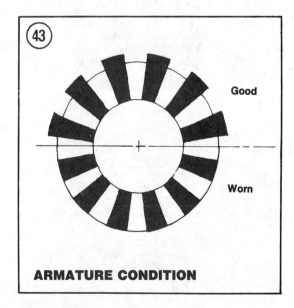

ARMATURE CONDITION

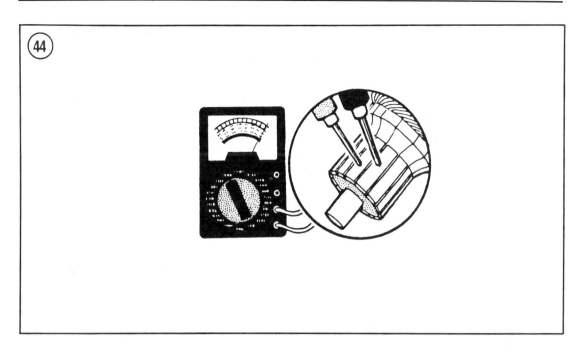

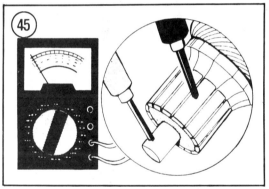

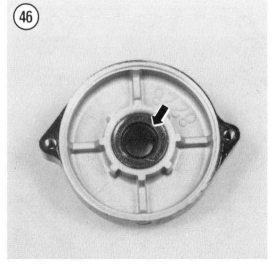

4. Turn the ignition switch ON.

5. Press the START button. The solenoid should click. If it does not click, the solenoid may be faulty and should be checked further.

6. Slide off the rubber protective boots and disconnect the electrical wires (**Figure 49**) from the terminals on top of the solenoid.

7. Disconnect the electrical connector from the starter solenoid.

8. Connect a 12-volt battery to the electrical connectors as follows (**Figure 50**):

   a. Yellow/red wire to the positive (+) battery terminal.

   b. Light green/red wire to the negative (–) battery terminal.

9. With the 12-volt battery connected, connect an ohmmeter between the positive and negative terminals on top of the solenoid and check for continuity. If there is continuity (low resistance) the solenoid is okay. If there is no continuity (infinite resistance), the solenoid is faulty and must be replaced.

10. Disconnect the 12-volt battery from the electrical connectors.

11. Install both electrical wires to the solenoid and tighten the nuts securely. Make sure the electrical connectors are on tight and that the rubber boot is properly installed to keep out moisture.

Removal/Installation

1. Remove the seat and rear fender as described in Chapter Fifteen.

2. Remove the junction box cover (**Figure 48**).

3. Disconnect the battery negative lead (**Figure 51**).

4. Slide off the rubber protective boots and disconnect the electrical wires (**Figure 49**) from the top terminals of the solenoid.

5. Remove the solenoid from the rubber mount on the frame.

6. Replace by reversing these removal steps, noting the following.

7. Install both electrical wires to the solenoid and tighten the nuts securely. Make sure the electrical

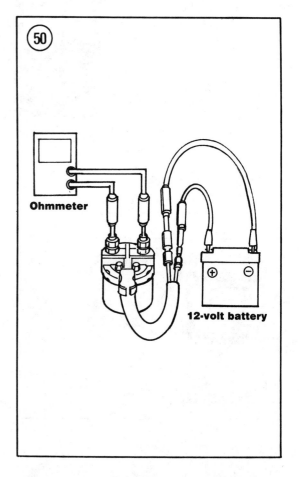

Ohmmeter

12-volt battery

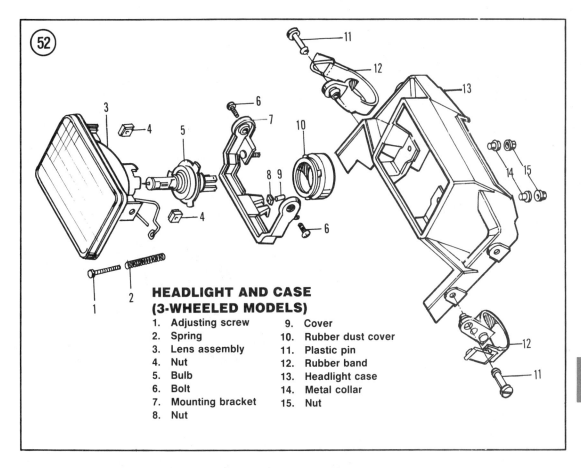

**HEADLIGHT AND CASE
(3-WHEELED MODELS)**

1. Adjusting screw
2. Spring
3. Lens assembly
4. Nut
5. Bulb
6. Bolt
7. Mounting bracket
8. Nut
9. Cover
10. Rubber dust cover
11. Plastic pin
12. Rubber band
13. Headlight case
14. Metal collar
15. Nut

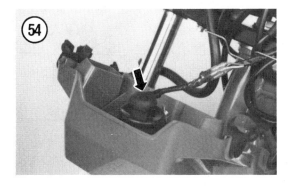

connectors are on tight and that the rubber boot is properly installed to keep out moisture.

LIGHTING SYSTEM

The lighting system consists of a headlight, taillight and indicator lights (4-wheeled models only). **Table 4** lists replacement bulbs for these components.

Always use the correct wattage bulb as indicated in this section. The use of a larger wattage bulb will give a dim light and a smaller wattage bulb will burn out prematurely.

**Headlight Replacement
and Headlight Case
Removal/Installation
(3-wheeled Models)**

Refer to **Figure 52** for this procedure.

1. Unhook the case rubber band (**Figure 53**) on each side securing the headlight case to each fork leg.

2. Pull the headlight case down and set it on the front fender.

3. Disconnect the electrical connector (**Figure 54**) from the backside of the bulb.

4. Remove the rubber dust cover (**Figure 55**).

CAUTION
Carefully read all instructions shipped with the replacement quartz bulb. Do not touch the bulb glass with your fingers because any traces of skin oil on the quartz halogen bulb will drastically reduce bulb life. Clean any traces of oil from the bulb with a cloth moistened in alcohol or lacquer thinner.

5. Unhook the clip (**Figure 56**) and remove the light bulb; replace with a new bulb.
6. To remove the headlight lens assembly, perform the following:
   a. Remove the adjusting screw (A, **Figure 57**) and the headlight mounting nuts (B, **Figure 57**).
   b. Remove the headlight assembly from the headlight case.
   c. Remove the screw on each side securing the headlight lens assembly to the headlight mounting bracket and remove the headlight lens assembly.
7. Install by reversing these removal steps.

Headlight Replacement
(4-wheeled Models)

Refer to **Figure 58** for this procedure.
1. Remove the bolt (A, **Figure 59**) on each side securing the headlight lens and the headlight case and guard.
2. Pull the headlight lens unit (B, **Figure 59**) out of the case and set it an the front fender.
3. Disconnect the electrical connector from the backside of the bulb.
4. Remove the rubber dust cover.
5. Rotate the socket assembly and remove the socket assembly from the lens assembly.
6. Remove the light bulb and replace with a new bulb.
7. Install by reversing these removal steps, noting the following.
8. Install the dust cover with the UP mark facing up.

Headlight, Headlight Case
and Mounting Bracket
Removal/Installation
(4-wheeled Models)

1. Remove the headlight assembly as described in this chapter.
2. Remove the bolt (A, **Figure 59**) on each side securing the headlight case to the mounting bracket.

3. Pull the headlight case (B, **Figure 59**) forward and carefully work the electrical wires out the rear opening of the headlight case.
4. Remove the bolts securing the mounting bracket (A, **Figure 60**) to the upper fork bridge.
5. Carefully remove the control cables and hoses (B, **Figure 60**) from the mounting tabs on the headlight mounting bracket.
6. Remove the headlight mounting bracket from the lower fork bridge and remove the mounting bracket.
7. Install by reversing these removal steps.

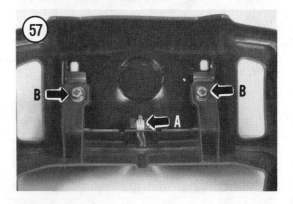

Taillight Replacement
(3-wheeled Models)

Refer to **Figure 61** for this procedure.

1. Remove the screws (**Figure 62**) securing the lens and remove the lens. Place your finger on the backside of the screw, as there is a loose nut that will fall off when the screw is removed.

2. Wash off the inside and outside of the lens with a mild detergent and wipe dry.

3. Inspect the lens gasket and replace it if damaged or deteriorated.

4. Remove the bulb from the socket and replace the bulb.

5. Make sure the metal collar is in place in the rubber mounting bracket on each side.

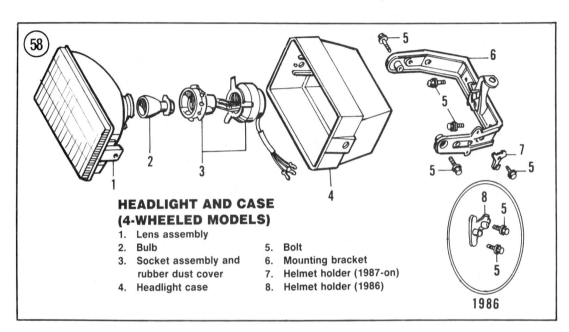

HEADLIGHT AND CASE
(4-WHEELED MODELS)
1. Lens assembly
2. Bulb
3. Socket assembly and rubber dust cover
4. Headlight case
5. Bolt
6. Mounting bracket
7. Helmet holder (1987-on)
8. Helmet holder (1986)

1986

8

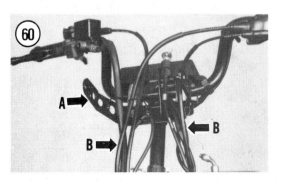

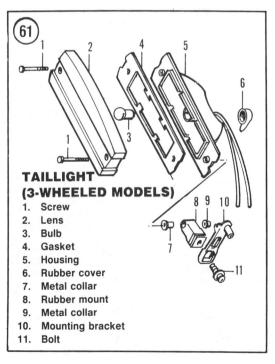

TAILLIGHT
(3-WHEELED MODELS)
1. Screw
2. Lens
3. Bulb
4. Gasket
5. Housing
6. Rubber cover
7. Metal collar
8. Rubber mount
9. Metal collar
10. Mounting bracket
11. Bolt

6. Install the lens. Do not overtighten the screws as the lens may crack.

Taillight Replacement (4-wheeled Models)

The taillight design was changed during the 1986 model year. The first taillight design was fitted to 1986 frame serial numbers TE030-GK000080 through GK054377. The later taillight design was fitted to the 1986 frame serial number TE030-GK054378 through GK064061 and all 1987-on models.

Refer to **Figure 63** for this procedure.

1986 frame serial numbers TE030-GK000080 through GK054377

1. Remove the screws securing the lens and remove the lens. Place your finger on the backside of the screw, as there is a loose washer and nut that will fall off when the screw is removed.
2. Wash off the inside and outside of the lens with a mild detergent and wipe dry.
3. Inspect the lens gasket and replace it if damaged or deteriorated.
4. Remove the bulb from the socket and replace the bulb.
5. Make sure the metal collar is in place in the rubber mounting bracket on each side.
6. Install the lens. Do not overtighten the screws as the lens may crack.

1986 frame serial number TE030-GK054378 through GK064061 and all 1987-on models

1. Carefully remove the plastic mounting pins (**Figure 64**) securing the rubber mount to the frame.
2. Disconnect the taillight electrical connectors (**Figure 65**).
3. Rotate the bulb socket assembly (**Figure 66**) out of the backside of the taillight assembly.

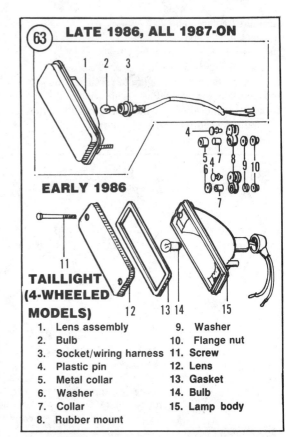

63 **LATE 1986, ALL 1987-ON**

EARLY 1986

TAILLIGHT (4-WHEELED MODELS)

1. Lens assembly
2. Bulb
3. Socket/wiring harness
4. Plastic pin
5. Metal collar
6. Washer
7. Collar
8. Rubber mount
9. Washer
10. Flange nut
11. Screw
12. Lens
13. Gasket
14. Bulb
15. Lamp body

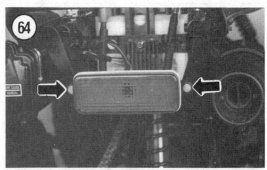

64

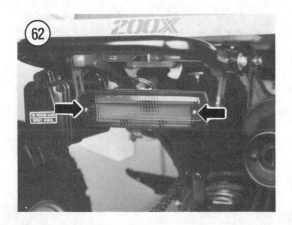

62

65

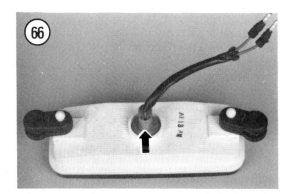

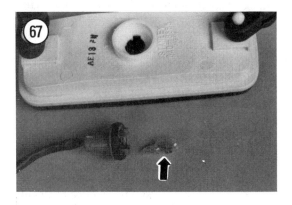

4. Carefully pull the bulb out of the socket (not a screw-in type bulb) and replace the bulb (**Figure 67**).

5. Insert the bulb socket assembly into the taillight assembly. Rotate the socket assembly and align the index arrows (**Figure 68**) on both parts.

6. Connect the taillight electrical connectors.

7. Install the taillight assembly onto the frame and install the plastic mounting pins.

Indicator Lights
(4-wheeled Models)

1. Carefully pry the trim strip (**Figure 69**) from the handlebar cover.

2. Remove the screws (**Figure 70**) securing the handlebar cover and move the cover off the handlebar.

3. Carefully withdraw the indicator light/socket assembly (A, **Figure 71**) from the handlebar cover.

4. Replace the bulb(s) and reinstall the handlebar cover and trim strip.

SWITCHES

Left-hand Combination Switch

The left-hand switch assembly is a combination switch containing the engine kill switch,

8

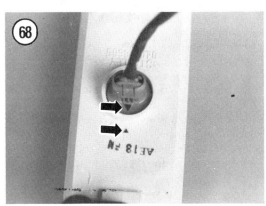

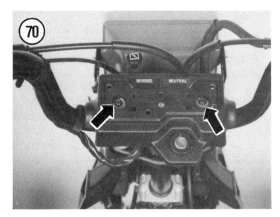

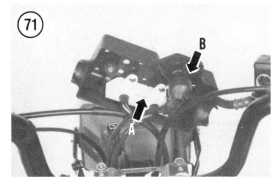

lighting/dimmer switch and on 4-wheeled models the starter switch. If any one part of the switch is faulty the entire switch assembly must be replaced. The individual switches are not serviceable.

Engine kill switch testing

1. Disconnect the electrical connectors from the engine kill switch (wire color black/white and green).
2. Use an ohmmeter set at R×1 and connect the 2 leads of the ohmmeter to these 2 electrical connectors of the switch.
3. Turn the kill switch button to one of the OFF positions. If the switch is good there will be continuity (low resistance).
4. Repeat Step 3 for the other OFF position.
5. Turn the switch to the RUN position. If the switch is good, there will be no continuity (infinite resistance).
6. If the switch fails either of these tests, the switch is faulty and must be replaced.

Lighting switch testing

1A. On 3-wheeled models, remove the headlight as described in this chapter. The electrical connectors are located within the headlight case.
1B. On 4-wheeled models, remove the front fenders as described in Chapter Fifteen. The electrical connections are located just ahead of the ignition coil.
2. Disconnect the electrical connectors from the lighting switch as follows:
    a. 3-wheeled models: white/yellow and brown.
    b. 4-wheeled models: black/brown and brown.
3. To test the lighting portion of the switch, use an ohmmeter set at R×1 and connect the 2 leads of the ohmmeter to the following electrical connectors of the switch:
    a. 3-wheeled models: white/yellow and brown.
    b. 4-wheeled models: black/brown and brown.
4. Turn the lighting switch to the ON position. If the switch is good, there will be continuity (low resistance).
5. Turn the switch to the OFF position. If the switch is good, there will be no continuity (infinite resistance).
6. If the switch fails either of these tests, the switch is faulty and the entire left-hand switch assembly must be replaced.

Dimmer switch testing

1A. On 3-wheeled models, remove the headlight as described in this chapter. The electrical connectors are located within the headlight case.

1B. On 4-wheeled models, remove the front fenders as described in Chapter Fifteen. The electrical connections are located just ahead of the ignition coil.
2. Disconnect the electrical connectors from the dimmer switch as follows:
    a. 3-wheeled models: brown, blue and white.
    b. 4-wheeled models: blue and white.
3. Turn the dimmer switch to the HI position. Use an ohmmeter set at R×1 and connect the 2 leads of the ohmmeter to the following electrical connectors of the switch:
    a. 3-wheeled models: brown and blue.
    b. 4-wheeled models: blue and the interconnector wire.
    c. If the switch is good, there will be continuity (low resistance).
4. Turn the lighting switch to the (N) position. Use an ohmmeter set at R×1 and connect the 2 leads of the ohmmeter to the following electrical connectors of the switch.
    a. 3-wheeled models: brown and blue, then brown and white and then blue and white.
    b. 4-wheeled models: blue and the interconnector wire, then blue and white and then white and the interconnector wire.
    c. If the switch is good, there will be continuity (low resistance).
5. Turn the lighting switch to the LO position. Use an ohmmeter set at R×1 and connect the 2 leads of the ohmmeter to the following electrical connectors of the switch.
    a. 3-wheeled models: brown and white.
    b. 4-wheeled models: white and the interconnector wire.
    c. If the switch is good, there will be continuity (low resistance).
6. If the switch fails any of these tests, the switch is faulty and the entire left-hand switch assembly must be replaced.

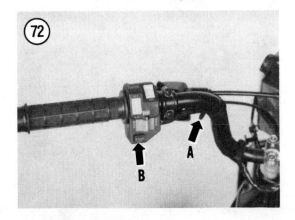

Starter switch testing (4-wheeled models)

1. Remove the front fenders as described in Chapter Fifteen. The electrical connections are located just ahead of the ignition coil.

2. Disconnect the black/brown and yellow/red electrical connectors from the starter switch.

3. Push in on the starter switch. Use an ohmmeter set at R×1 and connect the 2 leads of the ohmmeter to the black/brown and yellow/red electrical connectors of the switch.

4. If the switch is good, there will be continuity (low resistance).

5. If the switch fails this test, the switch is faulty and the entire left-hand switch assembly must be replaced.

Left-hand Combination Switch Removal/Installation

1A. On 3-wheeled models, remove the headlight as described in this chapter. The electrical connectors are located within the headlight case.

1B. On 4-wheeled models, remove the front fenders as described in Chapter Fifteen. The electrical connections are located just ahead of the ignition coil.

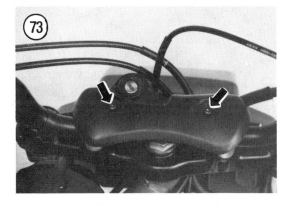

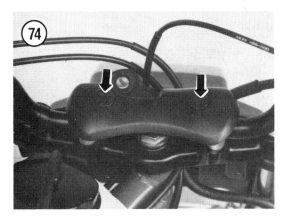

2. Disconnect all of the electrical connectors from the left-hand combination switch.

3. Remove the bands (A, **Figure 72**) securing the switch electrical harness to the handlebar and frame.

4. Remove the screws securing the left-hand switch assembly (B, **Figure 72**) together and separate the switch assembly.

5. Remove the switch assembly from the handlebar.

6. Install by reversing these removal steps, noting the following.

7. Make sure all electrical connectors are tight and free of corrosion.

Ignition Switch Testing (1987 3-wheeled Models)

1. Remove the seat/rear fender assembly as described in Chapter Fifteen.

2. Remove the fuel tank as described in Chapter Seven.

3. The electrical connectors are located next to the carburetor.

4. Disconnect the black and the green electrical connectors from the ignition switch.

5. Turn the ignition switch to the OFF position. Use an ohmmeter set at R×1 and connect the 2 leads of the ohmmeter to the black and green electrical connectors of the switch.

6. If the switch is good, there will be continuity (low resistance).

7. If the switch fails this test, the switch is faulty and the ignition switch assembly must be replaced.

Ignition Switch Removal/Installation (1987 3-wheeled Models)

> *CAUTION*
> *The caps are not a screw-on/off type.*
> *Rotate them slightly in either direction*
> *to release their locking lugs from the*
> *cover.*

1. Use a large coin and carefully rotate the caps (**Figure 73**) on the handlebar cover. Carefully pry the caps out of the handlebar cover and remove them.

2. Remove the bolts (**Figure 74**) securing the handlebar cover and remove the cover.

3. Remove the fuel tank as described in Chapter Seven.

4. Remove the headlight case as described in this chapter. The electrical connectors are located within the headlight case.

5. Disconnect the electrical connectors for the ignition switch within the headlight case. Carefully

withdraw the electrical wires from the backside of the headlight case.

6. Push the lugs on the ignition switch in and disengage the switch from the handlebar cover. Remove the ignition switch.

7. Install by reversing these removal steps, noting the following.

8. Make sure all electrical connectors are tight and free of corrosion.

Ignition Switch Testing (4-wheeled Models)

1. Remove the front fender assembly as described in Chapter Fifteen.

2. The electrical connectors are located next to the ignition coil.

3. Disconnect the black/white, green, red and black electrical connectors from the ignition switch.

4. Turn the ignition switch to the OFF position. Use an ohmmeter set at $R \times 1$ and connect the 2 leads of the ohmmeter to the black/white and green electrical connectors of the switch.

5. If the switch is good there will be continuity (low resistance).

6. Turn the ignition switch to the ON position. Use an ohmmeter set at $R \times 1$ and connect the 2 leads of the ohmmeter to the red and black electrical connectors of the switch.

7. If the switch is good, there will be continuity (low resistance).

8. If the switch fails either of these tests, the switch is faulty and the ignition switch assembly must be replaced.

Ignition Switch Removal/Installation (4-wheeled Models)

1. Carefully pry the trim strip (**Figure 69**) from the handlebar cover.

2. Remove the screws (**Figure 70**) securing the handlebar cover and move the cover off the handlebar.

3. Remove the front fender assembly as described in Chapter Fifteen.

4. The electrical connectors are located next to the ignition coil. Disconnect the electrical connectors from the ignition switch.

5. Push the lugs on the ignition switch in and disengage the switch from the handlebar cover (B, **Figure 71**). Remove the ignition switch.

6. Install by reversing these removal steps, noting the following.

7. Make sure all electrical connectors are tight and free of corrosion.

NEUTRAL and REVERSE Switch Testing (4-wheeled Models)

1. Remove the rear fender as described in Chapter Fifteen.

2. Remove the electrical junction box cover (**Figure 48**) and remove the cover.

3. Test the NEUTRAL switch as follows:

   a. Shift the transmission into NEUTRAL.

   b. Disconnect the light green/red electrical wire going to the switch (**Figure 75**).

   c. Connect an ohmmeter to the light green/red wire and ground. There should be continuity (low resistance).

   d. If there is no continuity (infinite resistance), the switch is faulty and must be replaced.

4. Test the reverse switch as follows:

   a. Shift the transmission into REVERSE.

   b. Disconnect the gray electrical wire going to the REVERSE switch (**Figure 75**).

   c. Connect an ohmmeter to the gray wire and ground. There should be continuity (low resistance).

d. If there is no continuity (infinite resistance), the switch is faulty and must be replaced.

WARNING
The wires must be connected to the correct terminals on the switch. If the wires are interchanged, the NEUTRAL indicator (on the handlebar cover) will indicate that the transmission is in NEUTRAL while it is actually in REVERSE and the vehicle will reverse suddenly when the throttle is opened.

5. Connect the electrical wires to the correct

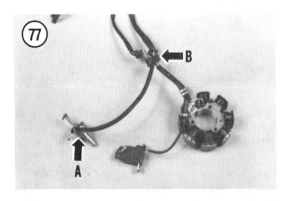

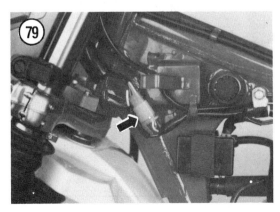

terminals on the NEUTRAL/REVERSE switch.

NEUTRAL and REVERSE Switch
Removal/Installation
(4-wheeled Models)

1. Remove the left-hand crankcase cover as described under *Left-hand Crankcase Cover Removal (4-wheeled Models)* in Chapter Four.
2. Remove the E-clip and NEUTRAL indicator from the exterior of the left-hand crankcase cover.
3. Remove the alternator stator assembly from the left-hand crankcase cover as described under *Alternator Stator Removal (4-wheeled Models)* in this chapter.
4. Remove the bolt (A, **Figure 76**) securing the switch wiring harness to the crankcase cover.
5. Remove the bolt (B, **Figure 76**) securing the switch to the crankcase cover.
6. Remove the bolts securing the alternator stator assembly (C, **Figure 76**) to the cover.
7. Carefully remove the switch, wiring harness and grommet (D, **Figure 76**) from the left-hand crankcase cover.
8. Separate the NEUTRAL switch's (A, **Figure 77**) wiring harness from the alternator stator wiring harness at the rubber grommet (B, **Figure 77**).
9. Install by reversing these removal steps, noting the following.
10. Make sure the spring pin (**Figure 78**) is in place in the switch.
11. Fill the engine with the recommended type and quantity of engine oil as described under *Engine Oil Change* in Chapter Three.

AC REGULATOR
(3-WHEELED MODELS)

Testing

1. Disconnect the engine kill switch/lighting switch electrical connector (**Figure 79**) just in front of the fuel tank on the left-hand side.
2. Connect a DC voltmeter to the white/yellow and green wire terminals on the wiring harness side of the connector.
3. Start the engine and let it idle. The voltage reading should be as follows:
   a. 1986 models: 13.5-14.5 volts.
   b. 1987 models: 12.5-13.5 volts.
4. If the voltage is not within specifications, inspect the AC regulator.
5. Shut off the engine and disconnect the voltmeter.
6. Remove the seat/rear fender assembly as described in Chapter Fifteen.

8

7. Disconnect the electrical connector (A, **Figure 80**) from the AC regulator.

8. Remove the AC regulator (B, **Figure 80**) from the rubber mount on the air filter air box.

9. Use an ohmmeter set at R×1,000 ohms and check the resistance between the electrical wire connectors on the AC regulator. The specified resistance is 100 k—infinity ohms.

10. If the AC regulator resistance does not meet this specification, the unit is bad and must be replaced.

11. Install the AC regulator into the rubber mount on the air filter air box. Connect the electrical connectors.

12. Reconnect the engine kill switch/lighting switch electrical connector.

13. Install the seat/rear fender as described in Chapter Fifteen.

FUSES

The 3-wheeled models are not equipped with any fuses.

The 4-wheeled models are equipped with one 15-amp main fuse that is located next to the starter solenoid. The fuse is in a fuse holder (**Figure 81**) that also holds a spare fuse.

NOTE
Always carry a spare fuse.

Whenever the fuse blows, find out the reason for the failure before replacing the fuse. Usually, the trouble is a short circuit in the wiring. This may be caused by worn-through insulation or a disconnected wire shorted to ground.

WIRING DIAGRAMS

Wiring diagrams for all models are located at the end of this book.

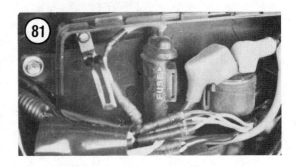

Table 1 VOLTAGE REGULATOR TEST POINTS (4-WHEELED MODELS)

Test probe Positive (+)	Negative (−)	Value K ohms
Yellow	yellow	infinity
Yellow	green	1-20
Yellow	red	infinity
Yellow	black	1-50
Yellow	yellow	infinity
Yellow	green	1-20
Yellow	red	infinity
Yellow	black	1-50
Green	yellow	infinity
Green	yellow	infinity
Green	red	infinity
Green	black	0.2-10
Red	yellow	1-20
Red	yellow	1-20
Red	green	3-100
Red	black	3-10
Black	yellow	infinity
Black	yellow	infinity
Black	green	0.2-20
Black	red	infinity

Table 2 CDI TROUBLESHOOTING

Symptoms	Probable Cause
Weak spark	Poor connections (clean and retighten) High voltage leak (replace defective wire) Defective coil (replace ignition coil)
No spark	Wiring broken (replace wire) Defective ignition (replace coil) Defective pulser coil in magneto (replace coil)

Table 3 STARTER TROUBLESHOOTING

Symptom	Probable Cause	Remedy

Starter does
  not work
	Low battery
	Worn brushes
	Defective relay
	Defective switch
	Defective wiring
	  or connection
	Internal short circuit
		Recharge battery
		Replace brushes
		Repair or replace
		Repair or replace
		Repair wire or clean
		  connection
		Repair or replace
		  defective component

Starter action
  is weak
	Low battery
	Pitted relay contacts
	Worn brushes
	Defective connection
	Short circuit in
	  commutator
		Recharge battery
		Clean or replace
		Replace brushes
		Clean and tighten
		Replace armature

Starter runs continuously	Stuck relay	Replace relay

Starter turns;
  does not turn engine
	Defective starter
	  clutch
		Replace starter
		  clutch

8

Table 4 REPLACEMENT BULBS

Item and model	Voltage/wattage

Headlight
  3-wheeled models
  4-wheeled models
	12V 60/55W
	12V 45/45W

Taillight
  3-wheeled models
    1986
    1987
  4-wheeled models
	
	12V 5W
	12V 8W
	12V 5W

NEUTRAL indicator	12V 3W
REVERSE indicator	12V 3W

CHAPTER NINE

FRONT SUSPENSION AND STEERING
(3-WHEELED MODELS)

This chapter describes repair and maintenance of the front wheel, hub, forks and steering components. Refer to **Table 1** for torque specifications for the front suspension components. **Tables 1-5** are at the end of this chapter.

FRONT WHEEL

Removal

1. Place the ATV on level ground and set the parking brake. Block the rear wheels so the vehicle will not roll in either direction.
2. On the left-hand side, loosen the nuts securing the front axle holder (**Figure 1**).
3. Loosen the front axle (**Figure 2**).
4. Loosen all wheel lug nuts (**Figure 3**).
5. Jack up the front of the vehicle with a small hydraulic or scissor jack. Place the jack under the frame with a piece of wood between the jack and the frame.
6. Place wood block(s) under the frame to support the ATV securely with the front wheel off the ground.
7. Remove all wheel lug nuts (**Figure 3**).
8. Completely unscrew the front axle (**Figure 2**) from the left-hand fork leg.
9. Withdraw the axle from the right-hand side. Don't lose the axle spacer on the right-hand side.
10. Carefully move the wheel forward and down.

This allows the brake disc to slide out of the caliper assembly on the right-hand fork leg.
11. Roll the wheel forward. Hold onto the front hub, as it is no longer attached to the front rim, and remove the wheel and front hub.
12. Remove the front hub from the front wheel.

NOTE
Insert a piece of vinyl tubing or wood in the caliper in place of the brake disc. That way if the brake lever is

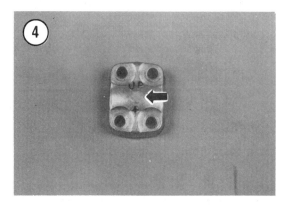

inadvertently squeezed, the piston will not be forced out of the cylinder. If this does happen, the caliper may have to be disassembled to reseat the piston and the system will have to be bled. By using the wood, bleeding the brake is not necessary when installing the wheel.

Installation

1. Make sure the axle bearing surfaces of the fork slider are free from burrs and nicks.
2. Clean the axle in solvent and dry thoroughly. Make sure all axle-to-fork contact surfaces of the axle are clean and free from road dirt and old grease before installation.
3. Remove the vinyl tubing or pieces of wood from the brake caliper.
4. If removed, install the front axle holder with the UP mark facing up (**Figure 4**). Tighten the nuts only finger-tight at this time since the front axle must be inserted through the holder.
5. Position the front hub into the front wheel—do not install the lug nuts at this time.
6. Position the wheel so the air valve stem (**Figure 5**) is on the left-hand side. If the valve stem is on the right-hand side, the brake disc will hide it.
7. Position the wheel and front hub, then carefully insert the brake disc between the brake pads in the caliper assembly.
8. Make sure that the axle spacer is in place both sides of the hub.
9. Move the front hub into position and install the front axle from the left-hand side through the wheel hub.
10. Screw the front axle into the right-hand fork leg and hand tighten it at this time.
11. Install the lug nuts with the tapered end going on first (**Figure 6**). Tighten the nuts only finger-tight at this time.
12. Remove the wood blocks from under the engine and set the front wheel on the ground.

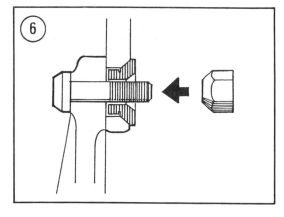

13. Tighten the wheel lug nuts to the torque specification listed in **Table 1**.

14. Tighten the front axle to the torque specification listed in **Table 1**.

15. Push down on the handlebar several times to seat the front axle correctly with the front forks.

16. Tighten the upper front axle holder nuts first and then the lower nuts to the torque specification listed in **Table 1**.

17. After the wheel is installed completely, rotate it; apply the brake several times to make sure that the wheel rotates freely and that the brake is operating correctly.

TIRES AND WHEELS

The ATV is equipped with tubeless, low pressure tires designed specifically for off-road use only. Rapid tire wear will occur if the ATV is ridden on paved surfaces. Due to their low pressure requirements, ATV tires should be inflated only with a hand-operated air pump instead of using an air compressor or a service station air hose.

> *CAUTION*
> *Do not overinflate the stock tires as they will be permanently distorted and damaged. If overinflated, they will bulge out like an inner tube that is not within the constraints of a tire and will **not** return to their original contour.*

> *NOTE*
> *Additional inflation pressure in the stock tires will not improve the ride or the handling characteristics of the ATV. For improved handling, aftermarket tires will have to be installed.*

To guard against punctures from *small* objects, install a commercially available liquid tire sealer into all tires though the valve stem. It's a good idea to carry a cold patch tire repair kit and hand-held pump in the tow vehicle.

Removing the tires from the rims is different than removal from a motorcycle or automobile wheel.

> *CAUTION*
> *Do **not** use conventional motorcycle tire irons for tire removal as the tire sealing bead will be damaged when forced away from the rim flange.*

Tire Changing

The rims used on all models (front and rear) are of the 1-piece type and have a very deep built-in ridge to keep the tire bead seated on the rim under severe riding conditions. Unfortunately it also tends to keep the tire on the rim during tire removal.

A special tool is required for tire changing on these models and is shown in use in this procedure. The special tool from Honda is the Universal Bead Breaker (part No. GN-AH-958-BB1). The use of this specific tool or equivalent is necessary as it directs all of the applied pressure to a very small section of the tire bead at a time. Most other aftermarket bead breakers spread out the applied pressure over a larger section of the tire bead and therefore are unable to break the bead loose from this type of rim.

If you are going to purchase this bead breaker and also have other ATV's with different rim sizes, the blade length (**Figure 7**) is important and the following blades are recommended:

a. Short blade for 7 in. and 8 in. rims.

b. Long blade for 9 in. and 11 in. rims.

The 3-wheeled models covered in this book use the long blade for 9 in. and 11 in. rims while the 4-wheeled models use the short blade for 8 in. rims.

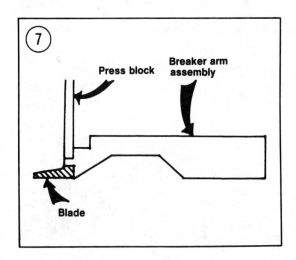

NOTE
One aftermarket bead breaker, called the "Bead Buster" (Figure 8) works very well on this type of rim and is less expensive than the Honda special tool. It is available from Jenco Products, P.O. Box 610, Glide, Oregon 97443.

CAUTION
The use of the improper size blade may damage the rim, tire or the blade.

1. Remove the valve stem cap and core and deflate the tire. Do not reinstall the core at this time.

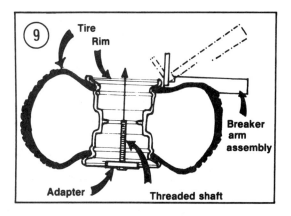

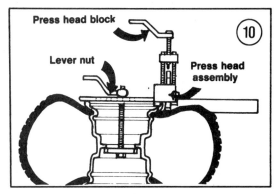

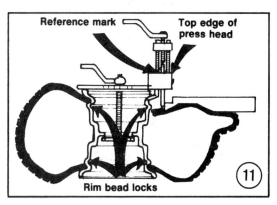

2. Install the correct size adapter onto the threaded shaft and place the wheel over this assembly (**Figure 9**).

3. Lubricate the tire bead and rim flanges with a liquid dish detergent or any rubber lubricant. Press the tire sidewall/bead down to allow the liquid to run into and around the bead area. Also apply lubricant to the area where the bead breaker arm will come in contact with the tire sidewall.

4. Hold the breaker arm at about 45° to the tire and insert the blade between the tire bead and the rim.

5. Push the breaker arm inward and downward until it is horizontal with the press block against the rim outer surface (**Figure 9**).

NOTE
*To completely seat the breaker arm, hold it horizontal and tap the end of the breaker arm with a soft-faced mallet to position the press block **completely** against the rim outer surface. This is necessary for the tool to work properly.*

6. With the breaker arm positioned correctly, place the breaker press head assembly over the press block of the breaker arm. Make sure the press head bolt is backed out all the way (**Figure 10**).

7. Position the nylon buttons on the press head against the inside edge of the rim.

8. Pull the threaded shaft and adapter assembly up and insert it into the breaker press head assembly. Install the bolts through the rim holes and the adapter to correctly position the adapter assembly to the center of the rim.

9. Slowly tighten the lever nut until both ends of the breaker press head assembly are in firm contact with the rim.

10. Slowly tighten the press head bolt until the reference mark on the press block is aligned with the top edge of the press head (**Figure 11**). At this point the tire bead *should* break away from the rim.

11. Using your hands, press down on the tire on either side of the breaker arm assembly and try to break the rest of the bead free from the rim.

12. If the rest of the tire bead cannot be broken loose, loosen the press head bolt and lever nut. Rotate the press head assembly about 1/8 to 1/4 of the circumference of the rim.

13. Repeat Steps 4-11 until the entire bead is broken loose from the rim.

14. Remove the tool assembly from the rim assembly. Turn the wheel over and repeat Steps 3-14 for the other rim flange.

15. Remove the tire from the rim using tire irons and rim protectors.

16. Inspect the rim sealing surface of the rim. If the rim has been severely hit it will probably leak air. Repair or replace any damaged rim.

17. Inspect the tire for cuts, tears, abrasions or any other defects.

18. Wipe the tire beads and rims free from any lubricating agent used in Step 3.

19. Apply clean water to the rim flanges, tire rim beads and onto the outer rim.

NOTE
Use only clean water and make sure the rim flange is clean. Wipe with a lint-free cloth before wetting down.

20. Install the tire onto the rim starting with the side opposite the valve stem. Use tire irons and rim protectors and install the tire onto the rim.

21. Install the valve stem core.

CAUTION
Do not use any mounting lubricant that contains silicone.

CAUTION
Do not inflate the tire past the maximum inflation pressure listed in **Table 3**.

22. Apply tire mounting lubricant or a liquid dish detergent to the tire bead and inflate the tire to the recommended tire pressure.

23. Deflate the tire and let it sit for about one hour.

24. Inflate the tire to the recommended air pressure, referring to **Table 3**.

25. Inspect the "rim line" of the tire in relation to the rim. It must be equally spaced from the rim all around the circumference. If the distance varies, this indicates that the bead is not properly seated and the tire must be reinstalled correctly on the rim. Repeat Steps 20-24.

26. Check for air leaks and install the valve cap.

Cold Patch Repair

This is the method that Honda recommends for patching a tire. The rubber plug type of repair is recommended only for an emergency repair, or until the tire can be patched correctly with the cold patch method.

1. Remove the tire as described in this chapter.

2. Before removing the object that punctured the tire, mark the location of the puncture with chalk or crayon on the outside of the tire. Remove the object (**Figure 12**).

3. On the inside of the tire, roughen the area around the hole slightly larger than the patch (**Figure 13**). Use the cap from the tire repair kit or pocket knife. Do not scrape too vigorously or you may cause additional damage.

4. Clean the area with a non-flammable solvent. Do not use an oil base solvent as it will leave a residue rendering the patch useless.

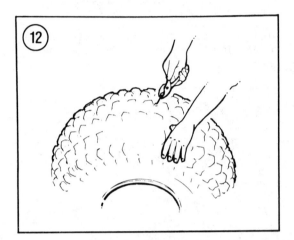

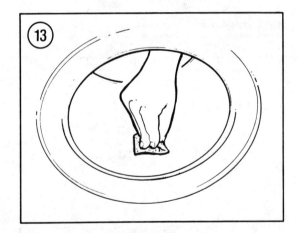

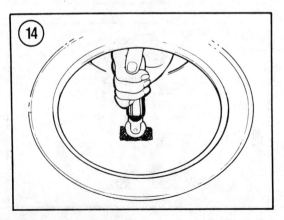

5. Apply a small amount of special cement to the puncture and spread it with your finger.
6. Allow the cement to dry until tacky—usually 30 seconds or so is sufficient.
7. Remove the backing from the patch.

CAUTION
Do not touch the newly exposed rubber with your fingers or the patch will not stick firmly.

8. Center the patch over the hole. Hold the patch firmly in place for about 30 seconds to allow the cement to dry. If you have a roller, use it to help press the patch into place (**Figure 14**).
9. Dust the area with talcum powder.

FRONT HUB/BRAKE DISC AND AXLE

Inspection

Inspect each wheel bearing before removing it from the wheel hub.

CAUTION
Do not remove the hub bearings for inspection purposes as they will be damaged during the removal process. Remove the wheel bearings only if they are to be replaced.

1. Perform Steps 1-4 of *Disassembly* in this chapter.
2. Turn each bearing by hand. Make sure each bearing turns smoothly.

NOTE
Some axial play (end play) is normal, but radial play (side play) should be negligible. The bearing should turn smoothly.

3. On non-sealed bearings, check the balls for evidence of wear, pitting or excessive heat (bluish tint). Replace bearings if necessary; always replace as a complete set. When replacing, be sure to take your old bearings along to ensure a perfect matchup.

NOTE
Fully sealed bearings are available from many good bearing specialty shops. Fully sealed bearings provide better protection from dirt and moisture that may get into the hub.

4. Check the axle for signs of fatigue, fractures and straightness. Use V-blocks and a dial indicator as shown in **Figure 15**. If the runout exceeds the service limit listed in **Table 2**, the axle should be replaced.
5. Inspect the grease seals. Replace the seals if they are deteriorating or starting to harden.

9

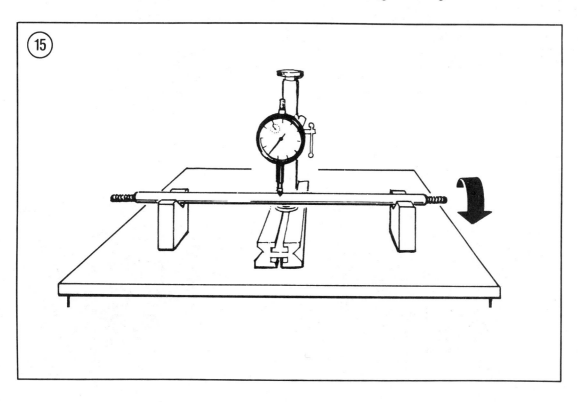
(15)

Disassembly

Refer to **Figure 16** for this procedure.

1. Remove the front wheel as described in this chapter.

2. On the right-hand side, remove the axle spacer (**Figure 17**).

3. Remove the nuts (**Figure 18**) securing the brake disc to the front hub and remove the brake disc.

4. On the right-hand side, remove the grease seal (**Figure 19**).

5. On the left-hand side, remove the axle spacer (**Figure 20**) and grease seal (**Figure 21**).

6. Before proceeding any further, inspect the wheel bearings as described in this chapter.

7. To remove the left and right-hand bearings and distance collar, insert a soft aluminum or brass drift into one side of the hub. Push the distance

collar over to one side and place the drift on the inner race of the lower bearing. Tap the bearing out of the hub with a hammer working around the perimeter of the inner race.

8. Remove the center collar and tap out the opposite bearing.

9. Thoroughly clean out the inside of the hub with solvent and dry with compressed air or a shop cloth.

Assembly

1. On non-sealed bearings, pack the bearings with a good quality bearing grease. Work the grease thoroughly in between the balls. Turn the bearing by hand a couple of times to make sure the grease is distributed evenly inside the bearing.

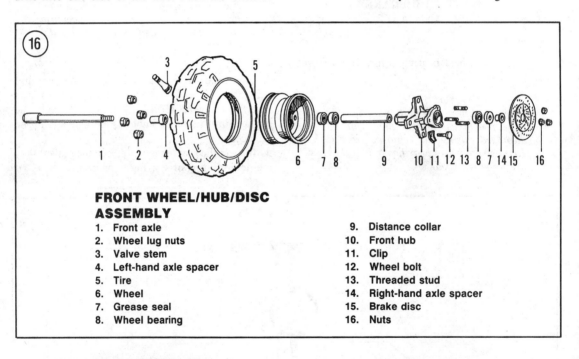

FRONT WHEEL/HUB/DISC ASSEMBLY

1. Front axle
2. Wheel lug nuts
3. Valve stem
4. Left-hand axle spacer
5. Tire
6. Wheel
7. Grease seal
8. Wheel bearing
9. Distance collar
10. Front hub
11. Clip
12. Wheel bolt
13. Threaded stud
14. Right-hand axle spacer
15. Brake disc
16. Nuts

2. Pack the wheel hub and distance collar with multipurpose grease.

CAUTION
*Install the wheel bearings with the sealed side facing out. During installation, tap the bearings squarely into place and tap on the outer race only. Use a socket (**Figure 22**) that matches the outer race diameter. Do not tap on the inner race or the bearing may be damaged. Be sure that the bearings are completely seated.*

3. Install the left-hand bearing.

4. Install the distance collar and the right-hand bearing.

5. Apply a light coat of multipurpose grease to both grease seals.

6. Install the grease seal on each side of the hub.

7. Install the axle spacer on the right- and left-hand side.

8. Position the brake disc with the DRIVE mark facing toward the outside and install the nuts. Tighten the nuts to the torque specification listed in **Table 1**.

9. Install the front wheel as described in this chapter.

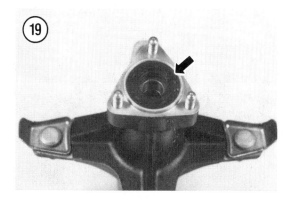

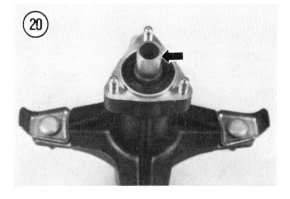

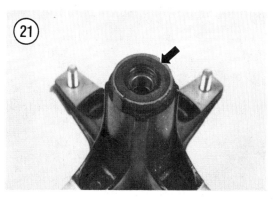

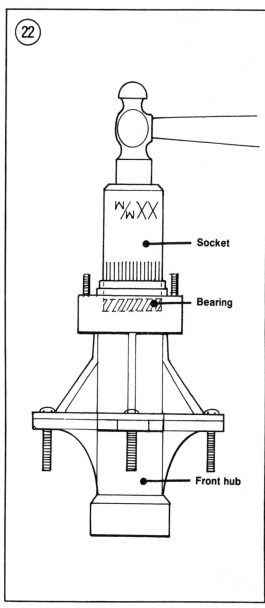

Socket

Bearing

Front hub

8

HANDLEBAR

Removal

1. Remove the bolts securing the throttle assembly (A, **Figure 23**) and carefully lay the throttle assembly and cable over the fender or back over the frame. Be careful that the cable does not get crimped or damaged.

> *CAUTION*
> *Cover the frame with a heavy cloth or plastic tarp to protect it from accidental spilling of brake fluid. Wash any spilled brake fluid off painted or plated surfaces immediately, as it will destroy the finish. Use soapy water and rinse thoroughly.*

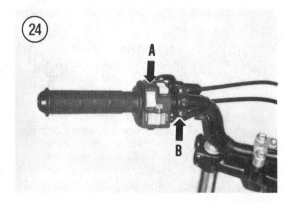

2. Remove the bolts (B, **Figure 23**) securing the brake master cylinder and lay it over the frame. Keep the reservoir in the upright position to minimize loss of brake fluid and to keep air from entering into the brake system. It is not necessary to remove the hydraulic brake line.

3. Remove the screws securing the left-hand switch assembly (A, **Figure 24**) and remove the switch assembly.

4. Remove the screws (B, **Figure 24**) and clamp securing the left-hand clutch/parking brake lever and remove the assembly.

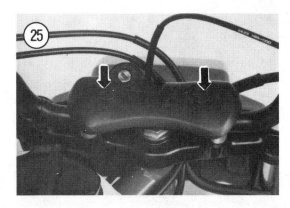

5. Withdraw the fuel filler cap breather hose from the steering stem.

6A. On 1986 models, remove the bolts securing the handlebar upper holders and remove the holders.

> *CAUTION*
> *The caps are not a screw-on/off type. Rotate them slightly in either direction to release their locking lugs from the cover.*

6B. On 1987 models, perform the following:
  a. Use a large coin and carefully rotate the caps (**Figure 25**) on the handlebar cover.
  b. Carefully pry the caps out of the handlebar cover and remove them.

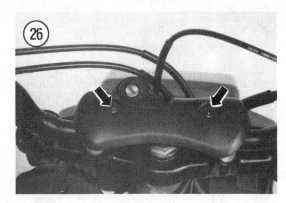

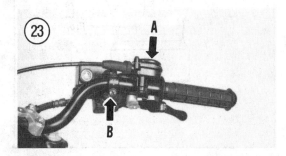

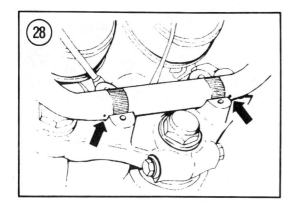

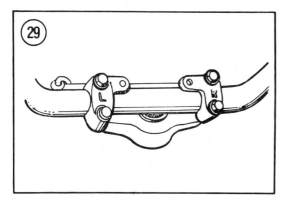

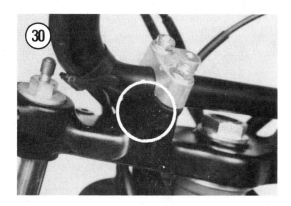

c. Remove the bolts (**Figure 26**) securing the handlebar cover and remove the cover.

d. Remove the bolts securing the handlebar upper holders (**Figure 27**) and remove the holders.

7. Remove the handlebar.

8. To maintain a good grip on the handlebar and to prevent it from slipping down, clean the knurled section of the handlebar with a wire brush. It should be kept rough so it will be held securely by the holders. The holders should also be kept clean and free of any metal that may have been gouged loose by handlebar slippage.

Installation

1. Position the handlebar on the handlebar lower holders so the punch mark on the handlebar is aligned with the top surface of the handlebar lower holders (**Figure 28**).

2A. On 1986 models, install the handlebar upper holders with the punch mark facing toward the front.

2B. On 1987 models, install the handlebar upper holders with the "L" or "R" marks (**Figure 29**) located on the correct side.

3. Install the handlebar holder bolts. Tighten the forward bolts first and then the rear bolts and tighten to the torque specification listed in **Table 1**.

4. After installation is complete, recheck the alignment of the punch mark on the handlebar (**Figure 30**); readjust if necessary.

5. On 1987 models, perform the following:

a. Install the handlebar holder cover and screws (**Figure 26**). Tighten the screws securely.

b. Align the lugs on the caps and install the caps (**Figure 25**) into the holder cover. Using a large coin, rotate the caps and secure the caps to the cover.

6. Install the left-hand switch assembly onto the handlebar and locate the pin on the assembly with the hole in the handlebar. Install the screws and tighten the upper screw first, then the lower screw. Tighten the screws securely.

7. Install the left-hand clutch/parking brake lever assembly. Position the clamp with the UP mark (**Figure 31**) toward the top and install the bolts. Align the split mark of the housing with the punch mark on the handlebar. Tighten the upper bolt first, then the lower bolt. Tighten the bolts securely.

9

8. Install the master cylinder assembly. Position the clamp with the UP mark (**Figure 32**) toward the top and install the bolts. Align the split mark of the housing with the punch mark on the handlebar. Tighten the bolts securely.

9. Install the throttle housing onto the handlebar. Align the ridge on the housing with the mating

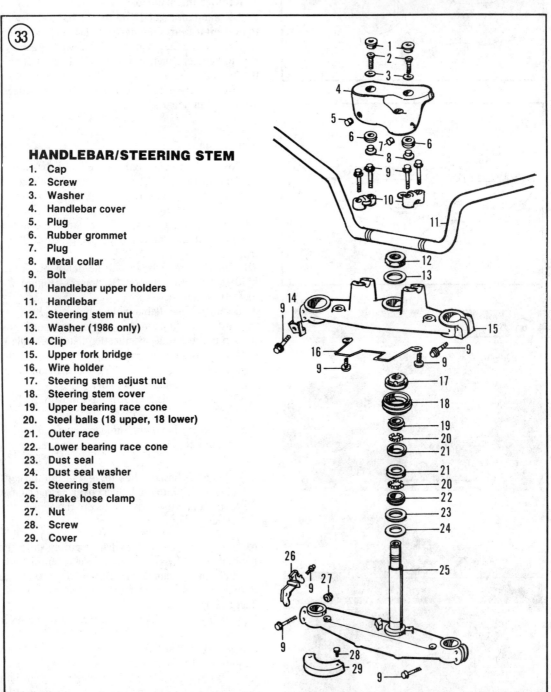

HANDLEBAR/STEERING STEM

1. Cap
2. Screw
3. Washer
4. Handlebar cover
5. Plug
6. Rubber grommet
7. Plug
8. Metal collar
9. Bolt
10. Handlebar upper holders
11. Handlebar
12. Steering stem nut
13. Washer (1986 only)
14. Clip
15. Upper fork bridge
16. Wire holder
17. Steering stem adjust nut
18. Steering stem cover
19. Upper bearing race cone
20. Steel balls (18 upper, 18 lower)
21. Outer race
22. Lower bearing race cone
23. Dust seal
24. Dust seal washer
25. Steering stem
26. Brake hose clamp
27. Nut
28. Screw
29. Cover

surface of the master cylinder body and clamp. Tighten the forward bolt first, then the rear bolt. Tighten the bolts securely.

10. After all assemblies have been installed, test each one to make sure it operates correctly with no binding. Correct any problem at this time.

STEERING STEM

The steering stem is equipped with loose ball bearings in both the top and bottom bearings. Refer to **Figure 33** for this procedure.

Disassembly

1. Remove the front wheel as described in this chapter.
2. Remove the headlight assembly as described in Chapter Eight.
3. Remove the bolts securing the front fender and remove the fender.
4. Remove the front forks as described in this chapter.
5. Remove the fuel tank as described in Chapter Seven.
6. Remove the bolts securing the headlight bracket and remove the headlight bracket.

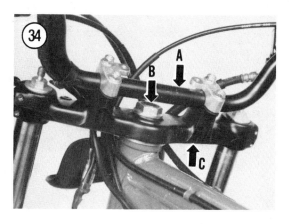

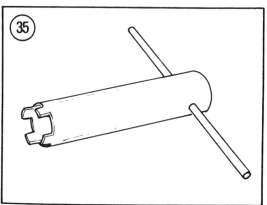

7. Remove the bolts securing the cable bracket on the upper fork bridge.
8. Remove the handlebar assembly (A, **Figure 34**) as described in this chapter.
9A. On 1986 models, remove the steering stem nut and washer.
9B. On 1987 models, remove the steering stem nut (B, **Figure 34**).
10. Remove the upper fork bridge (C, **Figure 34**).
11. Remove the bolts securing the steering stem cover on the lower fork bridge and remove the steering stem cover.
12. Loosen the steering head adjusting nut. Use a large drift and hammer or use the easily improvised tool shown in **Figure 35**.
13. Remove the steering head adjusting nut and upper bearing cone race.
14. On models so equipped, remove the steering stem seal.

NOTE
Have an assistant hold a large pan under the steering stem to catch the loose ball bearings while you carefully lower the steering stem.

15. Lower the steering stem assembly down and out of the steering head.
16. Remove the ball bearings from the upper and lower race. There are 18 ball bearings in each race.

Inspection

1. Clean the bearing races in the steering head, the steering stem races and the ball bearings with solvent.
2. Check the welds around the steering head for cracks and fractures. If any are found, have them repaired by a competent frame shop or welding service.
3. Check the balls for pitting, scratches or discoloration indicating wear or corrosion. Replace them in sets if any are bad.
4. Check the races for pitting, galling and corrosion. If any of these conditions exist, replace the races as described under *Steering Head Bearing Races* in this chapter.
5. Check the steering stem for cracks and check its race for damage or wear. If this race or any race is damaged, the bearings should be replaced as a complete bearing set. Take the old races and bearings to your dealer to ensure accurate replacement.

Steering Head Bearing Races

The headset and steering stem bearing races are pressed into place. Because they are easily bent, do not remove them unless they are worn and require replacement.

Headset bearing race removal/installation

> *NOTE*
> *The top and bottom bearing races are the same size and same Honda part number.*

To remove the headset race, insert a hardwood stick or soft punch into the head tube (**Figure 36**) and carefully tap the race out from the inside. After it is started, tap around the race so that neither the race nor the head tube is damaged.

To install the headset race, tap it in slowly with a block of wood, a suitable size socket or piece of pipe (**Figure 37**). Make sure that the race is squarely seated in the headset race bore before tapping it into place. Tap the race in until it is flush with the steering head surface.

Steering stem bearing race and grease seal removal/installation

Refer to **Figure 33** for this procedure.

1. To remove the steering stem race (bottom bearing lower race) try twisting and pulling it up by hand. If it will not come off, carefully pry it up with a screwdriver; work around in a circle, prying a little at a time.

2. Remove the bottom bearing lower race, dust seal and dust seal washer.

3. Install the dust seal washer and dust seal. Slide the bottom bearing lower race over the steering stem with the bearing surface pointing up.

4. Tap the lower race down with a piece of hardwood; work around in a circle so the race will not be bent. Make sure it is seated squarely and is all the way down.

Steering Stem Assembly

Refer to **Figure 33** for this procedure.

1. Make sure the steering head and stem races are properly seated.

2. Apply a coat of cold grease to the upper bearing race cone and fit 18 ball bearings around it (**Figure 38**).

3. Apply a coat of cold grease to the lower bearing race cone and fit 18 ball bearings around it (**Figure 39**).

4. Install the steering stem into the head tube and hold it firmly in place.

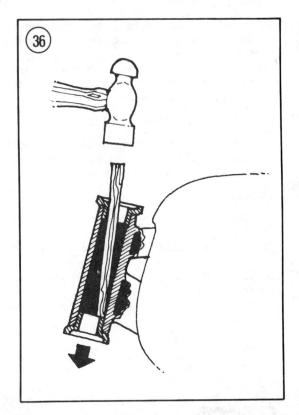

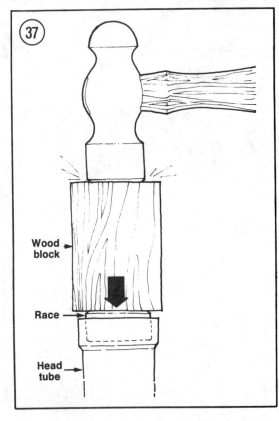

5. Install the upper race cone into the upper ball bearings.

6. Install the steering stem adjusting nut and tighten to the initial torque specification listed in **Table 1**.

7. Turn the steering stem from the extreme left to the extreme right 2-3 times to seat the ball bearings.

8. Loosen the steering stem adjusting nut and tighten to the final torque specification listed in **Table 1**.

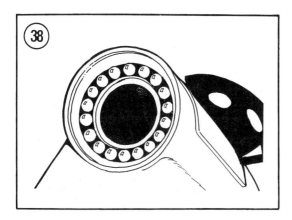

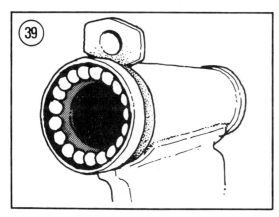

9. Install the steering stem cover onto the lower fork bridge and tighten the bolts to the torque specification listed in **Table 1**.

10. Install the upper fork bridge.

11A. On 1986 models, install the washer and steering stem nut finger-tight.

11B. On 1987 models, install the steering stem nut finger-tight.

NOTE
Steps 12-14 must be performed in this order to assure proper upper and lower fork bridge to fork alignment.

12. Slide the fork tubes into position and tighten the lower fork bridge bolts to the torque specification listed in **Table 1**.

NOTE
*Install the fork tubes so that the groove in the top of the fork tube aligns with the top surface of the upper fork bridge (**Figure 40**).*

13. Tighten the steering stem nut to the torque specification listed in **Table 1**.

14. Tighten the upper fork bridge bolts to the torque specification listed in **Table 1**.

15. Install the handlebar as described in this chapter.

16. Install the front fender and tighten the bolts securely.

17. Install the cable bracket and bolts to the upper fork bridge. Tighten the bolts securely.

18. Install the headlight assembly as described in Chapter Eight.

19. Install the front wheel as described in this chapter.

Steering Stem Adjustment

If play develops in the steering system, it may only require adjustment. However, don't take a chance on it. Disassemble the stem and look for possible damage. Then reassemble and adjust as described in Step 6 of the *Steering Head Assembly* procedure.

FRONT FORKS

The front suspension uses a spring controlled, hydraulically damped, telescopic fork.

Before suspecting major trouble, drain the front fork oil and refill with the proper type and quantity; refer to *Front Fork Oil Change (3-wheeled Models)* in Chapter Three. If you still have trouble, such as poor damping, a tendency to bottom or top out or leakage around the rubber seals, follow the service procedures in this section.

9

To simplify fork service and to prevent the mixing of parts, the legs should be removed, serviced and installed individually.

Removal/Installation

> *WARNING*
> *Always bleed off all air pressure; failure to do so may cause personal injury when disassembling the fork assembly.*

> *WARNING*
> *Release the air pressure gradually. If released too fast, fork oil will spurt out with the air. Protect your eyes and clothing accordingly.*

1. Remove the air valve cap (**Figure 41**) and bleed off *all* air pressure by depressing the valve stem (**Figure 42**).

> *NOTE*
> *The Allen screw at the base of the slider has been secured with Loctite and is often very difficult to remove because the damper rod will turn inside the slider. It sometimes can be removed with an air impact driver. If you are unable to remove it, take the fork tubes to a dealer and have the screws removed.*

2. If the fork assembly is going to be disassembled, perform the following:
   a. While an assistant holds the front brake on, compress the front forks and hold them in this position.
   b. Using a 6 mm Allen wrench, slightly loosen the Allen bolt at the base of the slider. If the bolt is loosened too much, fork oil may start to drain out of the slider.

3. Remove the front wheel as described in this chapter.

4. Remove the bolt (**Figure 43**) securing the front brake cable bracket to the fork leg. Move the brake cable out of the way.

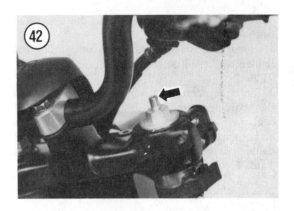

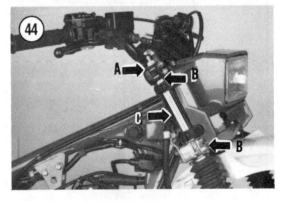

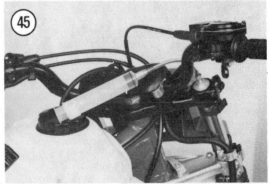

FRONT FORK ASSEMBLY

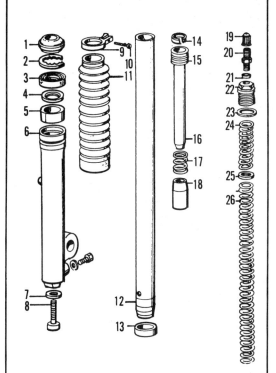

1. Dust seal
2. Circlip
3. Oil seal
4. Backup ring
5. Fork tube bushing
6. Fork slider
7. Washer
8. Allen bolt
9. Clamp
10. Screw
11. Rubber boot
12. Fork slider
13. Slider bushing
14. Piston seal
15. Piston seal holder
16. Damper rod
17. Rebound spring
18. Oil lock piece
19. Dust cap
20. Air valve
21. Gasket
22. Fork top cap
23. Seal
24. Upper spring "A"
25. Spring seat
26. Lower spring "B"

46

5. Loosen the clamping screw on the clamp securing the top of the rubber boot in place.

6. Loosen the top fork bolt/air valve assembly (A, **Figure 44**).

7. Loosen the upper and lower fork bridge bolts (B, **Figure 44**).

8. Remove the fork tube (C, **Figure 44**). It may be necessary to slightly rotate the fork tube while pulling it down and out.

9. Install by reversing these removal steps, noting the following.

10. Position the fork tube so that the groove near the top surface of the fork tube aligns with the top surface of the upper fork bridge (**Figure 40**).

11. Tighten the upper and lower fork bridge bolts to the torque specifications listed in **Table 1**.

12. Inflate the front forks to the standard air pressure listed in **Table 4**. Do not use compressed air; only use a small hand-operated air pump (**Figure 45**).

> *WARNING*
> *Never use any type of compressed gas as an explosion may be lethal. Never heat the fork assembly with a torch or place it near an open flame or extreme heat, as this will also result in an explosion.*

> *CAUTION*
> *Never exceed an air pressure of 1.0 kg/cm² (14 psi) as damage may occur to internal components of the fork assembly.*

13. Remove the wood blocks from under the engine skid plate. Apply the front brake and pump the forks several times.

Disassembly

Refer to **Figure 46** during the disassembly and assembly procedures.

1. If not already loosened, loosen the clamping screw at the top of the rubber boot. Remove the rubber boot (**Figure 47**) from the groove in the top of the slider. Slide the rubber boot off of the fork tube.

9

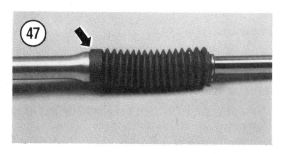

47

2. Clamp the slider in a vise with soft jaws.

3. If not loosened in Step 3 of *Removal/ Installation*, loosen the Allen head screw (**Figure 48**) in the base of the slider.

> *NOTE*
> *This screw has been secured with Loctite and is often very difficult to remove because the damper rod will turn inside the slider. It sometimes can be removed with an air impact driver. If you are unable to remove it, take the fork tubes to a dealer and have the screws removed.*

4. Remove the Allen head screw and washer.

> *WARNING*
> *Be careful when removing the fork top cap bolt as the springs are under pressure.*

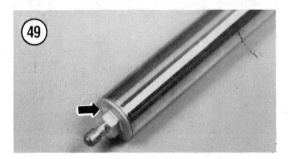

5. If not loosened during the removal sequence, hold the upper fork tube in a vise with soft jaws and loosen the fork top cap bolt/air valve assembly.

6. Remove the fork top cap bolt/air valve assembly (**Figure 49**) from the fork.

7. Remove the upper short spring "A," the spring seat and the lower long spring "B" (**Figure 50**).

8. Remove the fork from the vise, pour the fork oil out and discard it. Pump the fork several times by hand to expel most of the remaining oil.

9. Install the fork slider in a vise with soft jaws.

10. Remove the dust seal (**Figure 51**) and the circlip from the slider.

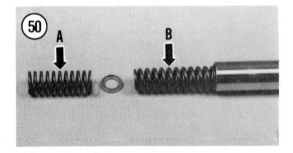

> *NOTE*
> *It may be necessary to slightly heat the area on the slider around the oil seal prior to removal. Use a rag soaked in hot water; do not apply a flame directly to the fork slider.*

11. Withdraw the fork tube from the slider.

12. Turn the fork tube upside down and slide off the oil seal, backup ring and fork slider bushing from the fork tube (**Figure 52**).

13. Remove the oil lock piece (**Figure 53**), the damper rod and rebound spring (**Figure 54**).

Inspection

1. Thoroughly clean all parts in solvent and dry them. Check the fork tube for signs of wear or scratches.

2. Check the damper rod for straightness. **Figure 55** shows one method. The rod should be replaced if the runout is warped to the service limit dimension in **Table 2** or greater.

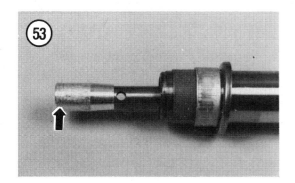

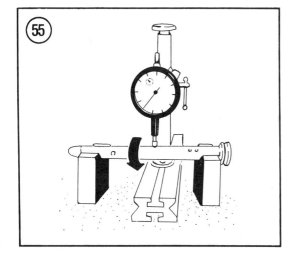

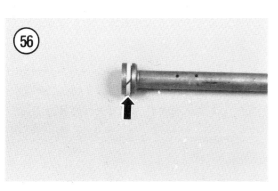

3. Check the damper rod and piston ring for wear or damage (**Figure 56**).

4. Check the fork tube for straightness. If bent or severely scratched, it should be replaced.

5. Check the slider (**Figure 57**) for dents or exterior damage that may cause the upper fork tube to hang up during riding; replace if necessary.

6. Inspect the oil seal area of the fork slider (**Figure 58**) for roughness or damage. If damaged, replace the fork slider.

7. Inspect the threaded studs (**Figure 59**) on the fork slider. If any are damaged, unscrew them and install new ones.

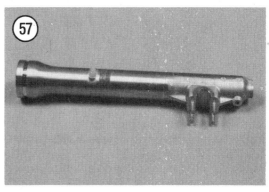

9

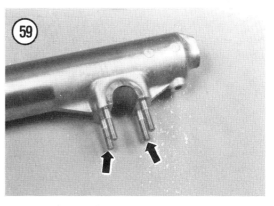

8. Inspect the fork oil seal (**Figure 60**) for wear or deterioration; replace if necessary.

9. Measure the uncompressed length of the fork short and long springs (not rebound spring) as shown in **Figure 61**. If the spring(s) has sagged to the service limit dimensions listed in **Table 2** or less, the spring(s) must be replaced.

10. Inspect the fork tube and slider bushings. If either is scratched or scored they must be replaced. If the Teflon coating is worn off so that the copper base material is showing on approximately 3/4 of the total surface, the bushing must be replaced. Also check for distortion on the check points of the backup ring; replace as necessary. Refer to **Figure 62**.

11. Any parts that are worn or damaged should be replaced. Simply cleaning and reinstalling unserviceable components will not improve the performance of the front suspension.

Assembly

1. Coat all parts with fresh automatic transmission fluid or fork oil before installation.

2. If removed, install a new fork tube bushing (A, **Figure 63**).

3. Install the rebound spring (**Figure 64**) onto the damper rod and insert this assembly into the fork tube (**Figure 54**).

4. Temporarily install the lower long fork spring "A," the spring seat, the upper short spring "B " (**Figure 50**) and the fork top cap bolt/air valve assembly (**Figure 65**) to hold the damper rod in place.

5. Install the oil lock piece onto the damper rod (**Figure 53**).

6. Install the upper fork assembly into the slider (**Figure 66**).

7. Make sure the gasket (A, **Figure 67**) is on the Allen head screw. Apply Loctite Lock N' Seal to the threads of the Allen head screw (B, **Figure 67**) before installation. Install it in the fork slider (**Figure 48**) and tighten to the torque specification listed in **Table 1**.

8. Slide the fork slider bushing (B, **Figure 63**) down the fork tube and rest it on the slider.

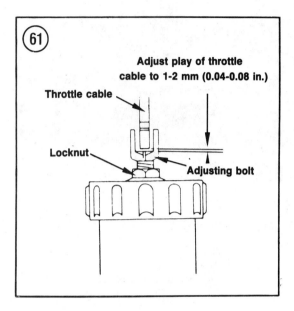

61

Adjust play of throttle cable to 1-2 mm (0.04-0.08 in.)

Throttle cable

Locknut

Adjusting bolt

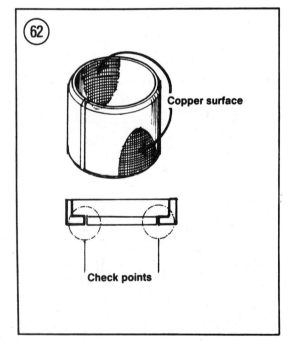

62

Copper surface

Check points

60

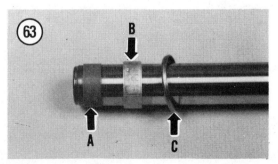

63

B

A   C

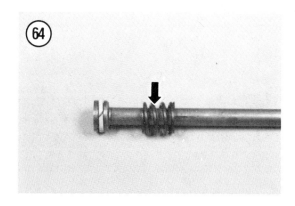

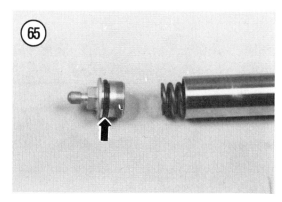

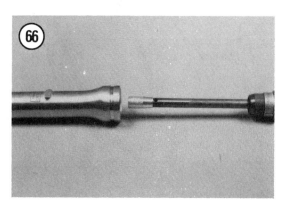

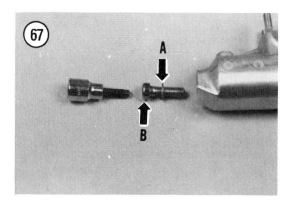

9. Slide the fork slider backup ring (flange side up) (C, **Figure 63**) down the fork tube and rest it on top of the fork slider bushing.

10. Place the old fork slider bushing on top of the backup ring. Drive the bushing into the fork slider with Honda special tool Fork Seal Driver (part No. 07747-0010100) and attachment (part No. 07747-0010501). Drive the bushing into place until it seats completely in the recess in the fork slider. Remove the installation tool and the old fork slider bushing.

11. Coat the new seal with automatic transmission fluid. Position the seal with the marking facing upward and slide it down onto the fork tube. Drive the seal into the fork slider with Honda special tool Fork Seal Driver (part No. 07747-0010101) and Attachment (part No. 07747-0010501). Refer to **Figure 68**. Drive the oil seal in until the groove in the slider can be seen above the top surface of the oil seal.

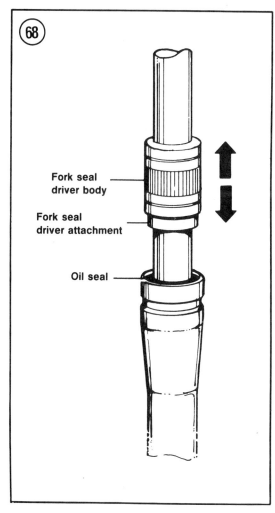

Fork seal driver body

Fork seal driver attachment

Oil seal

9

12. Install the circlip (**Figure 69**) with the sharp side facing up. Make sure the circlip is completely seated in the groove in the fork slider.

13. Install the dust seal (**Figure 70**).

14. Remove the fork top cap bolt/air valve assembly and the upper and lower fork springs.

15. Fill the fork tube with DEXRON automatic transmission fluid or SAE 10W fork oil. Refer to **Table 5** for the specific quantity for each fork leg.

16. Hold the fork upright and compress the fork several times.

17. Compress the fork completely and measure the fluid level from the top of the fork tube (**Figure 71**) after the fork oil has settled. Refer to **Table 5** for the specified fork level. Adjust fork oil level if necessary.

18. Wipe off each fork spring with a lint-free cloth.

19. Install the lower fork spring "B" with the tapered end in first.

20. Install the spring seat and the upper short fork spring "A."

21. Inspect the O-ring seal (**Figure 65**) on the fork top cap bolt/air valve assembly; replace if necessary.

22. Install the fork top cap bolt while pushing down on the springs. Start the bolt slowly; don't crossthread it.

23. Place the slider in a vise with soft jaws and tighten the top fork cap bolt to the torque specifications listed in **Table 1**.

24. Slide the rubber boot onto the fork tube with the clamping end going on last. Install the rubber boot into the groove in the top of the slider. Tighten the clamping screw at the top of the rubber boot.

25. Perform Steps 1-24 for the other fork assembly.

26. Install the fork assemblies as described in this chapter.

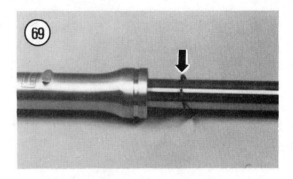

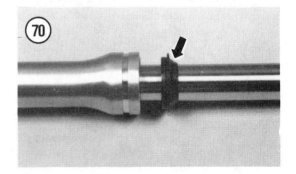

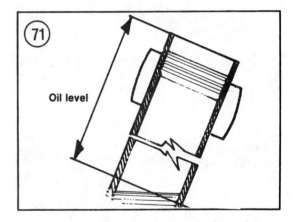

Oil level

Table 1 FRONT SUSPENSION TORQUE SPECIFICATIONS

Item and model	N·m	ft.-lb.
Wheel lug nuts	60-70	43-51
Front axle	70-110	51-80
Front axle holder nuts	10-14	7.2-10
Brake disc nuts	20-30	15-22
Handlebar upper holder bolts	18-30	13-22
Steering stem adjust nut		
Initial torque	25-35	18-25
Final torque	7-8	5.1-5.8
Steering stem cover bolts	1-2	0.7-1.4
Steering stem nut	90-120	65-87
Fork bridge bolts		
Upper and lower	18-25	13-18
Front forks		
Allen bolts	15-25	11-18
Top cap bolt/air valve		
valve assembly	15-30	11-22

Table 2 FRONT SUSPENSION SPECIFICATIONS

Item	Specification	Wear limit
Front axle runout	—	0.5 mm (0.02 in.)
Front fork		
Damper rod runout	—	0.2 mm (0.008 in.)
Fork springs		
Spring A	71.0 mm (2.80 in.)	67.3 mm (2.65 in.)
Spring B	465.9 mm (18.34 in.)	456.6 mm (17.98 in.)
Fork tube runout	—	0.2 mm (0.008 in.)

Table 3 TIRE INFLATION PRESSURE (COLD)*

Model	Tire size	Standard		Minimum		Maximum	
		kPa	psi	kPa	psi	kPa	psi
Front	23.5×11.0-8	25	3.6	22	3.2	28	4.1
Rear	22×10-9	17	2.5	14	2.0	20	2.9

* Tire inflation pressure for factory equipped tires. Aftermarket tires may require different inflation pressure.

Table 4 FRONT FORK AIR PRESSURE

Standard air pressure 0 kPa (0 psi)
Maximum air pressure 70 kPa (10 psi)

Table 5 FORK OIL CAPACITY

Year	Capacity		Dimension from top	
	cc	oz.	mm	in.
1986	216-221	7.3-7.5	178	7.0
1987	226-231	7.6-7.8	160	6.25

FRONT SUSPENSION AND STEERING (4-WHEELED MODELS)

This chapter describes repair and maintenance of the front wheels, hubs and steering components. Refer to **Table 1** for torque specifications for the front suspension components.

Tire removal and repair are covered in Chapter Nine.

Tables 1-3 are at the end of this chapter.

FRONT WHEEL

Removal/Installation

1. Place the ATV on level ground and set the parking brake. Block the rear wheels so the vehicle will not roll in either direction.
2. Remove the wheel cap (A, **Figure 1**).
3. Loosen the wheel lug nuts (B, **Figure 1**).
4. Jack up the front of the vehicle with a small hydraulic or scissor jack. Place the jack under the frame with a piece of wood between the jack and the frame.
5. Place wood block(s) under the frame to support the ATV securely with the front wheels off the ground.
6. Remove the lug nuts (B, **Figure 1**) securing the wheel to the hub/brake drum. Remove the front wheel.
7. Install the front wheel.

8. Install the lug nuts with the tapered end going on first (**Figure 2**). Tighten the nuts only finger-tight at this time.
9. Jack up the front of the vehicle up a little and remove the wood block(s).
10. Let the jack down and remove the jack and wood block(s).

> *WARNING*
> *Always tighten the lug nuts to the correct torque specification or the lug nuts may work loose, allowing the wheel to fall off.*

11. Use a torque wrench and tighten the lug nuts to the torque specification listed in **Table 1**.
12. Install the wheel cap (A, **Figure 1**).
13. Jack up the front of the vehicle up a little and install the wood block(s).
14. After the wheel is installed completely, rotate it. Apply the brake several times to make sure that the wheel rotates freely and that the brake is operating correctly.
15. Jack up the front of the vehicle a little and remove the wood block(s).
16. Let the jack down and remove the jack and wood block(s).

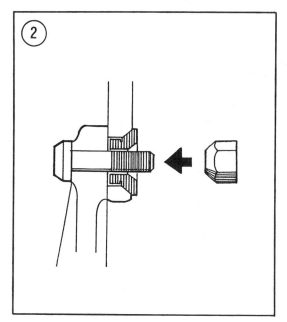

FRONT HUB/BRAKE DRUM

Inspection

Inspect each wheel bearing before removing it from the wheel hub.

> *CAUTION*
> *Do not remove the wheel bearings for inspection purposes as they will be damaged during the removal process. Remove the wheel bearings only if they are to be replaced.*

1. Perform Steps 1-5 of *Front Hub/Brake Drum Disassembly* in this chapter.
2. Turn each bearing by hand. Make sure each bearing turns smoothly.

> *NOTE*
> *Some axial play (end play) is normal, but radial play (side play) should be negligible. The bearing should turn smoothly.*

3. On non-sealed bearings, check the balls for evidence of wear, pitting or excessive heat (bluish tint). Replace bearings if necessary; always replace as a complete set. When replacing, be sure to take your old bearings along to ensure a perfect matchup.

> *NOTE*
> *Fully sealed bearings are available from many good bearing specialty shops. Fully sealed bearings provide better protection from dirt and moisture that may get into the hub.*

4. Inspect the grease seals. Replace if they are deteriorating or starting to harden.
5. Inspect the threaded studs on the front hub/brake drum assembly (A, **Figure 3**); replace as necessary.

Disassembly

Refer to **Figure 4** for this procedure.

1. Remove the front wheel as described in this chapter.

> *WARNING*
> *Do not inhale brake dust. It may contain asbestos, which can cause lung injury and cancer.*

10

2. Remove the cotter pin and hub nut (B, **Figure 3**) securing the front hub/brake drum assembly and remove the front hub/brake drum assembly (**Figure 5**) from the steering knuckle.

3. Remove the collar (A, **Figure 6**) and the grease seal (B, **Figure 6**) from the outside surface of the hub/brake drum.

4. Remove the grease seal (**Figure 7**) from the inside surface of the hub/brake drum.

5. Before proceeding any further, inspect the wheel bearings as described in this chapter.

6. To remove the inner and outer bearings and distance collar, insert a soft aluminum or brass drift into one side of the hub. Push the distance collar over to one side and place the drift on the inner race of the outer bearing. Tap the bearing out of the hub with a hammer working around the perimeter of the inner race.

FRONT WHEEL/HUB

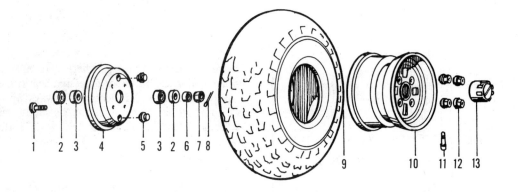

1. **Bolt**	8. **Cotter pin**
2. **Grease seal**	9. **Tire**
3. **Wheel bearing**	10. **Wheel**
4. **Front hub/drum**	11. **Valve stem**
5. **Rubber plug**	12. **Wheel lug nut**
6. **Collar**	13. **Rubber cap**
7. **Castellated nut**	

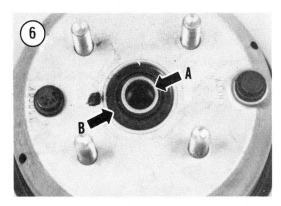

7. Remove the distance collar and tap out the inner bearing.

8. Thoroughly clean out the inside of the hub with solvent and dry with compressed air or a shop cloth.

9. Inspect the rubber seal (**Figure 8**) around the perimeter of the brake drum. If worn or starting to deteriorate, the front hub/brake drum must be replaced.

Assembly

1. On non-sealed bearings, pack the bearings with a good quality bearing grease. Work the grease in between the balls thoroughly. Turn the bearing by hand a couple of times to make sure the grease is distributed evenly inside the bearing.

2. Pack the wheel hub and distance collar with multipurpose grease.

CAUTION
Install the wheel bearings with the sealed side facing out. During installation, tap the bearings squarely into place and tap on the outer race only. Use a socket that matches the outer race diameter. Do not tap on the inner race or the bearing may be damaged. Be sure that the bearings are completely seated.

3. Install the outer bearing.

4. Install the distance collar and the inner bearing.

5. Apply a light coat of multipurpose grease to both grease seals.

6. Install both grease seals.

7. Install the collar onto the outside surface of the hub/brake drum.

8. Install the front hub/brake drum onto the steering knuckle.

9. Install the hub nut and tighten to the torque specification listed in **Table 1**.

WARNING
Always install new cotter pins. Never reuse an old one as it may break and fall out.

10. Install a new cotter pin and bend the ends over completely.

11. Install the front wheel as described in this chapter.

⑨

HANDLEBAR/STEERING SHAFT

1. Trim piece
2. Screw
3. Metal collar
4. Rubber grommet
5. Handlebar cover
6. Indicator light case
7. Indicator light
8. Screw
9. Indicator light
10. Socket/wire harness assembly
11. Bolt
12. Handlebar
13. Handlebar cover mounting bracket
14. Handlebar upper holders
15. Handlebar lower holders
16. Washer
17. Nut
18. Cap
19. Steering shaft
20. Steering shaft holder—inner
21. Rubber bushing
22. Steering shaft holder—outer
23. Dust seal
24. Bearing
25. Locknut
26. Washer
27. Nut
28. Cap
29. Clip
30. Cotter pin

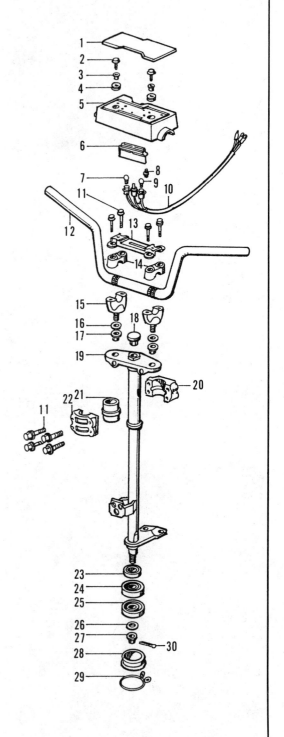

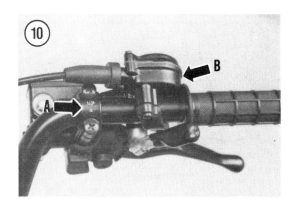

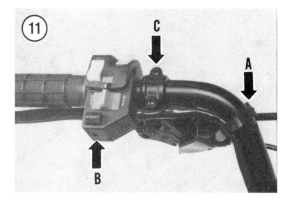

HANDLEBAR

Removal

Refer to **Figure 9** for this procedure.

> *CAUTION*
> *Cover the seat, fuel tank cover and front fender with a heavy cloth or plastic tarp to protect it from the accidental spilling of brake fluid. Wash any spilled brake fluid off any painted or plated surface immediately as it will destroy the finish. Use soapy water and rinse thoroughly.*

1. Remove the bolts securing the front master cylinder clamp (A, **Figure 10**) to the handlebar and lay it over the front fender. Keep the reservoir in the upright position to minimize loss of brake fluid and to keep air from entering the brake system. It is not necessary to remove the hydraulic brake line from the master cylinder.

2. Remove the screws and clamp securing the throttle assembly (B, **Figure 10**) to the handlebar and remove the assembly. Lay the assembly over the front fender. Be careful that the cable does not get crimped or damaged.

3. Remove the wire band (A, **Figure 11**) holding the brake and left-hand switch housing wires to the handlebar.

4. Remove the screws securing the left-hand switch assembly (B, **Figure 11**) and remove the switch assembly.

5. Remove the screws (C, **Figure 11**) and clamp securing the left-hand brake lever and remove the assembly.

6. Carefully pry the trim piece (**Figure 12**) from the handlebar cover.

7. Remove the screws (**Figure 13**) securing the handlebar cover and move the cover off the handlebar.

8. Remove the bolts (**Figure 14**) securing the handlebar cover bracket and upper holders and remove the handlebar cover bracket and holders.

10

9. Remove the handlebar.

10. To maintain a good grip on the handlebar and to prevent it from slipping down, clean the knurled section of the handlebar with a wire brush. It should be kept rough so it will be held securely by the holders. The holders should also be kept clean and free of any metal that may have been gouged loose by handlebar slippage.

Installation

1. Position the handlebar on the handlebar lower holders so the punch mark on the handlebar is aligned with the top surface of the handlebar lower holders (**Figure 15**).

2. Install the handlebar upper holders with the punch mark facing toward the front.

3. Install the handlebar cover bracket and the handlebar holder bolts. Tighten the forward bolts first and then the rear bolts and tighten to the torque specification listed in **Table 1**.

4. After installation is complete, recheck the alignment of the punch mark on the handlebar; readjust if necessary.

5. Install the handlebar cover and screws. Tighten the screws securely.

6. Install the trim strip in the handlebar cover.

7. Install the left-hand switch assembly onto the handlebar. Align the locating pin with the hole in the handlebar and install the screws. Tighten the screws securely.

8. Install the left-hand brake lever assembly. Position the clamp with the dot mark toward the top and install the screws. Align the end of the clamp with the punch mark on the handlebar. Tighten the upper screw first and then the lower screw. Tighten the screws securely.

9. Install the wire band holding the brake and left-hand switch housing wires to the handlebar.

10. Install the front master cylinder as follows:

   a. Place the master cylinder on the handlebar.

   b. Install the holder clamp with the UP arrow (A, **Figure 10**) pointing up and install the screws.

   c. Align the end of the clamp with the punch mark on the handlebar.

   d. Tighten the upper screw first and then the lower. Tighten the screws securely.

11. Install the throttle housing and holder onto the handlebar. Align the end of the housing with the punch mark on the handlebar and tighten the forward screw, first then the rear screw. Tighten the screws securely.

12. After all assemblies have been installed, test each one to make sure it operates correctly with no binding. Correct any problem at this time.

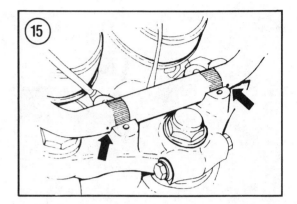

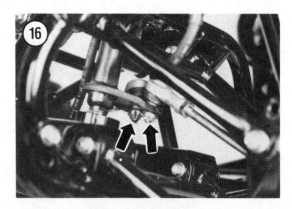

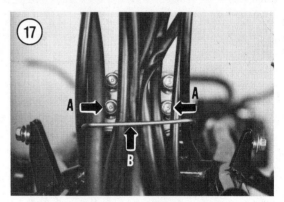

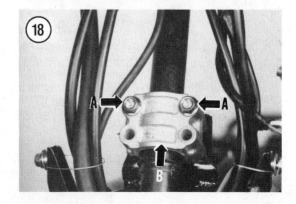

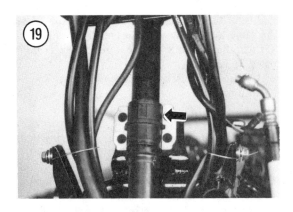

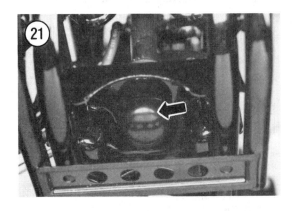

STEERING SHAFT

Steering Shaft Removal

Refer to **Figure 9** for this procedure.

1. Place the ATV on level ground and set the parking brake. Block the rear wheels so the vehicle will not roll in either direction.

2. Remove the seat and front fender as described in Chapter Fifteen.

3. Remove both front wheels as described in this chapter.

4. Disconnect both tie rods (**Figure 16**) from the steering shaft lower end as described in this chapter.

5. Remove the handlebar as described in this chapter.

6. Remove the headlight housing and mounting bracket as described in Chapter Eight.

7. Remove the fresh air intake case assembly as described under *Fresh Air Inlet Case (4-wheeled Models)* in Chapter Fifteen.

8. Remove the lower bolts (A, **Figure 17**) securing the steering shaft holder and wire clamp. Remove the wire clamp (B, **Figure 17**).

9. Move the electrical wires to the side and remove the upper bolts (A, **Figure 18**) securing the steering shaft holder. Remove the holder (B, **Figure 18**).

10. If worn or damaged, remove the bushing (**Figure 19**) from the steering shaft.

11. Remove the clip (**Figure 20**) and cap (**Figure 21**) from the base of the steering stem.

12. Remove the cotter pin, castellated nut (**Figure 22**) and washer securing the lower end of the steering shaft to the frame. Discard the cotter pin—never reuse a cotter pin.

13. Carefully lift the steering shaft up and out of the frame. Don't lose the back half of the steering shaft holder where it attaches to the frame.

Steering Shaft Inspection

1. Carefully inspect the entire steering shaft assembly, especially if the vehicle has been involved in a collision or spill. If the shaft is bent or twisted in any way it must be replaced. If a damaged shaft is installed in the vehicle, it will cause rapid and excessive wear to the lower bearing and upper rubber bushing as well as place undue stress on other components in the frame and steering system.

2. If not already removed, remove the rubber bushing from the steering shaft. Inspect the rubber bushing for wear or deterioration; replace if necessary.

10

3. Inspect the lower bearing in the frame for excessive play or wear; replace if necessary as described in this chapter.

4. Inspect the dust seal at the top surface of the lower bearing in the frame. If the seal is damaged in any way it should be replaced. A damaged seal will allow grit and moisture to enter the lower bearing.

Steering Shaft Bearing and Dust Seal Replacement

> *CAUTION*
> *The steering shaft bearing is pressed into place in the frame. Do not remove the bearing for inspection purposes as it will be damaged during the removal process. Remove the bearing only if it is to be replaced.*

1. Using Honda special tool (Lock Nut Wrench Adapter—part No. 07GMA-HA70200), unscrew the locknut securing the steering shaft bearing in the frame receptacle. Remove the locknut.

2. From the top surface of the frame, remove the dust seal.

3. To remove the steering shaft bearing, perform the following:

   a. Insert a long hardwood stick or soft punch into the top surface of the frame opening and carefully tap the race out from the top. After it is started, tap around the race so that the frame receptacle is damaged.

   b. Remove the bearing from the frame. Discard the bearing.

4. Clean the bearing receptacle in the frame with a shop cloth and cleaning solvent. Remove all dirt and grit.

5. Install a new steering shaft bearing as follows:

> *NOTE*
> *On 1987-on models, position the bearing with the sealed side facing in first, toward the frame.*

   a. Position the new bearing into the receptacle in the frame. Make sure the race is squarely seated in the receptacle before tapping it into place. During installation, tap the bearing squarely into place and tap on the outer race only.

   b. Use a socket that matches the outer race diameter. Do not tap on the inner race or the bearing will be damaged.

   c. Tap the bearing into place until it is completely seated.

6. Install a new dust seal into the surface of the frame above the bearing.

7. Install the steering shaft bearing locknut. Use the same tool set-up used during *Removal* Step 1. Tighten the locknut to the torque specification listed in **Table 1**.

8. Use a cold chisel and hammer and stake the locknut in place.

Steering Shaft Installation

1. Apply multipurpose grease to the steering shaft rubber bushing and install the bushing onto the steering shaft.

2. Apply multipurpose grease to the lips of the steering shaft bearing dust seal.

3. Carefully install the steering shaft into the frame and into the bearing in the base of the frame.

4. Position the steering shaft so the tie-rod mounting flange is facing toward the rear.

5. Install the steering shaft holder, wire clamp and bolts. Tighten the bolts only finger-tight at this time.

6. Install the tie-rod ends onto the mounting flange on the steering shaft as described in this chapter.

7. Install the washer and castellated nut onto the end of the steering shaft. Tighten the nut to the torque specification listed in **Table 1**. Bend both ends of the cotter pin over completely.

8. Install the plastic cap and clip.

9. Tighten the steering shaft holder bolts securely.

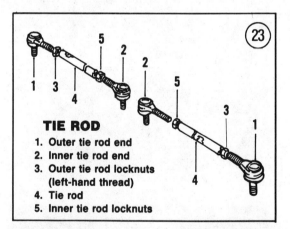

TIE ROD
1. Outer tie rod end
2. Inner tie rod end
3. Outer tie rod locknuts (left-hand thread)
4. Tie rod
5. Inner tie rod locknuts

10. Install the fresh air intake case assembly as described under *Fresh Air Inlet Case (4-wheeled Models)* in Chapter Fifteen.

11. Install the headlight mounting bracket and housing as described in Chapter Eight.

12. Install the handlebar as described in this chapter.

13. Install both front wheels as described in this chapter.

14. Install the seat and front fender as described in Chapter Fifteen.

TIE ROD

Removal

Both tie rod assemblies are the same. Refer to **Figure 23** for this procedure.

NOTE
This procedure is shown with the front hub/brake drum assembly removed for clarity. It is not necessary to remove it for this procedure.

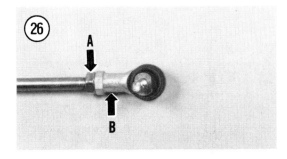

1. Place the ATV on level ground and set the parking brake. Block the rear wheels so the vehicle will not roll in either direction.

2. Remove the seat and front fender as described in Chapter Fifteen.

3. Remove both front wheels as described in this chapter.

4. Remove the cotter pin and castellated nut (**Figure 24**) securing the tie rod end to the steering knuckle. Discard the cotter pin as a new pin must be installed.

CAUTION
If the tie rod is difficult to remove from the steering knuckle, do not attempt to pry it out as the tie rod seal may be damaged.

5. Carefully disconnect the tie rod from the steering knuckle. If the tie end is difficult to remove, install the nut just enough to cover the threads on tie rod end and tap the tie rod end out of the steering knuckle with a soft-faced mallet.

6. Remove the cotter pin and castellated nut (**Figure 16**) securing the tie rod end to the steering shaft mounting flange. Discard the cotter pin as a new pin must be installed.

7. Carefully disconnect the tie rod from the steering shaft mounting flange and remove the tie rod assembly. If the tie rod is difficult to remove, use the procedure in Step 5 for this end of the tie rod.

8. Repeat Steps 4-7 for the other tie rod.

Inspection/Disassembly/Assembly

1. Inspect the rubber boot at each end of the tie rod end swivel joint (**Figure 25**). The swivel joints are permanently packed with grease. If the rubber boot is damaged, dirt and moisture can enter the swivel joint and destroy it. If the boot is damaged in any way, disassemble the tie rod assembly and replace the tie rod end(s). They can be replaced separately.

2. If the tie rod ends (swivel joints) are to be replaced, refer to **Figure 23** and perform the following for removal:

    a. Loosen the locknuts (A, **Figure 26**) securing the tie rod ends. The locknut securing the outside tie rod end has *left-hand* threads.

    b. Unscrew the damaged tie rod end(s) (B, **Figure 26**).

3A. On 1986 models, to install the tie rod ends, refer to **Figure 23** and perform the following:

    a. The inner tie rod is marked with an "L" (**Figure 27**). Install this tie rod end onto the end of the tie rod *without* the flat on it.

10

b. Install the new tie rod end and turn it in until the groove (interrupted thread) in the tie rod threads enters the tie rod end.

c. Screw the locknut up against the tie rod end, but do not tighten at this time. They will be tightened after the wheel alignment is adjusted.

d. Repeat for the other tie rod end if necessary.

3B. On 1987-on models, to install the tie rod ends, refer to **Figure 23** and perform the following:

a. The inner tie rod is marked with an "L" (**Figure 27**). Install this tie rod end onto the end of the tie rod *without* the flat on it.

b. Install the new tie rod end onto the tie rod and turn it in until the center-to-center of each ball-joint is 313 ± 1.5 mm (12.32 ± 0.06 in.) is obtained as shown in **Figure 28**.

c. Screw the locknut up against the tie rod end, but do not tighten at this time. They will be tightened after the wheel alignment is adjusted.

d. Repeat for the other tie rod end if necessary.

Installation

1. Position the tie rod assembly so the end with the flat (**Figure 29**) on the shaft is attached to the steering knuckle.

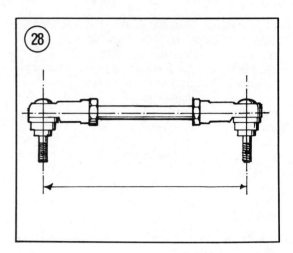

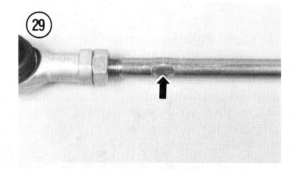

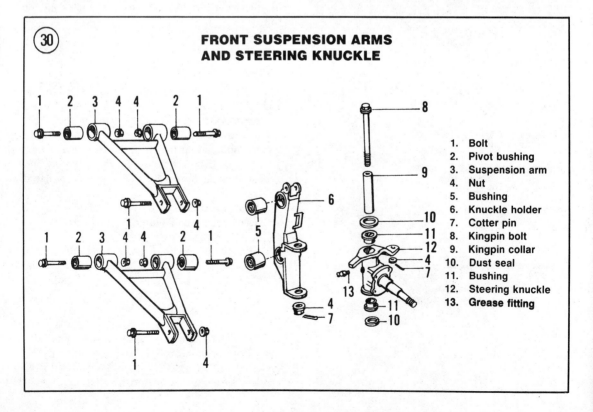

FRONT SUSPENSION ARMS AND STEERING KNUCKLE

1. Bolt
2. Pivot bushing
3. Suspension arm
4. Nut
5. Bushing
6. Knuckle holder
7. Cotter pin
8. Kingpin bolt
9. Kingpin collar
10. Dust seal
11. Bushing
12. Steering knuckle
13. Grease fitting

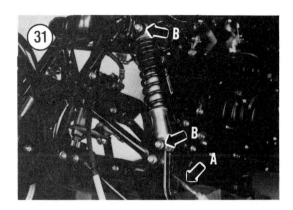

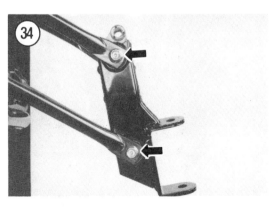

2. Attach the tie rod assembly to the steering shaft and to the steering knuckle. Install the castellated nuts and tighten to the torque specification listed in **Table 1**.

3. Install a new cotter pin at each location and bend both ends over completely.

4. Install both front wheels as described in this chapter.

5. Align the toe-in adjustment of the front wheels as described under *Front Wheel Toe-in Adjustment (4-wheeled Models)* in Chapter Three.

6. Tighten the tie rod end locknuts to the torque specification listed in **Table 1**.

7. Install the seat and front fender as described in Chapter Fifteen.

STEERING KNUCKLE AND STEERING KNUCKLE HOLDER

Removal

Refer to **Figure 30** for this procedure.

1. Place the ATV on level ground and set the parking brake. Block the rear wheels so the vehicle will not roll in either direction.

2. Remove the seat and front fenders as described in Chapter Fifteen.

3. Remove both front wheels as described in this chapter.

4. Remove the front brake assemblies as described under *Front Brake Panel Removal/Installation* in Chapter Thirteen.

5. Remove the tie rod assembly (A, **Figure 31**) from the steering knuckle as described in this chapter.

6. Remove the bolts and nuts securing the shock absorber (B, **Figure 31**) to the frame and the steering knuckle holder. Remove the shock absorber.

7. Remove the cotter pin and castellated nut (**Figure 32**) from the kingpin bolt.

8. Withdraw the kingpin bolt (A, **Figure 33**) and remove the steering knuckle (B, **Figure 33**) from the knuckle holder.

9. Remove the bolts and nuts (**Figure 34**) securing the knuckle holder to the upper and lower suspension arms. Remove the knuckle holder.

Installation

1. Install the knuckle holder into the suspension arms, then install the bolts and nuts. Tighten the nuts and bolts to the torque specification listed in **Table 1**.

10

2. If removed, apply multipurpose grease to the kingpin collar (A, **Figure 35**) and install it into the steering knuckle.

3. Apply multipurpose grease to the lips of the steering knuckle dust seals (B, **Figure 35**).

4. Apply multipurpose grease to the kingpin bolt.

5. Install the steering knuckle into the steering knuckle holder and install the kingpin bolt from the top (B, **Figure 33**).

6. Install the castellated nut onto the kingpin bolt and tighten to the torque specification listed in **Table 1**.

7. Install a new cotter pin (**Figure 32**) and bend the ends over completely.

8. Install the shock absorber and the mounting bolts and nuts (B, **Figure 31**). Tighten the nuts to the torque specification listed in **Table 1**.

9. Install the tie rod assembly (A, **Figure 31**) onto the steering knuckle as described in this chapter.

10. Install the front brake assemblies as described under *Front Brake Backing Plate Removal/ Installation* in Chapter Thirteen.

11. Install both front wheels as described in this chapter.

12. Install the seat and front fenders as described in Chapter Fifteen.

Steering Knuckle
Inspection and Bushing Replacement

Refer to **Figure 30** for this procedure.

1. Inspect the dust seal (**Figure 36**) at each end of the steering knuckle for wear or damage; replace if necessary.

2. Check each kingpin pivot bushing (**Figure 37**) for wear or damage; replace if necessary.

3. Measure the inside diameter of the kingpin bushings (**Figure 38**). If worn to the service limit dimension in **Table 2** or greater, replace both bushings. Replace both bushings even if only one is worn.

4. Measure the outside diameter of the kingpin (**Figure 39**). If worn to the service limit dimension in **Table 2** or less, replace the kingpin.

5. Inspect the kingpin bolt and nut (**Figure 40**) for straightness, wear or damage; replace if necessary.

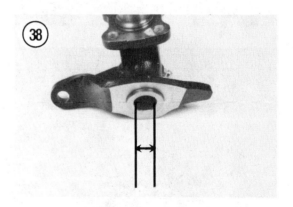

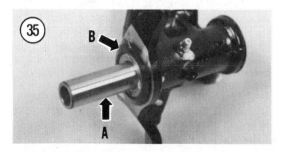

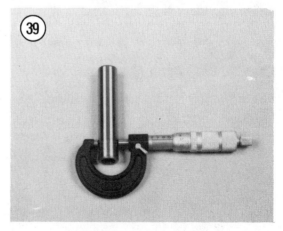

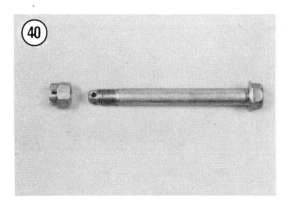

6. To remove the kingpin pivot bushings, perform the following:
   a. Support the steering knuckle.
   b. Insert an aluminum or brass drift into one side of the steering knuckle and place the end on the end of the bushing.
   c. Using a hammer, work around the perimeter and carefully drive out the old bushing.
   d. Repeat for the other bushing.

7. To install the new pivot bushing perform the following:
   a. Pack the inside surface of the steering knuckle with multipurpose grease.
   b. Tap the new bushing into the steering knuckle squarely with a block of wood and hammer. Make sure the bushing is completely seated in the steering knuckle.

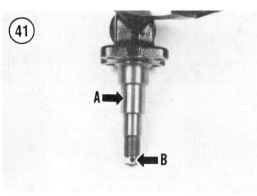

8. Inspect the spindle portion of the steering knuckle (A, **Figure 41**) for wear or damage. A hard spill or collision may cause the spindle portion to bend or fracture. If the spindle is damaged in any way, replace the steering knuckle as described in this chapter.

9. Check the hole (B, **Figure 41**) at the end of the steering knuckle where the cotter pin fits. Make sure there are no fractures or cracks leading out toward the end of the steering knuckle. If any are present, replace the steering knuckle.

Steering Knuckle Holder
Inspection and Bushing Replacement

Refer to **Figure 30** for this procedure.

1. Inspect the shock absorber mounting holes (**Figure 42**) for wear or elongation. If worn, replace the knuckle holder.

2. Inspect the kingpin bolt mounting holes (**Figure 43**) for wear or elongation. If worn, replace the knuckle holder.

3. Inspect the kingpin bolt mounting tabs. They must be parallel to each other (**Figure 44**). If uneven or damaged, replace the knuckle holder.

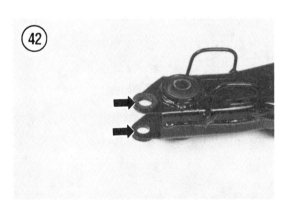

10

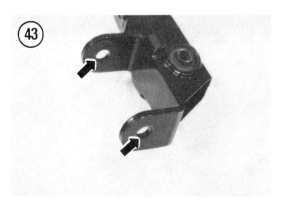

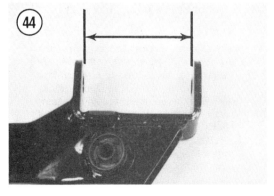

4. Check each steering knuckle holder pivot bushing (**Figure 45**) for wear or damage; replace if necessary.

5. To replace the pivot bushing perform the following:

   a. Support the steering knuckle holder and carefully drive out the old bushing with a suitable size socket and hammer.

   b. Install the new pivot bushing using the same tool setup used for removal. Tap the bushing in until it is centered or flush with each side.

6. Apply a coat of waterproof grease to the pivot bolt opening in the pivot bushing.

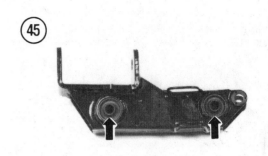

FRONT SUSPENSION ARM

Removal

1. Remove the steering knuckle and knuckle holder as described in this chapter.

> *NOTE*
> *The suspension arms must be reinstalled into the frame at the same angle from true horizontal. The pivot bushing inner ends are serrated. When the suspension arm mounting bolts and nuts are tightened, the pivot bushing and arm will stay in that position, relative to the frame.*

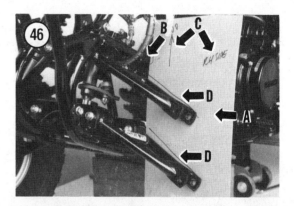

2. Before loosening the bolts and nuts securing the steering arms to the frame, perform the following and make an installation template:

   a. Tape a piece of stiff cardboard (A, **Figure 46**) to the frame directly behind the steering arms.

   b. Make a mark on the cardboard at the top surface of the frame (B, **Figure 46**). Also mark an UP arrow and whether it is the right- or left-hand side of the vehicle (C, **Figure 46**).

   c. Using a fine-point marking pen, draw a line on the cardboard directly above the top surface of each arm (D, **Figure 46**).

> *NOTE*
> *The top and bottom suspension arms are identical. If working on a vehicle with many miles on it, reinstall the arms in their original positions. Parts take a wear pattern after a period of time. Also, the arms can be installed backwards if not properly identified. If installed incorrectly the shock absorber mount (on the knuckle holder) will be offset and the shock absorber cannot be installed.*

3. Place a piece of masking tape onto the arms. Mark each arm as to location top or bottom and with an arrow pointing to the front (**Figure 47**).

4. Remove the pivot bolts and nuts (**Figure 48**) securing the suspension arms to the frame and remove the assembly. Note that the bolts are installed from the inner surface of the pivot points.

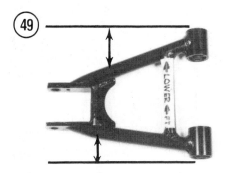

Installation

1. If the suspension arm was not labeled during the removal sequence, refer to **Figure 49**. The front of the suspension arm has a greater angle as shown.

2. Install the suspension arm into the mounting tabs (**Figure 50**) in the frame.

3. Install the bolts from the inner surface of the pivot points and install the nuts. Do not tighten the bolts and nuts at this time.

NOTE
The suspension arms must be reinstalled into the frame at the same angle from true horizontal. The pivot bushing inner ends are serrated. When the mounting bolts and nuts are tightened, the pivot bushing and arm will stay in that position in relation to the frame.

4. Position the suspension arm to the angle noted during *Removal* Step 2 (D, **Figure 46**).

5. Tighten the bolts and nuts to the torque specification listed in **Table 1**.

6. Repeat for all suspension arms.

7. Remove the piece of cardboard and the masking tape from the arms.

8. Install the steering knuckle holder and steering knuckle as described in this chapter.

Front Suspension Arms
Inspection and Bushing Replacement

Refer to **Figure 30** for this procedure.

NOTE
The pivot bushing is laminated rubber and metal and does not rotate. The outer portion must be a tight fit in the suspension arm.

1. Check each front suspension arm pivot bushing (**Figure 51**) for wear or damage; replace if necessary.

2. To replace the pivot bushing, perform the following:

    a. Support the suspension arm and carefully drive out the old bushing with a suitable size socket and hammer.

    b. Install the new pivot bushing using the same tool setup used for removal. Tap the bushing in until it is centered or flush with each side.

3. Inspect the steering knuckle holder mounting holes (**Figure 52**) for wear or elongation. If worn, replace the suspension arm.

10

SHOCK ABSORBER

Removal/Installation

1. Remove the front wheel as described in this chapter.
2. Remove the bolts and nuts (**Figure 53**) securing the shock absorber to the frame and steering knuckle holder.
3. Install by reversing these removal steps. Tighten the mounting bolts and nuts to the torque specifications listed in **Table 1**.
4. Repeat for the other side.

Disassembly/Inspection/Assembly

Refer to **Figure 54** for this procedure.

The shock is spring-controlled and hydraulically damped. The shock damper unit is sealed and cannot be serviced. Service is limited to removal and replacement of the damper unit and the spring.

A special tool and 2 additional items are needed for disassembly and assembly of the shock absorber. These tools are available from a Honda dealer and are as follows:

   a. Shock absorber compressor (Honda part No. 07959-3290001).
   b. Collar (Honda part No. 07967-GA70101).
   c. Spring compressor adaptor (Honda part No. 07967-VM50100).

> *WARNING*
> *Without the proper tools, this procedure can be dangerous. The spring can fly loose, causing injury. For a small bench fee, a dealer can do the job for you.*

1. Install the collar into the spring compressor.
2. Install the shock absorber into a compression tool as shown in **Figure 55**.
3. Install the adaptor onto the shock absorber spring and into the upper portion of the spring compressor. Tighten the clamp securing the adaptor.
4. Compress the shock spring just enough to gain access to the locknut.
5. Place the upper joint in a vise with soft jaws and loosen the locknut.
6. Completely unscrew the upper joint. This part may be difficult to break loose as thread locking agent was applied during assembly.
7. Release the spring tension and remove the shock from the compression tool.

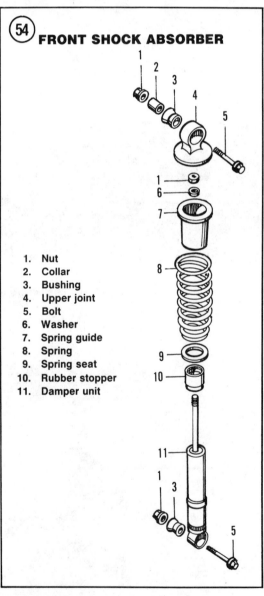

FRONT SHOCK ABSORBER

1. Nut
2. Collar
3. Bushing
4. Upper joint
5. Bolt
6. Washer
7. Spring guide
8. Spring
9. Spring seat
10. Rubber stopper
11. Damper unit

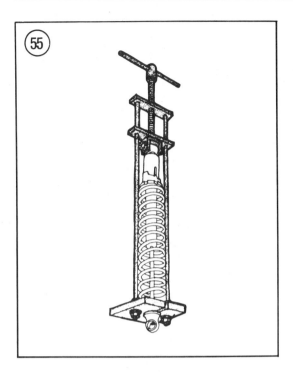

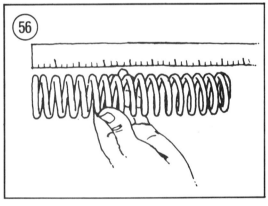

8. Remove the spring guide, spring and spring seat from the damper unit.

9. Measure the spring free length (**Figure 56**). The spring must be replaced if it has sagged to the service limit listed in **Table 2** or less.

10. Check the damper unit for leakage and make sure the damper rod is straight.

NOTE
The damper unit cannot be rebuilt; it must be replaced as a unit.

11. Inspect the rubber bushings in the upper joint (**Figure 57**) and lower joint (**Figure 58**); replace if necessary.

12. Inspect the rubber stopper. If it is worn or deteriorated, remove the locknut and washer, then slide off the rubber stopper. Replace with a new one.

13. Assembly is the reverse of these disassembly steps, noting the following.

14. Apply Loctite Lock 'N Seal to the threads of the damper rod before installing the locknut. Temporarily screw the locknut all the way down and tight against the end of the threads.

15. Apply Loctite Lock N' Seal to the threads of the damper rod before installing the upper joint. Screw the upper joint on all the way. Secure the upper joint in a vise with soft jaws and tighten the locknut along with the damper rod against the upper joint. Tighten the locknut securely.

NOTE
After the locknut is tightened completely the locknut must be against the bottom surface of the upper joint and against the end of the threads on the damper rod.

10

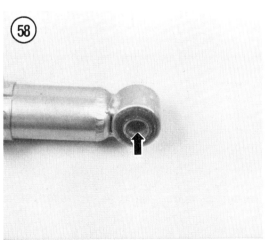

Table 1 FRONT SUSPENSION TORQUE SPECIFICATIONS

Item and model	N•m	ft.-lb.
Front wheel hub castellated nut	60-80	43-58
Wheel lug nuts	60-70	43-51
Handlebar upper holder bolts	18-30	13-22
Steering shaft bearing locknut	40-60	29-43
Steering shaft castellated nut	50-70	36-51
Tie rods		
Castellated nuts	35-43	21-31
End locknuts	35-43	21-31
Suspension arms-to-steering knuckle holder bolts and nuts		
1986-1987	40-50	29-36
1988	35-45	25-33
Suspension arms-to-frame bolts and nuts	30-36	22-26
Shock absorber mounting bolts and nuts		
1986-1987	40-50	29-36
1988	35-45	25-33
Steering knuckle king pin bolt and nut	50-70	36-51

Table 2 FRONT SUSPENSION SPECIFICATIONS

Item	Specification	Wear limit
King pin OD	17.966-17.984 mm (0.7073-0.7080 in.)	17.90 mm (0.705 in.)
Knuckle bushing ID	18.045-18.075 mm (0.7104-0.7116 in.)	18.17 mm (0.715 in.)
Shock absorber spring free length	161.1 mm (6.34 in.)	159.5 mm (6.28 in.)

Table 3 TIRE INFLATION PRESSURE (COLD) *

Model	Tire size	Standard kPa	Standard psi	Minimum kPa	Minimum psi	Maximum kPa	Maximum psi
Front	20×7.0-8	21	3.0	18	2.6	24	3.5
Rear	22×11-8	17	2.5	14	2.0	20	2.9

* Tire inflation pressure for factory equipped tires. Aftermarket tires may require different inflation pressure.

CHAPTER ELEVEN

REAR AXLE AND SUSPENSION
(3-WHEELED MODELS)

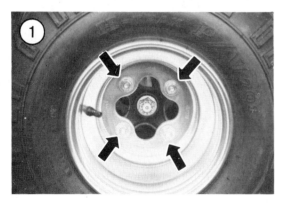

This chapter contains repair and replacement procedures for the rear wheel, rear hub and rear suspension. Service to the rear suspension consists of periodically checking bolt tightness, replacing swing arm bushings and checking the condition of the rear shock absorber. Tire removal and repair are covered in Chapter Nine.

Refer to **Table 1** and **Table 2** at the end of this chapter for rear suspension torque settings and specifications.

REAR WHEEL

Removal/Installation

1. Set the ATV on level ground and set the parking brake. Securely block the front wheel so the vehicle will not roll jn either direction.

2. Place wood blocks under the engine to support the ATV securely with the rear wheel off the ground.

3. Remove the lug nuts (**Figure 1**) securing the rear wheel to the hub and remove the rear wheel.

4. Install the rear wheel with the valve stem facing toward the outside.

5. Install the lug nuts with the tapered end going on first (**Figure 2**). Tighten the nuts only finger-tight at this time.

6. Remove the wood blocks from under the engine and set the rear wheel on the ground.

7. Tighten the wheel lug nuts to the torque specification listed in **Table 1**.

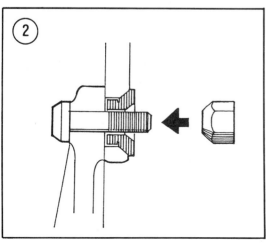

REAR HUB

Removal/Installation

1. Remove the rear wheel as described in this chapter.
2. Remove the cotter pin and hub nut (**Figure 3**) securing the wheel hub to the rear axle and remove the hub assembly.
3. Install the rear hub onto the rear axle.
4. Install the hub nut and tighten only finger-tight at this time.
5. Install the rear wheel as described in this chapter and set the vehicle on the ground.
6. Tighten the hub nut to the torque specification listed in **Table 1**.
7. Install a new cotter pin and bend the ends over completely. Never reuse a cotter pin as it may break and fall out.
8. Tighten the wheel nuts to the torque specification listed in **Table 1**.

REAR AXLE
AND DRIVEN SPROCKET

Removal

Refer to **Figure 4** for this procedure.
1. Place the ATV on level ground and set the parking brake.

2. Shift the transmission into NEUTRAL.
3. Remove the seat and rear fender as described in Chapter Fifteen.
4. To relieve drive chain tension, perform the following:
    a. Loosen the swing arm pinch bolts (A, **Figure 5**) securing the axle holder.
    b. Insert a drift or round bar into one of the holes (B, **Figure 5**) in the axle holder.
    c. Push the drift toward the front of the vehicle, rotating the top of the axle holder toward the front.

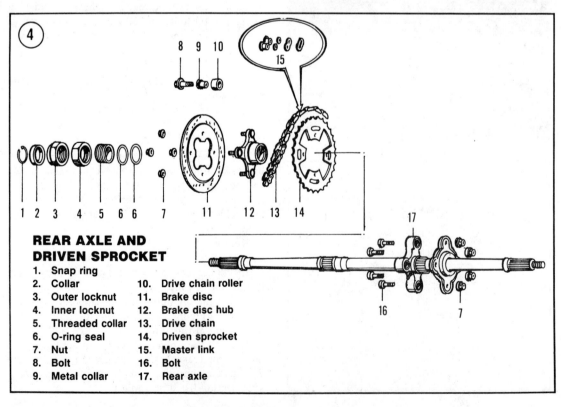

**REAR AXLE AND
DRIVEN SPROCKET**

1. Snap ring
2. Collar
3. Outer locknut
4. Inner locknut
5. Threaded collar
6. O-ring seal
7. Nut
8. Bolt
9. Metal collar
10. Drive chain roller
11. Brake disc
12. Brake disc hub
13. Drive chain
14. Driven sprocket
15. Master link
16. Bolt
17. Rear axle

d. Rotate the axle holder until there is the maximum amount of drive chain slack.

5. Remove both rear wheels as described in this chapter.

6. Remove both rear hubs as described in this chapter.

7. Remove the bolts securing the swing arm skid plate (**Figure 6**) and remove the skid plate.

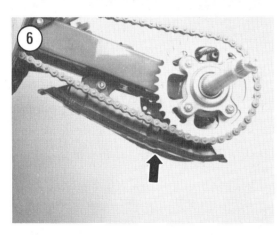

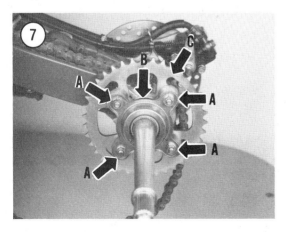

8. Grab the end of the rear axle and move the axle up and down and from side to side. Do this on each end of the axle. If there is excessive play, the bearings in the rear axle bearing housing need replacing. Replace the bearings as described in this chapter.

9. Remove the nuts (A, **Figure 7**) securing the drive chain guide plate and remove the guide plate (B, **Figure 7**).

10. Remove the bolts securing the driven sprocket and remove the driven sprocket (C, **Figure 7**) from the sprocket flange.

CAUTION
*The inner and outer locknuts have **left-hand** threads. To loosen the locknuts, turn the wrench **clockwise**.*

CAUTION
*The inner and outer locknuts have had Loctite applied during assembly and are tightened to 80-120 N•m (58-87 ft.-lb.). They are very hard to remove even with the correct size tool and a lot of force. Do **not** apply heat to the area in order to try to loosen the locknut and inner nut as this will ruin the heat-treated hardness of the axle.*

NOTE
A special flame cut 45 mm wrench is available from a Honda dealer or some mail order houses. The Honda part No. is 07916-187101 (available as a 2-wrench set).

11. Remove the brake disc as described in this chapter.

12. Place a 45 mm open end wrench on both the inner and outer locknuts.

NOTE
If you are unable to loosen the locknuts they will have to be chiseled off. Do not chisel all the way through into the threads of the threaded collar or the axle.

13. Temporarily install the left-hand hub and rear wheel. Have an assistant hold onto the left-hand wheel to keep the rear axle from turning.

14. Loosen the inner locknut and thread it all the way in toward the brake disc. It may be necessary to tap on the end of the wrench with a soft-faced mallet to break the locknut loose.

15. Place a 45 mm open-end wrench on the outer locknut and thread the outer locknut in toward the brake disc until the snap ring is accessible.

16. If installed, remove the left-hand wheel and hub.

11

17. Remove the snap ring (**Figure 8**) and slide the collar (**Figure 9**) off of the rear axle.

18. Slide the outer locknut, inner locknut and threaded collar as an assembly (**Figure 10**) off of the rear axle.

19. Slide the brake disc hub (**Figure 11**) off of the rear axle.

20. Remove the left-hand rear wheel.

21. Carefully tap on the right-hand end of the axle with a soft-faced mallet (**Figure 12**).

22. Pull the rear axle assembly out of the swing arm from the left-hand side (**Figure 13**).

23. Inspect the rear axle as described under *Rear Axle Inspection* in this chapter.

Installation

1. Make sure the axle bearing grease seals (**Figure 14**) are in place on each side of the rear axle bearing housing. Apply a light coat of multipurpose grease to the lips of the seals.

2. Install a new O-ring seal next to the driven sprocket mounting flange.

3. Install the rear axle assembly into the swing arm from the left-hand side with the driven sprocket mounting flange on the left-hand side.

4. Install a new O-ring seal (**Figure 15**) in the rear brake disc hub.

5. Position the rear brake disc assembly with the hub side going on first and slide the rear brake disc hub onto the rear axle. If necessary, carefully tap the hub into place with a soft-faced mallet.

6. Completely unscrew the inner and outer locknuts from the threaded collar (**Figure 16**). Use cleaning solvent and a stiff brush and clean off all old locking agent from all 3 parts. Inspect the parts as described in this chapter. Reassemble the 3 parts—do not apply any oil to any of these 3 parts as Loctite will be used during the installation procedure.

7. Slide on the inner locknut, outer locknut and threaded collar assembly with the inner locknut going on first (**Figure 17**).

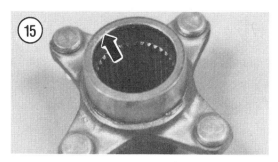

8. Install the collar (**Figure 9**) and the snap ring (**Figure 18**). Make sure the snap ring is correctly seated in the groove in the axle (**Figure 8**).

9. Apply blue Loctite Lock N' Seal to the threads of the threaded collar and the inner and outer locknuts.

10. Temporarily install the left-hand hub and rear wheel (**Figure 19**). Have an assistant hold onto the left-hand wheel to keep the rear axle from turning.

CAUTION
*The inner and outer locknuts have **left-hand** threads. To tighten the locknuts, turn the wrench **counter-clockwise**.*

11. Use a 45 mm open-end wrench and tighten the outer locknut out against the collar and snap ring in the axle. Tighten the locknut to the torque specification listed in **Table 1**.

12. Remove the left-hand rear wheel and hub.

13. Place a 45 mm open-end wrench on both the inner and outer locknut.

14. Tighten the inner locknut up against the outer locknut. Tighten to the torque specification listed in **Table 1**.

11

15. Install the driven sprocket. If the factory equipped sprocket is used, install it with the "number of teeth" mark (**Figure 20**) facing toward the outside.

16. Align the flats of the bolt heads with the grooves (**Figure 21**) in the driven sprocket and install the bolts into the driven sprocket and through the mounting flange.

17. Install the drive chain guide plate (B, **Figure 7**) and nuts (A, **Figure 7**). Tighten the nuts to the torque specification listed in **Table 1**.

18. Install the drive chain onto the driven sprocket.

19. Install the swing arm skid plate and bolts. Tighten the bolts securely.

20. Install both wheel hubs as described in this chapter.

21. Install the rear wheels as described in this chapter.

22. Adjust the drive chain as described under *Drive Chain Adjustment* in Chapter Three.

23. Install the seat and the rear fender as described in Chapter Fifteen.

REAR AXLE INSPECTION

1. Inspect the rear axle for signs of fatigue, fractures or damage.

2. Inspect the splines where the driven sprocket (**Figure 22**) and the disc brake hub (A, **Figure 23**) mesh with the axle. Replace the axle or brake hub as necessary.

3. Inspect the groove snap ring (B, **Figure 23**) for wear or damage. Repair the groove if possible, or replace the rear axle.

4. Check the hole at each end of the axle (A, **Figure 24**) where the cotter pin fits. Make sure there are no fractures or cracks leading out toward the end of the axle. If any are found, replace the axle.

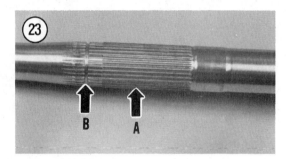

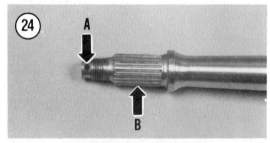

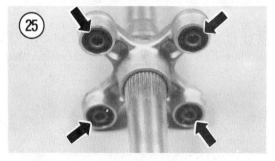

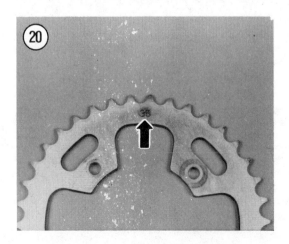

5. Inspect the splines where the rear hub (B, **Figure 24**) meshes with the axle. Replace the axle if necessary.

6. Inspect the rubber dampers (**Figure 25**) for wear or deterioration. If any are damaged, replace the rear axle.

7. Check the axle for straightness. Use V-blocks and a dial indicator as shown in **Figure 26**. Check the runout in the center of the axle and remember that the actual runout is 1/2 of the total runout reading from the dial indicator. If the runout is 3.0 mm (0.12 in.) or greater the axle must be replaced.

8. Completely unscrew the inner and outer locknuts from the threaded collar (**Figure 16**). Use cleaning solvent and a stiff brush and clean off all old locking agent from all 3 parts.

9. Inspect the threads (**Figure 27**) of both the inner and outer locknuts and the threaded collar. If the threads are damaged on any of the 3 parts, replace all 3 parts as a set. Reassemble the 3 parts—do not apply any oil to any of these 3 parts as Loctite will be used during the installation procedure.

10. Inspect the splines (**Figure 28**) of the threaded collar for wear or damage. If damaged, replace the threaded collar and the locknuts as a set.

11. Inspect the splines (A, **Figure 29**) and threaded studs (B, **Figure 29**) on the brake disc hub for wear or damage. If damaged, replace the brake disc hub.

DRIVEN SPROCKET

Removal

Refer to **Figure 4** for this procedure.

1. Place the ATV on level ground and set the parking brake.

2. Shift the transmission into NEUTRAL.

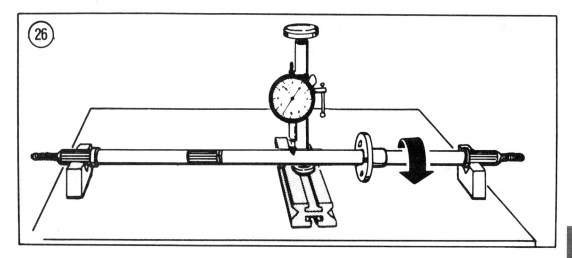

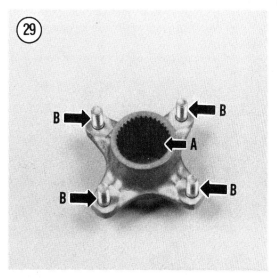

11

3. Remove the seat and rear fender as described in Chapter Fifteen.

4. To relieve drive chain tension, perform the following:

   a. Loosen the swing arm pinch bolts (A, **Figure 5**) securing the axle holder.

   b. Insert a drift or round bar into one of the holes (B, **Figure 5**) in the axle holder.

   c. Push the drift toward the front of the vehicle, rotating the top of the axle holder toward the front.

   d. Rotate the axle holder until there is the maximum amount of drive chain slack.

5. Remove the left-hand rear wheel as described in this chapter.

6. Remove the left-hand rear hub as described in this chapter.

7. Place a wood block under the swing arm to support it in the up position.

8. Remove the nuts (A, **Figure 7**) securing the drive chain guide plate and remove the guide plate.

9. Remove the bolts securing the driven sprocket and remove the driven sprocket from the sprocket flange (B, **Figure 7**).

Installation

1. Install the driven sprocket. If the factory equipped sprocket is used, install it with the "number of teeth" mark (**Figure 20**) facing toward the outside.

2. Align the flats of the bolt heads with the grooves (**Figure 21**) in the driven sprocket and install the bolts into the driven sprocket and through the mounting flange.

3. Install the drive chain guide plate (B, **Figure 7**) and nuts (A, **Figure 7**). Tighten the nuts to the torque specification listed in **Table 1**.

4. Install the drive chain onto the driven sprocket.

5. Install the left-hand wheel hub as described in this chapter.

6. Install the left-hand wheel as described in this chapter.

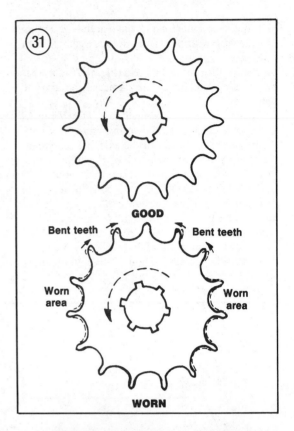

GOOD

Bent teeth   Bent teeth

Worn area   Worn area

WORN

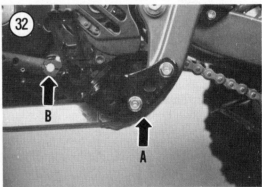

B

A

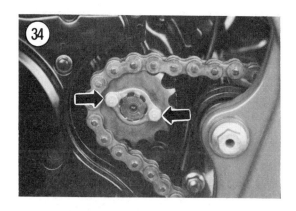

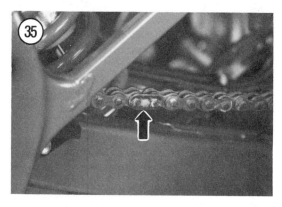

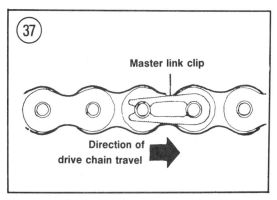

Master link clip

Direction of drive chain travel

7. Adjust the drive chain as described under *Drive Chain Adjustment* in Chapter Three.

8. Install the seat and the rear fender as described in Chapter Fifteen.

Driven Sprocket Inspection

Inspect the teeth of the driven sprocket (**Figure 30**). If the teeth are visibly worn (**Figure 31**), replace the driven sprocket with a new one.

If the driven sprocket requires replacement, the drive chain and the drive sprocket are probably worn also. Remove and replace the drive chain and drive sprocket as described in this chapter.

DRIVE SPROCKET AND CHAIN

Removal/Installation

1. Place the ATV on level ground and set the parking brake.

2. Remove the seat and the rear fender as described in Chapter Fifteen.

3. Remove the bolts securing the left-hand footpeg (A, **Figure 32**) and remove the footpeg assembly.

4. Remove the clamping bolt securing the gearshift lever (B, **Figure 32**) and remove the lever.

5. Remove the bolts securing the drive sprocket cover (**Figure 33**) and remove the cover.

6. To relieve drive chain tension, perform the following:

    a. Loosen the swing arm pinch bolts (A, **Figure 5**) securing the axle holder.

    b. Insert a drift or round bar into one of the holes (B, **Figure 5**) in the axle holder.

    c. Push the drift toward the front of the vehicle, rotating the top of the axle holder toward the front.

    d. Rotate the axle holder until there is the maximum amount of drive chain slack.

7. Have an assistant apply the rear brake to keep the drive chain taut and keep the drive sprocket from turning. Remove the bolts (**Figure 34**) securing the drive sprocket and plate.

8. Remove the master link (**Figure 35**) from the drive chain.

9. Rotate the drive sprocket plate in either direction to clear the splines of the transmission shaft and slide off the plate.

10. Remove the drive chain (A, **Figure 36**) from the drive sprocket.

11. Slide off the drive sprocket (B, **Figure 36**).

12. Install by reversing these removal steps, noting the following.

13. Install the drive chain master link clip with the closed end facing in the direction of travel (**Figure 37**).

14. Tighten the drive sprocket bolt securely.

11

15. Adjust the drive chain as described under *Drive Chain Adjustment* in Chapter Three.

Drive Sprocket Inspection

Inspect the teeth of the drive sprocket. If the teeth are visibly worn (**Figure 31**), replace the drive sprocket with a new one.

If the drive sprocket requires replacement, the drive chain is probably worn also. Remove and replace the drive chain as described in this chapter.

DRIVE CHAIN

Cleaning/Inspection/Lubrication

> *CAUTION*
> *The drive chain is equipped with O-rings. These rubber O-rings can easily be damaged. Do not use a steam cleaner, a high-pressure washer or any solvent that may damage the rubber O-rings.*

1. Remove the drive chain as described in this chapter.
2. Immerse the chain in a pan of kerosene or non-flammable solvent and allow it to soak for about half an hour. Move it around and flex it during this period so that the dirt between the links, pins, rollers and O-rings may work its way out.

> *CAUTION*
> *In the next step, do not use a wire brush or the O-rings will be damaged and the drive chain will have to be replaced.*

3. Scrub the rollers and side plates with a medium soft brush and rinse away loosened dirt. Do not scrub hard as the O-rings may be damaged. Rinse the chain a couple of times to make sure all dirt and grit are washed out. Dry the chain with a shop cloth, then hang it up and allow it to dry thoroughly.
4. After cleaning the chain, examine it carefully for wear or damage. If any signs are visible, replace the chain.

> *NOTE*
> *Always check both sprockets every time the chain is removed. If any wear is visible on the teeth, replace both sprockets. Never install a new chain over worn sprockets or a worn chain over new sprockets.*

5. Lubricate the chain with SAE 40 or 50 weight engine oil or a good grade of chain lubricant (specifically formulated for O-ring chains), following the manufacturer's instructions.
6. Reinstall the chain as described in this chapter.

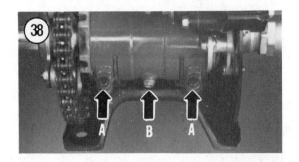

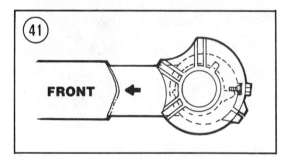

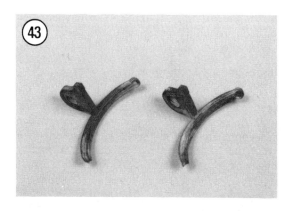

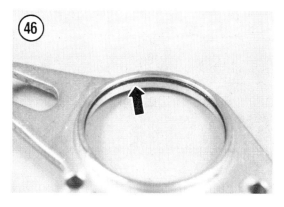

REAR AXLE BEARING HOUSING

The rear axle bearing housing is attached to the rear of the swing arm and contains the rear axle bearings and grease seals.

Removal

1. Completely loosen the rear axle bearing housing clamping bolts (A, **Figure 38**) at the rear of the swing arm.
2. Remove the large circlip (**Figure 39**) securing the brake caliper holder and remove the brake caliper holder.
3. Remove the rear axle as described in this chapter.
4. Inspect the axle bearings as described under *Bearing Preliminary Inspection* in this chapter.
5. Remove the rear axle bearing housing stopper bolt (B, **Figure 38**).

> *CAUTION*
> *Be careful not to damage the inner surfaces of the swing arm where the rear axle bearing housing rides. These surfaces must remain smooth so the rear axle bearing housing can rotate freely for drive chain adjustment.*

6. Using a soft-faced mallet, carefully tap the rear axle bearing housing out of the swing arm from the right-hand side. Note that the flanged side of the holder is on the left-hand side.
7. Remove and discard the O-ring seals (**Figure 40**) at each end of the housing.

Installation

1. Install new O-ring seals (**Figure 40**) on each end of the housing. Apply a light coat of multipurpose grease to the new O-rings.
2. Install the rear axle bearing housing from the left-hand side. Position the housing in the swing arm as shown in **Figure 41**.
3. Install the stopper bolt (**Figure 42**) and tighten to the torque specification listed in **Table 1**.
4. If removed, inspect the rubber seals (**Figure 43**) for deterioration. Replace seals as a pair if necessary. Install the rubber seals (**Figure 44**) into the swing arm.
5. Install a new O-ring seal (**Figure 45**) on the right-hand side of the bearing housing.
6. Install a new O-ring seal (**Figure 46**) into the caliper mounting plate.
7. Apply a light coat of waterproof grease to the backside of the caliper mounting plate and O-ring seal.

11

8. Make sure the locating post bushing (**Figure 47**) is in place on the pin on the swing arm.

9. Install the mounting plate onto the swing arm. Make sure the slot in the mounting plate is indexed correctly with the locating post bushing on the swing arm (**Figure 48**).

10. Install the rear axle as described in this chapter.

11. Position the large circlip with the OUTSIDE mark (**Figure 49**) facing toward the outside and install the circlip. Position the open end of the circlip facing upward as shown in **Figure 39**.

12. Install the rear axle bearing housing clamping bolts (A, **Figure 38**). Tighten only finger-tight at this time.

13. Adjust the drive chain as described under *Drive Chain Adjustment* in Chapter Three.

Bearing Preliminary Inspection

Before removing the rear axle bearing housing, perform the following.

1. Remove the rear axle as described in this chapter.

2. Wipe off all excessive grease from both bearings.

3. Turn each bearing by hand. Make sure the bearings turn smoothly. Check for roughness and free play. Some axial play (end play) is normal, but radial play (side play) should be negligible.

4. Replace the bearings, if necessary, as described in this chapter.

5. Inspect the grease seals. Replace if they are deteriorating or starting to harden.

Bearing Removal

Refer to **Figure 50** for this procedure.

1. Remove the rear axle bearing housing as described in this chapter.

2. Carefully remove the grease seal from each side of the rear axle bearing housing. Refer to **Figure 51** for the right-hand side or **Figure 52** for the left-hand side.

3. Insert a soft aluminum or brass drift into one side of the bearing housing.

4. Push the center collar over to one side and place the drift on the spacer next to the opposite bearing.

5. Tap the bearing out of the hub with a hammer working around the perimeter of the spacer.

6. Remove that bearing, spacer and the center collar.

7. Turn the rear axle housing over.

8. Insert a soft aluminum or brass drift into the opposite side of the bearing housing.

9. Place the drift on the spacer next to the opposite bearing.

10. Tap the bearing out of the hub with a hammer working around the perimeter of the spacer.

11. Remove the bearing and spacer.

Inspection and Lubrication

1. On non-sealed bearings, check the balls for evidence of wear, pitting or excessive heat (bluish tint). Replace bearings if necessary; always replace as a complete set. When replacing, be sure to take your old bearings along to ensure a perfect matchup.

NOTE
Fully sealed bearings are available from many bearing specialty shops. Fully sealed bearings provide better protection from dirt and moisture that may get into the housing.

2. Thoroughly clean the inside of the rear axle bearing housing with solvent and dry with compressed air or a shop cloth.
3. Do not clean sealed bearings. If non-sealed bearings are installed, thoroughly clean them in

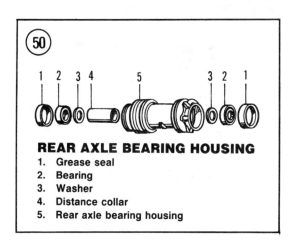

REAR AXLE BEARING HOUSING
1. **Grease seal**
2. **Bearing**
3. **Washer**
4. **Distance collar**
5. **Rear axle bearing housing**

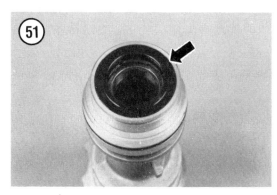

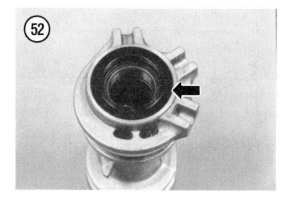

solvent and thoroughly dry with compressed air. Do not let the bearing spin while drying.
4. If non-sealed bearings are to be re-installed, pack the bearings with a good grade of waterproof grease, such as boat trailer wheel bearing grease, as follows:
   a. Spread some grease in the palm of your hand and scrape the open end of the bearing across your palm. Continue to add grease until the bearing is packed completely full of grease.
   b. Slowly spin the bearing a few times to determine if there are any areas that are void of grease. Thoroughly work the grease in between the balls.
   c. Turn the bearing by hand a couple more times to make sure the grease is distributed evenly inside the bearing.

Bearing Installation

Refer to **Figure 50** for this procedure.
1. Coat the outside of both bearings and inside of the rear axle bearing housing and the center collar with multipurpose grease.

CAUTION
During installation, tap the bearings squarely into place and tap on the outer race only. Use a socket that matches the outer race diameter. Do not tap on the inner race or the bearing may be damaged. Be sure that the bearings are completely seated.

2. On non-sealed bearings, position the bearing with the sealed surface facing outward. Non-sealed bearings have one sealed surface and this surface must face toward the outside.
3. Install the right-hand bearing.
4. Turn the bearing housing over and install the spacer and the center collar.
5. Install the left-hand bearing.
6. Apply a light coat of multipurpose grease to the grease seals.
7. Install a new grease seal into each side of the bearing housing. Drive the grease seals in until they are flush with the outer surface of the rear axle bearing housing.
8. Install the rear axle bearing housing and rear axle as described in this chapter.

SHOCK ABSORBER

Spring Preload Adjustment

There must be preload on the spring at all times. Never ride the vehicle without spring preload as loss of control may result.

11

The spring length (preload) must be maintained within the following dimensions:

    a. Standard dimension: 190 mm (7.48 in.).
    b. Minimum dimension: 185.5 mm (7.30 in.).
    c. Maximum dimension: 191.5 mm (7.53 in.).

1. Place wood block(s) under the frame to support the vehicle securely with both rear wheels off the ground.

2. Remove the seat/rear fender assembly as described in Chapter Fifteen.

3. Measure the existing spring length (**Figure 53**).

> *NOTE*
> *Special Honda tools are required for the locknut and the adjuster. These are pin spanners, part No. 89201-KA4-820 and part No. 89202-KA4-820.*

4. To adjust, loosen the locknut and turn the adjuster (**Figure 54**) in the desired direction. Tightening the adjuster *increases* spring preload and loosening it *decreases* preload.

5. On complete turn (360°) of the adjuster moves the spring 1.5 mm (0.06 in.).

> *NOTE*
> *Remember the spring length (preload) must be maintained within the previously listed dimensions.*

6. After the desired spring length is achieved, tighten the locknut to the torque specification listed in **Table 1**.

7. Install the seat/rear fender assembly as described in Chapter Fifteen.

Rebound Adjustment

Rebound damping can be adjusted to 4 different settings. The adjuster knob located at the base of

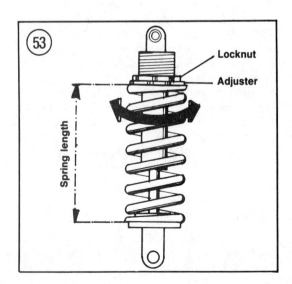

Locknut

Adjuster

Spring length

the shock absorber between the legs of the lower mounting bracket.

The rebound setting should be adjusted to personal preference to accommodate rider weight and riding conditions. The No. 1 setting is the softest while the No. 4 setting is the hardest.

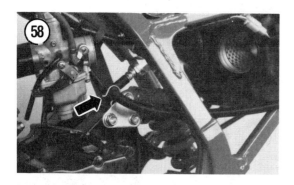

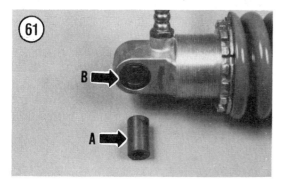

Make sure that the adjuster is located into one of the detents and not in between any 2 settings.

To change the setting slide the rubber boot (**Figure 55**) down and turn the adjuster (**Figure 56**) in either direction to achieve the desired amount of rebound.

Removal

1. Place the ATV on level ground and set the parking brake.
2. Place wood block(s) under the frame to support the ATV securely with the rear wheels off of the ground.
3. Remove the seat/rear fender assembly fender as described in Chapter Fifteen.
4. Remove both rear wheels as described in this chapter. It is not necessary to remove the wheels, but it makes shock absorber removal a lot easier.
5. Loosen the screws on the clamping bands of the carburetor-to-air filter air box interconnecting tube. Remove the interconnecting tube. Place a clean shop cloth in the carburetor throat to keep out any foreign matter.
6. Loosen the clamping screws and remove the clamps (**Figure 57**) securing the remote reservoir to the frame.
7. Remove the remote reservoir hose from the clamp on the engine rear hanger plate (**Figure 58**). Let the remote reservoir hang down.

NOTE
In the following steps, the rear axle is shown removed for clarity. It is not necessary to remove the axle to perform this procedure.

8. Remove the shock absorber cover from the swing arm.
9. Remove the bolt (**Figure 59**) securing the upper portion of the shock absorber to the frame. Let the swing arm and shock absorber swing down until they stop.
10. Remove the bolt and nut (**Figure 60**) securing the lower portion of the shock absorber to the swing arm.
11. Carefully remove the shock absorber assembly from the frame. Guide the remote reservoir oil hose through the frame.

Inspection

1. Remove the collar (A, **Figure 61**) from the bushing in the upper mount.
2. Remove the dust seal (B, **Figure 61**) from each side of the upper mount.

3. Inspect the bushing in the upper mount for wear or damage; replace if worn or damaged. If either the collar or bushing is worn or damaged, replace both parts as a set.

4. Install the dust seals and collar into the upper mount.

5. Remove the collar (A, **Figure 62**) from the bushing in the lower mount.

6. Inspect the O-ring seal (B, **Figure 62**) on each end of the collar. If worn or starting to deteriorate, replace both O-ring seals as a set.

7. Inspect the bushing in the lower mount for wear or damage; replace if worn or damaged. If either the collar or bushing is worn or damaged, replace both parts as a set.

8. Install the collar and O-ring seals into the lower mount.

9. Make sure the shock absorber spring nut and locknut (**Figure 63**) are tightened securely. Refer to **Table 1** for torque specifications.

10. Check the damper unit for dents, oil leakage or other damage. Make sure the damper rod (**Figure 64**) is straight. Replace the damper unit if any damage is found.

Installation

1. Apply a coat of molybdenum disulfide paste grease to the upper and lower mounting bushings on the shock absorber and to the upper and lower mounting yoke on the frame and the swing arm.

2. Make sure the dust seals are in place on the upper mount.

3. Position the shock absorber assembly in the frame with the remote reservoir oil hose facing *forward* and the adjuster on the lower mount facing toward the *rear*.

4. Install the shock absorber in the frame and install the shock absorber upper and lower mounting bolts and nuts. Tighten the bolts and nuts to the torque specification listed in **Table 1**.

5. Attach the oil hose to the engine rear hanger plate. Route the oil hose through the frame as shown in **Figure 65**.

6. Install the remote reservoir to the frame and tighten the clamping bolts (**Figure 57**). Make sure the oil hose is not kinked and has no sharp bends in it.

7. Remove the shop cloth from the carburetor throat.

8. Install the carburetor-to-air filter air box interconnecting tube. Tighten the screws on the clamping bands of the interconnecting tube.

9. Install both rear wheels as described in this chapter.

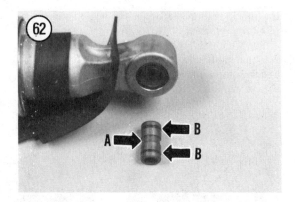

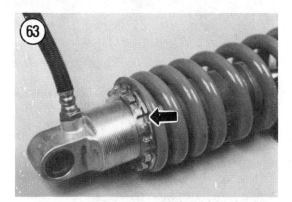

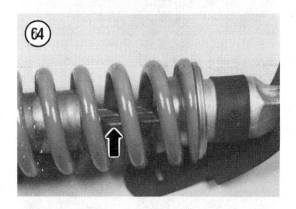

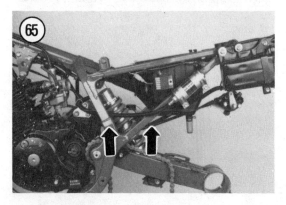

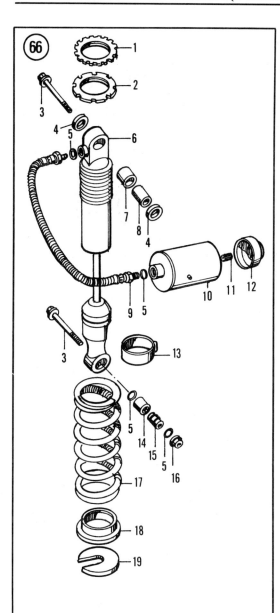

REAR SHOCK ABSORBER

1. Locknut
2. Adjust nut
3. Bolt
4. Dust seal
5. O-ring
6. Damper unit
7. Bushing
8. Collar
9. Oil hose
10. Remote reservoir

11. Valve stem cap
12. Cover
13. Rubber collar
14. Bushing
15. Collar
16. Nut
17. Spring
18. Spring seat
19. Spring seat stopper

10. Remove the wood blocks from under the frame.

11. Push down on the rear of the ATV and make sure the rear suspension is operating properly.

12. Install the seat/rear fender assembly as described in Chapter Fifteen.

Shock Absorber
Disassembly/Assembly

Refer to **Figure 66** for this procedure.

If you are satisfied with the existing spring preload setting and want to maintain it, measure the spring length (**Figure 67**) before disassembly.

1. Hold the shock absorber upside down and secure the upper mounting portion (A, **Figure 67**) of the shock absorber in a vise with soft jaws. Be careful not to kink or damage the remote reservoir hose.

NOTE
Special tools are required to loosen the locknut and the adjuster. These are pin spanners, Honda part No. 89201-KA4-820 and 89202-KA4-820.

2. Use special tools to loosen the locknut and spring adjuster (B, **Figure 67**). Unscrew them to almost the end of the threads. Do not completely unscrew either nut.

3. Slide out the spring seat stopper and spring seat.

4. Slide off the spring.

5. Inspect all components as described in this chapter.

6. Hold the shock absorber upside down and secure the upper mounting portion (A, **Figure 67**) of the shock absorber in a vise with soft jaws. Be careful not to kink or damage the remote reservoir hose.

7. Install the spring onto the damper unit.

8. Position the spring seat with the flange side away from the spring and install the spring seat.

9. Install the spring stopper.

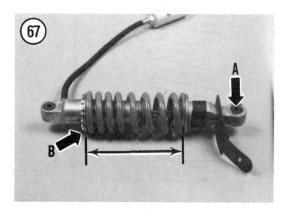

10. Screw the adjuster and locknut on by hand until they contact the spring.

11. Use the special Honda tools used during disassembly and tighten the adjuster to the dimension taken before disassembly or to the standard spring length listed in this procedure.

12. Hold onto the adjuster and tighten the locknut to the torque specification listed in **Table 1**.

13. Remove the shock absorber from the vise.

Inspection

1. Measure the free length of the spring (**Figure 68**). Replace the spring if it has sagged to the service limit listed in **Table 2** or less.

2. Check the remote reservoir hose for deterioration or damage. If damaged, have it replaced by a dealer.

3. Check the damper unit for dents, oil leakage or other damage. Make sure the damper rod is straight.

> *NOTE*
> *The damper unit cannot be rebuilt; it can be recharged with gas, as well as replacing the ATF fluid or the entire unit can be replaced.*

> *WARNING*
> *The shock absorber damper unit and remote reservoir contain nitrogen gas compressed to between 20-23 kg/cm² (284-327 psi). Do not tamper with or attempt to open the damper unit or disconnect the reservoir hose from either unit without first releasing the internal gas. Do not place it near an open flame or other extreme heat. Do not dispose of the damper assembly yourself. Take it to a dealer where it can be deactivated and disposed of properly.*

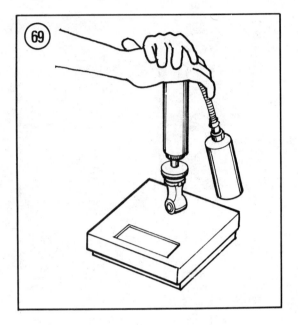

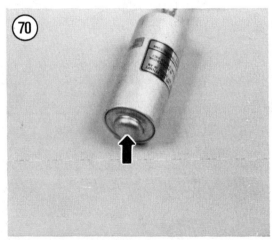

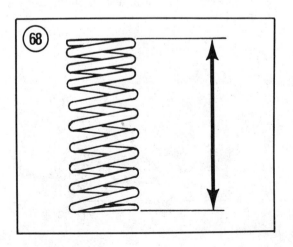

4. Check the remote reservoir hose for deterioration or damage. If damaged it must be replaced.

5. Place the damper unit on a scale; a bathroom scale will do. Write down the weight of the damper unit.

6. Compress the damper unit on the scale as shown in **Figure 69**. Note the amount of force (or scale weight) required to compress the damper unit 10 mm (0.14 in.).

7. The specified amount of force to compress the damper unit is 26-36 kg (57-79 lbs.). Remember to subtract the weight of the damper unit as noted in Step 5.

8. If the required force is less than specified, some of the nitrogen gas has leaked from the system. The system must be recharged as described in this chapter.

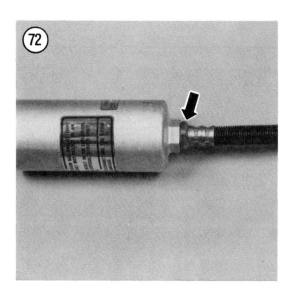

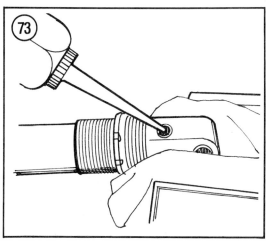

Damper Unit ATF Fluid Replacement and Nitrogen Gas Recharging

Recharging the nitrogen gas is best left to a dealer due to the high internal pressure within the shock absorber system.

This procedure is included if you choose to perform this task yourself. Read all WARNINGS included as this procedure is *dangerous*.

WARNING
Wear eye protection at all times. Use safety glasses or goggles.

1. Remove the cap (**Figure 70**) on the end of the remote reservoir.

2. Direct the remote reservoir valve end away from you and anyone else in the immediate vicinity.

WARNING
The system is pressurized to 20-23 kg/cm² (284-327 psi). Protect yourself accordingly in the next step.

WARNING
Bleed off the nitrogen gas gradually. If released too fast, oil will spurt out with the gas. Protect your eyes and clothing accordingly.

WARNING
Always bleed off all nitrogen gas pressure; failure to do so may cause personal injury when disassembling the components of the system.

3. Depress the valve stem and release *all* nitrogen gas from the system.

4. Unscrew the oil hose from the fitting on the damper unit (**Figure 71**) and the remote reservoir (**Figure 72**).

5. Drain out all ATF fluid from the damper unit, remote reservoir and oil hose. Discard the ATF—never reuse the ATF. Pump the damper unit several times to expel as much ATF as possible.

NOTE
Keep the damper unit in the vise in the horizontal position during Steps 6-17.

6. Position the damper unit horizontally and with the hole for the oil hose pointing straight up.

7. Secure the upper portion of the damper unit in a vise with soft jaws.

8. Pull the damper rod all the way out until it stops.

9. Fill the damper unit with fresh Dexron ATF until it is full (**Figure 73**).

11

10. After filling the damper unit with fresh ATF, bleed the air from the unit. Move the damper rod in and out slowly in short strokes (**Figure 74**) to expel air from the damper unit. Refill with ATF if necessary. The damper unit must be free of as much air as possible.

11. Fill the remote reservoir with fresh ATF until it is full (**Figure 75**). Slowly shake the remote reservoir back and forth to remove any air bubbles from the remote reservoir.

12. Install a new O-ring seal at each end of the oil hose.

13. Hold the oil hose in a "U" shape and fill with fresh ATF until it is full (**Figure 76**).

14. Hold your thumb over one end of the oil hose to help prevent the total loss of ATF from the oil hose.

15. Connect the other end of the oil hose to the damper unit. Tighten the oil hose to the damper unit to the torque specification listed in **Table 1**.

16. Some of the ATF drained out during Step 15. Hold the oil hose vertical and slowly refill the oil hose with fresh ATF (**Figure 77**).

> *NOTE*
> *The following step is tricky. Try not to let any air enter the remote reservoir or the oil hose. At the same time try not to let the ATF drain out of either unit while attaching the oil hose to the remote reservoir. Some ATF loss is expected—keep it to a minimum.*

17. Hold the remote reservoir at about a 45° angle and connect the oil hose to the remote reservoir. Tighten the oil hose to the torque specification listed in **Table 1**.

18. After the oil hose is attached to both units, check the damping action of the damper unit. Push and pull on the damper rod. The damping action should be even. If it is uneven there is air in the system and it must be bled off as follows:

    a. Hold the damper unit in the vertical position with the oil hose toward the top. Place the damper unit in a vise with soft jaws with the damper rod completely extended.

    b. Slightly loosen the oil hose fitting at the top of the damper unit.

    c. Slowly push up on the damper rod. This will expel ATF and air bubbles out of the oil hose fitting. This is similar to bleeding a brake system but without a bleeder valve.

    d. Continue to push up on the damper rod until there are no more air bubbles. Tighten the oil hose fitting to the torque specification listed in **Table 1**.

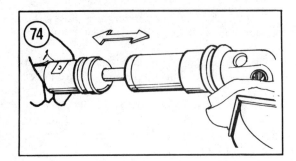

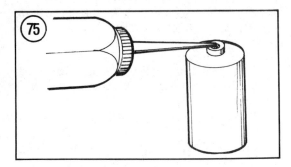

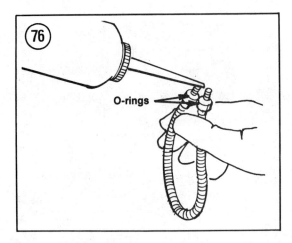

O-rings

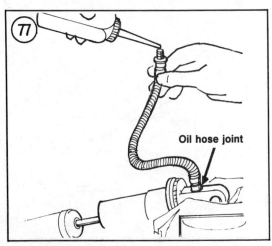

Oil hose joint

Honda does not specify the quantity of ATF for the damper unit and remote reservoir. If a considerable amount of ATF is lost during the bleeding procedure, refill the system by repeating Steps 9-18.

e. Recheck the damping action of the shock—it should be even. If the action is still uneven, bleed the shock again.

WARNING
*Refill the remote reservoir **only** with nitrogen gas. Do **not** use any other type of gas for this purpose. Other types of gas may be unstable and can cause a fire or explosion which could result in serious injury.*

19. Refill the system with nitrogen gas. This portion of the procedure is best left to a dealer who is experienced with the handling of high-pressure gas. Have the dealer fill the remote reservoir with 20-23 kg/cm² (284-327 lbs.) of nitrogen through the valve stem. Install the valve set cap then install the cover onto the remote reservoir.

SWING ARM

In time, the pivot needle bearings will wear and will have to be replaced. The condition of the needle bearings can greatly affect handling performance and if worn parts are not replaced they can produce erratic and dangerous handling. Common symptoms are wheel hop, pulling to one side during acceleration and pulling to the other side during braking.

Refer to **Figure 78** for this procedure.

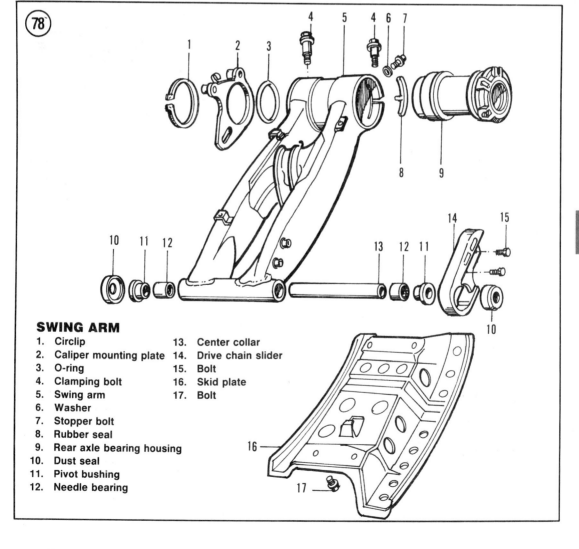

SWING ARM

1. Circlip
2. Caliper mounting plate
3. O-ring
4. Clamping bolt
5. Swing arm
6. Washer
7. Stopper bolt
8. Rubber seal
9. Rear axle bearing housing
10. Dust seal
11. Pivot bushing
12. Needle bearing
13. Center collar
14. Drive chain slider
15. Bolt
16. Skid plate
17. Bolt

11

Removal

1. Place the ATV on level ground. Block the front wheel so he vehicle will not roll in either direction.
2. Remove the seat/rear fender assembly as described in Chapter Fifteen.
3. Remove the rear wheels and axle as described in this chapter.
4. Remove the shock absorber as described in this chapter.
5. Grasp the rear end of the swing arm and try to move it from side to side in a horizontal arc. There should be no noticeable side play. If play is evident and the pivot bolt nut is tightened correctly, the bearings should be replaced.
6. Remove the hydraulic brake hose from the clips on the swing arm.
7. Remove and discard the pivot bolt self-locking nut (**Figure 79**).
8. Using a drift and hammer, tap the pivot bolt out of the frame and swing arm. Withdraw the pivot bolt from the left-hand side.
9. Pull back on the swing arm (**Figure 80**) and remove the swing arm from the frame.

> *NOTE*
> *Don't lose the dust seal caps on each side of both pivot points; they may fall off when the swing arm is removed.*

Disassembly/Inspection/Assembly

Refer to **Figure 78** for this procedure.
1. Remove the swing arm as described in this chapter.
2. If not already removed, remove the bolts securing the swing arm skid plate and remove the skid plate.
3. Remove the bolts securing the drive chain slider and remove the slider from the swing arm.
4. Remove the dust seals, from both pivot points, if they have not already fallen off during the removal sequence.
5. Remove the center collar (**Figure 81**).
6. Wipe off any excess grease from the needle bearings within each pivot area of the swing arm and inspect them as follows:
   a. The needle bearings wear very slowly and wear is very difficult to measure.
   b. Turn each bearing with your fingers; make sure they rotate smoothly.
   c. Check the rollers for evidence of wear, pitting or color change (bluish tint) indicating heat from lack of lubrication.

> *NOTE*
> *Always replace both needle bearings even though only one may be worn.*

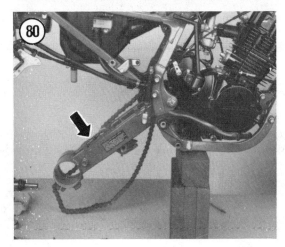

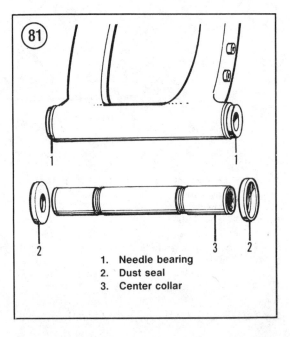

1. Needle bearing
2. Dust seal
3. Center collar

7. If the needle bearings need replacing, refer to *Needle Bearing Replacement* in this chapter. If the needle bearings are okay, proceed to the next step.

8. Install the drive chain slider and skid plate onto the swing arm.

9. Coat both needle bearings with molybdenum disulfide grease.

10. Coat the center collar with molybdenum disulfide grease.

11. Install the center collar into the swing arm.

12. Coat the inside of both dust seal caps with molybdenum disulfide grease and install them onto both pivot areas of the swing arm.

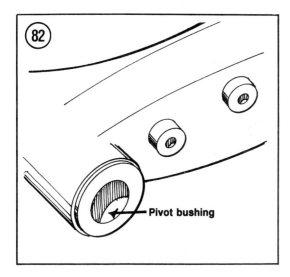

Pivot bushing

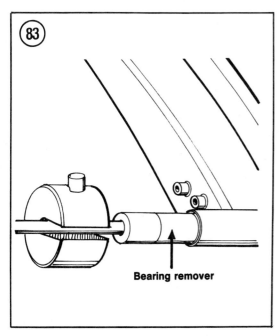

Bearing remover

13. Inspect the attachment points on the swing arm where the shock absorber is attached. If worn or damaged, the swing arm must be replaced.

14. Install the swing arm as described in this chapter.

**Pivot Bushing and
Needle Bearing Replacement**

The swing arm is equipped with a needle bearing at each end. The bearing is pressed in place and has to be removed with force. The bearing will get distorted when removed, so don't remove it unless absolutely necessary.

The bearings must be removed with special tools that are available from a Honda dealer. The special tools are as follows:

   a. Bearing remover: part No. 07936-3710600.

   b. Handle: part No. 07936-3710100.

   c. Slide hammer weight: part No. 07936-3710200.

1. Remove the swing arm as described in this chapter.

2. Remove the dust seal from each side of the swing arm.

3. Remove and discard the center collar (**Figure 81**).

4. Secure the swing arm in a vise with soft jaws.

5. Using a suitable size drift or extension and socket, tap the pivot bushing (**Figure 82**) out of one end of the swing arm.

6. Repeat Step 5 and remove the bushing from the other end.

NOTE
These special tools grab the inner surface of the bearing and then withdraw it from the swing arm with the use of a tool similar to a body shop slide hammer.

7. Either the right- or left-hand bearing race can be removed first.

8. Install the bearing remover through the hole in the bearing and expand the tool behind the bearing.

9. Attach the handle (slide hammer and handle) to the bearing remover.

10. Slide the weight on the hammer back and forth several times until the bearing and pivot bushing are withdrawn from the swing arm (**Figure 83**).

11. Remove the bearing from the special tools.

12. Turn the swing arm over in the vise and repeat Steps 9-12 for the other bearing.

13. Thoroughly clean out the inside of the swing arm with solvent and dry with compressed air.

11

14. Apply a light coat of molybdenum disulfide grease to all parts before installation.

NOTE
Either the right- or left-hand bearing race can be installed first.

CAUTION
For correct alignment the new needle bearings **should** *be pressed into place by a Honda dealer with the use of special tools and a hydraulic press. The following procedure is provided if you choose to perform this operation yourself. If done incorrectly, the needle bearing can be damaged during installation and may not be aligned correctly.*

WARNING
Never reinstall a needle bearing that has been removed. During removal it becomes slightly damaged and is no longer true to alignment. If installed, it will damage the center collar and create an unsafe riding condition.

15. Position the new needle bearing with its marks facing up toward the outside.
16. Place the bearing collar onto the needle bearing and place them onto the swing arm.
17. Use the following Honda special tools:
    a. 20 mm pilot: part No. 07746-0040500.
    b. 32×35 mm attachment: part No. 07746-0010100.
    c. Driver: part No. 07749-0010000.
18. Place the Honda special tools onto the bearing collar and the needle bearing (**Figure 84**).
19. Using a hammer, slowly and carefully drive the needle bearing and pivot bushing into place squarely. Make sure it is properly seated.
20. Remove the special tools.
21. Repeat Steps 15-20 for the other needle bearing.
22. Install a new center collar.
23. Install a new dust seal on each end of the swing arm.
24. Install the swing arm as described in this chapter.

Installation

1. Make sure that all dust seals are in place on each side of the swing arm.

2. Place the swing arm through the drive chain and position the swing arm into the mounting area. Align the holes in the swing arm with the holes in the frame. To help align the holes, insert a drift in from the right-hand side.

CAUTION
When tightening the pivot bolt nut, do **not** *exceed the torque specification listed in* **Table 1**. *If the nut is tightened more than specified, it may damage the internal parts of the pivot areas of the swing arm. If this happens the swing arm will* **not** *pivot freely and will greatly reduce the "road feel" of the rear suspension. This may give you a false impression that either the rear shock or the swing arm pivot bearings are defective which could lead to costly and unnecessary component replacement.*

3. Apply a light coat of grease to the pivot bolt and perform the following:
    a. After all holes are aligned, insert the pivot bolt from the left-hand side.
    b. Install a new self-locking nut and tighten to the torque specification listed in **Table 1**.
4. Install the rear axle as described in this chapter.
5. Install both rear wheels as described in this chapter.
6. Install the seat and rear fender as described in Chapter Fifteen.

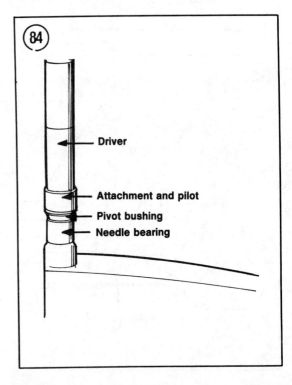

(84)

Driver

Attachment and pilot

Pivot bushing

Needle bearing

Table 1 REAR SUSPENSION TORQUE SPECIFICATIONS

Item and model	N·m	ft.-lb.
Rear wheel lug nuts	60-70	43-51
Rear axle castellated nut	120-170	87-123
Rear axle locknuts		
Inner locknut	100-120	72-87
Outer locknut	80-100	58-72
Driven sprocket nuts	30-40	22-29
Rear axle holder stopper bolt	8-11	5.8-8
Shock absorber		
Spring locknut	80-100	58-72
Mounting bolts and nuts	40-50	29-36
Oil hose-to-damper unit	20-25	14-18
Oil hose-to-remote reservoir	20-25	14-18
Swing arm pivot bolt and nut	70-110	51-80

Table 2 REAR SUSPENSION SPECIFICATIONS

Item	Specification	Wear limit
Rear axle runout	—	3.0 mm (0.12 in.)
Rear wheel runout		
Axial	—	4.0 mm (0.16 in.)
Radial	—	4.0 mm (0.16 in.)
Shock absorber spring free length	194 mm (7.64 in.)	190 mm (7.48 in.)
Shock absorber		
Damper rod compression force (travel 10 mm 0.4 in.)	26-36 kg (57.3-79.4 lb.)	—
Nitrogen pressure	2,000-2,300 kPa (284-327 psi)	—

11

CHAPTER TWELVE

REAR AXLE AND SUSPENSION
(4-WHEELED MODELS)

This chapter contains repair and replacement procedures for the rear wheel, rear hub and rear suspension. Service to the rear suspension consists of periodically checking bolt tightness, replacing swing arm bushings and checking the condition of the rear shock absorber. Tire removal and repair are covered in Chapter Nine.

Refer to **Table 1**, located at the end of this chapter, for rear suspension torque specifications.

REAR WHEEL

Removal/Installation

1. Set the ATV on level ground and set the parking brake. Also block the front wheels so the vehicle will not roll in either direction.

2. Place wood blocks under the engine to support the ATV securely with the rear wheel off the ground.

3. Remove the lug nuts (**Figure 1**) securing the rear wheel to the hub and remove the rear wheel.

4. Install the rear wheel with the valve stem facing toward the outside.

5. Install the lug nuts with the tapered end going on first (**Figure 2**). Tighten the nuts only finger-tight at this time.

6. Remove the wood blocks from under the engine and set the front wheel on the ground.

7. Tighten the wheel lug nuts to the torque specification listed in **Table 1**.

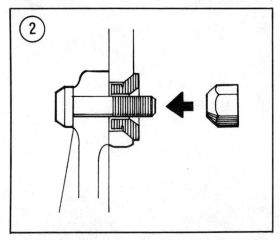

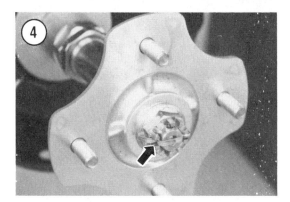

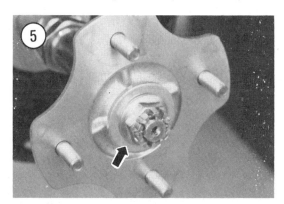

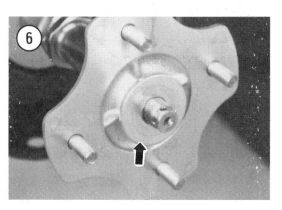

REAR HUB

Removal/Installation

1. Remove the rear wheel as described in this chapter.
2. Remove the hub cover (**Figure 3**).
3. Remove the cotter pin (**Figure 4**), hub nut (**Figure 5**) and washer (**Figure 6**) securing the wheel hub to the rear axle.
4. Remove the hub assembly (**Figure 7**).
5. Inspect the rear hub as described in this chapter.
6. Install the rear hub onto the rear axle.
7. Install the washer and hub nut.
8. Install the rear wheel and set the vehicle on the ground as described in this chapter.
9. Tighten the hub nut to the torque specification listed in **Table 1**.
10. Install a new cotter pin and bend the ends over completely. Never reuse a cotter pin as it may break and fall out.
11. Tighten the wheel nuts to the torque specification listed in **Table 1**.
12. Install the hub cover.

Inspection

1. Inspect the splines in the rear hub (**Figure 8**). If worn or damaged, the rear hub must be replaced.

12

2. Inspect the threaded studs on the rear hub (**Figure 9**). If worn or damaged, the rear hub must be replaced.

3. Inspect the rear hub splines and the axle nut threads on the rear axle. If worn or damaged, the rear axle must be replaced.

REAR AXLE AND DRIVEN SPROCKET

Removal

> *NOTE*
> *To remove just the driven sprocket, refer to **Driven Sprocket Removal** in this section.*

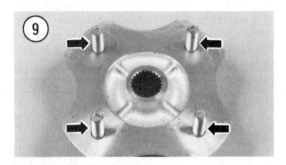

Refer to **Figure 10** for this procedure.

1. Place the ATV on level ground and set the parking brake.

2. Shift the transmission into NEUTRAL.

3. Remove the seat and rear fenders as described in Chapter Fifteen.

4. To relieve drive chain tension, perform the following:

　a. Loosen the axle housing lockbolts (**Figure 11**) on each side, securing the axle holder.

　b. Loosen the adjuster nuts (**Figure 12**) until there is sufficient slack in the drive chain.

5. Remove the bolts securing the skid plate (**Figure 13**) and remove the skid plate.

6. Remove both rear wheels as described in this chapter.

7. Remove both rear hubs as described in this chapter.

8. Grab the end of the rear axle and move the axle up and down and from side-to-side. Do this on each end of the axle. If there is excessive play, the bearings in the rear axle bearing holder need replacing. Replace the bearings as described in this chapter.

9. Place a wood block under the swing arm to support it in the up position.

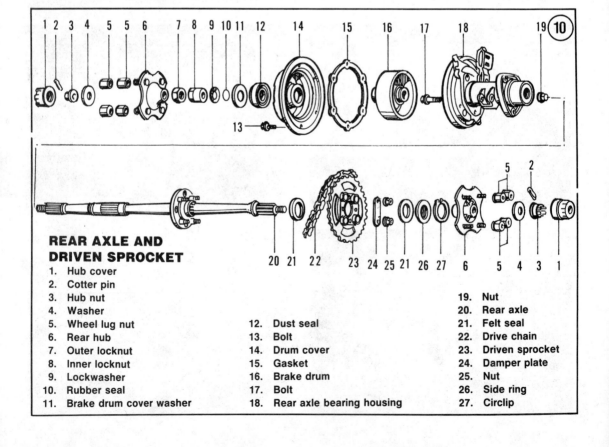

REAR AXLE AND DRIVEN SPROCKET

1. Hub cover
2. Cotter pin
3. Hub nut
4. Washer
5. Wheel lug nut
6. Rear hub
7. Outer locknut
8. Inner locknut
9. Lockwasher
10. Rubber seal
11. Brake drum cover washer
12. Dust seal
13. Bolt
14. Drum cover
15. Gasket
16. Brake drum
17. Bolt
18. Rear axle bearing housing
19. Nut
20. Rear axle
21. Felt seal
22. Drive chain
23. Driven sprocket
24. Damper plate
25. Nut
26. Side ring
27. Circlip

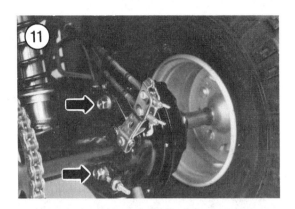

10. Remove the rear brake drum assembly as described under *Rear Brake Drum Removal* in Chapter Thirteen.

11. Remove the nuts (**Figure 14**) and damper plates (**Figure 15**) securing the driven sprocket to the mounting flange.

12. Remove the snap ring (**Figure 16**) securing the driven sprocket assembly.

13. Remove the side ring (**Figure 17**) and felt seal (**Figure 18**).

12

14. Derail the drive chain from the driven sprocket and slide the driven sprocket off the rear axle.

15. Remove the felt seal (**Figure 19**) from the mounting flange.

16. Carefully tap on the right-hand end of the axle with a soft-faced mallet.

17. Pull the rear axle assembly out of the swing arm from the left-hand side (**Figure 20**).

18. Inspect the rear axle as described under *Rear Axle Inspection*. Inspect the driven sprocket as described under *Driven Sprocket Inspection*.

Installation

1. Make sure the axle bearing oil seals are in place on each side of the rear axle bearing housing. Apply a light coat of multipurpose grease to the lips of the seals.

2. Install the rear axle assembly into the swing arm from the left-hand side.

3. Install the felt seal on the axle mounting flange.

4. Install the driven sprocket (A, **Figure 21**) onto the mounting flange and install the drive chain (B, **Figure 21**) onto the driven sprocket.

5. Install the felt seal (**Figure 18**).

6. Position the side ring with the flange side (**Figure 22**) facing toward the inside and install the side ring (**Figure 17**).

7. Position the circlip (**Figure 23**) with the sharp side facing toward the outside and install the circlip (**Figure 16**). Make sure the circlip is properly seated in the groove in the rear axle.

8. Install the damper plates (**Figure 15**) and driven sprocket mounting nuts (**Figure 14**). Tighten the mounting nuts to the torque specification listed in **Table 1**.

9. Install the rear brake drum assembly as described under *Rear Brake Drum Installation* in Chapter Thirteen.

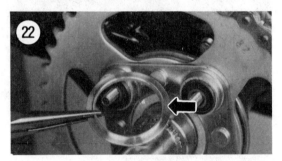

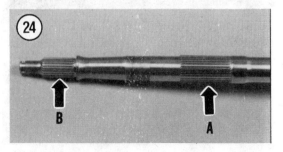

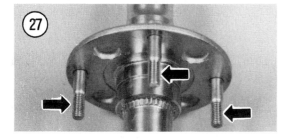

10. Install both wheel hubs as described in this chapter.

11. Install the rear wheels as described in this chapter.

12. Adjust the drive chain as described under *Drive Chain Adjustment* in Chapter Three.

13. Install the seat and the rear fender as described in Chapter Fifteen.

Rear Axle Inspection

1. Inspect the rear axle for signs of fatigue, fractures or damage.

2. Inspect the splines where the rear hub (A, **Figure 24**) and brake drum (B, **Figure 24**) mesh with the axle. If either is damaged, the axle must be replaced.

3. Check the hole at each end of the axle (**Figure 25**) where the cotter pin fits. Make sure there are no fractures or cracks leading out toward the end of the axle. If any are found, replace the axle.

4. Inspect the portion of the axle (**Figure 26**) where it rides in the left-hand bearing in the bearing housing. If worn or damaged, replace the axle.

5. Inspect the threaded studs (**Figure 27**) for the driven sprocket. Replace the stud(s) if worn or damaged.

6. Check the axle for straightness. Use V-blocks and a dial indicator as shown in **Figure 28**. Check the runout in the center of the axle and remember that the actual runout is 1/2 of the total runout reading from the dial indicator. If the runout is 3.0 mm (0.12 in.) or greater, the axle must be replaced.

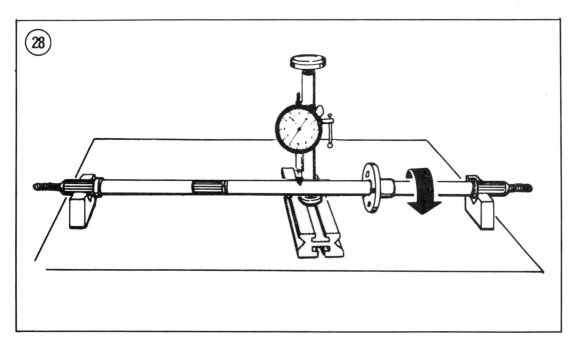

12

7. Inspect the inner and outer locknuts (**Figure 29**) for wear or damage. Replace as a set if either is damaged.

Driven Sprocket Removal

This procedure is used to remove just the driven sprocket. To remove the axle and driven sprocket together, refer to *Rear Axle and Driven Sprocket, Removal*, in this chapter.

1. Place the ATV on level ground and set the parking brake.
2. Shift the transmission into NEUTRAL.
3. Remove the seat and rear fenders as described in Chapter Fifteen.
4. To relieve drive chain tension, perform the following:
   a. Loosen the axle housing lockbolts (**Figure 11**) on each side, securing the axle holder.
   b. Loosen the adjuster nuts (**Figure 12**) until there is sufficient slack in the drive chain.
5. Remove the bolts securing the skid plate (**Figure 13**) and remove the skid plate.
6. Remove the left-hand rear wheel as described in this chapter.
7. Remove the left-hand rear hub as described in this chapter.
8. Place a wood block under the swing arm to support it in the up position.
9. Remove the nuts (**Figure 14**) and damper plates (**Figure 15**) securing the driven sprocket to the mounting flange.
10. Remove the snap ring (**Figure 16**) securing the driven sprocket assembly.
11. Remove the side ring (**Figure 17**) and felt seal (**Figure 18**).
12. Derail the drive chain (B, **Figure 21**) from the driven sprocket and slide the driven sprocket (A, **Figure 21**) off the rear axle.

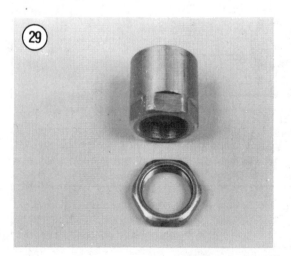

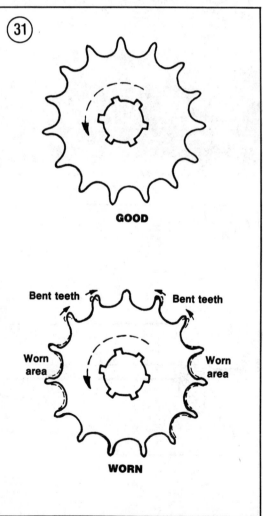

GOOD

Bent teeth   Bent teeth

Worn area   Worn area

WORN

13. Don't lose the felt seal (**Figure 19**) on the mounting flange.

Driven Sprocket Installation

1. Make sure the felt seal (**Figure 19**) is installed on the axle mounting flange.

2. Install the driven sprocket (A, **Figure 21**) onto the mounting flange and install the drive chain (B, **Figure 21**) onto the driven sprocket.

3. Install the felt seal (**Figure 18**).

4. Position the side ring with the flange side (**Figure 22**) facing toward the inside and install the side ring (**Figure 17**).

5. Position the circlip (**Figure 23**) with the sharp side facing toward the outside and install the circlip (**Figure 16**). Make sure the circlip is properly seated in the groove in the rear axle.

6. Install the damper plates (**Figure 15**) and driven sprocket mounting nuts (**Figure 14**). Tighten the mounting nuts to the torque specification listed in **Table 1**.

7. Install the left-hand wheel hub as described in this chapter.

8. Install the left-hand rear wheel as described in this chapter.

9. Adjust the drive chain as described under *Drive Chain Adjustment* in Chapter Three.

10. Install the seat and the rear fender as described in Chapter Fifteen.

Driven Sprocket Inspection

Inspect the teeth of the driven sprocket (**Figure 30**). If the teeth are visibly worn (**Figure 31**), replace the driven sprocket with a new one.

Drive Sprocket Removal/Installation

1. Place the ATV on level ground and set the parking brake.

2. Remove the seat and the rear fenders as described in Chapter Fifteen.

3. Remove the recoil starter as described under *Recoil Starter (4-wheeled Models) Removal/Installation* in Chapter Four.

4. Remove the bolts (**Figure 33**) securing the drive sprocket cover and guide, then remove the cover and guide.

5. To relieve drive chain tension perform the following:

    a. Loosen the axle housing pinch bolts (**Figure 34**) on each side, securing the axle holder.

    b. Loosen the adjuster nuts (**Figure 35**) until there is sufficient slack in the drive chain.

6. Have an assistant apply the rear brake to keep the drive chain taut and keep the drive sprocket from turning. Remove the bolts (**Figure 36**) securing the drive sprocket and plate.

7. Rotate the drive sprocket plate (A, **Figure 37**) in either direction to clear the splines of the transmission shaft and slide off the plate.

8. Remove the master link from the drive chain.

9. Remove the drive chain (B, **Figure 37**) from the drive sprocket.

10. Slide off the drive sprocket.

11. Remove the metal collar (**Figure 38**) from the transmission shaft.

12. Install by reversing these removal steps, noting the following.

13. Tighten the drive sprocket bolt securely.

14. Install the drive chain master link clip with the closed end facing in the direction of travel (**Figure 39**).

15. Adjust the drive chain as described under *Drive Chain Adjustment* in Chapter Three.

Drive Sprocket Inspection

Inspect the teeth of the drive sprocket. If the teeth are visibly worn (**Figure 40**), replace the drive sprocket with a new one.

If the drive sprocket requires replacement, the drive chain is probably worn also. Remove and replace the drive chain as described in this chapter.

DRIVE CHAIN

Cleaning/Inspection/Lubrication

> *CAUTION*
> *The drive chain is equipped with O-rings. These rubber O-rings can easily be damaged. Do not use a steam cleaner, a high-pressure washer or any solvent that may damage the rubber O-rings.*

1. Remove the drive chain as described in this chapter.

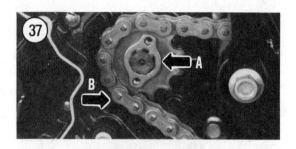

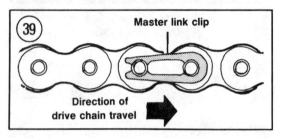

Master link clip

Direction of drive chain travel

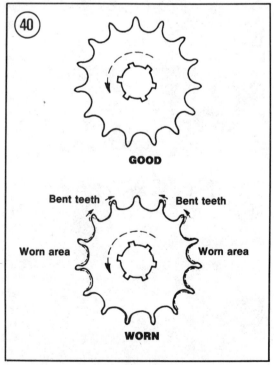

GOOD

Bent teeth   Bent teeth

Worn area   Worn area

WORN

2. Immerse the chain in a pan of kerosene or non-flammable solvent and allow it to soak for about half an hour. Move it around and flex it during this period so that the dirt between the links, pins, rollers and O-rings may work its way out.

CAUTION
In the next step, do not use a wire brush or the O-rings will be damaged and the drive chain will have to be replaced.

3. Scrub the rollers and side plates with a medium soft brush and rinse away loosened dirt. Do not scrub hard as the O-rings may be damaged. Rinse the chain a couple of times to make sure all dirt and grit are washed out. Dry the chain with a shop cloth, then hang it up and allow it to dry thoroughly.
4. After cleaning the chain, examine it carefully for wear or damage. If any signs are visible, replace the chain.

NOTE
Always check both sprockets every time the chain is removed. If any wear is visible on the teeth, replace both sprockets. Never install a new chain over worn sprockets or a worn chain over new sprockets.

5. Lubricate the chain with SAE 40 or 50 weight engine oil or a good grade of chain lubricant (specifically formulated for O-ring chains), following the manufacturer's instructions.
6. Reinstall the chain as described in this chapter.

REAR AXLE BEARING HOUSING

The rear axle bearing housing is attached to the rear of the swing arm and contains the rear axle bearings and grease seals.

Removal

1. Remove the rear axle as described in this chapter.
2. Inspect the bearings as described under *Bearing Preliminary Inspection* in this chapter.
3. Completely unscrew both brake adjusters (**Figure 41**) and pivot pin from each brake cable.
4. Withdraw each brake cable from the brake actuating arm (**Figure 42**). Reinstall the pivot pin and brake adjuster onto each brake cable so they will not get misplaced.
5. Remove the brake cables from the receptacles on the rear axle bearing housing.
6. Remove the brake shoes, brake actuating arm and camshaft as described in Chapter Thirteen.
7. Disconnect the breather hose (A, **Figure 43**) from the housing.
8. Remove the bolt and nut (A, **Figure 44**) securing the lower portion of the rear shock absorber to the rear axle bearing housing.
9. Remove the bolts and washers (B, **Figure 43**) on each side, securing the rear axle bearing housing to the swing arm.

10. Remove the rear axle bearing housing (B, **Figure 44**) from the swing arm.

11. Inspect the bearings as described in this chapter.

Installation

1. Install the rear axle bearing housing into the swing arm.

2. Install the rear axle bearing housing mounting bolts and washers. Tighten the bolts to the torque specification listed in **Table 1**.

3. Install the bolt and nut (A, **Figure 44**) securing the lower portion of the shock absorber to the rear axle bearing housing. Tighten the bolt and nut to the torque specification listed in **Table 1**.

4. Attach the vent hose to the housing.

5. Install the brake camshaft, brake actuating arm and brake shoes as described in Chapter Thirteen.

6. Install the brake cables into the receptacles on the rear axle bearing housing.

7. Install each brake cable into the brake actuating arms. Install the pivot pin and brake adjuster onto each brake cable.

8. Install the rear axle as described in this chapter.

9. Adjust the drive chain as described under *Drive Chain Adjustment* in Chapter Three.

Bearing Preliminary Inspection

Before removing the rear axle bearing housing, perform the following.

1. Remove the rear axle as described in this chapter.

2. Wipe off all excessive grease from both bearings.

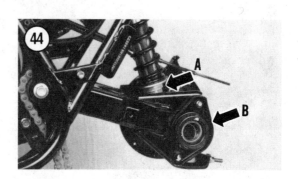

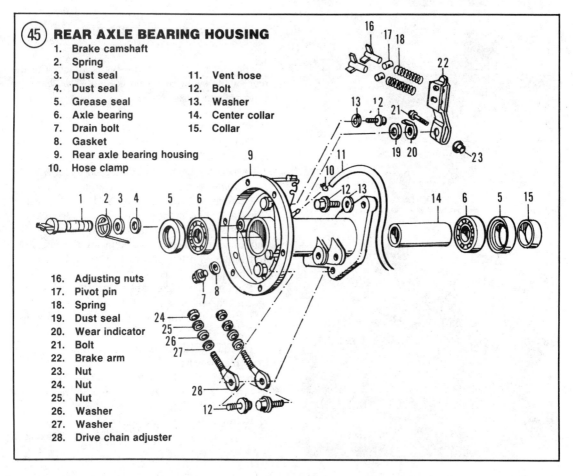

45 REAR AXLE BEARING HOUSING

1. Brake camshaft
2. Spring
3. Dust seal
4. Dust seal
5. Grease seal
6. Axle bearing
7. Drain bolt
8. Gasket
9. Rear axle bearing housing
10. Hose clamp
11. Vent hose
12. Bolt
13. Washer
14. Center collar
15. Collar
16. Adjusting nuts
17. Pivot pin
18. Spring
19. Dust seal
20. Wear indicator
21. Bolt
22. Brake arm
23. Nut
24. Nut
25. Nut
26. Washer
27. Washer
28. Drive chain adjuster

3. Turn each bearing by hand. Make sure the bearings turn smoothly. Check for roughness and free play. Some axial play (end play) is normal, but radial play (side play) should be negligible.

4. Replace the bearings, if necessary, as described in this chapter.

5. Inspect the grease seals. Replace if they are deteriorating or starting to harden.

Bearing Removal

Refer to **Figure 45** for this procedure.

1. Remove the rear axle bearing housing as described in this chapter.

2. Carefully remove the right-hand grease seal (**Figure 46**) and the left-hand grease seal (**Figure 47**) from the rear axle bearing housing.

3. Insert a soft aluminum or brass drift into one side of the bearing housing.

4. Push the center collar over to one side and place the drift on the inner race of the opposite bearing.

5. Tap the bearing out of the hub with a hammer working around the perimeter of the bearing.

6. Remove that bearing and the center collar.

7. Turn the rear axle housing over.

8. Insert a soft aluminum or brass drift into the opposite side of the bearing housing.

9. Place the drift on the opposite bearing.

10. Tap the bearing out of the hub with a hammer working around the perimeter of the bearing and tap out the bearing.

Inspection and Lubrication

1. On non-sealed bearings, check the balls for evidence of wear, pitting or excessive heat (bluish tint). Replace bearings if necessary; always replace as a complete set. When replacing, be sure to take your old bearings along to ensure a perfect matchup.

> *NOTE*
> *Fully sealed bearings are available from many bearing specialty shops. Fully sealed bearings provide better protection from dirt and moisture that may get into the housing.*

2. Thoroughly clean the inside of the rear axle bearing housing with solvent and dry with compressed air or a shop cloth.

3. Do not clean sealed bearings. If non-sealed bearings are installed, thoroughly clean them in solvent and dry thoroughly with compressed air. Do not let the bearing spin while drying.

4. If non-sealed bearings are to be re-installed, pack the bearings with a good grade of waterproof grease, such as boat trailer wheel bearing grease as follows:

   a. Spread some grease in the palm of your hand and scrape the open end of the bearing across your palm. Continue to add grease until the bearing is packed completely full of grease.

   b. Slowly spin the bearing a few times to determine if there are any areas that are void of grease. Thoroughly work the grease in between the balls.

   c. Turn the bearing by hand a couple more times to make sure the grease is distributed evenly inside the bearing.

Bearing Installation

Refer to **Figure 45** for this procedure.

1. Coat the outside of both bearings and inside of the rear axle bearing housing and the center collar with multipurpose grease.

> *CAUTION*
> *During installation, tap the bearings squarely into place and tap on the outer race only. Use a socket that matches the outer race diameter. Do not tap on the inner race or the bearing may be damaged. Be sure that the bearings are completely seated.*

12

2. On non-sealed bearings, position the bearing with the sealed surface facing outward. Non-sealed bearings have one sealed surface and this surface must face toward the outside.

3. Install the right-hand bearing.

4. Turn the bearing housing over and install the center collar.

5. Install the left-hand bearing.

6. Apply a light coat of multipurpose grease to the grease seals.

7. Install a new grease seal into each side of the bearing housing. Drive the grease seals in until they are flush with the outer surface of the rear axle bearing housing.

8. Install the rear axle bearing housing and rear axle as described in this chapter.

SHOCK ABSORBER

Removal

1. Place the ATV on level ground and set the parking brake.

2. Place wood block(s) under the frame to support the ATV securely with the rear wheels off of the ground.

3. Remove the seat and rear fender as described in Chapter Fifteen.

4. Remove both rear wheels as described in this chapter. It is not necessary to remove the wheels, but it makes shock absorber removal a lot easier.

5. Remove the bolt and nut (**Figure 48**) securing the upper portion of the shock absorber to the frame.

6. Remove the bolt and nut securing the lower portion of the shock absorber to the swing arm.

7. Carefully remove the shock absorber assembly (**Figure 49**) from the frame.

Installation

1. Apply a coat of molybdenum disulfide paste grease to the upper and lower mounting bushings on the shock absorber and to the upper and lower mounting yoke on the frame and the swing arm.

2. Make sure the dust seals and caps (**Figure 50**) are in place on the lower mount.

> *CAUTION*
> *Be sure to install the shock absorber unit with the damper unit portion (**Figure 50**) positioned toward the top. If installed upside down the seals will be damaged and leak damper fluid.*

3. Position the shock absorber with the damper unit portion toward the top and install the shock absorber in the frame.

4. Install the shock absorber upper and lower mounting bolts and nuts. Tighten the bolts and nuts to the torque specification listed in **Table 1**.

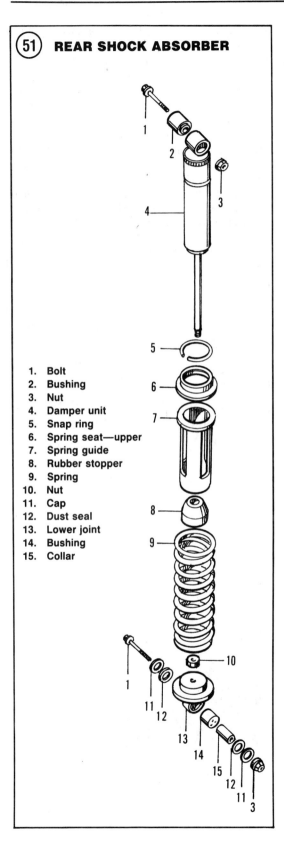

1. Bolt
2. Bushing
3. Nut
4. Damper unit
5. Snap ring
6. Spring seat—upper
7. Spring guide
8. Rubber stopper
9. Spring
10. Nut
11. Cap
12. Dust seal
13. Lower joint
14. Bushing
15. Collar

5. Install both rear wheels as described in this chapter.
6. Remove the wood blocks from under the frame.
7. Push down on the rear of the ATV and make sure the rear suspension is operating properly.
8. Install the seat and rear fenders as described in

**Shock Absorber
Disassembly/Inspection/Assembly**

Refer to **Figure 51** for this procedure.

The shock is spring-controlled and hydraulically damped. The shock damper unit is sealed and cannot be serviced. Service is limited to removal and replacement of the damper unit (A, **Figure 52**) and the spring (B, **Figure 52**).

A special tool and 2 additional items are needed for disassembly and assembly of the shock absorber. The compressor is the same tool used for the front shock absorber. The 2 additional items are unique to the rear shock. These tools are available from a Honda dealer and are as follows:

 a. Shock absorber compressor (Honda part No. 07959-3290001).

 b. Base (Honda part No. 07959-MB10000).

 c. Spring compressor adaptor (Honda part No. 07967-KC10000).

> *WARNING*
> *Without the proper tools, this procedure can be dangerous. The spring can fly loose, causing injury. For a small bench fee, a dealer can do the job for you.*

12

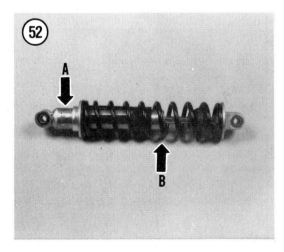

(52)

1. Install the base into the spring compressor.

2. Install the shock absorber into a compression tool as shown in **Figure 53**.

3. Install the adaptor onto the shock absorber spring and into the upper portion of the spring compressor. Tighten the clamp securing the adaptor.

4. Compress the shock spring just enough to gain access to the locknut.

5. Place the upper joint in a vise with soft jaws and loosen the locknut.

6. Completely unscrew the upper joint. This part may be difficult to break loose as thread locking agent was applied during assembly.

7. Release the spring tension and remove the shock from the compression tool.

8. Remove the spring, spring guide and spring seat from the damper unit.

9. Measure the spring free length (**Figure 54**). The spring must be replaced if it has sagged to the service limit listed in **Table 1** or less.

10. Check the damper unit for leakage and make sure the damper rod is straight. Replace the damper unit if any damage is found.

NOTE
The damper unit cannot be rebuilt; it must be replaced as a unit.

11. Remove the dust seal cap and dust seal from each side of the lower mount.

12. Remove the collar (**Figure 55**) from the bushing in the upper mount.

13. Inspect the bushing (**Figure 50**) in the upper mount for wear or damage. Replace if worn or damaged. If either the collar or bushing is worn or damaged, replace both parts as a set.

14. Inspect the bushing in the lower mount for wear or damage. Replace if bushing is worn or damaged.

15. Inspect the rubber stopper. If it is worn or deteriorated, remove the locknut and washer, then slide off the rubber stopper; replace with a new one.

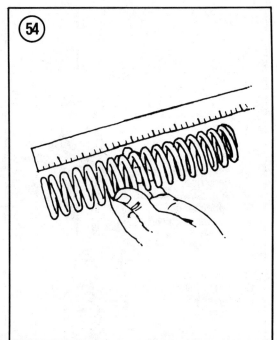

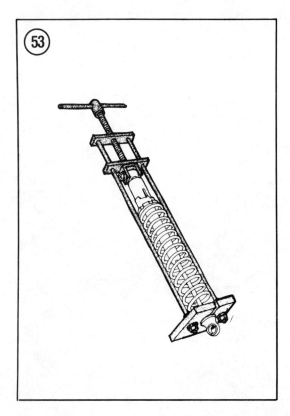

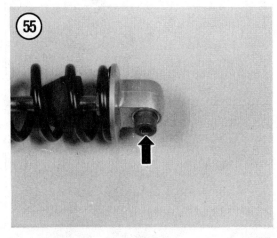

16. Assembly is the reverse of these disassembly steps, noting the following.

17. Apply Loctite Lock 'N Seal to the threads of the damper rod before installing the locknut. Temporarily screw the locknut all the way down and tight against the end of the threads.

18. Apply Loctite Lock N' Seal to the threads of the damper rod before installing the upper joint. Screw the upper joint on all the way. Secure the upper joint in a vise with soft jaws and tighten the locknut along with the damper rod against the upper joint. Tighten the locknut securely.

NOTE
After the locknut is tightened completely, the locknut must be against the bottom surface of the upper joint and against the end of the threads on the damper rod.

SWING ARM

In time, the pivot bushings will wear and will have to be replaced. The condition of the pivot bushings can greatly affect handling performance and if worn parts are not replaced they can produce erratic and dangerous handling. Common symptoms are wheel hop, pulling to one side during acceleration and pulling to the other side during braking.

Refer to **Figure 56** for this procedure.

Removal

1. Place the ATV on level ground. Block the front wheels so the vehicle will not roll in either direction.

2. Remove the seat and rear fenders as described in Chapter Fifteen.

3. Remove the rear axle as described in this chapter.

4. Remove the shock absorber as described in this chapter.

5. Grasp the rear end of the swing arm and try to move it from side to side in a horizontal arc. There should be no noticeable side play. If play is evident and the pivot bolt nut is tightened correctly, the pivot bushings should be replaced.

6. Remove the rear axle bearing housing as described in this chapter.

7. Remove the rear brake pedal as described under *Rear Brake Pedal Removal* in Chapter Thirteen.

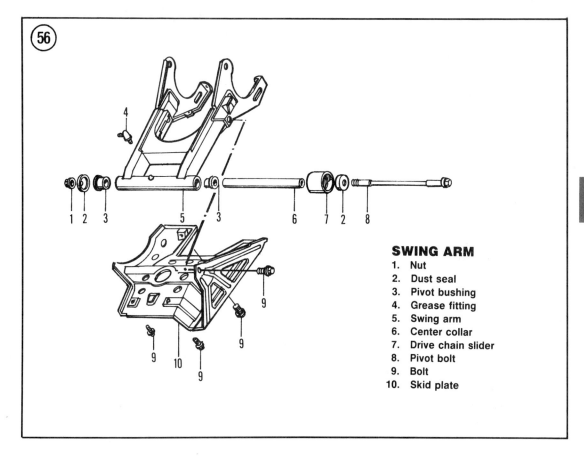

56

SWING ARM
1. Nut
2. Dust seal
3. Pivot bushing
4. Grease fitting
5. Swing arm
6. Center collar
7. Drive chain slider
8. Pivot bolt
9. Bolt
10. Skid plate

12

8. Remove and discard the pivot bolt self-locking nut (**Figure 57**).

9. Using a drift and hammer, tap the pivot bolt out of the frame and swing arm. Withdraw the pivot bolt from the left-hand side.

10. Pull back on the swing arm and remove the swing arm from the frame.

NOTE
Don't lose the dust seal caps on each side of both pivot points; they usually fall off when the swing arm is removed.

Disassembly/Inspection/Assembly

Refer to **Figure 56** for this procedure.

1. Remove the swing arm as described in this chapter.

2. Remove the bolts securing the swing arm skid plate and remove the skid plate.

3. Remove the dust seal caps, from both pivot points, if they have not already fallen off during the removal sequence.

4. Remove the drive chain roller from the left-hand side of the swing arm.

5. Remove the center collar from the swing arm (**Figure 58**).

NOTE
Honda does not provide any service information for the wear limit dimensions on either the center collar or the pivot bushings.

6. Inspect the center collar and pivot bushings in the swing arm for wear or damage. If considerable amount of side play is evident as noted in Step 5, *Removal*, then refer to *Pivot Bushing Replacement* in this chapter. If the pivot bushings are okay, proceed to next step.

NOTE
Always replace both pivot bushings even though only one may be worn.

7. Install the skid plate onto the swing arm.

8. Coat both pivot bushings with molybdenum disulfide grease.

9. Coat the center collar with molybdenum disulfide grease.

10. Install the center collar into the swing arm.

11. Install the chain roller onto the left-hand end of the swing arm.

12. Coat the inside of both dust seal caps with molybdenum disulfide grease and install them onto both pivot areas of the swing arm.

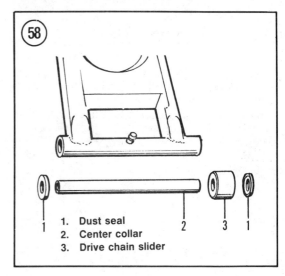

1. Dust seal
2. Center collar
3. Drive chain slider

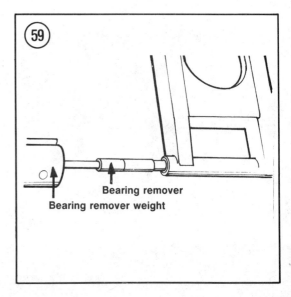

Bearing remover
Bearing remover weight

13. Inspect the attachment points on the swing arm where the shock absorber is attached. If worn or damaged, the swing arm must be replaced.

14. Install the swing arm as described in this chapter.

Pivot Bushing Replacement

The swing arm is equipped with a pivot bushing at each end. The bushing is pressed in place and has to be removed with force. The bushing will be distorted during removal so don't remove it unless absolutely necessary.

The bushing must be removed with special tools that are available from a Honda dealer. The special tools are as follows:

    a. Bearing remover: part No. 07936-3710600.

    b. Handle: part No. 07936-3710100.

    c. Slide hammer weight: part No. 07936-3710200.

1. Remove the swing arm as described in this chapter.

2. Remove the dust seal from each side of the swing arm.

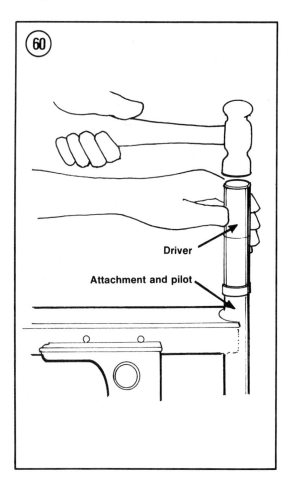

3. Remove and discard the center collar (**Figure 58**).

4. Remove the drive chain roller from the left-hand side of the swing arm.

5. Secure the swing arm in a vise with soft jaws.

NOTE
These special tools grab the inner surface of the bushing and then withdraw it from the swing arm with the use of a tool similar to a body shop slide hammer.

6. Either the right- or left-hand bushing can be removed first.

7. Install the bushing remover through the hole in the bushing and expand the tool behind that bushing.

8. Attach the handle (slide hammer and handle) to the bushing remover.

9. Slide the weight on the hammer back and forth several times until the bushing is withdrawn from the swing arm (**Figure 59**).

10. Remove the bushing from the special tools.

11. Turn the swing arm over in the vise and repeat Steps 7-10 for the other bushing.

12. Thoroughly clean out the inside of the swing arm with solvent and dry with compressed air.

13. Apply a light coat of molybdenum disulfide grease to all parts before installation.

NOTE
Either the right- or left-hand bushing race can be installed first.

CAUTION
Never reinstall a bushing that has been removed. During removal it becomes slightly damaged and is no longer true to alignment. If installed, it will damage the pivot collar and create an unsafe riding condition.

14. Place the bushing onto the swing arm.

15. Use the following Honda special tools:

    a. 20 mm pilot: part No. 07746-0040500.

    b. 32×35 mm attachment: part No. 07746-0010100.

    c. Driver: part No. 07749-0010000.

16. Place the Honda special tools onto the bushing (**Figure 60**).

17. Using a hammer, slowly and carefully drive the bushing into place squarely. Make sure it is properly seated.

18. Remove the special tools.

19. Repeat Steps 14-18 for the other bushing.

12

20. Install a new center collar.

21. Install a new dust seal on each end of the swing arm.

22. Install the swing arm as described in this chapter.

Installation

1. Make sure that all dust seals are in position.

2. Place the swing arm through the drive chain and position the swing arm into the mounting area. Align the holes in the swing arm with the holes in the frame. To help align the holes, insert a drift in from the right-hand side.

> *CAUTION*
> *When tightening the pivot bolt nut, do* ***not*** *exceed the torque specification listed in* ***Table 1****. If the nut is tightened more than specified, it may damage the internal parts of the pivot areas of the swing arm. If this happens the swing*

arm will ***not*** *pivot freely and will greatly reduce the "road feel" of the rear suspension. This may give you a false impression that either the rear shock or the swing arm pivot bearings are defective, which could lead to costly and unnecessary component replacement.*

3. Apply a light coat of grease to the pivot bolt and perform the following:

    a. After all holes are aligned, insert the pivot bolt from the left-hand side.

    b. Install a new self-locking nut and tighten to the torque specification listed in **Table 1**.

4. Install the rear brake pedal as described under *Rear Brake Pedal Installation* in Chapter Thirteen.

5. Install the rear axle bearing housing as described in this chapter.

6. Install the rear axle as described in this chapter.

7. Install the seat and rear fenders as described in Chapter Fifteen.

Table 1 REAR SUSPENSION TORQUE SPECIFICATIONS

Item and model	ft.-lb.	N•m
Rear wheel lug nuts	43-51	60-70
Rear axle castellated (hub) nut	58-72	80-120
Driven sprocket nuts	22-26	30-36
Rear axle bearing holder (housing) mounting bolts	58-72	80-100
Shock absorber mounting bolts and nuts	29-36	40-50

Table 2 REAR SUSPENSION SPECIFICATIONS

Item	Specification	Wear limit
Rear axle runout	—	3.0 mm (0.12 in.)
Rear wheel runout		
Axial	—	4.0 mm (0.16 in.)
Radial	—	4.0 mm (0.16 in.)
Shock absorber free length	262.5 mm (10.33 in.)	260 mm (10.24 in.)

CHAPTER THIRTEEN

DRUM BRAKES

The 4-wheeled models are equipped with drum brakes on both the front and rear. These models are also equipped with a parking brake that is cable operated and is integrated into the rear brake assembly. The front brakes are hydraulically operated and activated by the master cylinder and lever on the right-hand side of the handlebar. The mechanical rear brake is activated either by the hand lever on the left-hand side of the handlebar or by the foot brake on the right-hand side.

WARNING
*When working on the brake system, do **not** inhale brake dust. It may contain asbestos, which can cause lung injury and cancer.*

Lever and pedal free play must be maintained on both brakes to minimize brake drag and premature brake wear and maximize braking effectiveness. Refer to Chapter Three for complete adjustment procedures.

Both rear brake cables must be inspected and replaced periodically as they will stretch with use until they can no longer be properly adjusted.

Refer to **Table 1** for drum brake specifications. **Table 1** and **Table 2** are located at the end of this chapter.

The front drum brakes are actuated by hydraulic fluid and controlled by a hand lever on the handlebar mounted master cylinder.

When working on hydraulic brake systems, it is necessary that the work area and all tools be absolutely clean. Any tiny particles of foreign matter and grit in the wheel cylinder assembly or the master cylinder can damage the components. Also, sharp tools must not be used inside the wheel cylinder or on the pistons. If there is any doubt about your ability to correctly and safely carry out major service on the brake components, take the job to a dealer or brake specialist.

There is no recommended mileage interval for changing the brake linings. Lining wear depends greatly on riding habits and conditions. The linings should be checked for wear every 6 months (600 miles or 1,000 km) and replaced when worn to the service limit dimension (or less) listed in **Table 2**.

13

FRONT BRAKES

Brake Shoe Replacement

Refer to **Figure 1** for this procedure.

> *WARNING*
> *Do **not** inhale brake dust. It may
> contain asbestos, which can cause lung
> injury and cancer.*

1. Remove the front wheels and the front hub/brake drum assembly as described under *Front Hub/Brake Drum Disassembly* in Chapter Ten.
2. Push in on the spring and using a pair of pliers, rotate the brake shoe tension pins 90° and remove the pin holders (A, **Figure 2**).
3. Pull the brake shoes out of the notches in the brake shoe adjuster (B, **Figure 2**) and the wheel cylinder (C, **Figure 2**).

> *NOTE*
> *Place a clean shop rag on the linings to
> protect them from oil and grease during
> removal.*

4. Remove the brake shoes (D, **Figure 2**) from the backing plate by firmly pulling out and up on the center of each shoe.
5. Remove the return springs and separate the shoes.
6. Inspect the brake components as described in this chapter.
7. Assemble the brake by reversing the disassembly steps, noting the following.
8. Apply a light coat of silicone grease to the brake shoe locating notches in the wheel cylinder and the brake shoe anchor.
9. Apply a light coat of silicone grease to the raised pads on the backside of the brake shoe metal plate where the brake shoes ride on the brake backing plate. Avoid getting any grease on the brake linings.

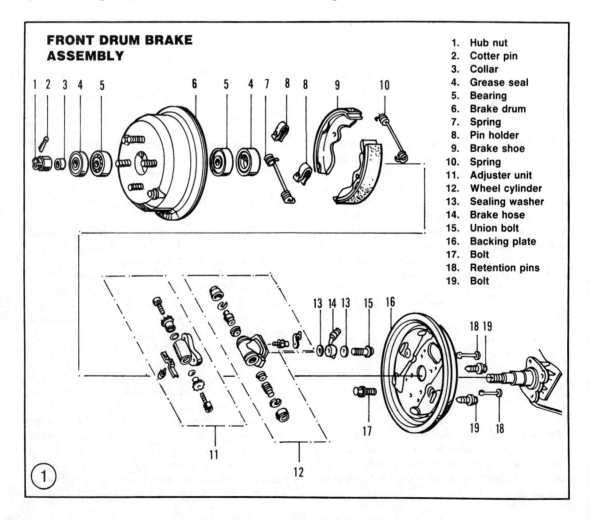

FRONT DRUM BRAKE ASSEMBLY

1. Hub nut
2. Cotter pin
3. Collar
4. Grease seal
5. Bearing
6. Brake drum
7. Spring
8. Pin holder
9. Brake shoe
10. Spring
11. Adjuster unit
12. Wheel cylinder
13. Sealing washer
14. Brake hose
15. Union bolt
16. Backing plate
17. Bolt
18. Retention pins
19. Bolt

1

10. Hold the brake shoes in a "V" information with the return springs attached (black spring on the adjuster side) and snap them in place into the brake shoe anchor and wheel cylinder on the brake backing plate. The black spring must be on the outside surface of the brake shoes (**Figure 3**). Make sure they are firmly seated on the brake backing plate.

NOTE
If new linings are being installed, file off the leading edge of each shoe a little so that the brake will not grab when applied.

11. Inspect the rubber seal (**Figure 4**) on the brake drum. Check for wear or deterioration and replace if necessary.

12. Install the front hub/brake drum assembly and front wheel as described under *Front Hub/Brake Drum Assembly* in Chapter Ten.

13. Adjust the front brakes as described in Chapter Three.

Brake Backing Plate
Removal/Installation

1. Disconnect the union bolt (**Figure 5**) and sealing washers securing the hydraulic brake hose to the wheel cylinder.

2. Remove the bolts (**Figure 6**) securing the brake backing plate to the steering knuckle and remove the brake panel.

3. Install by reversing these removal steps, noting the following.

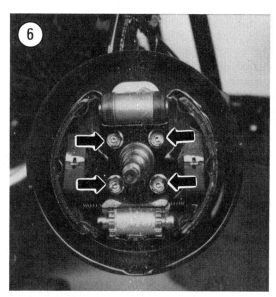

13

4. Make sure the locating pin on the brake hose indexes into the notch in the backing plate (**Figure 7**).

5. Tighten the bolts securing the brake backing plate securely.

6. Be sure to install a sealing washer on each side of the hydraulic brake hose fitting and tighten the union bolt to the torque specification listed in **Table 2**.

7. Bleed the brakes as described in this chapter.

Wheel Cylinder
Removal/Installation

1. Remove the brake linings as described in this chapter.

2. Remove the brake backing plate as described in this chapter.

3. Remove the bolts (A, **Figure 8**) securing the wheel cylinder to the brake backing plate and remove the wheel cylinder (A, **Figure 9**).

4. Clean off the area where the wheel cylinder attaches to the brake backing plate.

5. Apply a light coat of Gasgacinch, Three Bond No. 1104 or equivalent to the back of the wheel cylinder and its mounting area of the brake backing plate.

6. Install the wheel cylinder and bolts. Tighten the bolts securely.

7. Install the brake backing plate as described in this chapter.

8. Install the brake linings as described in this chapter.

9. Bleed the brakes as described in this chapter.

Wheel Cylinder Rebuilding

The wheel cylinder should be replaced with a new unit instead of rebuilding it. This procedure is included in case you choose to rebuild instead of replacing the wheel cylinder. If worn, leaking or damaged in any way, rebuild or replace the wheel cylinder assembly.

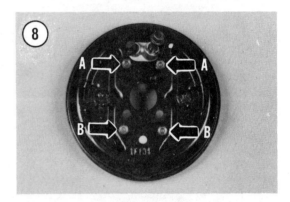

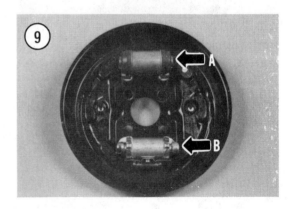

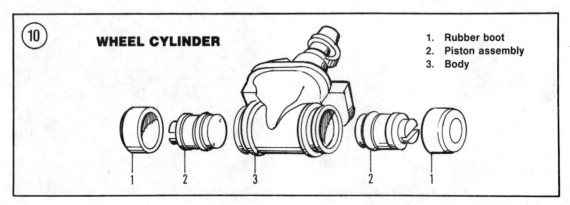

WHEEL CYLINDER

1. Rubber boot
2. Piston assembly
3. Body

Refer to **Figure 10** for this procedure.

1. Remove the wheel cylinder as described in this chapter.

2. Remove the rubber boot from each end of the wheel cylinder.

3. Withdraw the piston assemblies from the wheel cylinder.

4. Wash all parts in denatured alcohol or fresh brake fluid.

NOTE
If the piston cups are worn or damaged, replace the wheel cylinder assembly—do not replace the individual parts.

5. Inspect the cylinder bore and the piston assemblies for signs of wear and damage.

6. Measure the inside diameter of the wheel cylinder body (A, **Figure 11**). Replace the wheel cylinder body if worn to the service limit dimension listed in **Table 2** or greater.

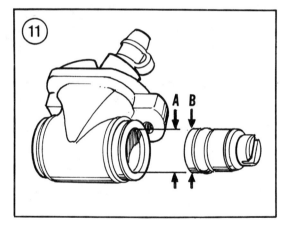

7. Measure the outside diameter of the piston assembly (B, **Figure 11**). Replace the piston assemblies as a pair if either is worn to the service limit dimension listed in **Table 2** or less.

8. Inspect the union bolt threads in the wheel cylinder body. If damaged, replace the wheel cylinder body.

9. Coat the inside bore surface of the wheel cylinder and the outside surfaces of the piston assemblies with fresh brake fluid before assembly.

10. Install the piston assemblies into the wheel cylinder.

11. Install the rubber boot onto each end of the wheel cylinder.

12. Rotate the piston assemblies so the notch that accepts the brake linings is vertical.

Adjuster Unit
Removal/Inspection/Installation

Refer to **Figure 12** for this procedure.

1. Remove the brake linings as described in this chapter.

2. Remove the brake backing plate as described in this chapter.

3. Remove the bolts (B, **Figure 8**) securing the adjuster unit to the brake backing plate and remove the adjuster unit (B, **Figure 9**).

4. Remove the screw securing the lockspring plate and remove the lockspring plate.

5. Withdraw both adjusters from the body.

6. Clean all parts in solvent and dry thoroughly with compressed air.

7. Inspect all parts for wear or damage.

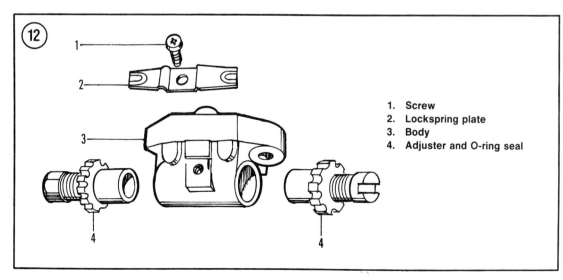

1. Screw
2. Lockspring plate
3. Body
4. Adjuster and O-ring seal

13

8. Make sure the adjuster screw turns smoothly in the adjuster nut. If not, completely unscrew the adjuster screw from the adjuster nut. Clean both parts in solvent and apply silicone grease to the screw threads. Screw the adjuster screw back into the adjuster nut.

9. Inspect the O-ring seal on each adjuster and replace if necessary.

10. Apply a light coat of high-temperature silicone grease to each adjuster where it rides in the adjuster unit body.

11. Install both adjusters into the body and install the lockspring plate and screw. Tighten the screw securely.

12. Apply a light coat of Gasgacinch, Three Bond No. 1104 or equivalent to the back of the adjuster and its mounting area of the brake backing plate.

13. Install the adjuster unit and bolts. Tighten the bolts securely.

14. Install the brake backing plate as described in this chapter.

15. Install the brake linings as described in this chapter.

Brake Drum Inspection

1. Check the contact surface of the drum (**Figure 13**) for scoring. If there are grooves deep enough to snag a fingernail, the drum should be turned and new shoes fitted. This type of wear can be avoided to a great extent if the brakes are disassembled and thoroughly cleaned after riding the vehicle in water, mud or deep sand.

NOTE
If oil or grease is on the drum surface, clean it off with a clean rag soaked in lacquer thinner—do not use any solvent that may leave an oil residue.

2. Use a vernier caliper and check the inside diameter of the drum (**Figure 14**) for out-of-roundness or excessive wear. Leave the drum if it will still be within the service limit dimension. Replace the drum it is worn to the service limit listed in **Table 2** or greater.

3. If the drum is turned, the linings will have to be replaced and the new linings arced to the new drum contour.

4. Measure the brake linings with a vernier caliper (**Figure 15**). They should be replaced if worn to the service limit (distance from the metal backing plate) or less as listed in **Table 2**.

5. Inspect the wheel lug nut threaded studs (**Figure 16**) for wear or damage; replace as necessary.

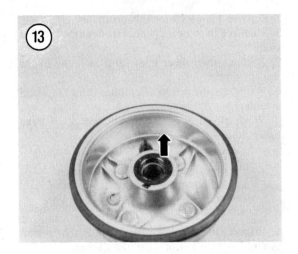

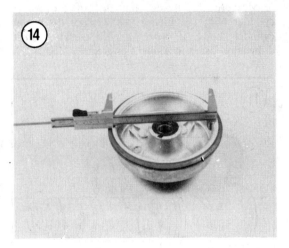

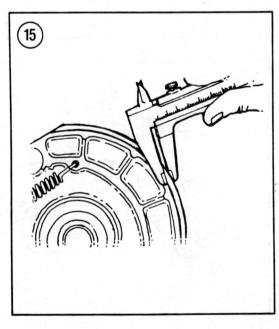

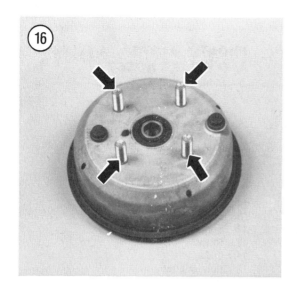

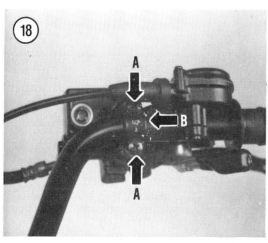

FRONT MASTER CYLINDER

Removal/Installation

1. Place the ATV on level ground and set the parking brake.

CAUTION
Cover the fuel tank and front fender with a heavy cloth or plastic tarp to protect them from accidental brake fluid spills. Wash any brake fluid off painted or plated surfaces immediately, as it will destroy the finish. Use soapy water and rinse completely.

2. Remove the union bolt (**Figure 17**) securing the brake hose to the master cylinder and remove the brake hose. Tie the brake hose up and cover the end to prevent the entry of foreign matter.

3. Remove the clamping bolts (A, **Figure 18**) and clamp securing the master cylinder to the handlebar and remove the master cylinder.

4. Install by reversing these removal steps, noting the following.

5. Position the clamp with the UP mark (B, **Figure 18**) facing up.

6. Tighten the upper clamping bolt first and then the lower bolt. Tighten both bolts securely.

7. Install the brake hose onto the master cylinder. Be sure to place a sealing washer on each side of the fitting and install the union bolt. Tighten the union bolt to the torque specification listed in **Table 2**.

8. Bleed the brake as described in this chapter.

Disassembly

Refer to **Figure 19** and **Figure 20** for this procedure.

1. Remove the master cylinder as described in this chapter.

2. Remove the bolt and nut securing the brake lever and remove the brake lever.

3. Remove the screws securing the cover and remove the cover, diaphragm plate and diaphragm. Pour out the brake fluid and discard it. *Never* reuse brake fluid.

4. Remove the rubber boot from the area where the hand lever actuates the internal piston.

5. Using circlip pliers, remove the internal circlip and washer from the body (**Figure 21**).

6. Remove the piston/primary cup assembly.

7. Remove the spring.

Inspection

1. Clean all parts in denatured alcohol or fresh brake fluid. Inspect the cylinder bore and piston

13

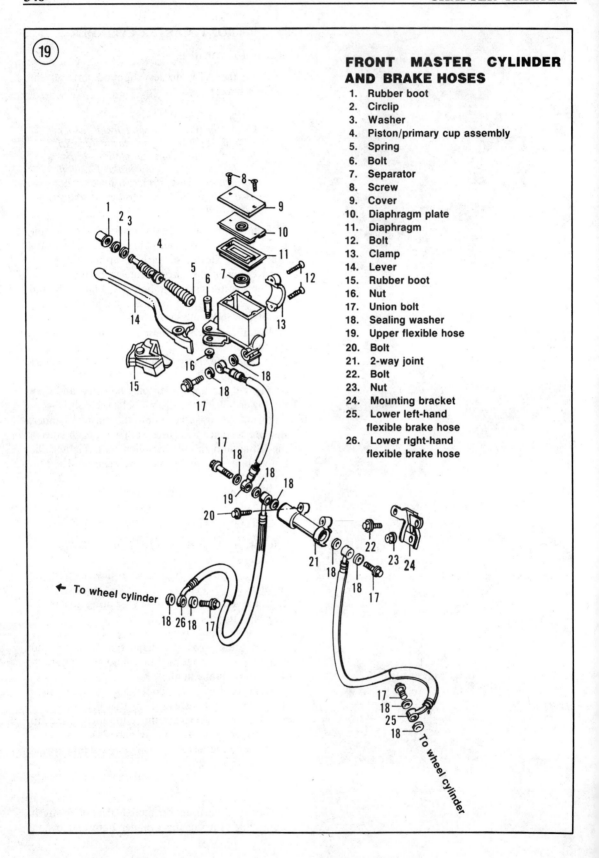

⑲

**FRONT MASTER CYLINDER
AND BRAKE HOSES**
1. Rubber boot
2. Circlip
3. Washer
4. Piston/primary cup assembly
5. Spring
6. Bolt
7. Separator
8. Screw
9. Cover
10. Diaphragm plate
11. Diaphragm
12. Bolt
13. Clamp
14. Lever
15. Rubber boot
16. Nut
17. Union bolt
18. Sealing washer
19. Upper flexible hose
20. Bolt
21. 2-way joint
22. Bolt
23. Nut
24. Mounting bracket
25. Lower left-hand
    flexible brake hose
26. Lower right-hand
    flexible brake hose

← To wheel cylinder

To wheel cylinder

contact surfaces for signs of wear and damage. If either part is less than perfect, replace it.

2. Check the end of the piston for wear caused by the hand lever. Replace the piston assembly if either cup is worn or damaged.

3. Inspect the pivot hole in the hand lever. If worn or elongated, it must be replaced.

4. Make sure the passages in the bottom of the brake fluid reservoir are clear. Check the reservoir cap, diaphragm plate and diaphragm for damage and deterioration and replace as necessary.

5. Inspect the threads in the bores for the brake line.

6. Check the front brake hand lever pivot lug on the master cylinder body for cracks.

7. Measure the cylinder bore (**Figure 22**). Replace the master cylinder if the bore exceeds the service limit listed in **Table 2**.

8. Measure the outside diameter of the piston assembly with a micrometer as shown in **Figure 23**. Replace the piston assembly if it is less than the service limit listed in **Table 2**.

Assembly

1. Soak the new piston assembly in fresh brake fluid for at least 15 minutes to make the cups pliable. Coat the inside of the cylinder with fresh brake fluid before the assembly of parts.

CAUTION
When installing the piston assembly, do not allow the cups to turn inside out as they will be damaged and allow brake fluid leakage within the cylinder bore.

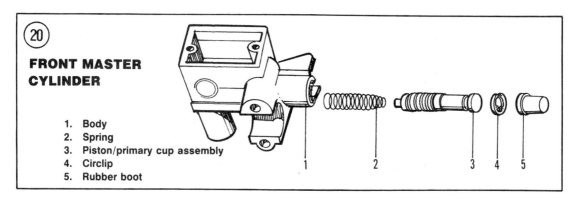

20

FRONT MASTER CYLINDER

1. Body
2. Spring
3. Piston/primary cup assembly
4. Circlip
5. Rubber boot

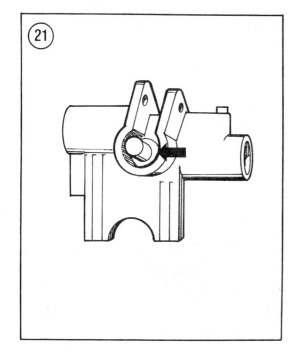

21

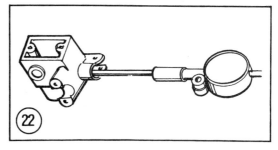

22

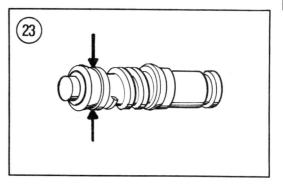

23

13

2. Install the spring and the piston assembly into the cylinder together. The spring's tapered end faces toward the piston assembly (**Figure 20**).

3. Install the washer and the circlip. Slide in the rubber boot.

4. Install the diaphragm, diaphragm plate and cover. Do not tighten the cover screws at this time as fluid will have to be added later.

5. Install the brake lever onto the master cylinder body.

6. Install the master cylinder as described in this chapter.

FRONT BRAKE HOSE

There is no factory-recommended replacement interval but it is a good idea to replace the flexible brake hoses every four years or when they show signs of cracking or damage.

Removal/Installation

Refer to **Figure 19** for this procedure.

> *CAUTION*
> *Cover the fuel tank with a heavy cloth or plastic tarp to protect it from accidental spilling of brake fluid. Wash any brake fluid off of plastic, painted or plated surfaces immediately, as it will destroy the finish. Use soapy water and rinse completely.*

1. Place the ATV on level ground and set the parking brake.

2. Remove both front wheels as described under *Front Wheel Removal/Installation* in Chapter Ten.

3. Remove the front fender as described in Chapter Fifteen.

4. To prevent the spilling of brake fluid on the steering knuckle and brake backing plate, perform the following:
   a. Connect a bleed hose to the bleed valve on one of the wheel cylinders. Place the other end in a container.
   b. Open the bleed valve and pump the master cylinder until brake fluid stops coming out. Close the bleed valve.
   c. Disconnect the bleed hose from the one wheel cylinder and reconnect it to the bleed valve on the other wheel cylinder. Place the other end in a container.
   d. Open the bleed valve and pump the master cylinder until brake fluid stops coming out. Close the bleed valve.
   e. Dispose of this brake fluid—*never* reuse brake fluid.

5. Place a container under the brake line at the caliper.

6. Remove the union bolt and sealing washers (**Figure 7**) securing the lower flexible brake hose to the wheel cylinder.

7. Remove the brake hose and let any remaining brake fluid drain out into the container. Dispose of this brake fluid—*never* reuse brake fluid.

> *WARNING*
> *Dispose of this brake fluid—never reuse brake fluid. Contaminated brake fluid can cause brake failure.*

8. To prevent the entry of moisture and dirt, cap the wheel cylinder where the brake line attaches.

9A. On the right-hand side, remove the union bolt and sealing washers securing the lower flexible brake hose to the 3-way joint.

9B. On the left-hand side, remove the union bolt and sealing washers (A, **Figure 24**) securing the upper (B, **Figure 24**) and the lower (C, **Figure 24**) flexible brake hoses to the 3-way joint.

10. Remove the lower flexible brake hose.

11. Repeat Steps 5-10 for the other lower flexible brake hose on the other side of the ATV.

12. Remove the union bolt and sealing washers (**Figure 17**) securing the upper flexible brake hose to the master cylinder and remove the hose.

13. Install new flexible brake hose, sealing washers and union bolts in the reverse order of removal. Be sure to install new sealing washers in the correct positions; refer to **Figure 19**.

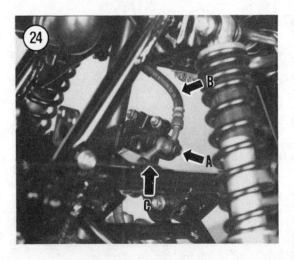

14. Tighten all union bolts and fittings on the metal brake lines to the torque specification listed in **Table 1**.

> *WARNING*
> *Use brake fluid from a sealed container marked DOT 3 or DOT 4 only (specified for disc brakes). Other types may vaporize and cause brake failure. Do not intermix different brands or types as they may not be compatible. Do not intermix a silicone based (DOT 5) brake fluid as it can cause brake component damage leading to brake system failure.*

15. Refill the master cylinder with fresh brake fluid marked DOT 3 or DOT 4 only. Bleed the brake as described in this chapter.

> *WARNING*
> *Do not ride the ATV until you are sure that the brakes are operating properly.*

REAR BRAKE

Brake Shoe Replacement

Refer to **Figure 25** for this procedure.
1. Place the ATV on level ground and set the parking brake.
2. Remove the brake drum as described in this chapter.
3. Using a vernier caliper, measure the brake lining thickness (**Figure 15**). The linings should be replaced if worn to the service limit (distance from the metal backing plate) listed in **Table 2** or less.

> *NOTE*
> *Place a clean shop rag on the linings to protect them from oil and grease during removal.*

4. Remove the brake shoes (**Figure 26**) from the rear brake panel by pulling up on the center of each shoe.

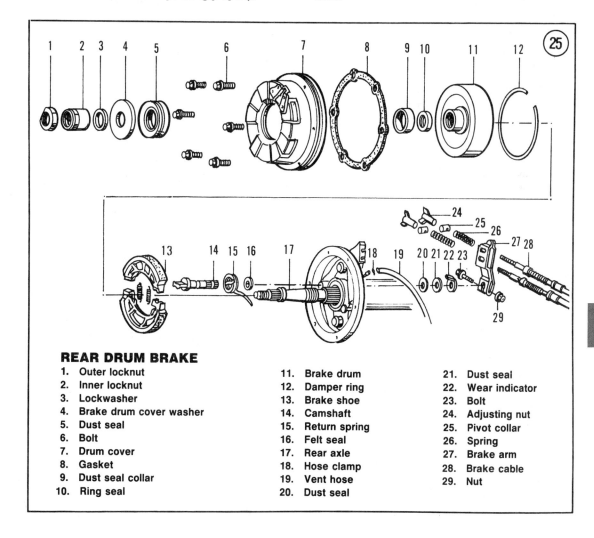

REAR DRUM BRAKE

1. Outer locknut
2. Inner locknut
3. Lockwasher
4. Brake drum cover washer
5. Dust seal
6. Bolt
7. Drum cover
8. Gasket
9. Dust seal collar
10. Ring seal
11. Brake drum
12. Damper ring
13. Brake shoe
14. Camshaft
15. Return spring
16. Felt seal
17. Rear axle
18. Hose clamp
19. Vent hose
20. Dust seal
21. Dust seal
22. Wear indicator
23. Bolt
24. Adjusting nut
25. Pivot collar
26. Spring
27. Brake arm
28. Brake cable
29. Nut

13

5. Remove the return springs and separate the shoes.

6. Apply a light coat of high temperature silicone grease to the brake camshaft and pivot post. Avoid getting any grease on the brake plate where the linings come in contact with it.

7. Attach the return springs to the brake shoes.

NOTE
Place a clean shop rag on the linings to protect them from oil and grease during installation.

8. Hold the brake shoes in a "V"-formation and snap them in place on the brake backing plate. Make sure they are firmly seated on it.

NOTE
*File off the leading edge of each shoe a little (**Figure 27**) so that the brake will not grab when applied.*

9. Install the rear brake drum as described in this chapter.

10. Adjust the rear brake as described under *Rear Drum Brake Adjustment* in Chapter Three.

Brake Drum Removal

Refer to **Figure 25** for this procedure.

1. Remove the right-hand rear wheel as described under *Rear Wheel Removal/Installation* in Chapter Twelve.

2. Remove the right-hand hub as described under *Rear Hub Removal/Installation* in Chapter Twelve.

CAUTION
*The outer locknut has had thread locking agent applied during assembly and is tightened to 120-140 N•m (87-101 ft.-lb.). It is very hard to remove even with the correct size tool and a lot of force. Do **not** apply heat to the area in order to try to loosen the locknut as this will ruin the heat-treated hardness of the axle.*

NOTE
A special set of flame cut 41 mm wrenches are necessary for this procedure and are available from a Honda dealer or some mail order houses.

3. The flame cut 41 mm wrenches required for this procedure are as follows:
   a. 41 mm locknut spanner: Honda part No. 07916-958020A.
   b. 41 mm locknut nut wrench: Honda part No. 07916-958010A.

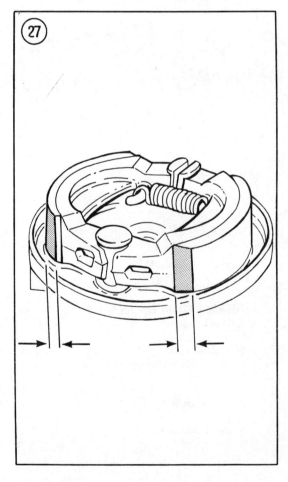

4. Place the 41 mm locknut spanner on the inner locknut (**Figure 28**).

5. Place the 41 mm locknut wrench on the outer locknut (**Figure 29**).

NOTE
If you are unable to loosen the locknuts they will have to be chiseled off. Do not chisel all the way through into the threads of the threaded collar or the axle.

6. Hold onto the inner locknut (A, **Figure 30**) and loosen the outer locknut (B, **Figure 30**). Completely unscrew the outer locknut and slide it off the rear axle. It may be necessary to tap on the end of the wrench with a soft-faced mallet to break the outer locknut loose.

7. Loosen the inner locknut (**Figure 31**). Completely unscrew inner locknut and slide it off the rear axle.

8. Slide off the lockwasher (**Figure 32**) and brake drum cover washer (**Figure 33**).

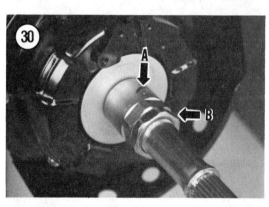

13

9. Remove the bolts securing the brake drum cover (**Figure 34**) and slide the cover off the rear axle.

> *NOTE*
> *In the next step, if you are unable to remove the brake drum, carefully tap around the perimeter of the brake drum with a soft-faced mallet to break the drum loose from the rear axle splines. If the splines are rusty, apply a **small** amount of Liquid Wrench to the open end of the brake drum in the drum/axle spline area. Let it set for 10-15 minutes and repeat this step.*

> *WARNING*
> *Do **not** inhale brake dust. It may contain asbestos, which can cause lung injury and cancer.*

> *CAUTION*
> *In the next step, do not slide the brake drum, with the rubber seal still in place, off of the rear axle. The axle splines will destroy the sealing ability of the rubber seal.*

10. Slide the brake drum (**Figure 35**) out and away from the brake shoe assembly. Push the brake drum back onto the brake shoe assembly and remove the rubber seal (**Figure 36**) from the brake drum.

11. Slide the brake drum off the rear axle.

12. Inspect the brake drum as described in this chapter.

Brake Drum Installation

1. Slide the brake drum onto the rear axle. Push it on all the way until it stops (**Figure 35**).

2. Install the rubber seal (**Figure 36**) and push it into the recess in the brake drum (**Figure 37**).

3. Install a new gasket (**Figure 38**) on the brake drum cover.

> *CAUTION*
> *In the next step don't apply too much grease to the dust seal or it will find its way into the brake drum and contaminate the brake linings.*

4. Apply a *light* coat of multipurpose grease to the lips of the brake drum cover dust seal (**Figure 39**).

5. Slide the brake drum cover onto the rear axle.

6. Install the brake drum cover bolts and tighten securely.

7. Slide on the brake drum cover washer (**Figure 33**).

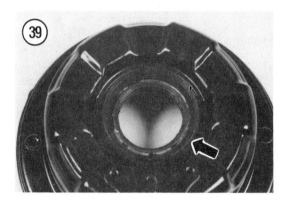

8. Position the lockwasher with the dished side facing toward the inside and slide the lockwasher (**Figure 32**) onto the rear axle.

9. Install the inner locknut (**Figure 31**). Use the 41 mm locknut wrench (**Figure 28**) and tighten the inner locknut to the torque specification listed in **Table 1**.

10. Spray the rear axle threads and outer locknut threads with contact cleaner to clean off any oil or grease residue.

11. Apply Loctite Lock N' Seal to the rear axle threads.

12. Install the outer locknut (B, **Figure 30**).

13. Place the 41 mm locknut spanner on the inner locknut (**Figure 28**).

14. Place the 41 mm locknut wrench on the outer locknut (**Figure 29**).

15. Hold onto the inner locknut and tighten the outer locknut to the torque specification listed in **Table 1**.

16. Install the right-hand wheel hub as described under *Rear Hub Removal/Installation* in Chapter Twelve.

17. Install the right-hand wheel as described under *Rear Wheel Removal/Installation* in Chapter Twelve.

Drum Brake Camshaft Removal

1. Remove the brake drum and linings as described in this chapter.

2. Completely unscrew both adjusting nuts (**Figure 40**) from both brake cables.

3. Unhook both brake cables from the receptacle (**Figure 41**) on the rear axle bearing housing.

4. Remove the pivot pin from each brake arm. To avoid misplacing these parts, install each pivot pin onto its respective brake cable and screw on the adjusting nuts.

13

5. Unscrew the bolt and nut (A, **Figure 42**) clamping the brake arm to the brake camshaft.

6. Remove the brake arm (B, **Figure 42**) and brake lining wear indicator (**Figure 43**) from the brake camshaft.

7. Remove the return spring (**Figure 44**) from the brake camshaft.

8. Remove the brake camshaft (**Figure 45**) from the rear axle bearing housing.

9. Remove the 2 inner dust seals and the outer dust seal from the recess in rear axle bearing housing where the brake camshaft pivots.

10. Inspect the brake parts as described in this chapter.

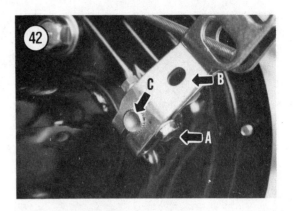

Drum Brake Camshaft
Installation

1. Apply a light coat of multipurpose grease to the camshaft dust seals.

2. Install 2 new inner dust seals and one outer dust seal (**Figure 46**) into the recess in rear axle bearing housing where the brake camshaft pivots.

3. Install the brake camshaft (**Figure 45**) into the rear axle bearing housing.

4. Install the camshaft return spring (**Figure 44**).

5. Align the flat on the brake lining wear indicator with the flat on the brake camshaft (**Figure 47**) and install the indicator onto the brake camshaft (**Figure 43**).

6. Align the punch marks (C, **Figure 42**) on the brake arm and brake camshaft and install the brake arm (B, **Figure 42**) onto the brake camshaft.

7. Install the clamping bolt and nut (A, **Figure 42**) securing the brake arm to the brake camshaft. Tighten the bolt and nut securely.

8. Insert both brake cables into the receptacles (**Figure 41**) on the rear axle bearing housing.

9. Remove the adjusting nut and the pivot pin from each brake cable. Install each pivot pin onto its respective slot in the brake arm.

10. Insert both brake cables into the pivot pins and install the adjusting nuts (**Figure 40**) onto both brake cables.

11. Install the brake drum and linings as described in this chapter.

12. Adjust the rear brake as described under *Rear Drum Brake Adjustment* in Chapter Three.

Brake Drum and Camshaft Inspection

1. Thoroughly clean and dry all parts except the linings.

2. Check the contact surface of the drum (**Figure 48**) for scoring. If there are grooves deep enough to snag a fingernail, the drum should be reground and new shoes fitted. This type of wear can be avoided to a great extent if the brakes are disassembled and thoroughly cleaned after riding the vehicle in water, mud or deep sand.

> *NOTE*
> *If oil or grease is on the drum surface, clean it off with a clean rag soaked in lacquer thinner—do not use any solvent that may leave an oil residue.*

3. Inspect the splines (**Figure 49**) on the brake drum for wear or damage. The drum must be replaced if the splines are damaged. Also check the splines on the rear axle where the brake drum is positioned.

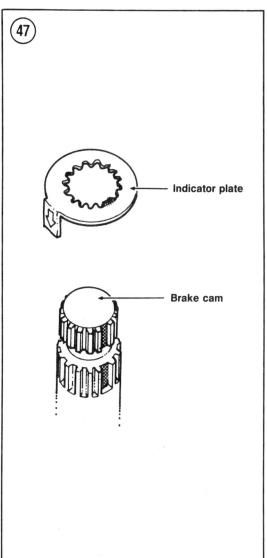

Indicator plate

Brake cam

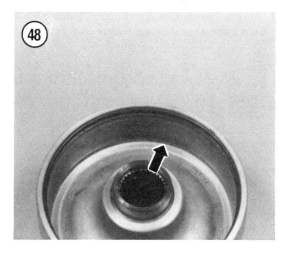

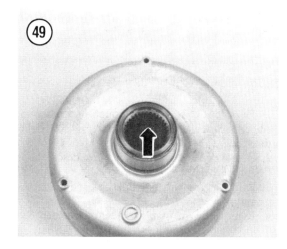

13

4. Use a vernier caliper and check the inside diameter of the drum for out-of-roundness or excessive wear (**Figure 50**). Have the drum turned if it will still be within the service limit dimension. Replace the drum it is worn to the service limit listed in **Table 2** or greater.

5. If the drum is turned, the linings will have to be replaced and the new linings arced to the new drum contour.

6. Inspect the camshaft lobe (A, **Figure 51**) and the pivot pin area (B, **Figure 51**) of the shaft for wear and corrosion. Minor roughness can be removed with fine emery cloth.

7. Inspect the brake shoe return springs for wear. If they are stretched, they will not fully retract the brake shoes from the drum, resulting in a power-robbing drag on the drums and premature wear of the linings. Replace shoes as necessary and always replace as a pair.

8. Inspect the dust seal (**Figure 39**) in the brake drum cover for wear or deterioration; replace if necessary.

9. Inspect the damper ring (**Figure 52**) in the brake drum for wear or damage; replace as necessary.

BRAKE CABLE REPLACEMENT

Brake cable adjustment should be checked periodically as the cables stretch with use and increase brake lever or pedal free play. Free play is the distance that the brake lever or pedal travels between the released position and the point when the brake shoes come in contact with the drum.

If the rear brake adjustment, as described in Chapter Three, can no longer be achieved the cable(s) must be replaced.

The rear drum brake can be activated either by the cable operated left-hand lever or by the cable actuated foot pedal on the right-hand side of the vehicle. The parking brake is cable operated and is controlled by the left-hand brake lever.

Rear Brake Cable Replacement
(Left-hand Lever Cable)

1. Place the ATV on level ground and block the wheels so the vehicle will not roll in either direction.

2. Remove the seat/rear fender as described in Chapter Fifteen.

3. Remove the front fender as described in Chapter Fifteen.

4. Remove the fuel tank as described under *Fuel Tank Removal/Installation* in Chapter Seven.

5. At the left-hand lever, perform the following:
  a. Slide back the rubber boot.
  b. Loosen the locknut and adjusting nut (A, **Figure 53**) on the brake cable.
  c. Pull the brake lever (B, **Figure 53**) all the way to the grip, then remove the cable nipple from the receptacle in the lever.

6. At the rear brake arm, perform the following:
  a. Completely unscrew the upper adjusting nut (A, **Figure 54**) from the brake cable.
  b. Unhook the brake cable from the receptacle (**Figure 55**) on the rear axle bearing housing.

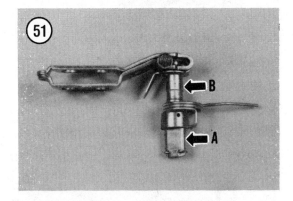

c. Remove the pivot pin from the brake arm. To avoid misplacing these parts, install the pivot pin onto the brake cable and screw on the adjusting nut.

d. Remove the cable from the receptacle on the rear axle bearing housing.

NOTE
The piece of string attached in the next step will be used to pull the new brake cable back through the frame so it will be routed in the exact same position.

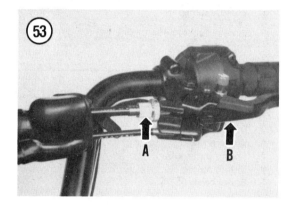

7. Tie a piece of heavy string or cord (approximately 1.8 m/6 ft. long) to the rear end of the brake cable. Wrap this end with masking or duct tape. Do not use an excessive amount of tape as it must be pulled through various frame loops (some models) during removal. Tie the other end of the string to the frame or rear axle.

8. Loosen the metal bands or remove any plastic tie wraps (B, **Figure 54**) securing the cable to the frame or to the brake drum vent tube.

9. At the handlebar end of the cable, carefully pull the cable (and attached string) out from the frame. Make sure the attached string follows the same path as the cable through the frame.

10. Remove the tape and untie the string from the old cable.

11. Lubricate the new cable as described under *Control Cables* in Chapter Three.

12. Tie the string to the brake mechanism end of the new brake cable and wrap it with tape.

13. Carefully pull the string back through the frame routing the new cable through the frame following the same path as the old cable.

14. Remove the tape and untie the string from the cable and the frame or rear axle.

15. Attach the metal bands or plastic tie wraps to the new cable in the exact same position on the frame.

16. At the rear brake arm, perform the following:

a. Insert the brake cable into the upper receptacle (**Figure 55**) on the rear axle bearing housing.

b. Remove the adjusting nut and pivot pin from the brake cable. Install the pivot pin onto the upper slot in the brake arm.

c. Insert the brake cable into the pivot pin and install the adjusting nut (A, **Figure 54**) onto the brake cable.

17. At the left-hand lever, pull the brake lever (B, **Figure 53**) all the way to the grip, then install the cable nipple into receptacle in the lever.

18. Install the fuel tank, fenders and seat.

19. Adjust the rear brake as described under *Rear Drum Brake Adjustment* in Chapter Three.

13

Rear Brake Pedal Cable
Removal/Installation

1. Place the ATV on level ground and block the wheels so the vehicle will not roll in either direction.

2. Remove the seat and the rear fender as described in Chapter Fifteen.

3. At the brake assembly, completely unscrew the lower adjusting nut (**Figure 40**) from the end of the brake cable.

4. Remove the cable and pivot pin from the brake arm.

5. Reinstall the pivot pin and adjusting nut onto the brake cable to avoid misplacing it.

6. Remove the cable from the receptacle (A, **Figure 56**) on the brake pedal.

7. Remove the cable from the receptacle (B, **Figure 56**) on the rear axle bearing housing.

8. Remove the brake cable from the frame.

9. Insert the pivot pin into the brake arm and slide the return spring onto the cable. Attach the cable to the brake arm and brake lever.

10. Adjust the rear brake as described in Chapter Three.

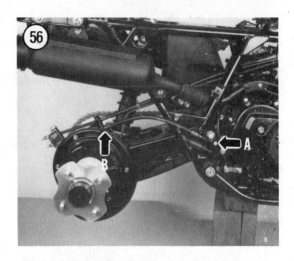

REAR BRAKE PEDAL

Removal/Installation

Refer to **Figure 57** for this procedure.

1. At the brake assembly, completely unscrew the lower adjusting nut (**Figure 40**) from the end of the brake cable.

2. Remove the cable and pivot pin from the brake arm. Reinstall the pivot pin and adjusting nut onto the brake cable to avoid misplacing them.

3. Remove the cable from the receptacle (A, **Figure 58**) on the brake pedal.

4. Using Vise Grips, unhook the return spring (B, **Figure 58**) from the brake pedal.

5. Remove the cotter pin and washer (C, **Figure 58**) securing the brake pedal to the pivot shaft on the frame. Discard the cotter pin. Never reuse a cotter pin as the ends may break off and the pin may fall out.

6. Slide the brake pedal (D, **Figure 58**) off the pivot shaft.

7. Inspect the dust seals on each side of the brake pedal; replace if necessary.

8. Install by reversing these removal steps, noting the following.

9. Apply grease to the pedal pivot shaft before installing the brake pedal.

10. Install a new cotter pin and bend the ends over completely.

11. Be sure that the return spring is properly attached.

12. Insert the pivot pin into the brake arm and slide the return spring onto the cable. Attach the cable to the brake arm and brake lever.

13. Adjust the rear brake as described under *Rear Drum Brake Adjustment* in Chapter Three.

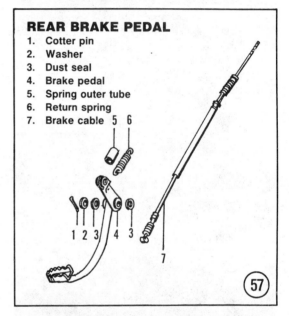

REAR BRAKE PEDAL
1. Cotter pin
2. Washer
3. Dust seal
4. Brake pedal
5. Spring outer tube
6. Return spring
7. Brake cable

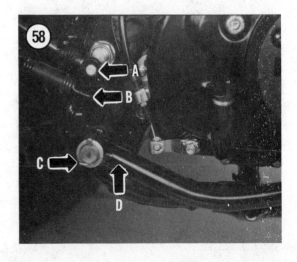

BLEEDING THE SYSTEM

This procedure is not necessary unless the brakes feel spongy, there has been a leak in the system, a component has been replaced or the brake fluid has been replaced.

Brake Bleeder Process

This procedure uses a brake bleeder that is available from motorcycle or automotive supply stores or from mail order outlets.

NOTE
Front wheel removal is not necessary but it does allow additional work room.

1. Remove the front wheels as described under *Front Wheel Removal/Installation* in Chapter Ten.

NOTE
It doesn't make any difference which wheel cylinder is bled first.

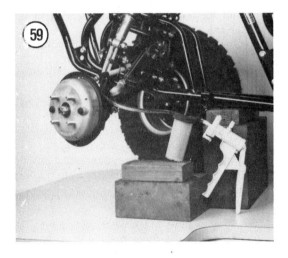

2. Remove the dust cap from the bleed valve on the wheel cylinder.
3. Connect the bleed hose of the brake bleeder to the bleed valve on the wheel cylinder (**Figure 59**).

CAUTION
Cover the front suspension arms with a heavy cloth or plastic tarp to protect it from the accidental spilling of brake fluid. Wash any brake fluid off of plastic, painted or plated surfaces immediately as it will destroy the finish. Use soapy water and rinse completely.

4. Clean the top of the master cylinder of all dirt and foreign matter.
5. Remove the screws securing the reservoir top (**Figure 60**) and remove the reservoir top, the diaphragm plate and the diaphragm.
6. Fill the reservoir almost to the top lip. Insert the diaphragm plate, the diaphragm and the top loosely. Leave the top in place during this procedure to prevent the entry of dirt.

WARNING
Use brake fluid from a sealed container marked DOT 3 or DOT 4 only (specified for disc brakes). Other types may vaporize and cause brake failure. Do not intermix different brands or types as they may not be compatible. Do not intermix a silicone based (DOT 5) brake fluid as it can cause brake component damage leading to brake system failure.

7. Open the bleed valve about one-half turn and pump the brake bleeder lever.

NOTE
If air is entering the brake bleeder hose from around the bleed valve, apply several layers of Teflon tape to the bleed valve. This should make a good seal between the bleed valve and the brake bleeder hose.

8. As the fluid enters the system and exits into the brake bleeder, the level will drop in the reservoir. Maintain the level at about 3/8 inch from the top of the reservoir to prevent air from being drawn into the system.
9. Continue to pump the lever until the fluid emerging from the hose is completely free of bubbles. At this point, tighten the bleed valve.

NOTE
Do not allow the reservoir to empty during the bleeding operation or more air will enter the system. If this occurs, the entire procedure must be repeated.

13

10. When the brake fluid is free of bubbles, tighten the bleed valve, remove the brake bleeder tube and install the bleed valve dust cap.

11. Repeat Steps 2-10 for the other wheel's brake assembly.

12. If necessary, add fluid to correct the level in the reservoir. It should be to the upper level line.

13. Install the diaphragm plate, diaphragm and the reservoir top. Tighten the screws securely.

14. Test the feel of the brake lever. It should be firm and should offer the same resistance each time it's operated. If it feels spongy, it is likely that there is still air in the system and it must be bled again. When all air has been bled from the system and the fluid level is correct in the reservoir, double-check for leaks and tighten all fittings and connections.

WARNING
Before riding the ATV, make certain that the brakes are operating correctly by operating the lever or pedal several times.

15. Test ride the ATV slowly at first to make sure that the brakes are operating properly.

Without a Brake Bleeder

NOTE
Front wheel removal is not necessary but it does allow additional work room.

1. Remove the front wheels as described under *Front Wheel Removal/Installation* in Chapter Ten.

NOTE
It doesn't make any difference which wheel cylinder is bled first.

2. Remove the dust cap from the bleed valve on the wheel cylinder.

3. Connect a length of clear tubing to the bleed valve on the wheel cylinder (**Figure 61**).

CAUTION
Cover the front suspension arms with a heavy cloth or plastic tarp to protect it from the accidental spilling of brake fluid. Wash any brake fluid off of plastic, painted or plated surfaces immediately, as it will destroy the finish. Use soapy water and rinse completely.

4. Place the other end of the tube into a clean container. Fill the container with enough fresh brake fluid to keep the end submerged. The tube should be long enough so that a loop can be made higher than the bleed valve to prevent air from being drawn into the caliper during bleeding.

5. Clean the top of the master cylinder of all dirt and foreign matter.

6. Remove the screws securing the reservoir top (**Figure 60**). Remove the reservoir top, the diaphragm plate and the diaphragm.

7. Fill the reservoir almost to the top lip. Insert the diaphragm plate, the diaphragm and the top loosely. Leave the top in place during this procedure to prevent the entry of dirt.

WARNING
Use brake fluid from a sealed container marked DOT 3 or DOT 4 only (specified for disc brakes). Other types may vaporize and cause brake failure. Do not intermix different brands or types as they may not be compatible. Do not intermix a silicone based (DOT 5) brake fluid as it can cause brake component damage leading to brake system failure.

8. Slowly apply the brake lever times as follows:
   a. Pull the lever in and hold the lever in the applied position.
   b. Open the bleed valve about one-half turn. Allow the lever to travel to its limit.
   c. When this limit is reached, tighten the bleed screw.

9. As the fluid enters the system, the level will drop in the reservoir. Maintain the level at about 3/8 inch from the top of the reservoir to prevent air from being drawn into the system.

10. Continue to pump the lever or pedal and fill the reservoir until the fluid emerging from the hose is completely free of bubbles.

NOTE
Do not allow the reservoir to empty during the bleeding operation or more air will enter the system. If this occurs, the entire procedure must be repeated.

11. Hold the lever in, tighten the bleed valve, remove the bleed tube and install the bleed valve dust cap.

12. Repeat Steps 2-11 for the other wheel's brake assembly.

13. If necessary, add fluid to correct the level in the reservoir. It should be to the upper level line.

14. Install the diaphragm plate, diaphragm and reservoir top. Tighten the screws securely.

15. Test the feel of the brake lever. It should be firm and should offer the same resistance each time it's operated. If it feels spongy, it is likely that there is still air in the system and it must be bled again. When all air has been bled from the system and the fluid level is correct in the reservoir, double-check for leaks and tighten all fittings and connections.

WARNING
Before riding the ATV, make certain that the brakes are operating correctly by operating the lever or pedal several times.

16. Test ride the ATV slowly at first to make sure that the brakes are operating properly.

Table 1 DRUM BRAKE TORQUE SPECIFICATIONS

Item	N·m	ft.-lb.
Front brake		
Union bolt @ wheel cylinder and master cylinder	25-35	18-25
Rear brake drum cover		
Inner locknut	35-45	23-33
Outer locknut	120-140	87-101
Front wheel hub castellated nut	60-80	43-58
Right-hand footpeg and		
brake pedal mounting bolts	60-70	43-51

Table 2 DRUM BRAKE SPECIFICATIONS

Model	New	Service limit
Front brake drum I.D.	130 mm (5.12 in.)	131 mm (5.16 in.)
Rear brake drum I.D.	140 mm (5.5 in.)	141 mm (5.6 in.)
Brake shoe lining thickness		
Front and rear	4.0 mm (0.16 in.)	2.0 mm (0.08 in.)
Front master cylinder		
Cylinder bore I.D.	12.700-12.743 mm (0.5000-0.5017 in.)	12.755 mm (0.5022 in.)
Piston O.D.	12.657-12.684 mm (0.4983-0.4994 in.)	12.645 mm (0.4978 in.)
Front wheel cylinder		
Cylinder bore I.D.	14.907-14.333 mm (0.5626-0.5643 in.)	14.343 mm (0.5647 in.)
Piston O.D.	14.247-14.274 mm (0.5606-0.5620 in.)	14.237 mm (0.5605 in.)

13

CHAPTER FOURTEEN

DISC BRAKES

Both the front and rear wheels are equipped with disc brakes on the 3-wheeled models. These models are equipped with a cable-operated parking brake integrated into the rear brake assembly. The brake is activated by the hand lever on the left-hand side of the handlebar.

WARNING
*When working on the brake system, do **not** inhale brake dust. It may contain asbestos, which can cause lung injury and cancer.*

Lever and pedal free play must be maintained on both brakes to minimize brake drag and premature brake wear and maximize braking effectiveness. Refer to Chapter Three for complete adjustment procedures.

The parking brake cable must be inspected and replaced periodically as it will stretch with use until it can no longer be properly adjusted.

Refer to **Table 1** for tightening torques and **Table 2** for disc brake specifications. **Table 1** and **Table 2** are at the end of this chapter.

The front disc brake is actuated by hydraulic fluid and is controlled by a hand lever on the handlebar-mounted master-cylinder. The rear disc brake is actuated by hydraulic fluid and is controlled by a foot-operated brake pedal and master-cylinder. As the brake pads wear, the piston extends farther from the caliper bore and brake fluid fills the larger space which is left in the caliper. The brake fluid level drops in the reservoir and automatically adjusts for wear.

When working on hydraulic brake systems, it is necessary that the work area and all tools be absolutely clean. Any tiny particles of foreign matter and grit in the caliper assembly or the master cylinder can damage the components. Also, sharp tools must not be used inside the caliper or on the piston. If there is any doubt about your ability to correctly and safely carry out major service on the brake components, take the job to a dealer or brake specialist.

There is no recommended mileage interval for changing the friction pads in the disc brake. Pad wear depends greatly on riding habits and conditions. The pads should be checked for wear every 6 months (600 miles or 1,000 km) and replaced when worn to the bottom of the wear indicator groove. To maintain an even brake pressure on the disc, always replace both pads in the caliper at the same time.

CAUTION
Watch the pads more closely when the pads wear close to the wear limit dimension. If pad wear happens to be uneven for some reason, the backing plate may come in contact with the disc and cause damage.

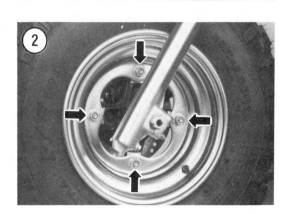

FRONT CALIPER
1. Rubber plug
2. Pin
3. Mounting bolt
4. Spring washer
5. Bleed valve
6. Cap
7. Pin boot
8. Caliper body
9. Pin bushing
10. Pin bolt
11. Wave washer
12. Mounting bracket
13. Piston seal
14. Dust seal
15. Piston
16. Pad spring
17. Shim
18. Outboard brake pad
19. Inboard brake pad
20. Lockwasher
21. Pad pin bolt

FRONT BRAKE PAD REPLACEMENT

Refer to **Figure 1** for this procedure.

1. Place the ATV on level ground and set the parking brake.

2. Place wood block(s) under the skid plate to support the ATV with the front wheel off the ground.

3. Remove the front wheel lug nuts (**Figure 2**).

4. Pull the front wheel off the threaded studs on the front hub and rest the front wheel against the left-hand fork leg.

5. Remove the bolt and clamp (**Figure 3**) securing the flexible brake hose to the lower fork bridge.

6. Remove the bolt and clamp (**Figure 4**) securing the flexible brake hose to the right-hand front fork slider.

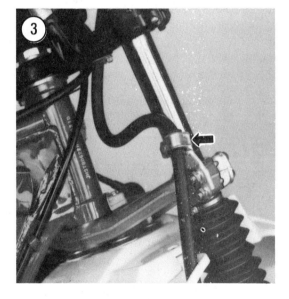

14

7. Remove the bolts (**Figure 5**) securing the caliper assembly to the right-hand fork slider.

8. Slide the caliper assembly off the brake disc.

9. Turn the brake caliper assembly around and re-attach it to the mounting tab on the fork slider (**Figure 6**).

10. Straighten the locking tabs on the lockwasher (**Figure 7**).

11. Loosen the pad pin bolts (A, **Figure 8**).

12. Remove the pad pin bolts and lockwasher (B, **Figure 8**).

13. Remove both brake pads and the pad spring.

14. Clean the pad recess and the end of the piston (**Figure 9**) with a soft brush. Do not use solvent, a wire brush or any hard tool which would damage the cylinder or the piston.

15. Carefully remove any rust or corrosion from the disc.

16. Lightly coat the end of the piston and the backs of the new pads *(not the friction material)* with disc brake lubricant.

> *NOTE*
> *When purchasing new pads, check with your dealer to make sure the friction compound of the new pad is compatible with the disc material. Honda recommends replacment brake pads that are marked "N18FF." Remove any roughness from the backs of the new pads with a fine cut file; wipe them clean with a clean soft cloth.*

17. When new pads are installed in the caliper, the master cylinder brake fluid level will rise as the caliper piston is repositioned. Perform the following:

   a. Clean the top of the master cylinder of all dirt and foreign matter.

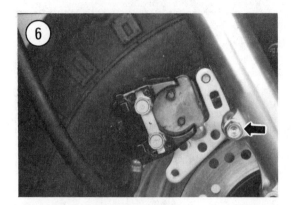

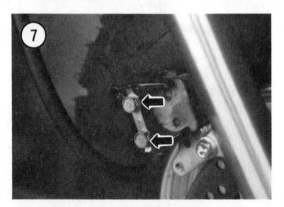

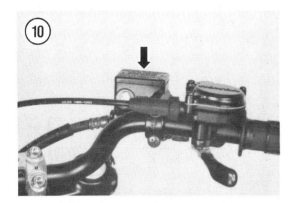

b. Remove the screws securing the cap (**Figure 10**) and remove the cap, diaphragm plate and the diaphragm from the master cylinder. Slowly push the caliper piston (**Figure 11**) into the caliper to make room for the new pads.

c. Constantly check the reservoir to make sure brake fluid does not overflow. Remove fluid, if necessary, before it overflows.

d. The caliper piston should move freely. If it doesn't, and there is evidence of it sticking in the cylinder, the caliper should be removed and serviced as described under *Caliper Rebuilding* in this chapter.

18. Install the brake pad spring (**Figure 12**) in the caliper.

19. Make sure the shim (**Figure 13**) is installed on the inboard brake pad.

20. Install the inboard pad (**Figure 14**) and then the outboard pad (A, **Figure 15**).

21. Push both brake pads into the caliper and install one of the pad pin bolts and new lockwasher (B, **Figure 15**).

22. Install the other pad pin bolt.

23. Tighten the pad pin bolts to the torque specification listed in **Table 1**. Bend one of the locking tabs up against a flat of each pad pin bolt head (**Figure 7**).

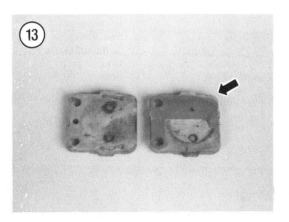

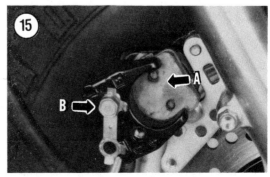

14

24. Remove the bolt securing the caliper to the fork slider and remove the caliper.

25. Carefully install the caliper assembly onto the disc. Be careful not to damage the leading edge of the pads during installation.

26. Install the front caliper assembly and mounting bolts onto the right-hand fork slider. Tighten the bolts to the torque specification listed in **Table 1**.

27. Install the flexible brake hose, bolt and clamp (**Figure 4**) securing the flexible brake hose to the right-hand front fork slider. Tighten the bolt securely.

28. Install the flexible brake hose, bolt and clamp (**Figure 3**) securing the flexible brake hose to the lower fork bridge. Tighten the bolt securely.

29. Position the front wheel onto the threaded studs on the front hub.

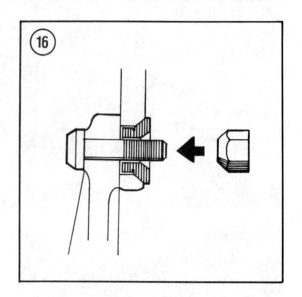

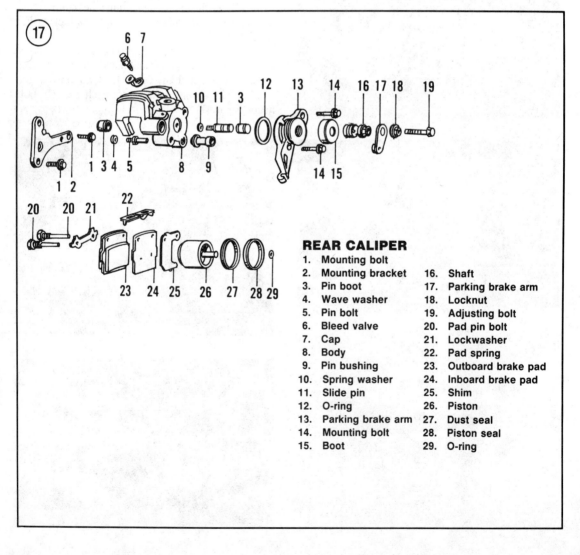

REAR CALIPER

1. Mounting bolt
2. Mounting bracket
3. Pin boot
4. Wave washer
5. Pin bolt
6. Bleed valve
7. Cap
8. Body
9. Pin bushing
10. Spring washer
11. Slide pin
12. O-ring
13. Parking brake arm
14. Mounting bolt
15. Boot
16. Shaft
17. Parking brake arm
18. Locknut
19. Adjusting bolt
20. Pad pin bolt
21. Lockwasher
22. Pad spring
23. Outboard brake pad
24. Inboard brake pad
25. Shim
26. Piston
27. Dust seal
28. Piston seal
29. O-ring

30. Install the front wheel lug nuts with the tapered end going on first (**Figure 16**). Tighten the lug nuts only finger-tight at this time.

31. Spin the front wheel and activate the brake lever as many times as it takes to refill the cylinder in the caliper and correctly locate the pads.

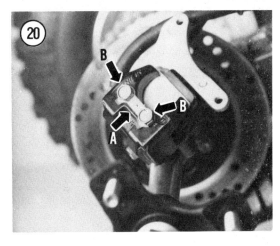

WARNING
Use brake fluid from a sealed container marked DOT 3 or DOT 4 only (specified for disc brakes). Other types may vaporize and cause brake failure. Do not intermix different brands or types as they may not be compatible. Do not intermix a silicone based (DOT 5) brake fluid as it can cause brake component damage leading to brake system failure.

32. Refill the master cylinder reservoir, if necessary, to maintain the correct fluid level. Install the diaphragm, diaphragm plate and top cap. Tighten the screws securely.

WARNING
Do not ride the ATV until you are sure the brake is operating correctly with full hydraulic advantage. If necessary, bleed the brake as described in this chapter.

33. Bed the pads in gradually for the first 10 days of riding by using only light pressure as much as possible. Immediate hard application will glaze the new friction pads and greatly reduce the effectiveness of the brake.

34. Remove the wood block(s) from under the skid plate and lower the front wheel to the ground.

35. Tighten the wheel lug nuts to the torque specification listed in **Table 1**.

REAR BRAKE PAD REPLACEMENT

Refer to **Figure 17** for this procedure.

1. Place the ATV on level ground. Block the front wheel so the ATV cannot move in either direction.

2. Place wood block(s) under the skid plate to support the ATV with the rear wheels off the ground.

3. Remove the seat/rear fender assembly as described in Chapter Fifteen.

4. Remove the bolt and clamp (**Figure 18**) securing the flexible brake hose to the swing arm.

NOTE
Figure 19 is shown with the parking brake lever removed for clarity. It is not necessary to remove the lever for this procedure.

5. Remove the bolts (**Figure 19**) securing the caliper assembly to the caliper mounting bracket.

6. Carefully slide the caliper assembly up and off the brake disc.

7. Straighten the locking tabs on the lockwasher (A, **Figure 20**) and remove the pad pin bolts (B, **Figure 20**).

8. Remove both brake pads, shim and the brake spring from the caliper.

9. Clean the pad recess and the end of the piston (**Figure 21**) with a soft brush. Do not use solvent, a wire brush or any hard tool which would damage the cylinder or piston.

10. Carefully remove any rust or corrosion from the disc.

11. Lightly coat the end of the piston and the backs of the new pads *(not the friction material)* with disc brake lubricant.

> *NOTE*
> *When purchasing new pads, check with your dealer to make sure the friction compound of the new pad is compatible with the disc material. Honda recommends replacment brake pads that are marked "N18FF." Remove any roughness from the backs of the new pads with a fine cut file; wipe them clean with a clean soft cloth.*

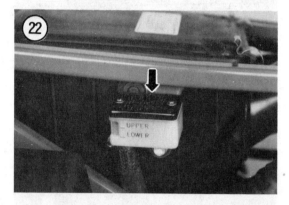

12. When new pads are installed in the caliper, the master cylinder brake fluid level will rise as the caliper piston is repositioned. Perform the following:

  a. Clean the top of the master cylinder of all dirt and foreign matter.
  b. Remove the screws securing the cap (**Figure 22**). Remove the cap, the diaphragm plate and the diaphragm from the master cylinder.
  c. Slowly push the caliper piston into the caliper.
  d. Constantly check the reservoir to make sure brake fluid does not overflow. Remove fluid, if necessary, before it overflows.
  e. The caliper piston should move freely. If it doesn't, and there is evidence of it sticking in the cylinder, the caliper should be removed and serviced as described under *Caliper Rebuilding* in this chapter.

13. Push the caliper piston (**Figure 21**) in all the way to allow room for the new pads.

14. Install the pad spring (**Figure 23**) into the caliper.

15. Install the shim (**Figure 24**) onto the inboard pad and install the inboard pad into the caliper (**Figure 25**).

16. Install the outboard pad (**Figure 26**) into the caliper.

17. Push both brake pads down into the caliper.

18. Install a new lockwasher and one of the pad pin bolts (**Figure 27**).

19. Install the other pad pin bolt (**Figure 28**).

20. Tighten the pad pin bolts to the torque specification listed in **Table 1**. Bend one of the locking tabs up against a flat of each pad pin bolt head.

21. Carefully install the caliper assembly onto the disc. Be careful not to damage the leading edge of the pads during installation.

22. Install the caliper mounting bolts and tighten to the torque specification listed in **Table 1**.

23. Install the clamp and bolt securing the flexible brake hose to the swing arm. Tighten the bolt securely.

24. Shift the transmission into NEUTRAL.

25. Spin the rear wheels and activate the brake pedal as many times as it takes to refill the cylinder in the caliper and correctly locate the pads.

WARNING
Use brake fluid from a sealed container marked DOT 3 or DOT 4 only (specified for disc brakes). Other types may vaporize and cause brake failure. Do not intermix different brands or types as they may not be compatible. Do not intermix a silicone based (DOT 5) brake fluid as it can cause brake component damage leading to brake system failure.

26. Refill the master cylinder reservoir, if necessary, to maintain the correct fluid level. Install the diaphragm plate, diaphragm and top cap. Tighten the screws securely.

WARNING
Do not ride the ATV until you are sure the brake is operating correctly with full hydraulic advantage. If necessary, bleed the brake as described in this chapter.

27. Bed the pads in gradually for the first 10 days of riding by using only light pressure as much as possible. Immediate hard application will glaze the new friction pads and greatly reduce the effectiveness of the brake.

FRONT MASTER CYLINDER

Removal/Installation

1. Place the ATV on level ground and set the parking brake.

CAUTION
Cover the fuel tank and front fender with a heavy cloth or plastic tarp to protect them from accidental brake fluid spills. Wash any brake fluid off painted or plated surfaces immediately, as it will destroy the finish. Use soapy water and rinse completely.

14

2. Remove the union bolt (**Figure 29**) securing the brake hose to the master cylinder and remove the brake hose. Tie the brake hose up and cover the end to prevent the entry of foreign matter.

3. Remove the clamping bolts (A, **Figure 30**) and clamp securing the master cylinder to the handlebar and remove the master cylinder.

4. Install by reversing these removal steps, noting the following.

5. Position the clamp with the UP mark (B, **Figure 30**) facing up.

6. Tighten the upper clamping bolt first and then the lower bolt. Tighten the bolts securely.

7. Install the brake hose onto the master cylinder. Be sure to place a sealing washer on each side of the fitting and install the union bolt. Tighten the union bolt to the torque specification listed in **Table 1**.

8. Bleed the brake as described in this chapter.

Disassembly

Refer to **Figure 31** and **Figure 32** for this procedure.

1. Remove the master cylinder as described in this chapter.

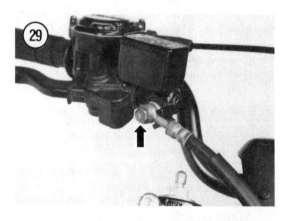

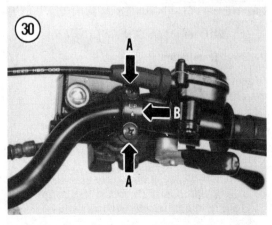

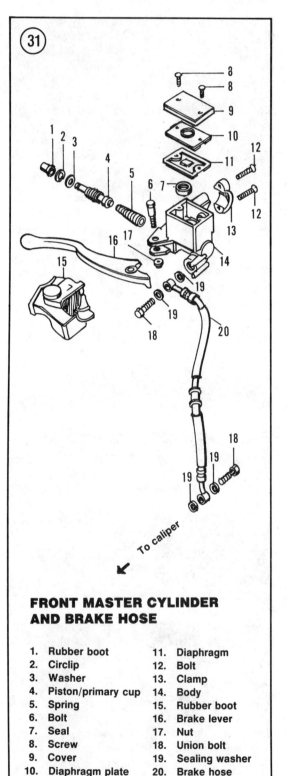

FRONT MASTER CYLINDER AND BRAKE HOSE

1.	Rubber boot	11. Diaphragm
2.	Circlip	12. Bolt
3.	Washer	13. Clamp
4.	Piston/primary cup	14. Body
5.	Spring	15. Rubber boot
6.	Bolt	16. Brake lever
7.	Seal	17. Nut
8.	Screw	18. Union bolt
9.	Cover	19. Sealing washer
10.	Diaphragm plate	20. Brake hose

2. Remove the bolt and nut securing the brake lever and remove the brake lever.

3. Remove the screws securing the cover. Remove the cover, the diaphragm plate and the diaphragm. Pour out the brake fluid and discard it. *Never* reuse brake fluid.

4. Remove the rubber boot from the area where the hand lever actuates the internal piston.

5. Using circlip pliers, remove the internal circlip and washer from the body (**Figure 33**).

6. Withdraw the piston/primary cup assembly from the body.

7. Withdraw the spring from the body.

Inspection

1. Clean all parts in denatured alcohol or fresh brake fluid. Inspect the cylinder bore and piston contact surfaces for signs of wear and damage. If either part is less than perfect, replace it.

2. Check the end of the piston for wear caused by the hand lever. Replace the piston assembly if either cup is worn or damaged.

3. Inspect the pivot hole in the hand lever. If worn or elongated, the lever must be replaced.

4. Make sure the passages in the bottom of the brake fluid reservoir are clear. Check the reservoir cap, diaphragm plate and diaphragm for damage and deterioration and replace as necessary.

5. Inspect the threads in the bore for the brake line.

6. Check the front brake hand lever pivot lug for cracks.

7. Measure the cylinder bore (**Figure 34**). Replace the master cylinder if the bore exceeds the service limit listed in **Table 2**.

8. Measure the outside diameter of the piston assembly with a micrometer as shown in **Figure 35**. Replace the piston assembly if it is less than the service limit listed in **Table 2**.

Assembly

1. Soak the new piston assembly in fresh brake fluid for at least 15 minutes to make the cups pliable. Coat the inside of the cylinder with fresh brake fluid before assembling parts.

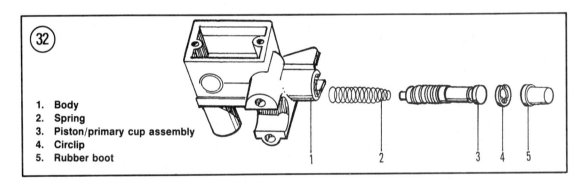

32

1. Body
2. Spring
3. Piston/primary cup assembly
4. Circlip
5. Rubber boot

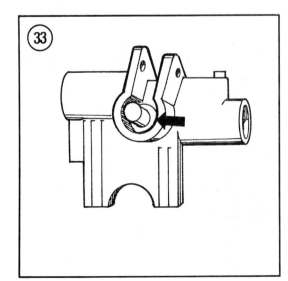

33

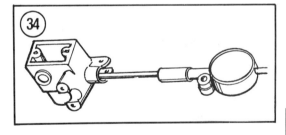

34

14

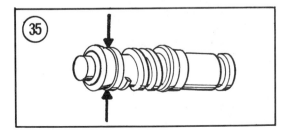

35

CAUTION
When installing the piston assembly, do not allow the cups to turn inside out as they will be damaged and allow brake fluid leakage within the cylinder bore.

2. Install the spring and the piston assembly into the cylinder together. The spring's tapered end faces toward the piston assembly (**Figure 32**).
3. Install the washer and the circlip. Slide in the rubber boot.
4. Install the diaphragm plate, the diaphragm and cover. Do not tighten the cover screws at this time as fluid will have to be added later.
5. Install the brake lever onto the master cylinder body.
6. Install the master cylinder as described in this chapter.

REAR MASTER CYLINDER

Removal/Installation

1. Place the ATV on level ground and set the parking brake.
2. Remove the seat and the rear fender assembly as described in Chapter Fifteen. It is not necessary to remove the rear fender, but it does allow additional work room.

CAUTION
Cover the surrounding frame with a heavy cloth or plastic tarp to protect it from accidental brake fluid spills. Wash any brake fluid off painted or plated surfaces immediately, as it will destroy the finish. Use soapy water and rinse completely.

3. Place a container under the reservoir hose.
4. Remove the hose clamp (A, **Figure 36**) securing the reservoir brake hose to the master cylinder.

NOTE
Drain the fluid from the hose and discard it—never reuse brake fluid. Contaminated brake fluid may cause brake failure.

5. Place a golf tee in the reservoir hose to prevent the entry of dirt and foreign matter.
6. Remove the union bolt (B, **Figure 36**) securing the brake hose to the top of the master cylinder and remove the brake hose. Don't lose the sealing washers on each side of the brake hose fitting.

NOTE
Drain the fluid from the hose and discard it—never reuse brake fluid.

Contaminated brake fluid may cause brake failure.

7. Remove the cotter pin and remove the pivot pin (C, **Figure 36**) from the rod eye at the bottom of the master cylinder.
8. Remove the bolts (D, **Figure 36**) securing master cylinder to the frame.
9. Remove the master cylinder from the frame.
10. To remove the reservoir, remove the flange bolt (**Figure 37**) securing it to the frame and remove the reservoir. Don't lose the metal collar in the mounting rubber grommet.
11. Install by reversing these removal steps, noting the following.
12. Inspect the brake actuating rod boot on the bottom of the master cylinder. Replace boot if it is cracked or deteriorated.
13. Install a new cotter pin on the pivot pin and bend the ends over completely. Never reuse an old cotter pin.
14. Install the brake hose onto the master cylinder. Be sure to place a sealing washer on each side of the fitting and install the union bolt. Tighten the union bolt to the torque specification listed in **Table 1**.
15. Bleed the brake as described in this chapter.

Disassembly

Refer to **Figure 38** and **Figure 39** for this procedure.

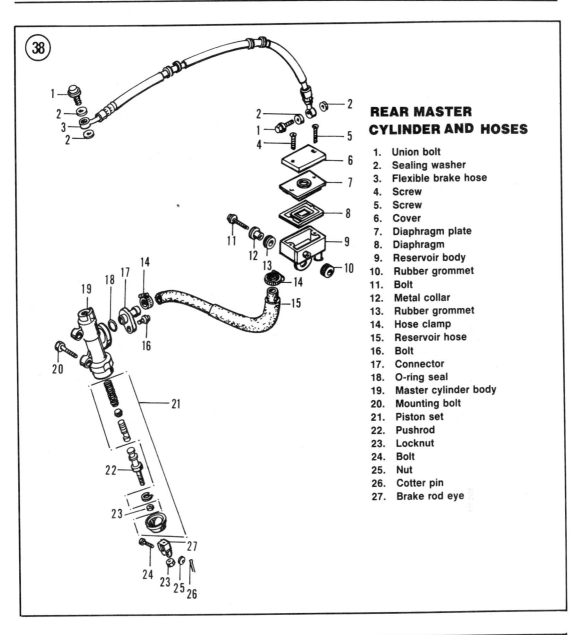

③⑧

REAR MASTER CYLINDER AND HOSES

1. Union bolt
2. Sealing washer
3. Flexible brake hose
4. Screw
5. Screw
6. Cover
7. Diaphragm plate
8. Diaphragm
9. Reservoir body
10. Rubber grommet
11. Bolt
12. Metal collar
13. Rubber grommet
14. Hose clamp
15. Reservoir hose
16. Bolt
17. Connector
18. O-ring seal
19. Master cylinder body
20. Mounting bolt
21. Piston set
22. Pushrod
23. Locknut
24. Bolt
25. Nut
26. Cotter pin
27. Brake rod eye

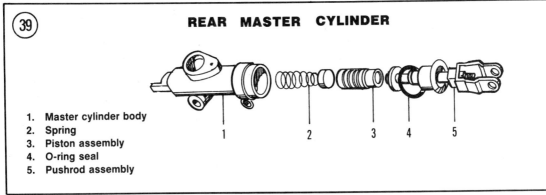

③⑨

REAR MASTER CYLINDER

1. Master cylinder body
2. Spring
3. Piston assembly
4. O-ring seal
5. Pushrod assembly

14

1. Remove the master cylinder as described in this chapter.

2. Slide the rubber boot down the master cylinder piston rod.

3. Using circlip pliers, remove the internal circlip from the body (**Figure 40**).

4. Remove the piston rod, the piston/cup assembly and the spring from the body.

> *NOTE*
> *If the piston assembly is difficult to remove from the body, apply a **small** amount of air pressure to the brake hose receptacle in the body. Hold your hand over the opening in the end of the body. Catch the piston assembly and spring as they are forced out by the air pressure.*

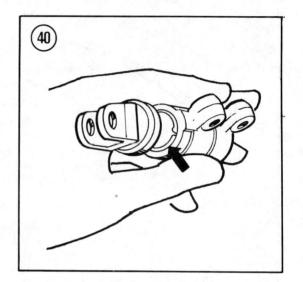

Inspection

1. Clean all parts in denatured alcohol or fresh brake fluid. Inspect the cylinder bore and piston contact surfaces for signs of wear and damage. If either part is less than perfect, replace it.

2. Check the end of the piston for wear caused by the pushrod. Replace the piston assembly if worn or damaged.

3. Make sure the passages in the bottom of the brake fluid reservoir are clear. Check the reservoir cap and diaphragm for damage and deterioration and replace as necessary.

4. Inspect the threads in the bore for the brake line.

5. Measure the cylinder bore (**Figure 41**). Replace the master cylinder if the bore exceeds the service limit listed in **Table 2**.

6. Measure the outside diameter of the piston assembly with a micrometer as shown in **Figure 42**. Replace the piston assembly if the diameter is less than the service limit listed in **Table 2**.

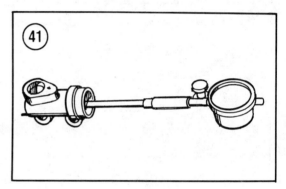

Assembly

1. Soak the new piston assembly in fresh brake fluid for at least 15 minutes to make the cups pliable. Coat the inside of the cylinder with fresh brake fluid before assembling the parts.

> *CAUTION*
> *When installing the piston assembly, do not allow the cups to turn inside out as they will be damaged and allow brake fluid leakage within the cylinder bore.*

2. Install the spring and the piston assembly into the cylinder together. The spring's tapered end faces toward the piston assembly (**Figure 39**).

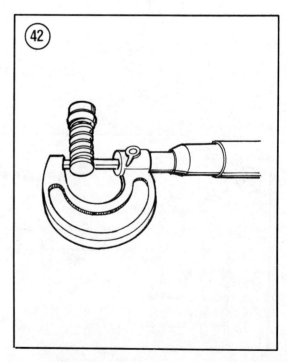

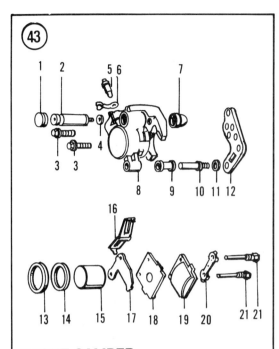

FRONT CALIPER

1.	Rubber plug	12.	Mounting bracket
2.	Pin	13.	Piston seal
3.	Mounting bolt	14.	Dust seal
4.	Spring washer	15.	Piston
5.	Bleed valve	16.	Pad spring
6.	Cap	17.	Shim
7.	Pin boot	18.	Outboard brake pad
8.	Caliper body	19.	Inboard brake pad
9.	Pin bushing	20.	Lockwasher
10.	Pin bolt	21.	Pad pin bolt
11.	Wave washer		

3. Install the piston rod assembly and install the circlip. Slide the rubber boot into position.

4. Install the master cylinder as described in this chapter.

FRONT CALIPER

Removal

Refer to **Figure 43** for this procedure.

> *CAUTION*
> *Do not spill any brake fluid on the painted portion of the steering knuckle or front wishbone. Wash any spilled brake fluid off immediately, as it will destroy the finish. Use soapy water and rinse completely.*

1. Place the ATV on level ground and set the parking brake.

2. Place wood block(s) under the skid plate to secure the vehicle with the front wheel off the ground.

3. Remove the front wheel lug nuts (**Figure 44**).

4. Pull the front wheel off the threaded studs on the front hub and rest the front wheel against the left-hand fork leg.

5. Place a container under the brake line at the caliper.

6. Remove the union bolt and sealing washers (A, **Figure 45**) securing the brake line to the caliper assembly.

7. Remove the brake line and let the brake fluid drain out into the container. Dispose of this brake fluid—*never* reuse brake fluid. To prevent the entry of moisture and dirt, cap the end of the brake line and tie the loose end up to the front fork.

8. Remove the rubber cap (B, **Figure 45**) and loosen the Allen bolt under the rubber cap.

9. Remove the bolts (C, **Figure 45**) securing the caliper assembly to the right-hand fork leg. Push on the caliper while loosening the bolts to push the piston back into the caliper.

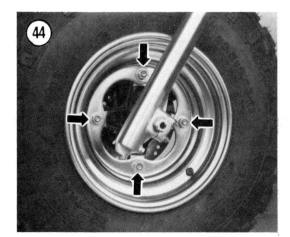

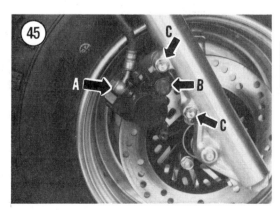

14

10. Slide the caliper assembly off the brake disc.

11. Remove the caliper assembly.

Installation

1. Carefully install the caliper assembly onto the disc. Be careful not to damage the leading edge of the pads during installation.

2. Tighten the caliper mounting bolts and the Allen bolt to the torque specification listed in **Table 1**.

3. Install the rubber cap over the Allen bolt.

4. Install the brake hose, with a sealing washer on each side of the fitting, onto the caliper. Install the union bolt and tighten to the torque specification listed in **Table 1**.

5. Position the front wheel onto the threaded studs on the front hub.

6. Install the front wheel lug nuts with the tapered end going on first (**Figure 46**). Tighten the lug nuts only finger-tight at this time.

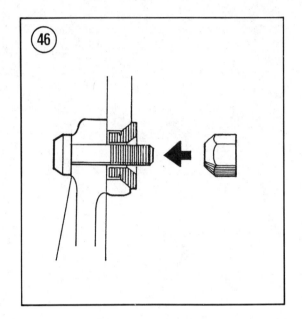

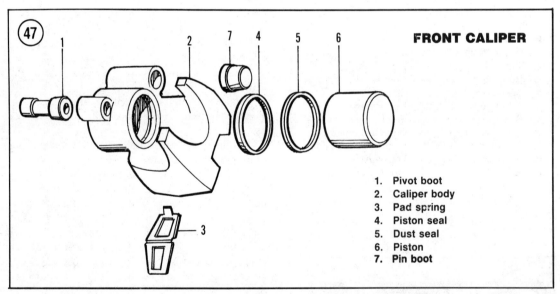

FRONT CALIPER

1. Pivot boot
2. Caliper body
3. Pad spring
4. Piston seal
5. Dust seal
6. Piston
7. Pin boot

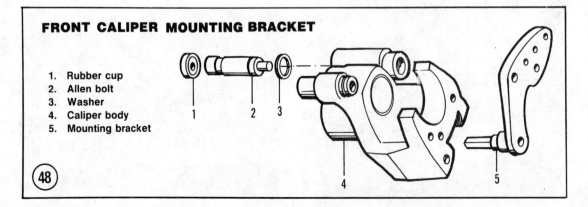

FRONT CALIPER MOUNTING BRACKET

1. Rubber cup
2. Allen bolt
3. Washer
4. Caliper body
5. Mounting bracket

7. Spin the front wheel and activate the brake lever as many times as it takes to refill the cylinder in the caliper and correctly locate the pads.

WARNING
Use brake fluid from a sealed container marked DOT 3 or DOT 4 only (specified for disc brakes). Other types may vaporize and cause brake failure. Do not intermix different brands or types as they may not be compatible. Do not intermix a silicone based (DOT 5) brake fluid as it can cause brake component damage leading to brake system failure.

8. Refill the master cylinder reservoir, if necessary, to maintain the correct fluid level. Install the diaphragm, diaphragm plate and top cap. Tighten the screws securely.

WARNING
Do not ride the ATV until you are sure the brake is operating correctly with full hydraulic advantage. If necessary, bleed the brake as described in this chapter.

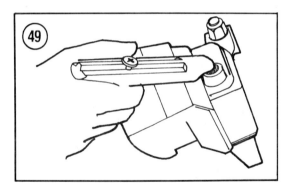

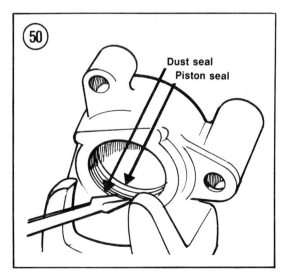

Dust seal
Piston seal

9. Bed the pads in gradually for the first 10 days of riding by using only light pressure as much as possible. Immediate hard application will glaze the new friction pads and greatly reduce the effectiveness of the brake.
10. Remove the wood block(s) from under the skid plate and lower the front wheel to the ground.
11. Tighten the wheel lug nuts to the torque specification listed in **Table 1**.

Caliper Rebuilding

Refer to **Figure 43** and **Figure 47** for this procedure.
1. Remove the caliper and brake pads as described in this chapter.
2. Remove the Allen bolt and washer securing the caliper body to the caliper mounting bracket (**Figure 48**).
3. Separate the caliper mounting bracket from the caliper body.
4. If not already removed, remove the brake pad spring.
5. Place a shop cloth or piece of soft wood in the area normally occupied by the brake pads.
6. Place the caliper assembly on the workbench with the piston facing down.

WARNING
*In the next step, the piston may shoot out of the caliper body like a bullet. Keep your fingers out of the way. Wear shop gloves and apply air pressure gradually. Do **not** use high pressure air or place the air hose nozzle directly against the hydraulic line fitting inlet in the caliper body. Hold the air nozzle away from the inlet, allowing some of the air to escape.*

7. Apply the air pressure in short spurts to the hydraulic line fitting inlet (**Figure 49**) and force the piston out. Use a service station air hose if you don't have a compressor.

CAUTION
In the following step, do not use a sharp tool to remove the dust and piston seals from the caliper cylinders. Do not damage the cylinder surface.

8. Use a piece of plastic or wood and carefully push the dust and piston seals in toward the caliper cylinder and out of their grooves (**Figure 50**). Remove the dust seal and piston seal from the cylinder and discard the seals.
9. Inspect the caliper body for damage. Replace the caliper body if necessary.

14

10. Inspect the cylinder and the piston for scratches, scoring or other damage. Light dirt may be removed with a cloth dipped in rubbing alcohol or clean brake fluid. If rust is present, replace the caliper assembly.

11. If serviceable, clean the caliper body with rubbing alcohol and rinse with clean brake fluid.

12. Measure the inside diameter of the caliper cylinder with an inside micrometer (**Figure 51**). If worn to the service limit dimension listed in **Table 2**, or greater, replace the caliper assembly.

13. Measure the outside diameter of the piston with a micrometer as shown in **Figure 52**. If worn the service limit dimension listed in **Table 2**, or less, replace the piston.

> *NOTE*
> *Never reuse the old dust seals and piston seals. Very minor damage or age deterioration can make the seals useless.*

14. Coat the new dust seals and piston seals with fresh DOT 3 or DOT 4 brake fluid.

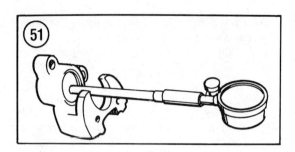

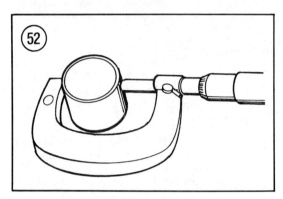

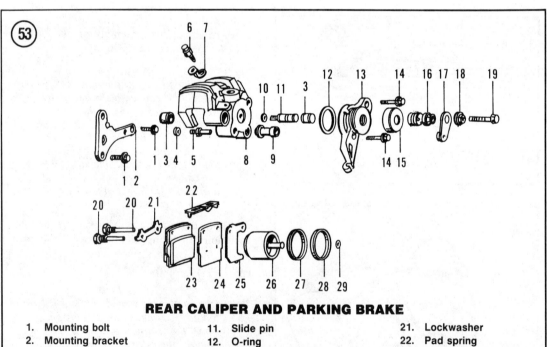

REAR CALIPER AND PARKING BRAKE

1. Mounting bolt	11. Slide pin	21. Lockwasher
2. Mounting bracket	12. O-ring	22. Pad spring
3. Pin boot	13. Parking brake base	23. Outboard brake pad
4. Wave washer	14. Mounting bolt	24. Inboard brake pad
5. Pin bolt	15. Boot	25. Shim
6. Bleed valve	16. Shaft	26. Piston
7. Cap	17. Parking brake arm	27. Dust seal
8. Body	18. Locknut	28. Piston seal
9. Pin bushing	19. Adjusting bolt	29. O-ring
10. Spring washer	20. Pad pin bolt	

15. Position the new dust seal and piston seal with the smaller diameter end *facing in* toward the caliper.

16. Carefully install the new dust seal and piston seal in the grooves in the caliper cylinder. Make sure the seals are properly seated in their respective grooves.

17. Coat the piston and caliper cylinder with fresh DOT 3 or DOT 4 brake fluid.

18. Position the piston with the flush side facing out toward the brake pads and install the piston into the caliper cylinder. Push the piston in until it bottoms out.

19. Apply silicone grease to the caliper rubber pivot boots. Install the boots onto the caliper body.

20. Install the caliper mounting bracket onto the caliper body. Push it on until it bottoms out. Install the Allen bolt and washer and tighten only finger-tight at this time.

21. Install the brake pads and the caliper as described in this chapter.

REAR CALIPER

Removal/Installation

Refer to **Figure 53** for this procedure.

> *CAUTION*
> *Do not spill any brake fluid on the painted portion of the swing arm or axle bearing housing. Wash any spilled brake fluid immediately, as it will destroy the finish. Use soapy water and rinse completely.*

1. Place the ATV on level ground. Block the front wheel so the ATV will not roll in either direction.

2. Place wood block(s) under the skid plate to support the ATV with the rear wheels off the ground.

3. Remove the seat/rear fender assembly as described in Chapter Fifteen.

4. Loosen the parking brake adjusting bolt locknut (A, **Figure 54**) and remove the adjusting bolt and locknut (B, **Figure 54**).

5. Remove the arm from the caliper assembly. Withdraw the parking brake cable from the receptacle (A, **Figure 55**) on the parking brake housing.

6. Place a container under the brake line at the caliper. Remove the union bolt and sealing washers (B, **Figure 55**) securing the brake line to the caliper assembly.

7. Remove the brake line and let the brake fluid drain out into the container. Dispose of this brake fluid—*never* reuse brake fluid.

8. To prevent the entry of moisture and dirt, cap the end of the brake line and tie the loose end up to the frame.

9. Loosen the Allen bolt (C, **Figure 55**) securing the caliper assembly to the mounting bracket.

10. Remove the bolts securing the caliper mounting bracket to the swing arm (D, **Figure 55**).

11. Remove the caliper assembly.

Installation

1. Carefully install the caliper assembly onto the disc. Be careful not to damage the leading edge of the pads during installation.

2. Tighten the caliper mounting bolts to the torque specification listed in **Table 1**.

3. Install the brake hose, with a sealing washer on each side of the fitting, onto the caliper. Install the union bolt and tighten to the torque specification listed in **Table 1**.

4. Tighten the Allen bolt to the torque specification listed in **Table 1**.

5. Insert the parking brake cable into the receptacle in the parking brake housing.

14

6. Align the index mark on the parking brake arm with the index mark on the parking brake shaft (**Figure 56**). Install the parking brake arm onto the parking brake shaft in the caliper assembly.

7. Install the adjusting bolt and locknut. Temporarily tighten the locknut.

8. Shift the transmission into NEUTRAL.

9. Spin the rear wheels and activate the brake pedal as many times as it takes to refill the cylinder in the caliper and correctly locate the pads.

> *WARNING*
> *Use brake fluid from a sealed container marked DOT 3 or DOT 4 only (specified for disc brakes). Other types may vaporize and cause brake failure. Do not intermix different brands or types as they may not be compatible. Do not intermix a silicone based (DOT 5) brake fluid as it can cause brake component damage leading to brake system failure.*

10. Refill the master cylinder reservoir to maintain the correct fluid level. Install the diaphragm plate, diaphragm and top cap. Tighten the screws securely.

11. Adjust the parking brake as described under *Parking Brake Adjustment (Disc Brake Models)* in Chapter Three.

12. Bleed the brake as described in this chapter.

> *WARNING*
> *Do not ride the ATV until you are sure that the brake is operating properly.*

Caliper Rebuilding

Refer to **Figure 53** and **Figure 57** for this procedure.

1. Remove the caliper and brake pads as described in this chapter.

2. If not already removed, remove the brake pad spring.

3. Remove the Allen bolt and washer securing the caliper mounting bracket and remove the bracket (**Figure 58**).

4. Remove the rubber pivot boots from the caliper assembly.

5. Place a shop cloth or piece of soft wood in the area normally occupied by the brake pads.

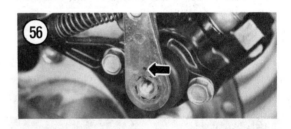

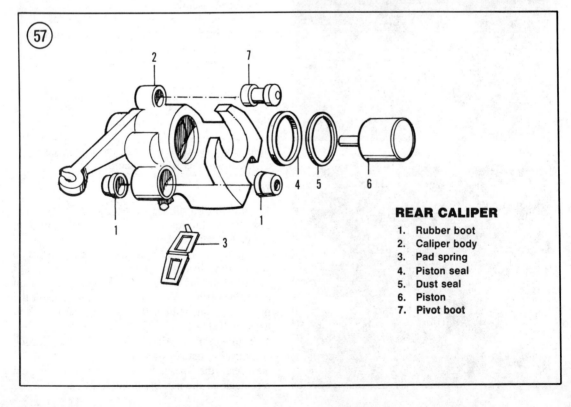

REAR CALIPER

1. Rubber boot
2. Caliper body
3. Pad spring
4. Piston seal
5. Dust seal
6. Piston
7. Pivot boot

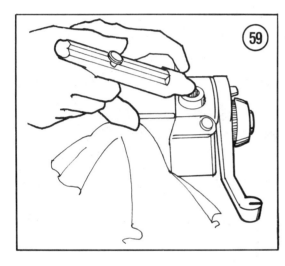

REAR CALIPER MOUNTING BRACKET

1. Allen bolt
2. Washer   3. Caliper mounting bracket

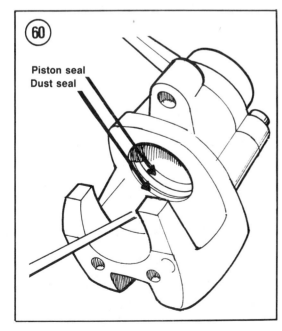

Piston seal
Dust seal

6. Place the caliper assembly on the workbench with the piston facing down.

WARNING
*In the next step, the piston may shoot out of the caliper body like a bullet. Keep your fingers out of the way. Wear shop gloves and apply air pressure gradually. Do **not** use high pressure air or place the air hose nozzle directly against the hydraulic line fitting inlet in the caliper body. Hold the air nozzle away from the inlet, allowing some of the air to escape.*

7. Apply the air pressure in short spurts to the hydraulic line fitting inlet and force the piston out (**Figure 59**). Use a service station air hose if you don't have a compressor.

CAUTION
In the following step, do not use a sharp tool to remove the dust seal and piston seal from the caliper cylinder. Do not damage the cylinder surface.

8. Use a piece of plastic or wood and carefully push the dust seal and piston seal in toward the caliper cylinder and out of their grooves (**Figure 60**). Remove the dust seal and piston seal from the cylinder and discard all seals.

9. Inspect the caliper body for damage. Replace the caliper body if necessary.

10. Inspect the cylinder and the piston for scratches, scoring or other damage. Light dirt can be removed with a cloth dipped in rubbing alcohol or fresh brake fluid. If rust is present, replace the caliper assembly.

11. If serviceable, clean the caliper body with rubbing alcohol and rinse with clean brake fluid.

12. Measure the inside diameter of the caliper cylinder with an inside micrometer as shown in **Figure 61**. If worn to the service limit dimension listed in **Table 2**, or greater, replace the caliper assembly.

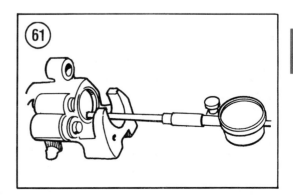

14

13. Measure the outside diameter of the piston with a micrometer as shown in **Figure 62**. If worn to the service limit dimension listed in **Table 2**, or less, replace the piston.

NOTE
Never reuse the old dust seals and piston seals. Very minor damage or age deterioration can make the seals useless.

14. Coat the new dust seals and piston seals with fresh DOT 3 or DOT 4 brake fluid.
15. Position the new dust seal and piston seal with the smaller diameter end *facing in* toward the caliper.
16. Carefully install the new dust seal and piston seal in the grooves in the caliper cylinder. Make sure the seals are properly seated in their respective grooves.
17. Coat the piston and caliper cylinder with fresh DOT 3 or DOT 4 brake fluid.
18. Position the piston with the flush side facing out toward the brake pads and install the piston into the caliper cylinder. Push the piston in until it bottoms out.
19. Apply silicone grease to the caliper rubber pivot boots. Install the boots onto the caliper body.
20. Install the caliper mounting bracket onto the caliper body. Push it on until it bottoms out. Install the Allen bolt and washer and tighten only finger-tight at this time.
21. Install the brake pads and the caliper as described in this chapter.

PARKING BRAKE

Removal/Disassembly

Refer to **Figure 53** for this procedure.
1. Place the ATV on level ground. Block the front wheel so the ATV will not roll in either direction.
2. Place wood block(s) under the skid plate to support the ATV with the rear wheels off the ground.
3. Remove the seat/rear fender assembly as described in Chapter Fifteen.
4. Loosen the parking brake adjusting bolt locknut (A, **Figure 54**) and remove the adjusting bolt (B, **Figure 54**) and locknut.
5. Remove the arm from parking brake shaft in the caliper assembly. Withdraw the parking brake cable (A, **Figure 63**) from the receptacle on the parking brake housing.
6. Remove the bolts (B, **Figure 63**) securing the parking brake base to the caliper body. Remove the parking brake base.

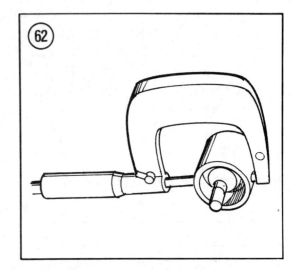

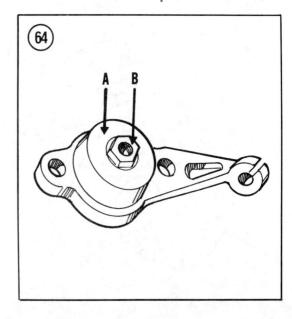

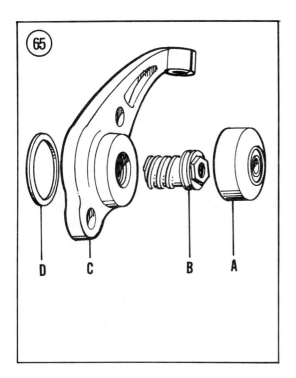

D C B A

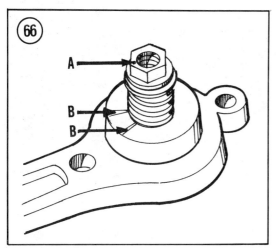

A
B
B

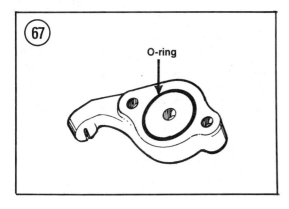

O-ring

7. Remove the rubber boot (A, **Figure 64**) from the parking brake base.

NOTE
*The parking brake shaft has **left-hand** threads.*

8. Unscrew the brake shaft (B, **Figure 64**) from the parking brake base.

9. Inspect the boot (A, **Figure 65**) for wear or deterioration; replace if necessary.

10. Inspect the shaft (B, **Figure 65**) and base (C, **Figure 65**) threads for wear or damage. If either is damaged, replace the base and the shaft as a pair.

11. Inspect the O-ring (D, **Figure 65**) for wear or deterioration; replace if necessary.

Installation

1. Apply a light coat of multipurpose grease to the parking brake shaft.

NOTE
*The parking brake shaft has **left-hand** threads.*

2. Position the parking brake shaft so the index mark (A, **Figure 66**) is placed in between the 2 index marks (B, **Figure 66**) on the parking brake base. Turn the shaft *counterclockwise* and screw the shaft into the base.

3. Screw the shaft in until it stops, then back it out 1/8 turn. Make sure the index mark on the shaft is positioned within the 2 index marks on the base. If alignment is incorrect, unscrew the shaft and repeat Step 2. This alignment is necessary for proper parking brake operation.

4. Install the rubber boot onto the shaft and base. Make sure the boot is properly seated in the groove in both the shaft and the base.

5. Install a new O-ring seal (**Figure 67**) in the groove in the base.

6. Install the parking brake base onto the caliper assembly.

7. Install the bolts and tighten to the torque specification listed in **Table 1**.

8. Insert the parking brake cable into the receptacle in the parking brake housing.

9. Align the index mark on the parking brake arm with the index mark on the parking brake shaft (**Figure 56**). Install the parking brake arm onto the parking brake shaft in the caliper assembly.

10. Install the adjusting bolt and locknut. Temporarily tighten the locknut.

11. Since air may have entered the brake system when the parking brake base was removed, bleed the rear brake system as described in this chapter.

14

12. Adjust the parking brake as described under *Parking Brake Adjustment (Disc Brake Models)* in Chapter Three.

13. Install the seat/rear fender assembly as described in Chapter Fifteen.

14. Remove the wood block(s) from under the skid plate.

FRONT BRAKE DISC

Removal/Installation

1. Remove the front wheel and front hub as described under *Front Wheel Removal* in Chapter Nine.

2. Remove the nuts (**Figure 68**) securing the brake disc to the front hub and remove the brake disc.

3. Position the brake disc with the DRIVE mark facing toward the outside and install the nuts. Tighten the nuts to the torque specification listed in **Table 1**.

4. Install the front wheel and front hub as described under *Front Wheel Installation* in Chapter Nine.

Brake Disc Inspection

It is not necessary to remove the disc from the wheel to inspect it. Small marks on the disc are not important, but deep radial scratches, deep enough to snag a fingernail, reduce braking effectiveness and increase brake pad wear. If these grooves are found, the disc should be replaced.

1. Measure the thickness of the disc at several locations around the disc with vernier calipers or a micrometer (**Figure 69**). The disc must be replaced if the thickness, in any area, is worn to the service limit (or less) listed in **Table 2**.

2. Clean the disc of any rust or corrosion and wipe clean with lacquer thinner. Never use an oil-based solvent that may leave an oil residue on the disc.

3. To inspect brake disc warpage or runout, perform the following:

    a. Place wood block(s) under the skid plate to support the ATV with the front wheel off the ground.

    b. Mount a dial indicator onto the front fork.

    c. Place the probe of the dial indicator against the brake disc. Position the probe toward the outer edge of the disc to avoid the drilled holes in the disc.

    d. Slowly rotate the front wheel and note the reading of the dial indicator. If the runout is to the service limit dimension listed in **Table 2** or greater, replace the brake disc as described in this chapter.

    e. Remove the dial indicator from the front fork.

REAR BRAKE DISC

Removal

1. Place the ATV on level ground and set the parking brake. Block the front wheel so the ATV will not roll in either direction.

2. Place wood block(s) under the frame to support the ATV with the rear wheels off the ground.

3. Remove the seat/rear fender assembly as described in Chapter Fifteen.

4. Place a wood block under the swing arm to support it in the up position.

5. Remove the left-hand rear wheel as described under *Rear Wheel Removal/Installation* in Chapter Eleven.

6. Remove the left-hand rear hub as described under *Rear Hub Removal/Installation* in Chapter Eleven.

7. Loosen the bolts securing the brake disc to the mounting flange on the axle.

8. Release the parking brake and remove the rear caliper assembly as described in this chapter. Tie the caliper assembly up to the frame with a wire or Bunjee cord.

9. Remove the bolts (**Figure 70**) securing the brake disc to the mounting flange on the axle.

10. Slide the brake disc and hub assembly off the right-hand side of the rear axle.

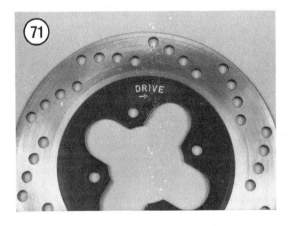

Installation

1. Position the rear brake disc with the DRIVE mark (**Figure 71**) facing toward the right-hand side and slide the rear brake disc onto the rear axle. Install the bolts securing the brake disc and tighten only finger-tight at this time.

2. Install the disc brake caliper assembly as described in this chapter.

3. Apply the parking brake.

4. Tighten the bolts to the specification listed in **Table 1**.

5. Install the left-hand wheel hub as described under *Rear Hub Removal/Installation* in Chapter Eleven.

6. Install the left-hand wheel as described under *Rear Wheel Removal/Installation* in Chapter Eleven.

7. Install the seat/rear fender as described in Chapter Fifteen.

Brake Disc Inspection

It is not necessary to remove the disc from the wheel to inspect it. Small marks on the disc are not important, but deep radial scratches, deep enough to snag a fingernail, reduce braking effectiveness and increase brake pad wear. If these grooves are found, the disc should be replaced.

1. Measure the thickness of the disc at several locations around the disc with vernier calipers or micrometer (**Figure 72**). The disc must be replaced if the thickness, in any area, is worn to the service limit (or less) listed in **Table 2**.

2. Clean the disc of any rust or corrosion and wipe clean with lacquer thinner. Never use a petroleum-based solvent that may leave residue on the disc.

3. To inspect brake disc warpage or runout, perform the following:

   a. Place wood block(s) under the skid plate to support the ATV with the rear wheels off the ground.

   b. Mount a dial indicator onto the swing arm.

   c. Place the probe of the dial indicator against the brake disc. Position the probe toward the outer edge of the disc to avoid the drilled holes in the disc.

   d. Slowly rotate the rear wheels and note the reading of the dial indicator. If the runout is to the service limit dimension listed in **Table 2** or greater, replace the brake disc as described in this chapter.

   e. Remove the dial indicator from the swing arm.

14

FRONT BRAKE HOSE

There is no factory-recommended replacement interval, but it is a good idea to replace the flexible brake hoses every four years or when they show signs of cracking or damage.

Removal/Installation

Refer to **Figure 73** for this procedure.

> *CAUTION*
>
> *Cover the front wheel, fender and fuel tank with a heavy cloth or plastic tarp to protect it from accidental spilling of brake fluid. Wash any brake fluid off of plastic, painted or plated surfaces immediately, as it will destroy the finish. Use soapy water and rinse completely.*

1. Place the ATV on level ground and set the parking brake.
2. Remove the headlight case as described under *Headlight Replacement and Headlight Case Removal/Installation* in Chapter Eight.
3. Place a container under the brake line at the caliper.
4. Remove the union bolt and sealing washers (**Figure 74**) securing the lower flexible brake hose to the caliper assembly.
5. Remove the brake hose and let the brake fluid drain out into the container. Dispose of this brake fluid—*never* reuse brake fluid.
6. To prevent the entry of moisture and dirt, cap the caliper assembly where the brake line attaches.

> *WARNING*
> *Dispose of this brake fluid—never reuse brake fluid. Contaminated brake fluid can cause brake failure.*

7. Remove the bolt and clamp (**Figure 75**) securing the flexible brake hose to the right-hand fork slider.
8. Remove the bolt and clamp (**Figure 76**) securing the flexible brake hose to the lower fork bridge.
9. Remove the union bolt and sealing washers (**Figure 77**) securing the flexible brake hose to the master cylinder and remove the hose.
10. Route the new hose through the upper and lower fork bridges as shown in **Figure 78**.
11. Install a new flexible brake hose (**Figure 79**), sealing washers and union bolts in the reverse order of removal.

12. Be sure to install a new sealing washer on each side of the brake hose fittings at the master cylinder and the front brake caliper.
13. Tighten all union bolts and fittings on the metal brake lines to the torque specification listed in **Table 1**.

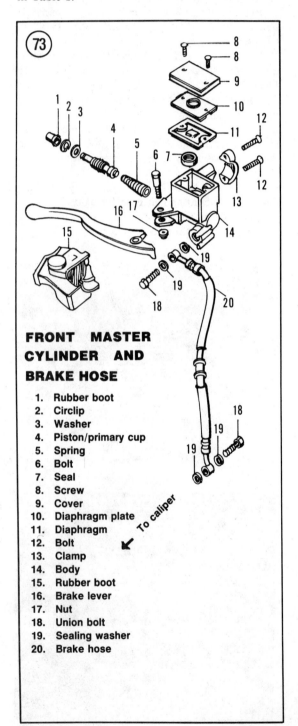

FRONT MASTER CYLINDER AND BRAKE HOSE

1. Rubber boot
2. Circlip
3. Washer
4. Piston/primary cup
5. Spring
6. Bolt
7. Seal
8. Screw
9. Cover
10. Diaphragm plate
11. Diaphragm
12. Bolt
13. Clamp
14. Body
15. Rubber boot
16. Brake lever
17. Nut
18. Union bolt
19. Sealing washer
20. Brake hose

WARNING
Use brake fluid from a sealed container marked DOT 3 or DOT 4 only (specified for disc brakes). Other types may vaporize and cause brake failure. Do not intermix different brands or types as they may not be compatible. Do not intermix a silicone based (DOT 5) brake fluid as it can cause brake component damage leading to brake system failure.

14. Refill the master cylinder with fresh brake fluid marked DOT 3 or DOT 4 only. Bleed the brake as described in this chapter.

WARNING
Do not ride the ATV until you are sure that the brake is operating properly.

REAR BRAKE HOSE REPLACEMENT

There is no factory-recommended replacement interval but it is a good idea to replace all brake hoses every four years or when they show signs of cracking or damage.

14

Refer to **Figure 80** for this procedure.

CAUTION
*Cover the swing arm and axle bearing
housing with a heavy cloth or plastic
tarp to protect it from accidental
spilling of brake fluid. Wash any brake
fluid off of plastic, painted or plated
surfaces immediately, as it will destroy
the finish. Use soapy water and rinse
completely.*

1. Place the ATV on level ground and set the
parking brake.

2. Remove the seat/rear fender assembly as
described in Chapter Fifteen.
3. Place a wood block under the swing arm to
support it in the up position.
4. Remove the right-hand rear wheel as described
in Chapter Eleven.
5. Place a container under the brake line at the
caliper. Remove the union bolt and sealing
washers (**Figure 81**) securing the flexible brake line
to the caliper assembly.
6. Remove the flexible brake line and let the brake
fluid drain out into the container.

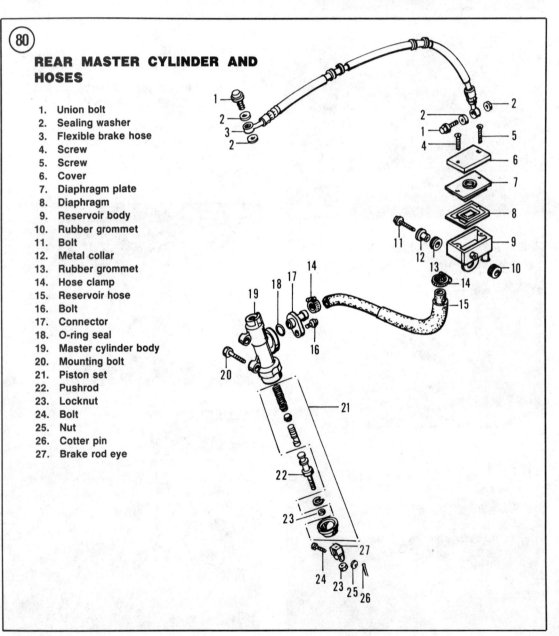

REAR MASTER CYLINDER AND HOSES

1. Union bolt
2. Sealing washer
3. Flexible brake hose
4. Screw
5. Screw
6. Cover
7. Diaphragm plate
8. Diaphragm
9. Reservoir body
10. Rubber grommet
11. Bolt
12. Metal collar
13. Rubber grommet
14. Hose clamp
15. Reservoir hose
16. Bolt
17. Connector
18. O-ring seal
19. Master cylinder body
20. Mounting bolt
21. Piston set
22. Pushrod
23. Locknut
24. Bolt
25. Nut
26. Cotter pin
27. Brake rod eye

7. Pump the rear brake pedal until the brake fluid is expelled into the container. Dispose of this brake fluid—*never* reuse brake fluid.

8. To prevent the entry of moisture and dirt, cap the brake hose opening in the caliper.

> *WARNING*
> *Dispose of this brake fluid—never reuse brake fluid. Contaminated brake fluid can cause brake failure.*

9. Remove the union bolt and sealing washers securing the flexible brake hose (**Figure 82**) to the master cylinder and remove the hose.

10. Remove the bolts and clamps (**Figure 83**) securing the flexible brake hose to the swing arm.

11 Remove the hose from the frame.

12. Install a new flexible brake hose, sealing washers and union bolts in the reverse order of removal. Be sure to install new sealing washers on each side of the union bolts. Refer to **Figure 80**.

13. Tighten the union bolts to the torque specification listed in **Table 1**.

> *WARNING*
> *Use brake fluid from a sealed container marked DOT 3 or DOT 4 only (specified for disc brakes). Other types may vaporize and cause brake failure. Do not intermix different brands or types as they may not be compatible. Do not intermix a silicone based (DOT 5) brake fluid as it can cause brake component damage leading to brake system failure.*

14. Refill the master cylinder with fresh brake fluid marked DOT 3 or DOT 4 only. Bleed the brake as described in this chapter.

> *WARNING*
> *Do not ride the ATV until you are sure that the brake is operating properly.*

15. Install the right-hand rear wheels as described under *Rear Wheel Removal/Installation* in Chapter Eleven.

16. Install the seat/rear fender assembly as described in Chapter Fifteen.

BLEEDING THE SYSTEM

This procedure is not necessary unless the brakes feel spongy, there has been a leak in the system, a component has been replaced or the brake fluid has been replaced.

This procedure pertains to both the front and rear brake systems.

Brake Bleeder Process

This procedure uses a brake bleeder that is available from motorcycle or automotive supply stores or from mail order outlets.

1. Remove the dust cap from the bleed valve on the caliper assembly.

14

2. Connect the bleed hose of the brake bleeder to the bleed valve on the caliper assembly. Refer to **Figure 84** for front brake or **Figure 85** for the rear brake.

> *CAUTION*
> *Cover the swing arm area with a heavy cloth or plastic tarp to protect it from the accidental spilling of brake fluid. Wash any brake fluid off of plastic, painted or plated surfaces immediately, as it will destroy the finish. Use soapy water and rinse completely.*

3. Clean the top of the master cylinder of all dirt and foreign matter.

4. Remove the screws securing the reservoir top and remove the reservoir top, diaphragm plate and the diaphragm. Refer to **Figure 86** for front brake or **Figure 87** for the rear brake.

5. Fill the reservoir almost to the top lip. Insert the diaphragm plate, diaphragm and the top loosely. Leave the top in place during this procedure to prevent the entry of dirt.

> *WARNING*
> *Use brake fluid from a sealed container marked DOT 3 or DOT 4 only (specified for disc brakes). Other types may vaporize and cause brake failure. Do not intermix different brands or types as they may not be compatible. Do not intermix a silicone based (DOT 5) brake fluid as it can cause brake component damage leading to brake system failure.*

6. Open the bleed valve about one-half turn and pump the brake bleeder lever.

> *NOTE*
> *If air is entering the brake bleeder hose from around the bleed valve, apply several layers of Teflon tape to the bleed valve. This should make a good seal between the bleed valve and the brake bleeder hose.*

7. As the fluid enters the system and exits into the brake bleeder the level will drop in the reservoir. Maintain the level at about 3/8 inch from the top of the reservoir to prevent air from being drawn into the system.

8. Continue to pump the lever on the brake bleeder until the fluid emerging from the hose is completely free of bubbles. At this point, tighten the bleed valve.

> *NOTE*
> *Do not allow the reservoir to empty during the bleeding operation or more*

air will enter the system. If this occurs, the entire procedure must be repeated.

9. When the brake fluid is free of bubbles, tighten the bleed valve, remove the brake bleeder tube and install the bleed valve dust cap.

10. If necessary, add fluid to correct the level in the reservoir. It should be to the upper level line.

11. Install the diaphragm plate, diaphragm and the reservoir top. Tighten the screws securely.

12. Test the feel of the brake lever or pedal. It should be firm and should offer the same resistance

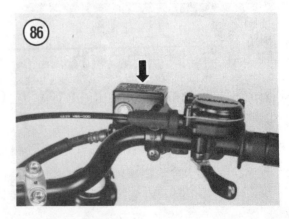

each time it's operated. If it feels spongy, it is likely that there is still air in the system and it must be bled again. When all air has been bled from the system and the fluid level is correct in the reservoir, double-check for leaks and tighten all fittings and connections.

> *WARNING*
> *Before riding the ATV, make certain that the brakes are operating correctly by operating the lever or pedal several times.*

13. Test ride the ATV slowly at first to make sure that the brakes are operating properly.

Without a Brake Bleeder

1. Remove the dust cap from the bleed valve on the caliper assembly.

2. Connect a length of clear tubing to the bleed valve on the caliper assembly. Refer to **Figure 88** for front brake or **Figure 89** for the rear brake.

> *CAUTION*
> *Cover the swing arm area with a heavy cloth or plastic tarp to protect it from the accidental spilling of brake fluid. Wash any brake fluid off of plastic, painted or plated surfaces immediately, as it will destroy the finish. Use soapy water and rinse completely.*

3. Place the other end of the tube into a clean container. Fill the container with enough fresh brake fluid to keep the end submerged. The tube should be long enough so that a loop can be made higher than the bleed valve to prevent air from being drawn into the caliper during bleeding.

4. Clean the top of the master cylinder of all dirt and foreign matter.

5. Remove the screws securing the reservoir top and remove the reservoir top, diaphragm plate and the diaphragm. Refer to **Figure 86** for front brakes or **Figure 87** for the rear brake.

6. Fill the reservoir almost to the top lip. Insert the diaphragm plate, diaphragm and the top loosely. Leave the top in place during this procedure to prevent the entry of dirt.

> *WARNING*
> *Use brake fluid from a sealed container marked DOT 3 or DOT 4 only (specified for disc brakes). Other types may vaporize and cause brake failure. Do not intermix different brands or types as they may not be compatible. Do not intermix a silicone based (DOT 5) brake fluid as it can cause brake component damage leading to brake system failure.*

7. Slowly apply the brake lever or pedal several times as follows:
   a. Pull the lever in or push the pedal down. Hold the lever or pedal in the applied position.
   b. Open the bleed valve about one-half turn. Allow the lever or pedal to travel to its limit.
   c. When this limit is reached, tighten the bleed screw.

8. As the fluid enters the system, the level will drop in the reservoir. Maintain the level at about 3/8 inch from the top of the reservoir to prevent air from being drawn into the system.

14

9. Continue to pump the lever or pedal and fill the reservoir until the fluid emerging from the hose is completely free of bubbles.

NOTE
Do not allow the reservoir to empty during the bleeding operation or more air will enter the system. If this occurs, the entire procedure must be repeated.

10. Hold the lever or pedal down, tighten the bleed valve, remove the bleed tube and install the bleed valve dust cap.
11. On drum brake models, repeat Steps 2-10 for the other wheel's brake assembly.
12. If necessary, add fluid to correct the level in the reservoir. It should be to the upper level line.
13. Install the diaphragm plate, diaphragm and reservoir top. Tighten the screws securely.
14. Test the feel of the brake lever or pedal. It should be firm and should offer the same resistance each time it's operated. If it feels spongy, it is likely that there is still air in the system and it must be bled again. When all air has been bled from the system and the fluid level is correct in the reservoir, double-check for leaks and tighten all fittings and connections.

WARNING
Before riding the ATV, make certain that the brakes are operating correctly by operating the lever or pedal several times.

15. Test ride the ATV slowly at first to make sure that the brakes are operating properly.

REAR BRAKE PEDAL

Removal/Installation

Refer to **Figure 90** for this procedure.
1. Place the ATV on level ground and set the parking brake.
2. Remove the seat/rear fender assembly as described in Chapter Fifteen.
3. Remove the cotter pin, washer and pivot pin (**Figure 91**) securing the master cylinder brake rod to the brake pedal. Discard the cotter pin.
4. Remove the bolts securing right-hand footpeg assembly (**Figure 92**) and remove the footpeg assembly.
5. Using Vise Grips, unhook the brake pedal return spring from the pin on the frame (A, **Figure 93**).
6. Withdraw the brake arm (B, **Figure 93**) and return spring from the frame.
7. Inspect the dust seals on each side of the brake pedal; repack if necessary.

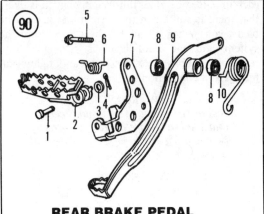

REAR BRAKE PEDAL
1. Bolt
2. Right-hand footpeg assembly
3. Washer
4. Cotter pin
5. Bolt
6. Spring
7. Mounting bracket
8. Dust seal
9. Brake pedal
10. Return spring

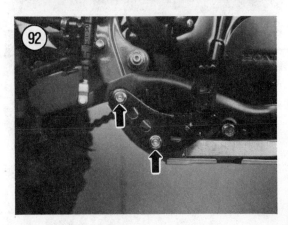

8. Install by reversing these removal steps, noting the following.

9. Apply multipurpose grease to the pivot shaft on the brake pedal before installing the brake pedal.

10. Tighten the bolts securing the right-hand footpeg assembly and brake pedal to the torque specification listed in **Table 1**.

11. Install new cotter pins and bend the ends over completely. Never reuse an old cotter pin.

12. Adjust the rear brake height as described under *Rear Disc Brake Pedal Height Adjustment* in Chapter Three.

Table 1 DISC BRAKE TORQUE SPECIFICATIONS

Item	N•m	ft.-lb.
Front wheel lug nuts	60-70	43-51
Front caliper		
Pad pin bolts	15-20	11-15
Mounting bolts	20-30	15-22
Allen bolts	15-20	11-15
Rear caliper		
Pad pin bolts	15-20	11-15
Mounting bolts	20-30	15-22
Allen bolts	15-20	11-15
Parking brake base		
mounting bolts	20-25	14-18
Rear axle locknut		
Inner locknut	100-120	72-87
Outer locknut	80-100	58-72
Union bolts	25-35	18-25
Right-hand footpeg and brake		
pedal mounting bolts	60-70	43-51
Front and rear brake disc		
mounting nuts	20-30	15-22

Table 2 is on the following page.

14

Table 2 DISC BRAKE SPECIFICATIONS

Model	New	Service limit
Front disc		
Thickness	3.8-4.2 mm (0.15-0.17 in.)	3.0 mm (0.12 in.)
Runout	—	0.3 mm (0.012 in.)
Front master cylinder		
Cylinder bore I.D.	12.700-12.743 mm (0.5000-0.5017 in.)	12.755 mm (0.5022 in.)
Piston O.D.	12.657-12.684 mm (0.4983-0.4994 in.)	12.645 mm (0.4978 in.)
Front caliper		
Cylinder bore I.D.	33.960-34.010 mm (1.3370-1.3390 in.)	34.020 mm (1.3394 in.)
Piston O.D.	33.878-33.928 mm (1.3338-1.3357 in.)	33.870 mm (1.3335 in.)
Rear disc		
Thickness	3.8-4.2 mm (0.15-0.17 in.)	3.0 mm (0.12 in.)
Runout	—	0.3 mm (0.012 in.)
Rear master cylinder		
Cylinder bore I.D.	14.000-14.043 mm (0.5512-0.5529 in.)	14.055 mm (0.5533 in.)
Piston O.D.	13.957-13.984 mm (0.5495-0.5506 in.)	13.945 mm (0.5490 in.)
Rear caliper		
Cylinder bore I.D.	33.960-34.010 mm (1.3370-1.3390 in.)	34.020 mm (1.3394 in.)
Piston O.D.	33.878-33.928 mm (1.3338-1.3357 in.)	33.870 mm (1.3335 in.)

CHAPTER FIFTEEN

BODY

This chapter contains removal and installation procedures for body panels and rear carry handle.

As soon as the part is removed from the vehicle, all mounting hardware (i.e. small brackets, bolts, nuts, rubber bushings, metal collars, etc.) should be reinstalled onto the removed part. Honda makes frequent changes during the model year, so your part and the way it is attached to the frame may differ slightly from the one used in the service procedures in this chapter.

> *CAUTION*
> *The metal collars that are used within the mounting holes in some of the plastic parts are very important and must be used. These collars are used as stops when the bolts and nuts are tightened. Without the metal collar, the bolt and nut would be tightened down onto the plastic part and fracture the plastic surrounding the mounting hole.*

FRONT FENDER

Removal/Installation
(3-wheeled Models)

1. Remove the bolts and washers securing the front fender to the lower fork bridge. Don't lose the rubber grommets and metal collars in the mounting holes in the front fender.

2. Make sure the metal spacers are installed in the mounting holes in the front fender.

3. Install the bolts and washers and tighten securely. Do not overtighten as the plastic fender may fracture. See the CAUTION at the beginning of this chapter.

Removal/Installation
(4-wheeled Models)

Refer to **Figure 1** for this procedure.

1. Pull up on the release lever on the left-hand side and remove the seat.

2. Remove the screw (**Figure 2**) securing the fuel shutoff valve handle and remove the handle.

3. Remove the fuel tank filler cap (**Figure 3**) and cover the opening with duct tape or clean shop cloth.

4. Remove the screws (**Figure 4**) securing the fuel tank cover stay.

5. Remove the screws and metal collars (**Figure 5**) securing the front portion of the air scoop grille.

6. Carefully unsnap and remove the fuel tank cover (**Figure 6**).

> *CAUTION*
> *Do not pull straight up on the air scoop grille or the locking tabs will **break off**.*

①

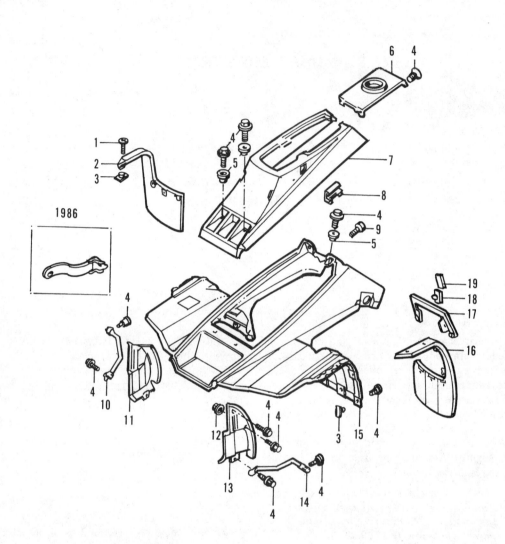

1986

FRONT FENDER
(4-WHEELED MODELS)
1. Screw
2. Mud guard—right-hand side
3. Special nut
4. Bolt
5. Metal collar
6. Fuel tank center cover
7. Air scoop grille
8. Rubber pad
9. Bolt
10. Mounting bracket
11. Front fender inner panel
    —right-hand side
12. Nut
13. Front fender inner
    panel—left-hand side
14. Mounting bracket
15. Front fender
16. Mud guard—left-hand side
17. Cover stay
18. Special nut
19. Rubber pad

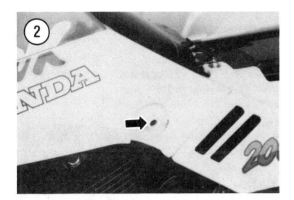

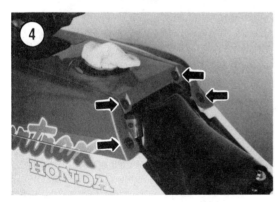

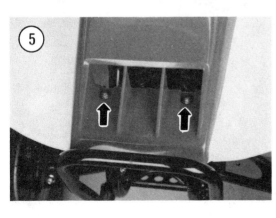

7. Carefully pull the air scoop grille toward the *rear* to disengage all of the locking tabs (**Figure 7**) from the front fender.

8. Carefully pull the rear sides of the air scoop grille out, pull the unit forward and remove the air scoop grille (**Figure 8**).

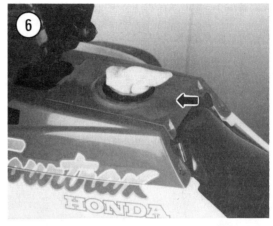

15

9. Remove the cover stay (**Figure 9**).

10. Remove the bolts and collars (**Figure 10**) securing the rear portion of the front fender to the frame.

11. Remove the screw (**Figure 11**) on each side, securing the rear fender and mud guard to the frame bracket.

12. Remove the screws (A, **Figure 12**) on each side, securing the front fender and the inner panels to the frame.

13. Carefully pull the rear sides of the front fender out, pull the assembly forward and remove the front fender assembly.

14. Unhook the inner panel (**Figure 13**) from the frame rail and remove the inner panel. Repeat for the other side.

15. Install by reversing these removal steps, noting the following.

16. Insert the front fender between the front fender inner panels and the frame (B, **Figure 12**).

17. Hook the rear side portions of the front fender into the locating slot on each side of the rear fender (**Figure 14**).

18. Hook the rear lower portions of the front fender into the locating slot on each side of the inner panels (**Figure 15**).

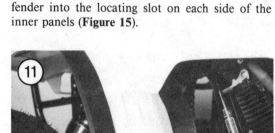

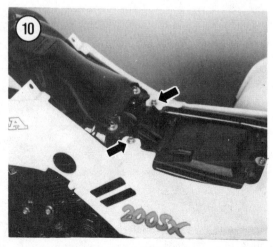

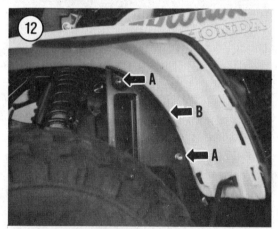

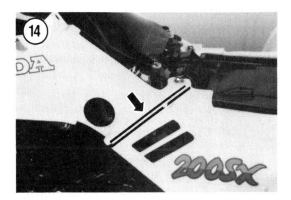

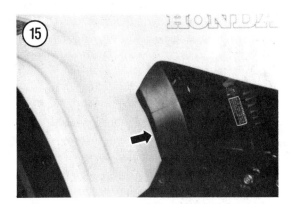

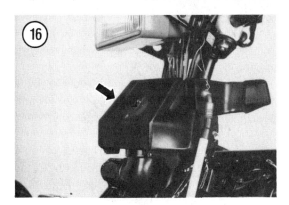

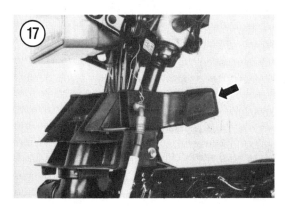

19. Tighten all bolts, nuts and screws securely. Do not overtighten as the plastic fender may fracture. See the CAUTION at the beginning of this chapter.

FRESH AIR INLET CASE (4-WHEELED MODELS)

1. Remove the front fender assembly as described in this chapter.
2. Remove the screws securing the cover (**Figure 16**) and remove the cover.
3. Remove the flexible air duct (**Figure 17**) from each side of the air inlet case.
4. Loosen the clamping screw (**Figure 18**) on the rubber elbow where it attaches to the frame fresh air inlet tube.
5. Remove the bolts and collars securing the inlet case (**Figure 19**) to the frame. Remove the case from the frame.
6. Install by reversing these removal steps.

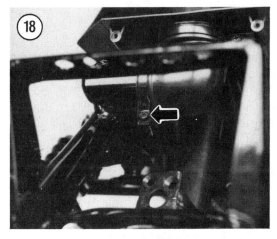

15

REAR FENDER/SEAT

Removal/Installation
(3-wheeled Models)

Refer to **Figure 20** for this procedure.
1. At the rear of the seat, move the lever (**Figure 21**) and release the rear fender/seat from the frame.
2. Raise the rear of the rear fender/seat assembly up and pull toward the rear. Remove the assembly from the frame.
3. Install by reversing these removal steps, noting the following.

4. Move the kickstarter out and away from the frame before installing the rear fender/seat. If the kickstarter is tucked back against the frame it will be trapped behind the rear fender assembly.

Removal/Installation
(4-wheeled Models)

Refer to **Figure 22** and **Figure 23** for this procedure.
1. Pull up on the release lever on the left-hand side and remove the seat.

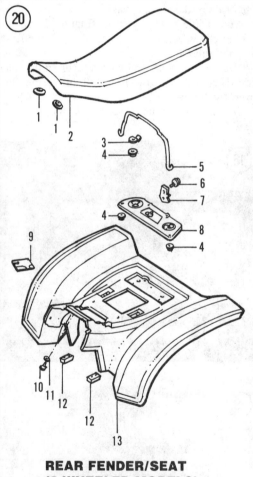

REAR FENDER/SEAT
(3-WHEELED MODELS)

1. Rubber stopper	8. Seat lockplate
2. Seat	9. Rubber guard
3. Support bracket	10. Bolt
4. Nut	11. Metal collar
5. Fender bracket	12. Rubber stopper
6. Bolt	13. Rear fender
7. Bracket	

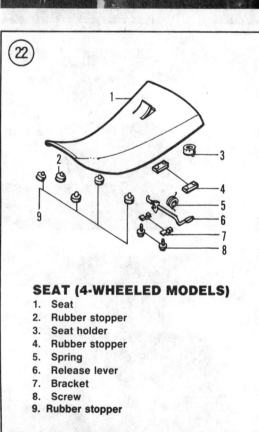

SEAT (4-WHEELED MODELS)
1. Seat
2. Rubber stopper
3. Seat holder
4. Rubber stopper
5. Spring
6. Release lever
7. Bracket
8. Screw
9. Rubber stopper

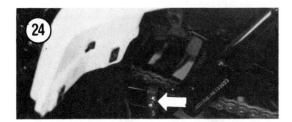

2. Remove the bolts (**Figure 10**) securing the front portion of the rear fender and the rear portion of the front fender.

3. Remove the bolt (**Figure 24**) on each side, securing the mud guard mounting bracket to the frame.

4. Remove the Phillips screw (**Figure 25**) on each side, securing the front section of the rear fender.

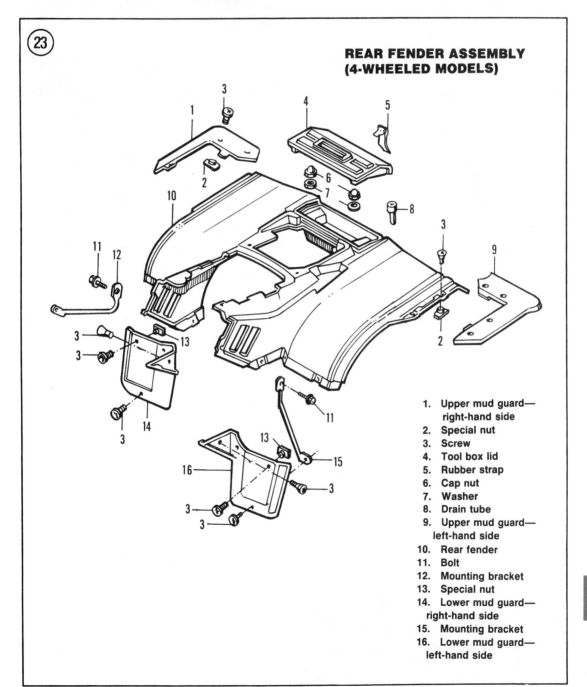

REAR FENDER ASSEMBLY (4-WHEELED MODELS)

1. Upper mud guard—
   right-hand side
2. Special nut
3. Screw
4. Tool box lid
5. Rubber strap
6. Cap nut
7. Washer
8. Drain tube
9. Upper mud guard—
   left-hand side
10. Rear fender
11. Bolt
12. Mounting bracket
13. Special nut
14. Lower mud guard—
   right-hand side
15. Mounting bracket
16. Lower mud guard—
   left-hand side

5. Open the tool box compartment lid.

6. Remove the cap nuts and washers (**Figure 26**) securing the rear section of the rear portion of the rear fender.

7. Carefully pull the rear fender up and remove the rear fender.

8. Install by reversing these removal steps, noting the following.

9. Hook the slot in the front portion of the rear fender into the locating tab on each side of the front fender (**Figure 14**).

10. Tighten all bolts and cap nuts securely. Do not overtighten as the plastic fender may fracture. Be sure to reinstall all spacers used within mounting holes, as they prevent overtightening which can damage plastic parts.

FRONT CARRY HANDLE (4-WHEELED MODELS)

Removal/Installation

NOTE
It is not necessary to remove the front fender, but it does give additional work room.

1. Remove the front fender as described in this chapter.

2. Remove the bolts and nuts (**Figure 27**) on each side, securing the front carrier to the frame and remove the carrier.

3. Install the front carrier and tighten the bolts and nuts securely.

4. Install the front fender as described in this chapter.

REAR CARRY HANDLE

Removal/Installation
(3-wheeled Models)

Refer to **Figure 28** for this procedure.

1. Remove the bolts and washers on each side, securing the rear carry handle to the frame. On the right-hand side, the front bolt also holds the muffler in place.

2. Remove the rear carry handle.

3. Install by reversing these removal steps, noting the following.

4. Be sure to install the rubber grommets in the receptacles in the rear carry handle.

5. Tighten the bolts securely.

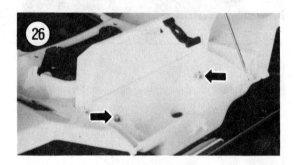

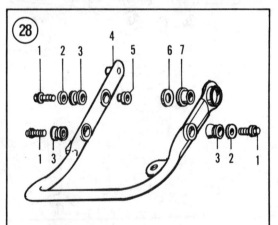

REAR HANDLE (3-WHEELED MODELS)
1. Bolt
2. Washer
3. Rubber grommet
4. Rear carry handle
5. Metal collar
6. Washer
7. Metal collar

**Removal/Installation
(4-wheeled Models)**

Refer to **Figure 29** for this procedure.

1. Remove the bolts and washers (**Figure 30**) on each side, securing the rear carry handle and the rear fender brackets to the frame.

2. Remove the rear fender brackets and rubber grommets at each attachment point.

3. Remove the rear carry handle.

4. Install by reversing these removal steps, noting the following.

5. Be sure to install the rubber grommets between the carry handle and the rear fender brackets.

6. Tighten the bolts securely.

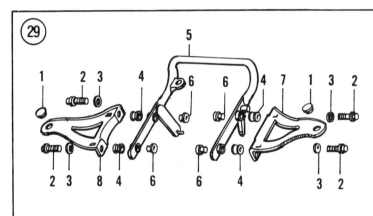

**REAR HANDLE
(4-WHEELED MODELS)**

1. Rubber cap
2. Bolt
3. Washer
4. Rubber grommet
5. Rear carry handle
6. Metal collar
7. Fender support—
   left-hand side
8. Fender support—
   right-hand side

15

INDEX

16

1986-1988 FOURTRAX 200SX

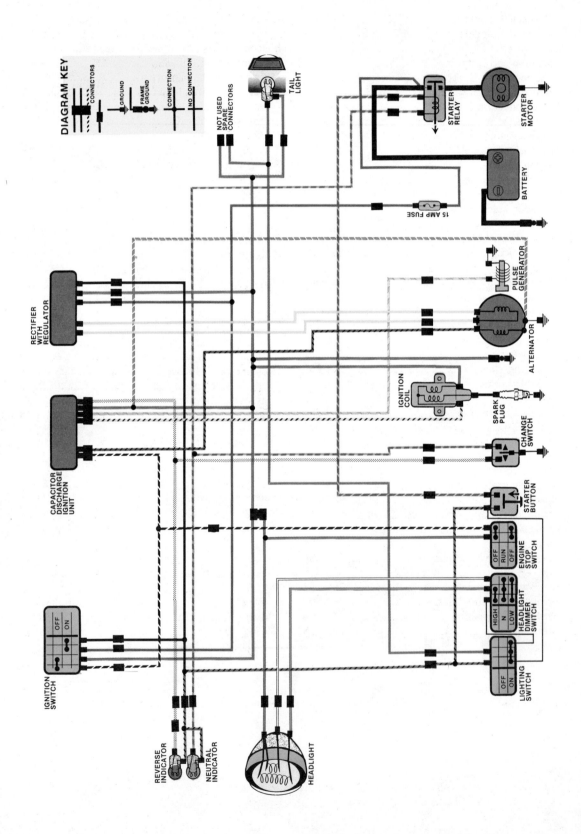

1986 ATC200X

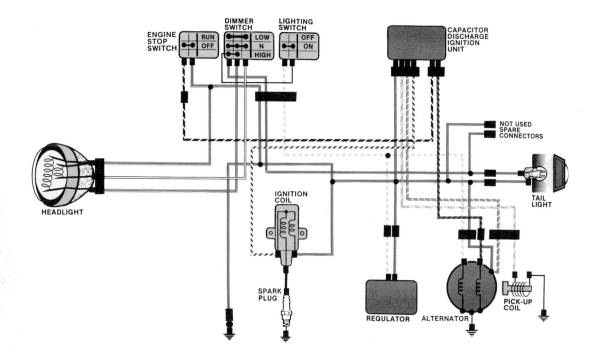

1987 ATC200X

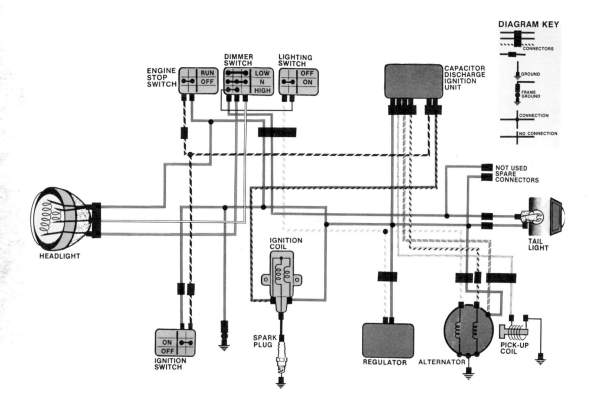